Right and Wronged i
International Relations

MW00813019

Brian C. Rathbun argues against the prevailing wisdom on morality in international relations, both the commonly held belief that foreign affairs is an amoral realm and the opposing notion that norms have gradually civilized an unethical world. By focusing on how states respond to being wronged rather than when they do right, Rathbun shows that morality is and always has been virtually everywhere in international relations – in the perception of threat, the persistence of conflict, the judgment of domestic audiences, and the articulation of expansionist goals. The inescapability of our moral impulses owes to their evolutionary origins in helping individuals solve recurrent problems in their anarchic environment. Through archival case studies of German foreign policy; the analysis of enormous corpora of text; and surveys of Russian, Chinese, and American publics, this book reorients how we think about the role of morality in international relations.

BRIAN C. RATHBUN is the author of four other books on international affairs and is a Distinguished Scholar of the International Studies Association. His latest book with Cambridge University Press, *Reasoning of State*, won the 2020 award for best book on foreign policy from the American Political Science Association.

Cambridge Studies in International Relations: 163

Right and Wronged in International Relations

Cambridge Studies in International Relations is a joint initiative of Cambridge University Press and the British International Studies Association (BISA). The series aims to publish the best new scholarship in international studies, irrespective of subject matter, methodological approach or theoretical perspective. The series seeks to bring the latest theoretical work in International Relations to bear on the most important problems and issues in global politics.

Other titles in the series are listed at the back of the book.

Right and Wronged in International Relations

Evolutionary Ethics, Moral Revolutions, and the Nature of Power Politics

BRIAN C. RATHBUN
University of Southern California

CAMBRIDGE
UNIVERSITY PRESS

Shaftesbury Road, Cambridge CB2 8EA, United Kingdom

One Liberty Plaza, 20th Floor, New York, NY 10006, USA

477 Williamstown Road, Port Melbourne, VIC 3207, Australia

314–321, 3rd Floor, Plot 3, Splendor Forum, Jasola District Centre, New Delhi – 110025, India

103 Penang Road, #05–06/07, Visioncrest Commercial, Singapore 238467

Cambridge University Press is part of Cambridge University Press & Assessment, a department of the University of Cambridge.

We share the University's mission to contribute to society through the pursuit of education, learning and research at the highest international levels of excellence.

www.cambridge.org
Information on this title: www.cambridge.org/9781009344715

DOI: 10.1017/9781009344722

First published 2023

A catalogue record for this publication is available from the British Library.

Library of Congress Cataloging-in-Publication Data
Names: Rathbun, Brian C., 1973– author.
Title: Right and wronged in international relations : evolutionary ethics, moral revolutions, and the nature of power politics / Brian C. Rathbun.
Description: Cambridge, United Kingdom ; New York, NY : Cambridge University Press, 2023. | Series: Cambridge studies in international relations ; 163 | Includes bibliographical references and index.
Identifiers: LCCN 2022050160 (print) | LCCN 2022050161 (ebook) | ISBN 9781009344715 (hardback) | ISBN 9781009344722 (ebook)
Subjects: LCSH: International relations – Moral and ethical aspects. | Germany – Foreign relations – 1871–1918. | Germany – Foreign relations – 1933–1945. | World War, 1914–1918 – Germany. | World War, 1939–1945 – Germany.
Classification: LCC JZ1306 .R37 2023 (print) | LCC JZ1306 (ebook) | DDC 327.43–dc23/eng/20230103
LC record available at https://lccn.loc.gov/2022050160
LC ebook record available at https://lccn.loc.gov/2022050161

ISBN 978-1-009-34471-5 Hardback
ISBN 978-1-009-34468-5 Paperback

Additional resources for this publication at www.cambridge.org/9781009344715

For Jay

Contents

Figures

Tables

Acknowledgments

For a long while, I suppose if you had asked me why I had become a political scientist as opposed to some other type of social or natural scientist, I would not have known the answer. I would have likely attributed the choice to various happenstances and chance encounters, and that is undoubtedly true. But I had no significant interest in politics as an adolescent and even less in international relations. When I began my undergraduate studies, I am quite sure I would have insisted that Marx was Russian. I was placed in my introduction to international relations course at university because cultural anthropology was full, and I stayed because the instructor had a good reputation. I got a B in the course.

Now I know the answer. Politics inevitably invokes morality, and morality has always been a central preoccupation of mine. I am sure this has to do with my Catholic upbringing. For four years, grades four through seven, I attended parochial school and as a consequence six masses a week, as Monday through Friday does not give you a pass on Sunday. But my parents are liberal Catholics; they think that the Pope should be a woman, priests should marry alongside same-sex couples, birth control is fine, the death penalty is more sacrilegious than abortion, and good Catholics should spend more time helping others in duress than chastising them for their moral failings. So I think I was raised thinking about how to determine what is right and wrong when various values conflict and that the voices of authority can be wrong, leading me to wonder why we spend so much time listening to them.

Morality is the thread that runs through all of my books. I began with humanitarian intervention, trying to figure out why some are more willing than others to help those beyond their borders. I then took up the role played by trust in international relations, but trust of a particular type – moralistic, the belief that others have good, ethical intentions. My book on diplomacy locates the sources of how decision-makers negotiate in their underlying moral codes.

The more I thought about politics, the more I realized that virtually every political issue and controversy is a moral one, or at least the public debate is inevitably ethical in tone. Even the tax code is inherently moral since it implicates issues of fairness, which can be interpreted in different ways. I should keep my million dollars because I worked hard for it and hard work is an indication that I do not free ride on others. Or I should take your million dollars because there are so many who do not have a hundred dollars. I would issue readers a challenge. Try to find a salient political issue within or between countries that is not cast in ethical terms. I cannot find one. Sometimes people distinguish between legal and moral justifications. We have to obey the law because it is the law and not because it is right in a particular instance. But even in those instances, there is concern for the respect of law, and law is inherently moral; laws allow a social stability that better allows societies to prosper, and that is a morally good thing. There is no escaping morality.

The study of international relations, more so than political science more generally, is preoccupied with the most basic moral questions, and now I know that this was why I inclined in this direction. Under what circumstances can we justify the use of physical violence? To what extent do we have an obligation to those outside of our local communities? All I had to do was to learn something about history, which has taken me about twenty years.

And yet international relations – paradoxically, I would say – still often characterizes itself as the study of the amoral sphere where right and wrong know no place. At its extreme, the contention is not that conceptions of right and wrong differ beyond territorial borders but that they do not exist there at all. To put it bluntly, this book makes the case that such a claim is simply preposterous. I do so by showing that the processes and phenomena associated with the basest power politics – conflict duration, status-seeking, crisis signaling, territorial expansion – are all inextricably intertwined with morality. And we see this in the countries most identified in the Western mind with amoral Machtpolitik: Wilhelmine Germany in its time and Russia and China today. What we are missing has been imagination. First, we have to understand that morality involves not just doing good for others, but also the way by which we respond to others who do bad, what is called moral condemnation. Second, we have to realize that we often feel special moral obligations to our groups. Once we widen our understanding of morality to the extent that it is experienced in the real world – which requires a willingness to see morality through the eyes of others – we see morality everywhere in international relations.

That alone would have been a book, but in thinking about morality's ubiquity I found myself going deeper into the literature on human evolution and the role that morality played in human success (if, at this point, you can call it that). I had a superficial knowledge of this field based on earlier projects on reciprocity and altruism, and I cannot remember the point at which I actively decided I was going to make a commitment to an ultimately material case for the origins of ethics. I am sure that my close friendship with Rose McDermott made me more open to it. Like most of us, however, I had an allergy to the ultimate implication of this literature – that morality is not the transcendence of material reality but rather the reflection of it. It seems to cheapen it, and my wife certainly disagrees with where I have come down. But I realized that such a position on ethics is not at all as pessimistic and deterministic as its reputation. If anything, it tells us that the nature of human beings is deeply cooperative and caring, but that this is accompanied by tendencies toward destructive behaviors that are themselves driven by competing moral impulses. We're complicated.

We're also full of it. To say that morality is everywhere is not to say that everyone is moral all the time. In fact, if we were, we wouldn't have the concept of morality at all. Morality helps us regulate our social relationships. It requires that we respond negatively when we or others are wronged. Everyone is therefore always acting in the shadow of morality; even when acting instrumentally we have to put our behavior in a different light. Congressional advocates of corporate tax breaks do not admit that they are taking campaign contributions with the implicit expectation that they benefit some small constituency. They have to make a moral argument about the just desserts of job creation. My personal theory about why Donald Trump drives so many of us so crazy is that he doesn't seem to feel that pressure. But of course, he is the narcissistic exception that proves the rule. And even he has to wrap his transactionalism in the flag, making America great again. So much of his foreign policy consisted of complaining about how the United States was treated unfairly by others, which is a moral argument.

This is a pandemic book, written mostly in the first twelve months of this global catastrophe. I fielded my survey in Russia the same week that California locked itself down (I must thank Evgeniia Iakhnis, my research assistant, profoundly for her translation of the instrument). As such it was written in relative isolation. I did not share drafts with colleagues as much as I had with previous projects, so I do not have an extensive list of people to thank, although Katy Powers and Rose McDermott were kind enough to provide some thoughts. It was, however, a time of deep collaboration with Caleb Pomeroy, who as I write this is just about to complete his dissertation at The Ohio State University. I brought him in, with a cold email, to help me implement the word embeddings analysis that became Chapter 4, and it has sparked one of the most fruitful partnerships in my career. Caleb and I have had many garage jam sessions, which sounds much cooler than it is. I have a finished studio in the backyard, without facilities, where Caleb has bunked down at several points.

As always the person who read everything was my wife, Nina Srinivasan Rathbun, and as always I owe her everything.

I dedicate this book to a close friend who passed away in November 2020. I met James "Jay" Mitchell during what was one of the most formative and transformative periods of my life. In the fall of 1992, I was part of a wind ensemble that spent the semester in Vienna. It is there that I first tried out my elementary German, learned about the European Union, and in general discovered there was a wide world that I had never really thought about. Part of the ensemble was Jay, who, although at a different university, came along for the semester after his close high school friend told him about it. Jay had an infectious and impish sense of humor, and I liked him instantly. He was one of the few people I have ever met who I wanted to be like, who made me want to change things about myself. And I think I did as a result.

At the time, I had no idea how incredibly smart Jay was. He went on to study molecular and cell biology at Berkeley, and when I arrived there, a year after he did, he was the only person I knew. He became my best friend. Jay worked long hours in the lab, and often I would just head over there in the evening to have a beer while he waited on his sample cells to do something or other. We had something of a standing date at his place to watch *Saturday Night Live*. We shared a deep affection for Norm MacDonald. Jay was there as I began my relationship with Nina, and he was a groomsman at my wedding. I went back to Vienna to attend his own marriage to Elisabeth, who had organized our wind ensemble's travel arrangement while we were there before, and who Jay had begun secretly seeing at the time.

After he and I left Berkeley, I lost touch with Jay. He was very much of the moment. If you were in his presence, you were the most important person in the world – but out of sight, out of mind, I came to realize. It turns out he was having a fabulously successful career, a trailblazer at Harvard in the study of diet's effect on aging. But I only found this out after he had died at forty-nine, and I did not know that he had passed away for many months after it happened. It makes me angry and sad of course to think about the opportunities I missed to rekindle the friendship.

When Jay and I were together, we never talked about our research. I couldn't really understand what he was doing and vice versa. But he came, at his insistence, to my very first large lecture when I, as a teaching assistant, subbed for our traveling professor. It seems fitting that I dedicate this particular book to him, given its heavy reliance on biology, even if at a much more macro level. I would love to talk to him about it someday. Maybe now we could do more than crack jokes. But maybe not, and isn't that better anyway?

The online appendix referred to in the book can be found at: www .cambridge.org/9781009344715 or directly from the author.

1 | *The Nature in and Nature of International Relations*

For as long as men and women have talked about war, they have talked about it in terms of right and wrong. And for almost as long, some among them have derided such talk, called it a charade, insisted that war lies beyond (or beneath) moral judgments. War is a world apart, where life itself is at stake, where human nature is reduced to its elemental forms, where self-interest and necessity prevail.

—Michael Walzer[1]

It's not surprising that the rediscovery of human nature has taken so long. Being everywhere we look, it tends to elude us. We take for granted such bedrock elements of life as gratitude, shame, remorse, pride, honor, retribution, empathy, love and so on – just as we take for granted the air we breathe, the tendency of dropped objects to fall, and other standard features of living on this planet.

—Robert Wright[2]

This curious dialectic of ethics and politics, which prevents the latter, in spite of itself, from escaping the former's judgment and normative direction, has its roots in the nature of man as both a political and a moral animal.

—Hans Morgenthau[3]

It is one of the great truisms of international relations: Foreign affairs is an amoral realm where everyday ethical norms know no place. Foreign policy is the pursuit of egoistic ends with little regard for others, often through the threat or use of violence. Since morality's primary function is to place restraints on selfish behavior, if egoism is the driving force of

[1] Walzer, Michael. 1977. *Just and Unjust Wars*. New York: Basic Books, 3.
[2] Wright, Robert. 1994. *The Moral Animal*. New York: Pantheon Books, 8.
[3] Morgenthau, Hans J. 1945. "The Evil of Politics and the Ethics of Evil." *Ethics* 56(1): 5.

international politics, then ethical considerations must be largely absent. As explained by Waltz, "Each state pursues its own interests, however defined, in ways it judges best. Force is a means of achieving the external ends of states because there exists no consistent, reliable process of reconciling the conflicts of interest that inevitably arise among similar units in a condition of anarchy. *A foreign policy based on this image of international relations is neither moral nor immoral*, but embodies merely a reasoned response to the world about us."[4] Morgenthau calls this the "autonomy of the political sphere," one in which there is no "relevance" or even "existence ... of standards of thought other than the political one."[5] This is what Walzer calls "the world apart."

In this view, the "private" morality that we utilize in our daily interactions and within the (hopefully) more predictable, ordered, and stable confines of domestic politics is fundamentally different from the "public" morality exercised by state leaders. As Morgenthau explains, "The argument starts with the observation that man as an actor on the political scene does certain things in violation of ethical principles, which he does not do, or at least not as frequently and habitually, when he acts in a private capacity. There he lies, deceives, and betrays, and he does so quite often. Here he does so, if at all, only as an exception and under extraordinary circumstances.... In other words, there is one ethics for the political sphere and there is another ethics for the private sphere."[6]

The empirical study of morality in international relations (IR), what is sometimes called the "norms" literature, aims to counter that great truism by documenting some degree of moral progress over the course of time.[7] Elites and national publics demonstrate increasing concern for the fate of others beyond their borders, which is evident in such phenomena as international criminal tribunals, foreign aid, decolonization, and human rights treaties.[8]

---

[4] Waltz, Kenneth. 1959. *Man, the State and War*. New York: Columbia University Press, 238 (emphasis added).

[5] Morgenthau, Hans J. 1948. *Politics among Nations: The Struggle for Power and Peace*. New York: A. A. Knopf, 10–11.

[6] Morgenthau, "The Evil of Politics," 6.

[7] This "positive" literature is different from the normative literature, which concerns itself with what constitutes ethical behavior in international relations – the "ought" rather than the "is" – and is much older.

[8] Skeptics reply that states are still preoccupied with their own self-interests, sacrificing little for others. Even democratic publics and leaders are willing to

All of these ethical phenomena are surely moral, and I would argue that they have systematically changed the nature of modern international relations. However, they are not all there is to morality in international relations. In fact, the norms literature does not even begin to scratch the surface. For all their differences, both optimists and pessimists rely on the same, overly truncated conception of morality, a liberal and cosmopolitan standard in which ethical action is that which demonstrates universal concern for individuals regardless of national origin. Liberal ethics are one standard of morality, but individualistic cosmopolitanism does not exhaust the set of moral foundations that might motivate state action in international relations. Missing that fact obscures the totality of morality in international politics. Scholars of international relations therefore drastically understate the presence of ethically minded and morally motivated action in international affairs. The largely universal embrace of liberal moral benchmarks in the positive literature on ethics in international relations leads to two particular blindspots.

First, we focus on moral conscience – our desire to do good for others – to the neglect of moral condemnation and punishment, our response to what we perceive to be the unethical behavior of others, not only vis-à-vis third parties but also ourselves.[9] Morality serves to restrain excessive egoism, but how do we respond when others act in an overly self-interested manner? In both everyday life and international relations, the response is generally to punish. Norms of justice and fairness aim at taming our most grandiose ambitions but also come with their own injunctions in the face of noncompliance. Passing moral judgment on others is ubiquitous in international politics and can give rise to fundamentally different, and sometimes even more violent, dynamics than a simple amoral conflict of interests. When states believe that others are behaving in a disproportionately egoistic manner, they are morally outraged.

kill large numbers of innocent civilians to accomplish national goals (Downes, Alexander. 2008. *Targeting Civilians in War*. Ithaca and London: Cornell University Press; Press, Daryl G., Scott D. Sagan, and Benjamin A. Valentino. 2013. "Atomic Aversion: Experimental Evidence on Taboos, Traditions, and the Non-use of Nuclear Weapons." *American Political Science Review* 107(1): 188–206.

[9] DeScioli, Peter and Robert Kurzban. 2009. "Mysteries of Morality." *Cognition* 112(2): 281–299; DeScioli, Peter and Robert Kurzban. 2013. "A Solution to the Mysteries of Morality." *Psychological Bulletin* 139(2): 477–496.

Second, the positive IR ethics and morality literature have not come to terms with moral principles that operate at the level of the group, binding them together. For many, even in Western countries, morality is communitarian in nature. When our group is engaged in a conflict with another, we owe it our loyalty. Betrayal is a universally recognized moral transgression. In such situations, we defer to the authorities out of moral obligation. They deserve our respect for their efforts to protect us. These so-called "binding foundations" are the morality that brings and keeps *groups* together.[10] They are particularly important for international relations since foreign affairs are a matter of intergroup interaction.

Binding morality and moral condemnation are highly linked in international relations in that a belief that other groups are dangerous to our own is more often than not equated to a belief that they are immoral. Binding the group together is necessary precisely because there are unethical individuals and groups inside and outside of the group. These are second-order moral beliefs, beliefs about the ethics of others. It is this combination that keeps international relations from resembling a set of billiard balls colliding with one another since states project moral expectations for others' behavior into the global sphere.

Such a perspective shifts the emphasis in our study of ethics from the liberal question of whether states do good – important, of course – to the question of what states do when other states do bad, particularly to them. It implies a shift from the study of moral judgment to moral judgmental-ism. These impulses, motivated by moral outrage and a feeling of anger, are not necessarily our better angels, which would have us turn the other cheek.[11] But they are angels nonetheless in the sense that they are sincerely held moral principles by many. To capture the nature of international relations adequately, we must retrain our focus from doing right to being wronged and the rights that states feel they have in those circumstances – that is, to our lesser angels.

---

[10] Graham, Jesse, Brian A. Nosek, Jonathan Haidt, Ravi Iyer, Spassena Koleva, and Peter H. Ditto. 2011. "Mapping the Moral Domain." *Journal of Personality and Social Psychology* 101(2): 366.

[11] On anger in international relations, see Hall, Todd H. 2017. "On Provocation: Outrage, International Relations, and the Franco–Prussian War." *Security Studies* 26(1): 1–29.

Once we cast our moral net more widely, we realize that morality is everywhere, more striking in the breach than the observance, as the opening epigraph from Wright suggests. As central as morality is to human interaction, sustained political action that pays no regard to morality is likely impossible. What we generally regard as the most striking manifestations of the lack of ethics, the use of violence for political purposes and other aspects of "power politics," are more often than not the very expression of moral principles, just not the ones we are used to. Even Morgenthau recognizes that "the very juxtaposition of 'power politics' and 'moral politics' is fundamentally mistaken" and ultimately rejects the private–public distinction (as we will see in the following text).[12]

Recognizing that not all morality is self-abnegating and that moral condemnation arises in response to the perception of excessive egoism by others, we see that what appears to be the naked expression of egoistic interests is quite often driven by a sense of injustice, such as when states object to threats to their honor and security or demand a fair share of a bargain. As we will see, the pursuit of fairness is often mistaken for status-seeking, perhaps the most self-regarding of all human (and therefore state) motivations. Morality is central to deterrence and war termination. Those who believe others are immoral feel the need to demonstrate resolve and frame situations as commitment problems so that the only solution in costly conflicts is to continue fighting. If our leaders do not demonstrate such determination, we fault them for not being loyal enough to the group's interest. When the "audience" judges leaders, it is finding fault with them ethically. Indeed the very groups that do the business of international relations – nation-states – are held together by moral glue. Morality also informs the extent and nature of military expansion and occupation. Not all conquest is the same, quantitatively and qualitatively. And moral coercion is one of the most potent sources of nonmaterial power in interstate diplomacy, even in negotiations about how to carve up the world.

In sum, we cannot understand much of anything in traditional security studies without morality; yet up to this point, the field has tried very hard to do just that. Both optimists and pessimists typically characterize ethics in international relations as a rare and delicate flower

---

[12] Quoted in Murray, A. J. H. 1996. "The Moral Politics of Hans Morgenthau." *Review of Politics* 58(1): 98.

just starting to gain a foothold in inhospitable soil. Morgenthau summarizes this traditional view: "[T]he morality of the political sphere, viewed from the standards of individual ethics,[13] is a residue from an immoral age which has been overcome in the individual sphere but still leads a ghostlike existence in the realm of politics."[14] To make my alternative case, in this book, I present evidence derived from analyses of massive textual corpora, thirteen non-experimental and experimental surveys of American, Chinese, and Russian samples, and six historical case chapters on German foreign policy based predominantly on primary texts and original archival sources.

This is not to say that individuals or groups always act morally by any ethical standard. Indeed if self-restraint based on a sense of moral obligation were universal, there would be no concept of morality at all. However, rarely do either everyday Joes, Janes or political actors simply take what they want and say so. Walzer writes, "If we had all become realists like the Athenian generals or like Hobbists in a state of war … [w]e would simply tell one another, brutally and directly, what we wanted to do or have done. But the truth is that one of the things most of us want, even in war, is to act or to seem to act morally."[15] Pinker has the same idea when he writes, "Other than devils and storybook villains, no one says, 'I believe murder is a heinous atrocity, and I do it whenever it serves my purposes.'"[16] Even if doing the right thing is at times performative, this shows that morality is real and serves as a restraint on the pursuit of selfish interests, both within and between societies, as we will see. This is because state action takes place, as much of human behavior does, in front of audiences. I call this the "shadow of morality."

The Nature in International Relations

There is a reason humans universally engage in moral condemnation and form groups to whom they feel they have moral obligations – our evolutionary origins. Evolutionary psychologists now agree that morality in all its predominant forms was central for the survival

---

[13] Morgenthau means liberal, individualistic ethics.
[14] Morgenthau, "The Evil of Politics," 7.   [15] Walzer, *Just and Unjust Wars*, 20.
[16] Pinker, Stephen. 2012. *The Better Angels of Our Nature: The Decline of Violence in History and Its Causes*. New York: Penguin Press, 623.

of individuals' genetic material in our distant past. By checking our most excessively egoistic impulses, morality allows us to reap the gains of cooperation without even knowing it, which in turn allows us and/or our kin to survive. Moral condemnation encouraged the development of moral conscience, backed by the emotion of guilt, which in turn acted as a credible signal of cooperativeness that paid material and therefore evolutionary dividends. Our humanitarianism is a genetic by-product of a biological but unconscious drive to survive. We are moral in all the ways we are because our genes are selfish. "A gene, in effect, looks beyond its moral bearer to interests of the potentially immoral set of its replicas existing in other related individuals."[17]

Binding morality also has evolutionary origins. Those humans who contributed to collective defense based on a sense of loyalty to a group and deference to authority would avoid the moral opprobrium of shirking their contribution to group welfare, which would have a potential genetic cost. Especially in extremely dangerous environments, those loyal to a group and deferential to authority could prosper to such a degree as to offset the competing incentives to shirk and free-ride within the group.

Even for those who do not have moral impulses, they are so universal that no one can ignore them, making humans extremely attentive to their moral reputation even in international relations.[18] Everyone – as we will see, even Hitler – operates under this *shadow of morality*. Evolutionary psychologists believe this attentiveness to audiences to be the manifestation of a genetic strategy to avoid moral condemnation that might have been materially and genetically costly. Being branded an egomaniac is bad for egoism. We have the evolved emotion of shame to protect us from self-defeat. In modern times, nation-states morally condemn other nation-states, generally for threats to the precursors of society – life, truth, and property.[19] And nation-states try to avoid this censure. Scholars of rhetorical coercion have already convincingly demonstrated how political actors attempt to

---

[17] Axelrod, Robert and William D. Hamilton. 1981. "The Evolution of Cooperation." *Science* 211(4489): 1390.

[18] Johnston, Alastair Iain. 2001. "Treating International Institutions as Social Environments." *International Studies Quarterly* 45(4): 487–515.

[19] Bull, Hedley. 1977. *The Anarchical Society*. New York: Columbia University Press.

entrap others into taking their preferred positions, and a close look at this literature shows that framing debates are about occupying the moral high ground.[20]

There is also moral condemnation based on the binding foundations. Within states, self-interested leaders face potential accusations from their publics for not adequately defending their national interests, which is an accusation of disloyalty. US politicians ask each other, "You don't hate America, do you?" Even authoritarian leaders try to avoid such censure.

Given its biological basis, a large-scale autonomous sphere of human interaction absent of ethical considerations is no more possible than one devoid of oxygen. As De Waal writes, "Given the universality of moral systems, the tendency to develop and enforce them must be an integral part of human nature. Since we are moral beings to the core, any theory of human behavior that does not take morality 100 percent seriously is bound to fall by the wayside."[21] International relations offer theories of human behavior, so De Waal's warning applies. Otherwise, we are not doing justice to international relations, literally and figuratively. I believe we miss the omnipresence of morality in international affairs because morality is so natural and intuitive to us that we do not even notice it is there, as Wright claims.

Rather than a transcendence of our material reality, morality is material reality. Morality serves the function of solving recurrent material problems in our evolutionary past, problems we still face today such as deterring threats or distributing resources. This is at odds with the strictly ideational manner in which morality is generally approached in international relations theory, particularly in liberal and constructivist thought.

It also stands in contrast to many of those applications of biological thought to international relations to date that have given short shrift to one of the most important factors in explaining human success. References to "human nature" in IR theory almost universally imply the ethical limitations of human beings; they are resignations

---

[20] Krebs, Ronald and Patrick Thaddeus Jackson. 2007. "Twisting Tongues and Twisting Arms: The Power of Political Rhetoric." *European Journal of International Relations* 13(1): 35–66.

[21] De Waal, Francis. 1996. *Good Natured: The Origins of Right and Wrong in Humans and Other Animals*. Cambridge: Harvard University Press, 2.

to our immoral nature. Humans are the scorpions who cannot help but sting the frog. Yet this is a strikingly incomplete understanding of what makes us human. We are "moral animals," to quote the title of Robert Wright's book, the same phrase used by Morgenthau in his quote at the very beginning of this book, ironically because the latter is so associated with the pessimistic, unethical, or amoral understanding of humankind. One of the aims of this book is to reclaim the use of human nature from those who do not understand it.

Humans' ethical sense is physically embodied in our emotions. Our feelings are evolved mechanisms that lead us to automatically experience outrage at injustice to ourselves and others, guilt for our moral transgressions, and shame at having them exposed. These have all had the effect of promoting human chances in the evolutionary process. While we might reach different moral conclusions through active deliberation, our first draft morally is always intuitive. And even if we, for instance, decide that what is most humanitarian is to refrain from all violence regardless of the consequences, while others decide that violence might lead to fewer deaths in the long run and is therefore justified on the basis of the same humanitarian benchmark, our very concern for others is not something we can reason our way to. It is already there. We "know" it because we feel it.

Morality originated under conditions of anarchy precisely because of its adaptive function in promoting material well-being. It is not despite anarchy, as structural realists maintain, but on account of anarchy that humans have an ethical sense. "[O]ur noble tendencies might not only have survived the ruthless pressures of the material world, but actually have been nurtured by them."[22] Therefore, there can be no amoral "autonomy of the political sphere." The environment selected for morality, a case of "first image reversed" causation.[23]

This is not to say that states apply moral principles objectively, impartially, and even-handedly any more than individuals do. Their claims of unfairness or harm are just as myopic, inclined to give themselves the moral benefit of the doubt. Actions we take are not

[22] Frank, Robert H. 1988. *Passions within Reason: The Strategic Role of the Emotions*. New York: Norton, ix.
[23] Kertzer, Joshua D. and Dustin Tingley. 2018. "Political Psychology in International Relations: Beyond the Paradigms." *Annual Review of Political Science* 21: 329–330.

as threatening as the same actions taken by others, as students of the security dilemma have long observed. Others' blows hurt more and are less justified than ours. States, made as they are of humans, are as self-righteous as they are righteous. Yet this should not distract from the phenomenology of morality, the subjective feeling that one is in the right, and its implications for understanding international relations. And as we will see, the combination of moral condemnation and binding morality inherent in self-righteousness is a potent and destructive ethical cocktail.

Evolutionary ethics has implications for both liberal and realist approaches to morality. A truncated understanding of morality confines the empirical and positive study of morality in international relations, restricting our focus to just a few distinct and largely modern phenomena such as humanitarian intervention and foreign aid. While important, they are hardly the whole story. This is only the (humanitarian) tip of the larger moral iceberg. The book should be read as a complement and a corrective to liberal accounts and tendencies, not a polemic. Yet it also demands that we allow for the likelihood that there are genuinely felt moral concerns on the part of others that we do not share. To properly understand morality, we need to try to escape our own subjectivity. This is not always easy. As we will see in Chapter 6, for instance, German leaders felt they had every right to complain that their imperial empire was unjustifiably small, a notion premised on the common assumption at the time that there was a natural distinction to be made between civilized and uncivilized nations. How the colonized felt about it was irrelevant to them.

The liberal position, however, is considerably stronger than the structural realist or rationalist position of the "autonomous sphere." Much of IR scholarship explicitly maintains or implicitly accepts that the anarchic nature of the international system differentiates anarchic international politics from interpersonal interactions within well-organized societies in a way that makes morality irrelevant to foreign affairs. Save references to "greedy states,"[24] generally ethically sanitized by relabeling them as "revisionists," there is no mention of ethics. Free-loading becomes "free-riding." Rationalists might write of "cheating," but this seems to evoke no outrage. After all, we can simply

---

[24] Glaser, Charles. 2000. *Rational Theory of International Politics*. Princeton University Press.

call it "defection." Morality is scrubbed away. In amoral accounts of international relations such as these, even killing on the part of the state is treated phlegmatically. It is "just business." Violence is used without moral qualms but also borne without moral condemnation. There are no vengeful fantasies, no declarations of just rights or claims of being unjustly wronged. Human beings, and their leaders in larger groups, neither see or speak evil. What happens in anarchy stays in anarchy.

This is at odds with what we know about the perpetration of violence at every level of human society. Fiske and Rai write that "most violence is *morally motivated*.... [T]he person doing the violence subjectively feels that what she is doing is right: she believes that she should do the violence." In fact, "she is actually moved by moral emotions such as loyalty or outrage,"[25] that is, the binding foundations and moral condemnation, respectively. This is known as "virtuous violence" and is much more common than pure, morally indifferent, and instrumental killing. By presuming instrumental violence, we are missing the fact that most use of physical force, from the "war room to death row,"[26] is moralistic. Pinker argues, "The world has far too much morality. If you added up all the homicides committed in pursuit of self-help justice, the casualties of religious and revolutionary wars, the people executed for victimless crimes and misdemeanors and the targets of ideological genocides, they would surely outnumber the fatalities from amoral predation and conquest."[27] Or, as Walzer asserts in one of this book's epigraphs, "For as long as men and women have talked about war, they have talked about it in terms of right and wrong."[28]

Predatory violence, based on a pure desire for gain and greed with no ethical inhibitions, does unfortunately exist both within states and without. Not all humans have an ethical sense; nor do all state leaders, the Nazi regime being the most prominent example. However, that is precisely the point. Hitler's Germany does not represent the

---

[25] Fiske, Alan Page and Tage Shakti Rai. 2014. *Virtuous Violence: Hurting and Killing to Create, Sustain, End, and Honor Social Relationships.* Cambridge: Cambridge University Press, 5.

[26] Slovic, Paul, C. K. Mertz, David M. Markowitz, Andrew Quist, and Daniel Västfjäll. 2020. "Virtuous Violence from the War Room to Death Row." *Proceedings of the National Academy of Sciences* 117(34): 20474–20482.

[27] Pinker, *The Better Angels of Our Nature*, 622.

[28] Walzer, *Just and Unjust Wars*, 3.

norm of international relations, as it would were the "autonomy of the political sphere" to accurately depict the nature of world politics. This extreme example of pure immorality reveals the essential moral quality of humankind. As De Waal writes, "A society lacking notions of right and wrong is about the worst thing we can imagine – if we can imagine it at all."[29]

It is important, however, not to push the biological argument too far. Very few evolutionary psychologists or theorists of moral psychology are biological determinists. They recognize the tremendous human potential for moral entrepreneurship and dizzying cultural variation in the application of moral values. Indeed this book will highlight two moral *revolutions* that have affected the very nature of international relations, seen at work in the case chapters on German foreign policy. Even within each moral foundation, there are a number of values that conflict with one another, tradeoffs and tensions resolved differently across space but also time. Think of the difficulties in reconciling liberty and equality in modern liberal states, even though both grow out of respect for the individual. The implications of particular moral principles, that is, the operationalization of moral foundations into specific moral norms, can also vary widely. Even if communist and liberal systems both aim at creating a more humane society, they are profoundly different. Ideologies and –isms (nationalism, Marxism, Gaullism, etc.) often perform this work of translation.

When it comes to the binding foundations, owing loyalty to a group does not tell us what constitutes the group in the first place, nor the basis on which authority rests. This reminds us not to take for granted the modern *nation*-state, in which citizens identify with others on the basis of certain shared characteristics. Not only does binding morality not identify these traits and attributes, the creation of nations themselves as "imagined communities"[30] in Europe was a moral revolution that called into question the basis of legitimate authority for royal sovereigns.

Nevertheless, there are limits to even moral revolutions. We are always working with a particular moral menu defined by our evolutionary origins. We reimagine and reconfigure these moral foundations

[29] De Waal, *Good Natured*, 3.
[30] The term is that of Anderson, Benedict. 2006. *Imagined Communities: Reflections on the Origin and Spread of Nationalism*. London: Verso Books.

into new constellations, but we cannot manufacture new moral impulses. I think of our biological inheritance as a set of ingredients that can be combined in an incredible diversity of ways to suit our cultural tastes. Yet there are some tastes that are universally appealing or unappealing to us. Although cultural and individual-level variation in moral definition abounds, there are certain moral universals such as honesty, fairness, reciprocity, and the condemnation of unjustified aggression that are so universal as to suggest a strong biological foundation. They literally make us human.

Not only does evolution inform what is morally universal; it also illuminates moral divides and individual-level variation. While the emotional feeling of concern for others in need is so common in the species that it seems to be universal across societies, this does not mean that it is felt to the same degree across individuals, and indeed some might lack this impulse entirely. The same is also true of the binding foundations. This, in addition to tensions between the two moral intuitions, creates plenty of room for ethical debate. I draw on Duckitt's "dual process model" of ideology, which shows that political divisions are largely reducible to two dimensions of moral conflict, one defined by a humanitarian motivation to provide for others' welfare, the other defined by a desire to protect the ingroup.[31] In contemporary politics, the former expresses itself in advocacy for cosmopolitan projects of multilateralism and global aid, the latter in hawkish foreign policy attitudes. These ideological differences frequently divide left from right in modern nation-states.

Each dimension is associated with foundational characterizations of the social environment – second-order moral beliefs, that is, perceptions about the morality of others. The motivation to protect is grounded in a notion of the world as a dangerous place in which the fine, upstanding, and honorable members of a community must bind together against wrongdoers. Those who lack the motivation to provide see the world as a competitive struggle of all-against-all in which individuals must be amoral and ruthless. A competitive world

---

[31] Duckitt, John. 2001. "A Dual-Process Cognitive-Motivational Theory of Ideology and Prejudice." *Advances in Experimental Social Psychology* 33: 41–113; Duckitt, John, Claire Wagner, Ilouize Du Plessis, and Ingrid Birum. 2002. "The Psychological Bases of Ideology and Prejudice: Testing a Dual Process Model." *Journal of Personality and Social Psychology* 83(1): 75.

is different from a dangerous one, in that belief in the latter is highly moralized, distinguishing between others who are good and bad, moral and immoral. It is only in the former that we find believers in the autonomy of the political sphere.

While we are accustomed to thinking of humanitarian and even multilateralist attitudes about foreign affairs as having an ethical core, this book shows that the foreign policy beliefs of what we now call the political right are just as moralistic. This is typically overlooked, I suspect because of the limited menu in an international relations scholarship predicated primarily on liberal values. Those who embrace what we today call a "conservative" perspective believe that strong authority is necessary to protect the innocent from the wicked. At home, strong law and order and strict adherence to moral norms are necessary to generate social stability and send a message that bad behavior will not be tolerated, something that seems unnecessary to those with more optimistic expectations about human behavior.[32] Abroad, a strong military is necessary.

Much of the resistance to the notion of a biological basis to morality is likely normative. It seems to cheapen our better angels, especially if we understand these as ultimately serving a selfish motive of survival, albeit one of which we are unconscious. And biological arguments have a (undeservedly) deterministic reputation; if human beings are just hardwired to act in certain ways, such as favor their ingroups, this seems to deny us the ability to effect change in moral values, not to mention a basis on which to condemn those who violate certain ethical maxims. We cannot blame others for things they cannot control. Plus, wasn't Hitler an evolutionist? That can't be good.

The arguments of this book hopefully clear up some of these misconceptions. More than that, I argue that understanding the biological basis of morality is much more normatively satisfying than the dominant understanding in international relations – that norms are purely the product of social construction. Constructivist approaches argue that what constitutes right and wrong is purely (or at least largely) the product of intersubjective agreement at any time and place. If this is all there

---

[32] Altemeyer, Robert A. 1998. "The Other 'Authoritarian Personality'." *Advances in Experimental Social Psychology* 30: 47–91; Feldman, Stanley. 2003. "Enforcing Social Conformity: A Theory of Authoritarianism." *Political Psychology* 24(1): 41–74.

is to morality, we are denied a firm foundation from which to ethically judge others' behavior, even Hitler. Humanitarianism, just as much as ingroup patriotism, lacks justification. Others have noted this tension in liberal norms scholarship. It implicitly assumes a humanitarian benchmark for assessing moral progress, yet taken to its logical theoretical conclusion, it has no external theoretical viewpoint by which to do so. Biology tells us that humanitarianism has material roots arising from the ways by which the exchange of reciprocal gestures, sanctioned by our feelings of right and wrong, that allowed human beings to thrive. This is precisely what Hitler, who dismissed humanitarianism as bourgeois, Christian morality with no basis in material reality, got wrong about evolution. Conversely, we must acknowledge the ubiquitous presence of ingroup favoritism. This is the price for liberal moralists. Yet the empirical findings of this book buttress those from other disciplines that outgroup hate and moral indifference to humanity are not equivalent to ingroup love; nor are they ingrained human traits. Hitler's was a perverted version of binding morality. I discuss the normative issues raised by the empirics of this book in the concluding chapter alongside an empirical evaluation of some of Hitler's worst immoral excesses.

Empirical Strategies and the Plan of the Book

My aim is to offer a new characterization of the nature, quite literally, of international relations, one informed by evolutionary ethics. Since anarchy "caused" the development of morality, there is no reason to believe that morality somehow disappears when countries enter the fray of international relations. Since the world is anarchic, states might engage in more self-help. But more often than not, this is "self-help justice," the same things that individuals would do, or feel justified doing, in the absence of established order. My evolutionary account considers IR to be just one more domain of human interaction, not an autonomous sphere, given the common denominator – human beings. In this way, looking for the difference between "public" and "private" morality is a false errand. This is just as true in power politics as it is in other aspects of international relations. To understand the nature *of* power politics, we must understand the nature *in* power politics. These types of paradigm-challenging contributions are often weak on empirics. I believe that the evidentiary standards should be proportional to the boldness of the claim. I have three main strategies.

An evolutionary account proves especially tricky to test, since the processes leading to the behaviors I uncover are unobservable. My first strategy is to take a number of theories from moral and social psychology grounded in evolutionary claims and show that they illuminate critical components of international relations and foreign policy behavior. Because binding morality creates cohesive groups that project moral expectations and standards onto other groups, we should witness the same moral dynamics at work between groups as within them. My second empirical strategy is to take advantage of the fact that universal behaviors that emerge from our biology are automatic and intuitive. I utilize these two strategies in the first two empirical chapters of this book, which rely wholly on quantitative data. The more universal the domains from which I find evidence – across different cultural and non-Western national contexts, at different levels of analysis, and in political and non-political environments – the stronger the claim that they have a basis in human evolution. My third strategy is the "least likely" case, demonstrating the centrality of morality in the behavior of perhaps the biggest, baddest bully in international relations – Germany following Bismarck's departure up to and including (in certain limited ways) the Nazi regime. Germany, perhaps more than any other country, ostensibly shows what happens when foreign policy is stripped of morality. In the last six chapters, I turn to the German case studies, which demonstrate many of the mechanisms highlighted by evolutionary accounts – the importance of audiences, the moral underpinnings of political ideology – in action.

Because moral condemnation is a part of our biology, when we talk about war and violence, we cannot help but moralize. Whenever humans talk about harm and threat, they automatically speak evil. To say that some individual, group, or country is threatening is *inherently* an act of moral condemnation, in a way that is not true of the way we think about threats from nonhuman sources. A bear stealing your picnic basket is scary. A 6'8" human doing the same is scary but also a bad man. With Caleb Pomeroy, I test this claim in Chapter 4 with a word embedding analysis of several large textual corpora. Word embedding analyses can be used to measure our implicit associations by looking for the company that particular words keep. Because harm and threat are so inextricably intertwined with moral condemnation and disapproval, utterances of words indicating these concepts have a consistent negative moral valence. Whether it be speeches before the United Nations or private deliberations of American foreign policy officials, when policymakers and politicians talk about harm and threat, they simultaneously use words indicating judgments of immorality. We find the same is true of a massive quotidian and nonpolitical corpus meant to represent the entire English language. Elites do not operate autonomously from moral considerations in ways that differentiate them from ordinary people.

Fiske's "warmth-competence" model identifies moral characteristics as the most important criteria by which we form our impressions of others.[33] We notice what might present material threats or opportunities for us, and someone's ethical character is the most important thing to know. In other words, we see evil (and good). Chapter 4 indicates that we do the same with other nation-states. An original survey experiment on the Russian public shows that moral attributes are the single most important basis by which respondents make threat assessments of both other individuals and other nation-states, outweighing even power. Yet morality is nowhere to be seen in theories of threat assessment in international relations, presumably because the political sphere is thought to be autonomous and impervious to ethics. Again with Caleb Pomeroy, I buttress these findings by analyzing two observational surveys of Chinese respondents. One shows that attributions of Americans as being warlike are extremely highly correlated with assignations of immorality, barbarity, arrogance, and insincerity. The other shows that the more citizens of this US rival make negative moral assessments about the character of Americans, the more concerned they are about American involvement in the Pacific region on a variety of issues, even while controlling for threat perception. This shows the broader generalizability and external validity of the Russian experiment, which did not ask respondents to answer questions about real-life foreign policy issues. Combined, the results reassure us that this is not just a WEIRD (Western, educated, industrialized, rich, and democratic) phenomenon, but a frequent complaint about psychological theories.[34]

---

[33] Fiske, Susan T., Amy J. C. Cuddy, and Peter Glick. 2007. "Universal Dimensions of Social Cognition: Warmth and Competence." *Trends in Cognitive Sciences* 11(2): 77–83.

[34] Henrich, Joseph, Steven J. Heine, and Ara Norenzayan. 2010. "Most People Are Not WEIRD." *Nature* 466(7302): 29.

If moral condemnation has a basis in evolution, then it should be easy to invoke and hard to avoid. A literature largely sympathetic to my claims maintains that individuals and publics develop mental pictures or "images" of specific others, more often than not containing moralized depictions, that subsequently inform interpretations of their behavior. I do not disagree, but such history is often unnecessary. The last survey experiment in Chapter 4 tests the response of the Russian and American public to fictional countries involved in a dispute over territory with valuable resources. Leaders of those countries who use force and cause casualties in occupying 50% of the territory, as opposed to making a diplomatic demand for an equal split, are morally judged as less trustworthy and greedier. Using force and causing harm to others matters much more than whether the country was pursuing oil or water, another manipulated aspect of the scenario meant to capture whether or not respondents were more forgiving of action in a "lifeboat" situation of material scarcity. Respondents in both countries judge the pursuit of water less harshly than oil, but this effect is small in comparison to the other treatments. Even in the absence of crystallized images, moral condemnation quickly emerges.

Recent advances in moral and social psychology have made clear that political ideology has moorings in the same moral foundations thought to have evolutionary roots. As previously mentioned, a number of different scholars have converged on what Duckitt has labeled a "dual process model" of political ideology, a two-dimensional framework for explaining the fundamental cleavages in politics. The first dimension captures binding morality, driven by a motivation to *protect* from threats. Linked with a narrower ingroup identity, the motivational goal of protection is associated with the moral foundations that bind groups together in order to meet challenges from inside and outside. The second dimension captures a motivation to *provide* for others' welfare, what we have called humanitarian morality, which defines virtue as taking care of others. Its absence indicates the amoralism we presume is omnipresent in international politics. These moral differences account for why some see the need for strong law-and-order policies (to protect) while others emphasize the need for a comprehensive welfare net for the weakest and most vulnerable (to provide).

Since there is no autonomous political sphere, however, these divisions over morality are not confined to domestic political controversies. We project these same cleavages onto foreign policy. In the second empirical chapter, I present evidence from surveys of Americans and Russians showing that the two-dimensional models of foreign policy belief systems found to structure foreign policy attitudes in the United States and other countries have moral roots. Militant internationalism (MI), our beliefs about the necessity of carrying a big stick and being willing to use it, is strongly associated with binding moral values, our motivation to protect. Cooperative internationalism (CI), our beliefs about the gains to be had from cooperation and our obligations to others outside our own borders, is strongly associated with the moral motivation to provide. CI and MI are enormously important dispositions, postures, and attitudinal orientations shown to help both masses and elites derive policy preferences on more specific foreign policy issues.[35] Yet these reduce to even more fundamental values that grow out of our evolutionary past. This is not just true in the liberal West, but also in Russia, as the chapter shows.

Any residual concern that this is just a WEIRD phenomenon should be dispelled by the focus here on binding morality, thought to be the more "traditional" and therefore more common set of ethical considerations, across the globe. Rather than deriving a moral theory from the Western experience and projecting it onto others, I am returning binding morality to its proper, central place in even the behavior of developed, industrialized countries.[36]

What is the least likely case to show that there is no such thing as an autonomous political sphere – the country that, if we were to show the centrality of morality, would upend our traditional depictions of international politics? It is easy to pick and choose instances of moral condemnation, binding morality, and the influence of morally judgmental audiences from the historical record. But my aim is bolder – to show the ubiquity of these processes. I choose Germany, case studies of whose behavior form the last six chapters of the book.

---

[35] Wittkopf, Eugene. 1990. *Faces of Internationalism*. Durham: Duke University Press.

[36] On one score, however, the manuscript can be properly criticized. I neglect gender and sex differences in morality and its evolution. Research has found that women are more committed to the care and fairness foundations, whereas men exhibit higher scores on authority and ingroup loyalty. Graham, Jesse, Brian A. Nosek, Jonathan Haidt, Ravi Iyer, Spassena Koleva, and Peter H. Ditto. 2011. "Mapping the Moral Domain." *Journal of Personality and Social Psychology* 101(2): 366. I consider the role of gendered stereotypes about what constitutes honor, however, below.

The reasoning is drolly captured by Norm MacDonald in his Netflix comedy special *Hitler's Dog, Gossip and Trickery*: "On the entire earth, there's only one country that really scares me. That's the country of Germany.... I don't know if you are students of history, but Germany, in the previous century, they decided to go to war. And who did they decide to go to war with? [dryly and with comic pause]: The *world*. So you think that would last about five seconds and the world would win, and that would be that. But it was actually close. Then 30 years pass, and Germany decides to go to war again. And, once again, they choose as their foe: the world.... And now this time, they *really* almost win." We might also remember that a fictionalized version of Erich Ludendorff, the German general in World War I who will make an appearance later, was featured as the bad guy in the *Wonder Woman* movie (the good one).

There is a large school of historical thought we can call the "Fischer school," which is frequently echoed in international relations scholarship and which maintains that "the entire German nation, with the exception of some small and unimportant groups, had to a greater or lesser degree become the victims of an overwhelmingly obsession with power, the desire to obtain for the German empire equality of status with the three great world powers."[37] This tendency went unbroken through Hitler: "[T]he whole of the recent German past, from the beginning of the twentieth century, was nothing more than the introductory phase of the 'greater Germany' imperialism of the national-socialists."[38] Amoralists, of course, love to dominate and do not feel any embarrassment in doing so. Wolfers notes that such amoralism was pervasive in Germany, penetrating even its theorists of international relations: "German writers have been particularly insistent that ethical standards which apply to private individuals cannot measure the behavior of states."[39] These were believers in the autonomy of the political sphere. The decisive break only came with German defeat in World War II, after which time it became a stable democracy based on Western commitments to human rights and a reliable force for good

[37] Mommsen, W. J. 1966. "The Debate on German War Aims." *Journal of Contemporary History* 1(3): 55.

[38] Ibid, 47.

[39] Wolfers, Arnold. 1949. "Statesmanship and Moral Choice." *World Politics* 1(2): 176.

in international politics. Germany was the "tamed power"[40] with a "culture of antimilitarism,"[41] committed to maintaining international peace and prosperity through multilateral cooperation, avoiding the *Sonderweg* (special path) it had taken before.

I instead show that very little of interest about German foreign policy can be understood *without* making morality central. The typical interpretation of German foreign policy suffers from the truncated understanding of morality symptomatic of political science, international relations, and perhaps much of the humanities and social sciences. Germany is indubitably guilty of hostility to liberal morality. As Mommsen notes, the typical depiction of German foreign policy pre-World War II is "based largely on ethical convictions ... reflected in the repeated condemnation of the extremism and recklessness of German nationalist and imperialist ambitions."[42] Once we widen our scope, however, to allow for the presence of binding morality as well as understand the centrality of moral condemnation in foreign affairs, we see German foreign policy (before Hitler at least) in an entirely different light. In closely analyzing Germany's foreign policy, in particular domestic political divisions over the right course to take, we also see in practice the utility of the dual-process model and the centrality of domestic and international audiences in instances of great historical importance.

These chapters proceed chronologically. The first two chapters in this section deal with Wilhelmine German foreign policy before the war, the third and fourth German domestic politics during World War I, and the last two Nazi foreign policy. Each chapter on German foreign policy is written in such a way as to be largely self-standing and to contribute to some theoretical or empirical controversy in international relations scholarship or German historiography, another way of showing that no one can avoid morality in this field, even if they tried (although they do try). Three of these chapters on pre-Nazi foreign policy are paired with a survey experiment of a contemporary population that allows me to identify the effect of morality at the microfoundational, individual level when it is particularly difficult to do so macrohistorically, which also adds to the external validity of my

---

[40] Katzenstein, Peter J. (ed.). 1997. *Tamed Power: Germany in Europe*. Ithaca and London: Cornell University Press.

[41] Berger, Thomas. 1998. *Cultures of Antimilitarism: National Security in Germany and Japan*. Baltimore: Johns Hopkins University Press.

[42] Mommsen, "The Debate on German War Aims," 48.

claims. It is entirely possible of course to read these without accepting any of what I claim about morality's evolutionary origins. Indeed
one of the central themes of these chapters is the way that morality
can change in revolutionary ways very quickly. However, I do believe
that the case of Germany is decisive in putting to bed the notion of an
autonomous political sphere, even in the context of intense imperial
competition, power politics, and war.

Wilhelmine foreign policy was excessively moralistic and self-
righteous. In Chapter 6, I show that German insistence on (a highly
subjective understanding of) fair treatment in early twentieth-century
world politics is mistaken for wanton status-seeking. The status dissatisfaction literature correctly turns our attention to the foreign policy consequences of perceived gaps between what states deserve and
what they have. However, we also know this as a particular form of
fairness, that of equity. Feeling unjustly rewarded for its great power
position, Wilhelmine leaders provoked two crises over the status of
Morocco, a nominally independent kingdom slowly falling under
French control. However, in the first, it did not seek any special
advantages for Germany, as it would have had it been a pure status-
seeker. Instead, Germany sought the moral high ground by forcing
the convocation of an international conference to settle the question
of Western countries' rights more generally. This strategy ultimately
backfired by denying the possibility of a bilateral deal with France
but also leaving the country without a moral leg to stand on when
no other Western power expressed dissatisfaction with French predominance at the Algeciras conference. Itself highly self-righteous,
Germany overstated the role that moral condemnation would play
for others. In the second crisis, Germany once again reacted strongly
to increasing French influence in Morocco without the compensation
that France had offered to other countries. To force a settlement,
the Germans clumsily tried to apply military leverage by deploying
a gunboat while simultaneously disavowing such intentions through
utterly transparent pretexts. This disingenuousness created suspicions
on the part of the English in particular (since morality is the main way
by we judge others) and generated a crisis wholly centered on who
was to blame. When the moral duel exploded into the public sphere,
the countries came to the brink of war. Even though no shots were
exchanged, the crisis crystallized and hardened the divisions between
Germany and its soon-to-be World War I adversaries.

The current literature bakes justice into the conception of status and does not provide a mechanism for distinguishing status and fairness. The key, I argue, is whether the actor in question is demanding exclusive rights for itself, consistent with a desire to occupy a rarefied rank that has more value the fewer who have it; or whether it is content to share a higher rank with others who have earned it. Based on what we know from fairness-seeking in moral psychology, I hypothesize that fairness is judged by whether or not one is excluded from a club which they feel entitled to join, but once included they do not begrudge the admission of others who deserve it. However, they do not feel the same outrage when others are excluded as when they are; they are self-righteous.

We see this in both Moroccan crises, but so as to more precisely distinguish between pure status-seeking and fairness-seeking, I supplement these case studies with two survey experiments of the Russian public. Asked about membership in the Group of Eight (G8), respondents find exclusion to be unfair but not threatening to Russian status. Respondents prefer a more inclusive organization that admits other countries who deserve to be included by virtue of their GDP to an organization in which only Russia is admitted beyond the existing members. When asked to create their own Group of X organization, they respond to experimental manipulations of fairness through alternative measures of GDP, even becoming less likely to include Russia when it is ranked lower in economic activity. Since Wilhelmine Germany and contemporary Russia are regarded as status-seekers par excellence, these findings should lead us to rethink the status quo on status-seeking in international relations.

Chapter 7 tackles a second explanation for Germany's aggressive and bellicose foreign policy during the Wilhelmine period – suspected efforts by entrenched elites to distract from the country's stunted democratic development by generating international threats to unify the country, of which the Moroccan crises were prominent examples. These accounts fail to come to terms with the moral revolution occurring in Germany at the time – the rise of nationalism. A focus on Germany brings home the ways by which political actors can create wholly new combinations of moral values in ways that dramatically affect foreign policy – that is, cultural construction on top of a biological foundation.

The identification of the group as the nation, and the understanding that the nation's welfare is the leader's primary concern, required a revolution in the basis of authority. The legitimacy of the ruler had to be grounded in the people's will rather than divine right, a process that even extended to those countries that retained their sovereigns and did not undergo democratic revolutions. This amounted to an assertion of the moral supremacy of ingroup loyalty over deference to authority and a severing of the de facto equivalence of the two captured in the pithy phrase "L'etat, c'est moi."

Although this moral revolution was not confined to Germany, when it did come to the Reich, it implied that the emperor owed loyalty to the people, even if they were not (and should not be, in the eyes of the nationalist right) equal participants in a democracy. For this reason, German elites could not (and would not have wanted to) invent new ideas that called into question the nature of monarchical rule and their very privileges. Indeed it is these very ideas that allowed German nationalists to begin to critique the emperor for his vacillating and indecisive foreign policy, criticism that would have been previously unthinkable on the part of the German right because it would have been seen as demonstrating insufficient loyalty to the sovereign. The nationalist right began to demand assertiveness in foreign policy and to question the indecisive policy of the Wilhelmine regime in a way that was previously ethically prohibited. In a dangerous world full of immoral enemies, it is natural for binding moralists to venerate will, determination, and resolve since these are thought to be the bases for prevailing in conflicts that safeguard the nation's interests. The second Moroccan crisis was decisive for the breakthrough of a vocal "nationalist opposition," which was previously an oxymoron. During this episode, Wilhelmine elites unsuccessfully tried to opportunistically incite nationalist agitation to use as bargaining leverage vis-à-vis France and England. However, they did not invent such an opposition in the first place.

The internal moral dynamics in Wilhelmine Germany have implications for models of international relations that try to capture the relationship between leaders and their audiences, such as the now well-known "audience cost" models. First, any tendency of elites to avoid censure by standing firm assumes a particular constellation of binding moral values, one in which the nation is felt to be a community to whom all owe loyalty, even the authority figure. Second, any model emphasizing the effect of domestic publics on leaders for lack of resolve or insufficient patriotism is implicitly moral since resolution is a virtue. Since the moral nature of accusations of insufficient resolve is difficult to establish empirically through qualitative case studies, I supplement this chapter with a survey experiment conducted on the American public. For those who hold dangerous world beliefs, four virtues generally thought to indicate "competence" – disciplined and hard-working, strong-willed and determined, tough and strong, and persistent and resolute – are actually used as moral benchmarks, particularly for leaders. The standards by which binding moralists in Germany held Wilhelm II are the same used by contemporary Americans for their leaders.

We also see Germany's excessive self-righteousness in World War I. Binding morality, I argue in Chapters 8 and 9, is directly responsible for Germany's self-defeating behavior during the conflict – its refusal to seek a negotiated settlement when it became clear to rational decision-makers that there was no hope of real victory. According to bargaining models of war, war reveals private information about resolve and power, to which decision-makers respond rationally by increasing or lowering their reservation price for settling. When we are in a hole, we stop digging. Germany during World War I presents a puzzle for this baseline rationalist expectation, and theoretical accounts offer three rational reasons as to why leaders in a losing situation might nevertheless continue to fight, a number dealing with Wilhelmine Germany as a central case. If others cannot be trusted to abide by any peace settlement, a commitment problem arises that makes fighting on rational. Even exploring diplomatic settlement could reveal private information about a lack of resolve. Self-interested leaders fearing that defeat will result in domestic turmoil, revolution, and the loss of their elite prerogatives might have incentives to "gamble for resurrection." This might even result in the inflation of war aims precisely as the battlefield and home-front situation are turning against them in an effort to buy off the ordinary public for its sacrifices.

While these explanations are all theoretically plausible in other contexts, I argue that German elites' resistance to seeking diplomatic settlement, the concern with domestic revolution, and the inflation of war aims are all more parsimoniously accounted for through a focus on morality. All three were the expression of the ethics of German nationalists. Binding morality has built-in escalatory dynamics that make it hard to admit defeat – in this case, literally. Fundamental to this "ethics of community" is an understanding of adversaries as

having largely insatiable demands, in other words, the excessive egoism that generates moral opprobrium. This generates the perception
of a commitment problem that makes anything other than victory
unacceptable; it even creates demands for territorial expansion so as
to secure the country in the future. Right-wing German nationalists
would not even allow the government to make peace overtures to
implacable enemies lest they infer a lack of resolve. The German right
scorned demands for further democratization during the war as selfish class politics indicating that the country was not unified enough –
bound together – for this existential struggle.

Chapter 9 shows that as the war dragged on and Germany's troubles accumulated, the German military, a bulwark of binding morality, even raised its wartime aspirations so as to adequately compensate
for the people's loyal sacrifices. As citizens starve, soldiers perish, and
property is destroyed, there is a natural tendency to accrue some gains
to justify the losses. Otherwise all was in vain, a betrayal of all those
whose sacrificed. This can lead to an increase in war aims when the
rational course is of course to cut losses. The binding foundations lead
individuals toward demanding more just as the objective situation on
the battlefield should be pushing them to settle for less.

This irrationality is best seen in relief, by comparing the nationalist right not only to the German left but also to the consequentialist
and realist ethics of the German chancellor, Bethmann-Hollweg, who
was eventually swept aside by conservative forces. Careful from the
beginning not to define German war aims too grandly, he adjusted
his expectations downward as Germany faltered at home and on the
fronts. The chancellor pragmatically advocated for domestic reform
precisely as a way of preserving German unity during the conflict and
avoiding the overthrow of the regime.

This effect of binding morality on increasing reservation price, the
most obvious manifestation of the irrationality induced by binding
moralism, is more difficult to establish than its other impacts. I therefore conducted a survey panel experiment, presented in Chapter 9,
on a sample of the Russian public, which induced the same inflation
dynamics found in World War I Germany. I presented respondents
with a hypothetical war with the United States in the Arctic over a
valuable piece of territory with natural resources, in which, like World
War I Germany, Russia is continually falling behind with dwindling
chances for victory. Those who identify as binding moralists persist

for much longer in the conflict. Those in the sample who stay in the conflict until the very end increase their reservation price over time, even as the Russians are suffering disproportionate casualties. This is irrational by any standard. This tendency is exacerbated further by an experimental treatment framing capitulation as a betrayal of fallen Russian soldiers. Whereas we might posit hidden ulterior and selfishly rational, motives for German generals trying to avoid a collapse of the German empire and save their hides, we cannot do so for ordinary Russian citizens answering questions about a hypothetical conflict.

Therefore, German foreign policy through World War I was delusional but (highly subjectively) righteous. Ultimately, Germany had far too much morality for its own good, with binding morality contributing to the very collapse of the authoritarian regime. If this exemplar of illiberal foreign policy is nevertheless morally motivated, it indicates that it is time to reevaluate the role played by ethics in foreign affairs. There is no greater liberal success story in international relations than post-war West Germany. Indeed its story is an exemplar of a broader narrative of the march of Western morality, which explains its empirical appeal to constructivist norms scholars. However, by mistaking a lack of liberalism for a lack of morality, we fundamentally misunderstand the dynamics of German policy up until Hitler.

The Nazis, however, were a fundamentally different type of right-wing force, led not by dangerous but by competitive world beliefs. Duckitt's dual-process model helps illuminate the difference. Believers in a competitive world, marked by material scarcity, lack the most basic and universal moral impulses – those of humanitarian concern – and are responsible for the type of predatory violence that treats others as mere objects no more worthy of moral condemnation than moral consideration. For such amoralists who see a dog-eat-dog world, predation, cheating, and violence are not lamentable lesser evils. These acts have no ethical valence at all. Hitler dismissed the very existence of humanitarian ethics as a mere social construction and illusion, refusing even the typical scorn more traditional German nationalists expressed vis-à-vis their wartime adversaries.

This is the second moral revolution explored in this book, a reconstitution of the political right on a racial basis under the Nazi Party. Chapter 10 shows that Hitler's regime explicitly redefined the national community not as a cultural and linguistic entity but as a biological one. Rather than a continuation of previous tendencies in German nationalism, it was a decisive moral break and led to a wholly different basis for, and type of, international aggression. These racial groups, he argued, competed for resources – their daily bread – in a scarce world.[43] He preached ingroup loyalty and deference to his absolute authority (the *Führerprinzip*) so that the Aryan race might act in a unified manner to scrape for resources in a materially limited world. By defining the ingroup racially, in which what bound individuals together was not shared history but blood, Hitler paved the way for practices previously unimaginable even for radical nationalists, such as forced sterilization to advance the race (from the Nazi perspective) and of course the genocide of the Jewish people.

Most important for this book, Hitler's version of binding morality did away with any humanitarian concern for those outside the group. His moral revolution was also a moral devolution. In this way, Hitler's version of binding morality was a perversion of the usual ethics of community since it contained no element of moral condemnation directed externally, only internally at traitors to the German racial group. He felt no need, at least in private, to justify harm to other nations' actions by virtue of their immoral nature. Hitler dismissed the ambitions of Weimar nationalists of the Wilhelmine variety, whose only interest was to rail against the injustices of the Versailles Treaty and demand the return of lost German lands that were rightly theirs, perhaps going as far as annexing the remnants of the German-speaking Austrian empire. For Hitler, who presumed amorality in international affairs, no one had any right to any piece of territory; one simply took it. As a consequence, he defined foreign policy goals that were fundamentally different from those in pre–World War I and even wartime Wilhelmine Germany. Rather than security from implacably hostile and immoral adversaries, Germany's fair share in the imperial division of the world, or the unification of a culturally defined people in a single country, Hitler sought *Lebensraum* (living space) to feed Germany's growing population. Devoid of humanitarianism, Hitler was free to identify goals for German continental expansion that went far beyond what anyone in Wilhelmine Germany had ever considered.

Chapter 11 demonstrates how Nazi amorality led Hitler and the Nazi regime to undertake a fundamentally different type of occupation

---

[43] In this way, Nazism is different from the more pedestrian "looking out for no. 1" attitudes of selfish individuals. It had a group basis.

in Eastern Europe compared to the German army in 1915–1917, in which he aimed not at the paternalistic civilizing of conquered peoples but rather the elimination, evacuation, and instrumentalization of non-Aryan populations. Not all occupation and conquest are the same; the difference is in the underlying moral assumptions of the expansionist. While the occupation of Eastern Europe by the Wilhelmine regime was brutal and therefore by definition inhumane, there is simply no comparison to what the Nazis did and what they would have in all likelihood continued to do had they not lost the war. The difference was the shift from demonization to dehumanization that occurred as the nature of the German right transformed.

As cruel and inhumane as Hitler was, however, his regime drives home a central point of this book. When we assert that international relations are an autonomous sphere or world apart in which morality stops at the edge of the ingroup, we (often unknowingly) presume that Hitlers will be the norm rather than the exception. The Führer exhibited the phlegmatic indifference to moral questions in international affairs that we are so often told to assume. Thankfully, this is not the case.

Most strikingly, however, is the way by which even Hitler operated under the shadow of morality. We will see in Chapter 10 that Hitler largely hid his lack of moral outrage vis-à-vis Germany's historical enemies from the German public during the 1920s, purposively instrumentalizing the Versailles Treaty for propaganda purposes. Following the election of 1930, after which the Nazi Party become a major force in German electoral politics, he entirely jettisoned his amoral biological worldview from his public comments, indicating that he understood it could not appeal widely enough to even a nationally minded electorate. This made it difficult for the British in particular to establish whether he was a (now garden-variety) German nationalist of the Wilhelmine sort or a racial nationalist intent on European domination. They lost crucial time.

This account contrasts sharply with frequent claims in political science and international relations, shared by constructivists and realists, that Hitler was simply a more virulent nationalist and militarist and that in any case some sort of revisionist expansion was inevitable in German foreign policy. By distinguishing between the highly moralized dangerous world beliefs of traditional German nationalists before and after World War I and the entirely amoral competitive world beliefs of

Hitler and the Nazis, the difference finally becomes clear. Both were expansionist but for entirely different reasons. The continuity school finds itself needing to explain away the Holocaust as a sort of side project for Hitler that ultimately does not say much about German foreign policy. My moral account implies that Nazi genocide cannot be extricated from the larger goal of Lebensraum. The comparison of the behavior of the Germany army in World War I and World War II in occupied Eastern Europe in the final chapter shows the human cost of the difference.

Before we turn to empirics, however, the next two chapters lay out the theoretical foundation. The first theoretical chapter exposes the often implicit moral standards that IR scholars bring to their study of ethics in foreign policy and the blindspots this creates. I contrast humanitarian morality with binding and realist ethics and note the central role played by moral condemnation. The second theoretical chapter reviews the evolutionary literature that accounts for these different moral foundations and contrasts my argument with prevailing international relations approaches.

2 | Lesser Angels
Moral Condemnation and Binding Morality in International Relations

When international relations (IR) scholars debate the role of morality, they are almost always talking about moral conscience.[1] Whether it be the transfer of national resources to boost development in lesser developed countries, the willingness to put one's own troops in harm's way to protect vulnerable populations overseas, or the self-imposed restrictions on weapons that do massive damage to civilians in other lands, the moral impulse is the same: caring for others. It is liberal in the sense that it is based on a conception of individuals, regardless of who they are, having inherent worth and dignity. Just as morality in our everyday life is the costly sacrifice of our interests for others around us, morality in international relations is the transcendence of our national egoism. Even skeptics utilize this yardstick.[2] They simply conclude that liberal morality is unattainable given the exigencies of the anarchic environment. The definition of morality is not in question, but rather the follow-through. When Morgenthau writes that statesmen are forced to do "evil" things, he has liberal morality in mind.[3]

Yet this is just one of many manifestations of morality. Human beings are angered by the same selfish behavior at the international level as they are at the interpersonal level. They react with moral condemnation, which justifies the assertion of their own egoistic interests not properly considered by others – that is, others' lack of conscience. In modern international relations, they do this in groups bound together by another set of moral foundations: deference to authority and loyalty to the ingroup. Anarchy might mean that, compared

---

[1] The classic is Lumsdaine, David. 1993. *Moral Vision in International Politics: The Foreign Aid Regime, 1949–1989*. Princeton: Princeton University Press.
[2] Downes, Alexander. 2008. *Targeting Civilians in War*. Ithaca and London: Cornell University Press.
[3] Morgenthau, "The Evil of Politics," 11.

to well-ordered nation-states, human beings take matters into their own hands. That states do not demonstrate the same humanitarian restraint as individuals does not indicate that the international environment is not moralized, however, only that the same options available to them at home are not available internationally.

In this chapter, I demonstrate first how our understanding of ethics in international relation is incomplete. Based on what is likely the most universal of our moral intuitions, humanitarianism and altruism, it has liberal roots that define moral action as that which guarantees equal concern and respect for all individuals, regardless of national origins. Its presence is increasingly evident in all the phenomena mentioned earlier, yet it also obscures the moral bases of much of what constitutes foreign affairs.

I then turn to moral condemnation, contrasting it with moral conscience and exploring the various triggers for our moral outrage: threats to our personal integrity, unfair treatment, and dishonesty and cheating. These have the common denominator of a low welfare tradeoff ratio (WTR) on the part of others. They are willing to do great damage to us for little gain for themselves. I explore how this moral condemnation might be feigned and used instrumentally given the presence of morally judgmental audiences, yet not how this very pretense indicates the power of morality.

Binding morality asks group members to come together to meet external and internal challenges to a community's welfare. Sometimes called "parochial" altruism, I show that it is more complicated than simply drawing a line at which humanitarian concern ends. I push our understanding of binding morality further, arguing that this moral foundation justifies group favoritism by virtue of threats coming from those who would do the group harm. In other words, moral condemnation is central to binding morality. Binding morality is driven by a belief in a dangerous world, second-order moral beliefs that generate a need to demonstrate resolve, and strength vis-à-vis duplicitous and aggressive adversaries. In this moral mindset, resolve becomes an ethical virtue. Because binding morality justifies ingroup favoritism (although not outgroup hate), it is overlooked as an ethical foundation, running afoul of the cosmopolitan nature of liberal morality that typically serves as the benchmark for moral action.

Finally, I compare both liberal and these alternative moral foundations to realist consequentialism. I locate the difference between realist and liberal ethics not so much in the underlying moral ends, which are humanitarian and cosmopolitan in both, but rather on the need to make difficult choices in favor of the lesser evil. Realism is consequentialist, which means something different from what it is typically thought to be in the norms scholarship. Consequentialist judgment is not simply national egoism but rather a highly rational process of ethical decision-making in which individuals are honest with themselves about the moral advantages and disadvantages of alternative courses of action. As such, realism is different from both binding morality and liberal morality in that it cautions against emotionally driven choice. However, as argued in the next chapter, our moral foundations, grounded as they are in our evolutionary past, appeal to us intuitively and automatically and are inextricably intertwined with our emotions. This makes the reasoned deliberation necessary for realist consequentialism hard and therefore rare.

I rely on Haidt's definition of morality as "interlocking sets of values, practices, institutions, and evolved psychological mechanisms that work together to suppress or regulate selfishness and make social life possible."[4] To this I would add, consistent with moral sentimentalism (described subsequently in the following text), that morality is known to human beings by the feelings that it evokes in us, by a literal sense of right and wrong. All ethical principles place limitations on excessive self-interest and encourage other-regarding behavior based on a sense of right and wrong.[5] We see this same definition in international

---

[4] Haidt, Jonathan. 2008. "Morality." *Perspectives on Psychological Science* 3(1): 70; see also Alexander, Richard. 1987. *The Biology of Moral Systems.* New York: De Gruyter, 81.

[5] This is even true of the moral foundation of purity. As Horberg et al. explain, "The domain of purity involves values and principles directed at protecting the sanctity of the body and soul. These values originally related to the evolutionary challenges of avoiding the consumption of toxins, parasites, or bacteria. What began as concerns over purity and contamination of the physical form, however, subsequently extended to include concerns over the purity of the individual's character and social conduct, thus promoting beliefs in the moral value of a physically and mentally pure lifestyle." Horberg, Elizabeth J., Christopher Oveis, Dacher Keltner, and Adam B. Cohen. 2009. "Disgust and the Moralization of Purity." *Journal of Personality and Social Psychology* 97(6): 964. Given that many violations of purity ethics, such as sexual experience before marriage, arguably harm no one, many argue that purity concerns do not fall under this definition of morality. Schein and Gray take issue with this understanding, arguing that purity and other "harmless

relations. Morgenthau writes, "The individual is under the moral obligation to be unselfish, that is, to consider the interest of others before his own or at least besides his own."[6] However, to which others we owe these sacrifices and what behaviors are prescribed and proscribed vary across different conceptions of good and bad, of which there are many. As we will see, both moral condemnation and binding morality are ethical under this same standard. The former tells us how to respond to the excessive selfishness of others in a manner other than saying, "Thank you, sir, may I have another?" The latter has us subjugate our personal interests to the benefit of the group.

Modal Morality: Altruism, Humanitarianism, and the Liberal Understanding of Ethics in International Relations

The most obvious, and likely the most universal, understanding of morality is demonstrating concern for others' welfare, particularly those most in need, such as the sick or the weak. Concern for others' welfare can entail both negative – refrain from killing – and positive – feed the hungry – obligations.[7] Humans have obligations to avoid harm to others but also to care for them. For this reason, Graham et al. call this moral foundation "harm/care."[8] The harm/care principle, whose manifestations include charity, benevolence, and generosity, is altruistic. Altruism

wrongs" are "best understood as 'transformations' or 'intermediaries' of harm, values whose violation leads to perceptions of concrete harm. For example, Anita Bryant believed that the 'purity' violation of gay rights would convince kids to be gay, which would not only destroy their vulnerable immortal souls but also undermine procreation and hence the American family, which would bankrupt the nation and eventually lead to anarchy." Therefore, he or she who protects chastity does a prosocial turn. Schein, Chelsea and Kurt Gray. 2018. "The Theory of Dyadic Morality: Reinventing Moral Judgment by Redefining Harm." *Personality and Social Psychology Review* 22(1): 34. Nevertheless, I do neglect purity in the rest of this book as its implications for international relations are less clear to me.

[6] Morgenthau, "The Evil of Politics," 12.

[7] Shue, Henry. 1996. *Basic Rights: Subsistence, Affluence, and US Foreign Policy*. Princeton: Princeton University Press.

[8] Graham, Jesse, Jonathan Haidt, and Brian A. Nosek. 2009. "Liberals and Conservatives Rely on Different Sets of Moral Foundations." *Journal of Personality and Social Psychology* 96(5): 1029; Graham, Jesse, Jonathan Haidt, Sena Koleva, Matt Motyl, Ravi Iyer, Sean P. Wojcik, and Peter H. Ditto. 2013. "Moral Foundations Theory: The Pragmatic Validity of Moral Pluralism." *Advances in Experimental Social Psychology* 47: 55–130.

is such a fundamental ethical value as to be equated with morality in much of the scientific literature, synonymous with being humane and thus a part of our very essence as humans.[9] Traven shows how what we conceive of as modern liberal norms of concern for innocent civilians in warfare are hardly unique to modern Western societies. They are much more universal and found in ancient societies as well.[10]

Altruism and caring are predicated on the belief and understanding that others are deserving of our concern. They have inherent value. In Western (but not solely Western) societies, we go so far as to declare that all individuals are fundamentally equal and, as such, entitled to certain inalienable rights.[11] This is *liberal* morality, in the classical and individualist sense. While not identical, the ethical principles of altruism and equality nevertheless share a similarity. Individuals, whether equal or not, are the fundamental units of moral value and the locus of ethical concern. Unsurprisingly, humanitarian and egalitarian attitudes are highly correlated in the psychological literature.[12] For this reason, Graham and Haidt identify two separate foundations of humanitarian morality – harm/care and fairness/reciprocity – that they combine under the category of the "individualizing" foundations. In the terms of this book, the individualizing foundations are particular, culturally defined, and historically contingent configurations of more basic elements of our moral menu.

The positive literature on morality in international relations rests on this altruistic and egalitarian conception of what constitutes right and wrong as the benchmark by which to empirically establish moral progress. Whereas the harm/care principle in our daily lives manifests itself in our donations to charitable giving or costly acts of generosity, in international relations, it is evident in the efforts by state and non-state actors to help those outside of our national borders, without any

---

[9] De Waal, *Good Natured*, 1.

[10] Traven, David. 2015. "Moral Cognition and the Law and Ethics of Armed Conflict." *International Studies Review* 17(4): 556–587.

[11] Dworkin, Ronald. 1978. *Taking Rights Seriously*. Harvard University Press; Rhoda E., Howard and Jack Donnelly. 1986. "Human Dignity, Human Rights and Political Regimes." *American Political Science Review* 80(3): 801–817.

[12] Schwartz, Shalom. 1992. "Universals in the Content and Structure of Values: Theoretical Advances and Empirical Tests in 20 Countries." *Advances in Experimental Social Psychology* 25:1–65. However, as we know, it is possible to believe in inequality while still being humanitarian; colloquially, we call this paternalism.

ulterior motive.[13] Most of the notable contributions in the "norms" literature, the most prominent body of positive research on international morality, document humanitarian phenomena such as decolonization, taboos and norms against weapons of mass destruction, and human rights advocacy.[14]

Moral progress in the norms literature, and therefore the standard for morality itself, is not only altruistic and humanitarian but also liberal and cosmopolitan, based on the commitment to fundamental equality for all individuals, regardless of national origin.[15] For Price, altruism and liberal egalitarianism are one and the same. Humanitarianism "has long been central to varieties of liberal and critical theories of IR, whose champions in different ways have laid claim to the moral high ground in pointing the ways to possibilities of positive moral change in world politics against skepticism."[16] Even realists' standard of morality relies on this liberal, cosmopolitan conception, as I will discuss later in the chapter.

Caring for others is undoubtedly moral and universally accepted as so, and the last few centuries have seen a marked increase in the application of that particular set of principles beyond the water's edge.

---

[13] Lumsdaine, *Moral Vision in International Politics*, 11.
[14] Crawford, Neta. 2002. *Argument and Change in World Politics*. Cambridge University Press; Tannenwald, Nina. 1999. "The Nuclear Taboo: The United States and the Normative Basis of Nuclear Non-Use." *International Organization* 53(3): 433–468; Finnemore, Martha. 1996. *National Interests in International Society*. Ithaca and London: Cornell University Press; Finnemore, Martha. 2003. *The Purpose of Intervention: Changing Beliefs about the Use of Force*. Ithaca: Cornell University Press; Jackson, Robert H. 1993. "The Weight of Ideas in Decolonization: Normative Change in International Relations." In: Judith Goldstein and Robert O. Keohane (eds.). *Ideas and Foreign Policy*. Ithaca: Cornell University Press, 111–139; Kaufmann, Chaim D. and Robert A. Pape. 1999. "Explaining Costly International Moral Action: Britain's Sixty-Year Campaign against the Atlantic Slave Trade." *International Organization* 53(4): 631–668; Audie, Klotz. 1995. "Norms Reconstituting Interests: The Global Racial Equality and U.S. Sanctions against South Africa." *International Organization* 49(30): 451–478; Joshua, Busby. 2010. *Moral Movements and Foreign Policy*. Cambridge: Cambridge University Press; Carpenter, Charli. 2014. *Lost Causes: Agenda-Vetting in Global Issue Networks and the Shaping of Human Security*. Ithaca: Cornell University Press.
[15] Barnett, Michael. 2009. "Evolution without Progress: Humanitarianism in a World of Hurt." *International Organization* 63(4): 621–663; Price, Richard. 2008. "Moral Limit and Possibility in World Politics." *International Organization* 62(2): 191–220.
[16] Price, "Moral Limit and Possibility," 192.

However, are there other important, perhaps equally universal, moral principles also evident in international relations that we are missing by virtue of our particular working definition? If this is the case, we might underestimate the presence of morality in international relations.

Based on the empirical study of morality in psychology, there are two strong candidates for other universal moral principles – the phenomenon of moralistic condemnation and punishment evident in such practices as retaliation, revenge, negative reciprocity and the pursuit of justice against immoral others – and the group-based morality that Graham et al. call the "binding" foundations.[17] There is likely a reason why both have largely escaped the view of those who investigate the ethics of international relations. Both involve defending self-interest against the impingement of others. Moral condemnation is the outrage we feel when others unjustifiably step on our toes. Binding morality asserts the importance of the group's interest; in the context of international relations, this equates to a selfish concern with our group as compared to the cosmopolitan whole. However, as Thomas writes, from within the norms literature itself, we should not equate morality with altruism. "Problems arise not from the assumption of egoism itself but from the derivative assumption that egoism is incompatible with ethical action, which is assumed to derive only from altruistic motives."[18]

Fighting Fire with Fire: Moral Condemnation as Moral Foundation

As a general principle, neither altruistic nor individualistic conception of ethics can provide guidance on one of the most central moral questions: What do we do when others behave in an overly selfish manner, one that disregards the interests of others and ourselves? What is the proper response to the immoral actions of others? To wrong? In this vein, Price laments, "[T]here is little satisfactory engagement with the problem of whether and how to deal ethically with the ubiquity of ruthlessly instrumental actors.... [W]hat does one do in a situation – indeed, in a world – confronted constantly with agents who do not

[17] Graham et al., "Liberals and Conservatives"; Graham et al., "Moral Foundations Theory."

[18] Thomas, Ward. 2001. *The Ethics of Destruction*. Ithaca: Cornell University Press, 13.

approach a negotiation or a crisis with the characteristics of the ethical encounter entailed in a dialogic ethic?"[19]

Liberal theorists are at a loss because they define ethics almost solely in terms of the harm/care principle. What for Price (and many liberally minded individuals like myself) is a normative challenge is not for many in the real world. When others act excessively egoistically, they respond in kind. In international relations, states literally fight fire with fire. Retaliation of this kind is as universal an ethical principle as caring for others. This can take many forms – social ostracism, the termination of relationships, and the levying of symbolic or material fines. Most importantly though, it can justify violence in the eyes of the aggrieved. Violence can be the most effective of punishments since, well, it hurts. This is "virtuous" violence; aggression justified in our minds by ethical violations.

DeScioli and Kurzban distinguish between moral *conscience* and moral *condemnation*. The former is the little voice in our heads or the feeling in our hearts that tells us to do the right thing and restrains our most selfish of impulses. The latter is the outrage and opprobrium with which we react to those who do not demonstrate such a concern for our own or others' interests when they steal, cheat, or freeload. It is the response to a lack of moral conscience. Moral condemnation has two components: it is the use of "moral concepts to *judge* and *punish* a perpetrator."[20] Both operate as a check on the excessive egoism of others. Moral condemnation encourages other-regarding behavior through external enforcement rather than an internal ethical compass. Yet, it is predicated on the same conception of immoral behavior found as the harm/care foundation – excessive self-concern to the detriment of others, or a lack of care. It simply tells us what to do in response.

Moralistic punishment is known by various names – retribution, revenge, and negative reciprocity – all of which entail retaliation against overly selfish behavior, although each with different goals.[21] Revenge is the most severe form of moralistic punishment. Whereas negative reciprocity might be measured in such a manner as to match the offense

---

[19] Price, Richard (ed.). 2008. *Moral Limit and Possibility in World Politics.* Cambridge: Cambridge University Press, 22.

[20] DeScioli and Kurzban, "Mysteries of Morality," 285.

[21] McDermott, Rose, Anthony C. Lopez, and Peter K. Hatemi. 2017. "Blunt Not the Heart, Enrage It: The Psychology of Revenge and Deterrence." *Texas National Security Review* 1(1): 68–88.

and move the offender back toward a mutually beneficial relationship, revenge's sole purpose is to harm in response to a perceived grievance.

Moral condemnation shifts our attention from what makes humans do good to how they respond to bad, from our better to our lesser angels. It involves ascribing moral labels to act and actors: good and evil, right and wrong, honest and dishonest, greedy and charitable. Deciding what it means to act ethically – that is, moral judgment – entails judging others. This is no less – and perhaps even more – true in international relations than in interpersonal relations. "Faithfulness, devotion, chastity, shame, adultery, seduction, betrayal; aggression, self-defense, appeasement, cruelty, ruthlessness, atrocity, massacre – all these words are *judgments*, and judging is as common a human activity as loving or fighting."[22]

If morality is merely caring for others and treating them with respect as equals, moralistic punishment would be unethical. Wright observes the "irreconcilable difference ... between saying 'Do unto others as you would have them do unto you' and saying 'Do unto others as they have done to you'; between saying 'Love your enemies' or 'Turn the other cheek' and saying 'An eye for an eye, a tooth for a tooth'."[23] Yet, this does not square with our commonsense notion that we are *justified* in defending our interests against the selfish assertions of others. Pure altruism, the kind in which we give the shirt off our back to the person trying to steal it, is rare in humankind and likely, as a consequence, uncommon in international relations.

In other words, acting in defense of *one's own interests* is not in and of itself immoral and in some cases is entirely morally justified. The harm/care principle expects self-sacrifice; our impulse toward moral condemnation tells us when enough is enough. As Stein explains it, moral condemnation like revenge is "self-help justice," what humans rely on to condemn and punish others in the absence of (or in lieu of) the impartial justice provided by institutions.[24] Equating altruism with morality, as Thomas argues, "imposes an unrealistic and unduly demanding criterion of moral assessment, holding states to a moral standard that in our everyday judgments we do not even apply to

---

[22] Walzer, *Just and Unjust Wars*, 3 (emphasis added).
[23] Wright, *The Moral Animal*, 347.
[24] Stein, Rachel M. 2019. *Vengeful Citizens, Violent States*. Cambridge: Cambridge University Press.

individuals in civil society."[25] We must give up this "rigid dichotomy between ethics and interests."[26]

Nevertheless, while retaliation might seem like a simple case of self-interested action in a repeated game of the kind familiar to international relations scholars, this repeated game logic does not account for how humans experience such situations phenomenologically. It misses the feeling of moral outrage that accompanies what a formal theorist might phlegmatically call "defection" and the feeling of pleasure that accompanies the levying of punishment.[27] Nor can rationalist models account for human willingness to pay personal costs to punish bad behavior that does not affect them at all, the phenomenon of "third party" punishment. Our tendency to automatically punish others in order to enforce norms that do not produce any direct benefit, whether it be second party or third party in nature, is called "strong reciprocity" so as to distinguish the phenomenon from the more rationalist understanding of reciprocity based on conscious calculation of self-interest.[28]

Retribution has received some significant attention in international relations.[29] Lebow estimates that it accounts for a quarter of wars involving major powers since 1648.[30] However, the significance of its underlying motivation is far greater than has been recognized. It is as universal a moral foundation as humanitarianism, a "core value" as Stein describes it.[31] What has not been shown is just how commonplace, central, and unavoidable moral condemnation are in international relations.

The norms literature in international relations has integrated moral condemnation into their accounts, most notably in the "naming and shaming" literature.[32] However, it is largely preoccupied with

---

[25] Thomas, *The Ethics of Destruction*, 15.   [26] Ibid, 16.

[27] Pinker, *The Better Angels of Our Nature*, 531 and 537.

[28] Bowles, Samuel and Herbert Gintis. 2004. "The Evolution of Strong Reciprocity: Cooperation in Heterogeneous Populations." *Theoretical Population Biology* 65(1): 17–28; Gintis et al. "Strong Reciprocity and the Roots of Human Morality."

[29] Liberman, Peter. 2006. "An Eye for an Eye: Public Support for War against Evildoers." *International Organization* 60(3): 687–722.

[30] Lebow, Richard Ned. 2010. *Why Nations Fight: Past and Future Motives for War*. Cambridge: Cambridge University Press.

[31] Stein, *Vengeful Citizens, Violent States*.

[32] Keck, Margaret and Kathryn Sikkink. 1998. *Activists beyond Borders: Advocacy Networks in International Politics*. Ithaca: Cornell University Press; Fariss, Christopher J. 2014. "Respect for Human Rights Has Improved over

the enforcement of cosmopolitan and liberal values such as human rights beyond national borders, such as in international tribunals and courts[33] – in other words, condemnation for a lack of cosmopolitan commitment to international norms.[34] This is moralistic punishment on behalf of others, not ourselves, and thereby naturally and justifiably attracts the interest of liberal norms scholars. Those who do not act as good citizens of the international community are stigmatized and treated as outcasts, something that ostracized others try to strategically contest by arguing like lawyers and exploiting loopholes and alternative interpretations of norms that cast their behavior in a better light.[35]

In the Wrong: Welfare Tradeoff Ratios and the Triggers of Moral Condemnation

What evokes moral condemnation of others? This is of course not an easy question to answer (and the difficulty in answering it often generates conflict in the first place). However, three particular types of actions consistently evoke ethically laden outrage: (1) unprovoked physical aggression, (2) unfair distributions of goods, and (3) cheating. There is a clear parallel here to the three elements identified by Hedley Bull for the existence of "society" – life, truth, and property. "First, all societies seek to ensure that life will be in some measure secure against violence resulting in death or bodily harm. Second, all societies seek to ensure that promises, once made, will be kept, or that agreements, once undertaken, will be carried out. Third, all societies pursue the goal of ensuring that the possession of things will remain

---

Time: Modeling the Changing Standard of Accountability." *American Political Science Review* 108(2): 297–318.

[33] Bass, Gary. 2000. *Stay the Hand of Vengeance*. Princeton: Princeton University Press.

[34] Adler-Nissen, Rebecca. 2014. "Stigma Management in International Relations: Transgressive Identities, Norms, and Order in International Society." *International Organization* 68(1): 143–176; Zarakol, Ayşe. 2014. "What Made the Modern World Hang Together: Socialisation or Stigmatisation?" *International Theory* 6(2): 311–332.

[35] Kinsella, Helen M. and Giovanni Mantilla. 2020. "Contestation before Compliance: History, Politics and Power in International Humanitarian Law." *International Studies Quarterly* 64(3): 649–656; Sandholtz, Wayne. 2008. "Dynamics of International Norm Change: Rules against Wartime Plunder." *European Journal of International Relations* 14(1): 101–131.

stable to some degree, and will not be subject to challenges that are constant and without limit."[36] These three goals are "universal in the sense that all actual societies appear to take account of them."[37] This is not surprising since, as we will see, morality is to a large degree the basis of human success, and human success is a product of our sociality. Importantly, many of us feel entirely ethically justified in retaliation in all three cases, even when the victim (of the aggression or the unfair behavior or the dishonesty) is ourselves.

Violations that trigger moral condemnation and outrage have the common denominator of indicating a low "welfare tradeoff ratio," which is "the ratio of values below which an individual will tradeoff another's welfare for their own benefit in any conflict of interests."[38] Shown to operate intuitively in human beings, a WTR of 0 indicates that I will impose a cost of any size upon you to obtain any benefit at all, whereas an altruist will have a ratio of infinity, willing to bear any cost for even the tiniest of benefit to the other. Anything less than 1, which indicates that we value others' welfare as we do our own, might be called selfish, whereas any value greater than 1 indicates sacrifice and selflessness on behalf of others. In an amoral sphere of politics, all would have a WTR of 0. This concept, which as we will see seems to exist in humans as more than just a post hoc theoretical construct, indicates how we can think of morality as a check on egoism without requiring entirely self-abnegating altruism. After all, retaliation is about "getting even." It operationalizes perfectly our understanding of the common basis of all moral foundations – restraining excessive egoism.

Since our physical security is the foundation of life, threats to it indicate a low WTR on the part of others. Some moral psychologists argue that "harm is the fundamental basis by which moral judgments are made"[39] and physical violence is the most obvious and salient form of harm. The moral condemnation that inevitably accompanies physical aggression is evident in that most fundamental of norms: self-defense against threats. Our morally sanctioned right to use force to protect ourselves, to do harm in order to avoid harm, is virtually uncontested

---

[36] Bull, Hedley. 1977. *The Anarchical Society: A Study of Order in World Politics.* New York: Columbia University Press, 4.

[37] Bull, *The Anarchical Society*, 5.

[38] Sell, Aaron N. 2011. "The Recalibrational Theory and Violent Anger." *Aggression and Violent Behavior* 16(5): 382.

[39] Schein and Gray, "The Theory of Dyadic Morality," 32.

in all societies even though it is dedicated to the promotion of our most basic egoistic interest – avoiding harm – and requires a violation of our most basic moral principle – caring for others. When we think of the moral grounding of self-defense solely through the lens of the harm/care principle, it becomes difficult to justify.[40] Moral condemnation solves that puzzle. When others violate the moral norm of harm/care, a "moral asymmetry" emerges between victim and aggressor.[41] They are wrong; we are right. This understanding is at the heart of just war theory.[42] The universal acceptance of the morality of protecting ourselves from harm explains why historically most wars are justified in terms of self-defense.[43]

Ethics are consistently implicated in the distribution of resources. How do human beings think about right and wrong when dividing a pie, literally or figuratively, aside from the fact that it is wrong to hit someone over the head and take it all? Fairness provides a benchmark for what constitutes excessive self-regard and is particularly relevant for distributional conflicts of the kind that are so common in international relations.

Equality serves as a natural benchmark that ensures against excessive self-interest. An equal distribution of some good means that no one is benefitting more than another. It indicates a WTR of 1. Insisting on any outcome tilted toward ourselves is selfish. Agreeing on anything that favors the other is charitable and deserving of moral praise but not necessarily expected of us. As we will see in Chapter 6, research shows that individuals generally judge 50/50 splits as the fairest and often prefer such equal divisions even compared to those in which they come out ahead.[44]

There is another conception of fairness relevant to international relations, however – not equality, but equity, in which individuals receive benefits proportionate to their efforts. This alternative

[40] Rodin, David. 2002. *War and Self-Defense*. Oxford: Oxford University Press, 49.
[41] Ibid, 50.   [42] Walzer, *Just and Unjust Wars*, 12.
[43] Hathaway, Oona A., William S. Holste, Scott J. Shapiro, Jacqueline Van De Velde, and Lisa Wang Lachowicz. 2018. "War Manifestos." *The University of Chicago Law Review* 85(5): 1139–1226; Brock, Lothar and Hendrik Simon (eds.). 2021. *The Justification of War and International Order: From Past to Present*. Oxford: Oxford University Press.
[44] Fehr, Ernst and Urs Fischbacher. 2002. "Why Social Preferences Matter – The Impact of Non-Selfish Motives on Competition, Cooperation and Incentives." *The Economic Journal* 112(478): C1–C33.

benchmark typically emerges when generating goods for distribution entails costs on the part of those making them. When things are fair, outputs match inputs.[45] Equity conceptions of fairness also police against excessive self-interest, in this case, free-riding on the work of others. In Rousseau's famous analogy, why should everyone have the same share of the stag if not everyone contributed to the effort to hunt it? One modern manifestation of equity concerns is the outrage felt by those who must surrender part of their earnings to help the poor whose circumstances reflect a lack of effort in their eyes. However, human beings seem always inclined to be on the lookout for behavior of this kind.[46] Discrepancy between what states feel entitled to and their current share provokes moral outrage.[47]

Finally, human beings universally condemn cheating and dishonesty, taking advantage of the sacrifices of others to gain a selfish advantage. In cooperative games, social psychologists have long documented the presence of "behavioral assimilation," whereby those who begin their social interactions with others with the goal of mutual (rather than purely selfish) gain do not tolerate the egoistic behavior by others that comes at their expense, even going so far as to forgo individual gains to punish behavior by others that disregards their interests.[48] There are limits to most people's regard for others. Helping others is generally predicated on the assumption that they would do the same for you were the roles reversed. Trust in others is typically moralistic in nature, based on an expectation of others' honesty rather than a calculation of interest.[49]

[45] Adams, J. Stacy. 1965. "Inequity in Social Exchange." *Advances in Experimental Social Psychology* 2: 267–299; Deutsch, Morton. 1975. "Equity, Equality, and Need: What Determines Which Value Will Be Used as the Basis of Distributive Justice?" *Journal of Social Issues* 31(3):137–149.

[46] Petersen, Michael Bang. 2012. "Social Welfare as Small-Scale Help: Evolutionary Psychology and the Deservingness Heuristic." *American Journal of Political Science* 56(1): 1–16.

[47] Welch, David. 1993. *Justice and the Genesis of War.* Cambridge: Cambridge University Press, 19.

[48] Kelley, Harold H. and Anthony J. Stahelski. 1970. "Social Interaction Basis of Cooperators' and Competitors' Beliefs about Others." *Journal of Personality and Social Psychology* 16(1): 66–91; Kertzer, Joshua D. and Brian C. Rathbun. 2015. "Fair Is Fair: Social Preferences and Reciprocity in International Politics." *World Politics* 67(4): 613.

[49] Rathbun, Brian C. 2012. *Trust in International Cooperation.* Cambridge: Cambridge University Press.

WTR gives us a sense of what we will ethically expect for our ingroups from outgroups (while recognizing that, unlike in laboratory experiments, there is no way to objectively measure the costs and benefits for ourselves and others). It also helps elucidate some seeming paradoxes of what evokes moral condemnation, such as why we morally excuse self-interest in life and death situations but simultaneously react strongly to mere words on the part of others as insults to our honor, which we will explore in the following text. If one grabs the last life vest in a sinking ship, that life vest presumably confers an extremely high benefit to all potential holders, so that its seizure indicates a WTR of around 1. In contrast, insults, while doing less harm, are the act of directly informing another of our low WTR.

Playing to the Gallery?: Foreign Policy before Audiences

The skeptic asks whether this is just a velvet glove over an iron fist, the cloaking of narrow egoism (which, as established, is what morality is supposed to regulate) in high-minded language. State leaders are especially guilty of moral hypocrisy, castigating unethical behavior by others while engaging in the very same behaviors they condemn. If this is the case, morality is a distraction to which international relations scholars and foreign policy practitioners justifiably pay no more heed than the tears of a crocodile.

However, as we will explore more in text that follows, the very act of even disingenuous moral justification (and there are many examples in the chapters that follow) raises the question of why this is necessary in the first place: To remain oblivious to the possibility of moral condemnation undermines one's own interests. Wolfers points to the exception that proves the rule, a case I will examine in this book: "If ever any country did employ Machiavellian principles consciously and methodically it was Hitler's Germany, but with the result that she lost her independence as conclusively as few great nations have done."[50] Even pure political egoists must find their way in the shadow of morality. We will see that Hitler was no exception.

Political actors almost never take what they want and simply say so. No one quotes Thucydides during conquest. Even the moral relativist Carr, who argues that morality is merely an expression of power

---

[50] Wolfers, "Statesmanship and Moral Choice," 189.

and interest, notes the "necessity, recognized by all politicians both in domestic and international affairs, for cloaking interests in a guise of moral principles."[51] Moral hypocrisy implies the real existence of moral constraints, not their absence. Walzer writes, "Hypocrisy is rife in wartime discourse, because it is especially important at such time to appear to be in the right. It is not only that the moral stakes are high ... more crucially, his actions will be judged by other people, who are not hypocrites, and whose judgments will affect their policies towards him. There would be no point to hypocrisy if this were not so, *just as there would be no point to lying in a world where no one told the truth.*"[52]

Since even state leaders cannot simply moralize anything, as morality is not entirely socially constructed, this puts ethical handcuffs on even the unethical. Morgenthau argues, "However devoid of positive ethical significance the individual political act may be, it is bound to be less than completely evil and can never be without ethical significance at all; for the necessity of justifying it in ethical terms carries with it the obligation for even the most cynical of actors to choose his measures so that they, however evil, will coincide at least at some point, however limited and superficial, with the standards of ethics.... These claims may be false, yet they cannot be completely and absolutely false, as long as the actor is concerned with the appearance of his act as just."[53] As we will see, there are evolutionary reasons for this attentiveness to audiences.

Constructivists have demonstrated the importance of audiences and the ways by which they restrict behavior even in the domain of power politics. Political actors engage in "rhetorical coercion," strategically deploying language to pursue their interests, all before an audience.[54] "The public plays a crucial role: [political opponents] must craft their appeals with an eye to some audience which sits in judgment of their rhetorical moves."[55] Opposing sides must justify their position.

---

[51] Carr, E. H. 1964. *The Twenty Years' Crisis, 1919–1939: An Introduction to the Study of International Relations.* London: Macmillan, 92.

[52] Walzer, *Just and Unjust Wars*, 20 (emphasis added).

[53] Morgenthau, "The Evil of Politics," 5.

[54] Krebs, Ronald and Patrick Thaddeus Jackson. 2007. "Twisting Tongues and Twisting Arms: The Power of Political Rhetoric." *European Journal of International Relations* 13(1): 35–66.

[55] Ibid, 44.

Krebs and Jackson argue that successful speakers will draw from a set of "rhetorical commonplaces" that resonate with audiences; they cannot just say anything.

Consistent with their constructivist inspiration, they are loathe to identify any sort of appeals that are effective "in general"; the challenge for rhetorical coercers is to "formulate arguments limited in time and space."[56] However, a review of the literature shows that these rhetorical battles are always about occupying the moral high ground. More than that, the moral high ground is generally defined in terms of a commitment to life, truth, and property – Bull's elements of society. Violations of these elicit moral condemnation, which political actors seek to avoid. Goddard shows how Bismarck was able to legitimize Germany's rise and avoid a counterbalancing coalition by legitimating his moves in Schleswig-Holstein with reference to the sanctity of treaties.[57] This is simply a formalization of a norm against cheating, a human universal. Members of the European Union were forced to allow the accession of new Eastern European members after the fall of communism because, well, they had promised.[58] Rhetorical coercion, we will see, generally takes the form of a moral duel based on ethical principles that virtually everyone can agree on, even if there remain disputes about how to judge conformity in practice. Good arguments in the international arena must resonate with universal moral intuitions.

For King and Country: Binding Moral Foundations and the Ethics of Community

What is this self that we might legitimately defend and protect against the excesses of others in international relations? Typically, it is nation-states, which have their own moral glue of what Graham et al. call the "binding" moralities.[59] This understanding of right

---

[56] Ibid, 47.

[57] Goddard, Stacie. 2019. *When Might Makes Right: Rising Powers and World Order*. Ithaca and London: Cornell University Press.

[58] Schimmelfennig, Frank. 2001. "The Community Trap: Liberal Norms, Rhetorical Action, and the Eastern Enlargement of the European Union." *International Organization* 55(1): 47–80.

[59] Graham et al., "Liberals and Conservatives"; Graham et al., "Moral Foundations Theory."

and wrong is based on an "ethics of community" in which morality involves repressing individual wants and desires in service of a
specific group.[60] This is a more "traditional" and "conservative"
understanding of morality. Rather than rights, binding moralities
emphasize duties. Individuals must subordinate their own personal
interests to a larger collective of individuals to make it more cohesive.
Haidt writes, "Traditional moralities more often aim to suppress and
regulate selfishness by binding people into larger collectives, such
as families, guilds, teams, and congregations. These societies, which
exemplify the Durkheimian virtues of cohesiveness, interdependence,
and limitations on choice and acquisitiveness (up to a point), exemplify what we might call a binding approach to morality because they
treat the group as the fundamental source of moral value and they
expect individuals to limit their desires and play their roles within
the group. These are the *Gemeinschaften* celebrated by Tonnies."[61]
The locus of moral concern is not individuals but groups, which are
more than the simple collections of autonomous actors that they are
in liberal thought.[62]

The ethics of community come with two moral imperatives relevant for international relations: respect for authority and loyalty to
the ingroup.[63] Both involve the regulation of selfish interests, just like
altruism, egalitarianism, or any other moral value. However, they do
so differently. Authoritarian morality requires obedience, the repression of self-interest, and subordination to the command of others.
Binding morality is hierarchical rather than egalitarian. In return for
their leadership in protecting the group, subordinates "respect, obey
and pay deference to the will of superiors" because of the leadership, wisdom, and service they provide for the group.[64] It is wrong
to defy the orders of one's father, one's church, or one's government.

[60] Shweder, R. A., N. C. Much, M. Mahapatra, and L. Park. 1997. "The 'Big
  Three' of Morality (Autonomy, Community, and Divinity), and the 'Big Three'
  Explanations of Suffering." In: A. Brandt and P. Rozin (eds.). *Morality and
  Health*. New York: Routledge, 119–169.

[61] Haidt, "Morality," 70. *Gemeinschaft* is opposed to a similar word,
  Gesellschaft, which is translated as "society," thought to characterize the more
  atomistic collection of individuals common to individualistic societies.

[62] Pinker, *The Better Angels of Our Nature*, 625.

[63] I neglect here a third binding foundation of purity, which has less relevance
  for the discussion. See footnote 5.

[64] Fiske and Rai, *Virtuous Violence*, 19.

It is right to know one's place and role and to do one's bit for the community. Hierarchy is morally sanctioned and common in many of our most basic social relationships: teacher/student, parent/child, and priest/congregation.

Ingroup loyalty demands that we favor our group over others. To do otherwise is to betray those in our community, a powerful moral indictment of excessive egoism. Loyalty demands costly sacrifice but to a specific group rather than others in general. It is "parochial" altruism.[65] Binding morality makes it possible for us to think of groups as quasi-persons with their own interests and attributes. Groups are attributed a cohesive status and morally screened and condemned just as individuals are. This phenomenon, called "entitativity"[66] or "anthropomorphization,"[67] is made obvious by the phenomenon of stereotypes. Pinker explains, "A part of an individual's personal identity is melded with the identity of the groups that he or she affiliates with. Each group occupies a slot in their minds that is very much like the slot occupied by an individual person, complete with beliefs, desires and praiseworthy or blameworthy traits."[68]

Closing Ranks: Second-Order Moral Beliefs, Threat, and Binding the Group

This begs the question, however. Toward what end group solidarity and cohesiveness? In other words, why are these binding values of value? Political psychology scholars point to the underlying motivation of threat. Binding morality is associated with a particular view of the world as dangerous and full of threats deserving of moral condemnation and punishment. Right-wing authoritarianism (which the dual-process model, as we will see, shows to be capturing the same underlying motivational complexes as binding moralism) is a product of "dangerous world beliefs," based on a core understanding that the "social world is a dangerous and threatening place in which good,

[65] Choi, Jung-Kyoo and Samuel Bowles. 2007. "The Co-Evolution of Parochial Altruism and War." *Science* 318(5850): 636–639.
[66] Campbell, Donald. T. 1958. "Common Fate, Similarity, and Other Indices of the Status of Aggregates of Persons as Social Entities." *Behavioral Science* 3: 14–25.
[67] Johnston, Alastair Iain. 2008. *Social States: China in International Institutions, 1980–2000.* Princeton: Princeton University Press, 95.
[68] Pinker, *The Better Angels of Our Nature*, 522.

decent people's values and way of life are threatened by bad people."[69]
If the world is a precarious place, individuals must bind together in
tight groups to face common enemies at home and abroad. For those
who perceive the world as safer and more secure, more leeway can be
given to individuals to define their own destinies. In Janoff-Bulman's
terms, the ethical motivations of charity, benevolence, and altruism are
about *providing*, whereas the ethics of community are about *protecting*.[70] Jost et al. call this the "existential" motivation behind "conservative" values.[71] At home, strong law-and-order and strict adherence
to moral norms are necessary to generate social stability and send a
message that bad behavior will not be tolerated, something that seems
unnecessary to those with more optimistic expectations about human
behavior.[72] Abroad a strong military is necessary, which explains the
strong correlation between binding moral foundations and "militant
internationalism" we see in the next chapter.[73]

Dangerous world beliefs are second-order moral beliefs, beliefs
about the morality of others. In social psychology, they are measured through agreement or disagreement with survey statements
such as "it seems that every year there are fewer and fewer truly
respectable people and more and more persons with no morals at
all who threaten everybody else" and "there are many dangerous
people in our society who will attack someone out of pure meanness,
for no reason at all."[74] As Janoff-Bulman notes, binding morality
emphasizes "blameworthiness"; it is "condemnatory and strict."[75]
Ethnocentrism research finds morality to be central to explaining why
individuals evaluate ingroups more favorably relative to outgroups.

---

[69] Duckitt, "A Dual-Process Cognitive-Motivational Theory."
[70] Janoff-Bulman, Ronnie. 2009. "To Provide or Protect: Motivational Bases of
Political Liberalism and Conservatism." *Psychological Inquiry* 20: 120–128.
[71] Jost, John T, Jack Glaser, Arie W. Kruglanski, and Frank J. Sulloway. 2003.
"Political Conservatism as Motivated Social Cognition." *Psychological
Bulletin* 129(3): 339.
[72] Altemeyer, "The Other 'Authoritarian Personality'"; Feldman, "Enforcing
Social Conformity."
[73] Kertzer, Joshua D, Kathleen E. Powers, Brian C. Rathbun, and Ravi Iyer.
2014. "Moral Support: How Moral Values Shape Foreign Policy Attitudes."
Journal of Politics 76(3): 825–840.
[74] Duckitt, "A Dual-Process Cognitive-Motivational Theory," 15.
[75] Janoff-Bulman, Ronnie and Nate C. Carnes. 2013. "Surveying the Moral
Landscape: Moral Motives and Group-Based Moralities." *Personality and
Social Psychology Review* 17(3): 220.

Pride in one's ingroup is more affected by its perceived morality than by its competence.[76]

Yet why does meeting dangers require a narrow group focus? What is the relationship between communal loyalty and danger? Janoff-Bulman explains that those attuned to threats are "especially interested in who can be trusted, which is essentially a matter of knowing who is in your group and who is not.... [I]ngroup–outgroup (i.e., us–them) boundaries become very important; normative adherence and conformity to the group's rules become signs of 'true' belonging and commitment to the community, and defiance of group norms become the basis for exclusion."[77] Research shows that less trusting individuals confine their cooperative relations to smaller set of partners who are like them.[78] Perceived threat induces us to close ranks. Those with more generalized trust believe that others are generally good and honest and broaden their social interactions to include those who they do not know, even in international relations.[79] Whereas egalitarianism and altruism are "approach" orientations that aim at providing positive gains, the binding foundations are "avoidance" orientations aimed at protecting the group against negative outcomes.

The phenomenon of entitativity makes any collective agent capable of intentional action a moral actor, vulnerable to moral condemnation.[80] This allows for the same interpersonal dynamics of moral condemnation to occur between groups. Just as self-interested action by individuals in defiance and defense of the excessive self-interest of others feels justified to the defender, the same is true in interactions between groups because individuals perceive groups as cohesive entities. Studies show that in intergroup conflicts, outgroups are criticized for violations of harm/care and fairness principles, not binding foundations, since the latter are internal to the group.[81] The right to physical

---

[76] Leach, Colin, Naomi Ellemers, and Manuela Barreto. 2007. "Group Virtue: The Importance of Morality (vs. Competence and Sociability) in the Positive Evaluation of In-Groups." *Journal of Personality and Social Psychology* 93(2): 234–249.

[77] Janoff-Bulman, "To Provide or Protect," 125; Stenner, Karen. 2009. "Three Kinds of 'Conservatism'." *Psychological Inquiry* 20(2–3): 142–159.

[78] Uslaner, Eric M. 2002. *The Moral Foundations of Trust.* Cambridge: Cambridge University Press.

[79] Rathbun, *Trust in International Cooperation.*

[80] Schein and Gray, "The Theory of Dyadic Morality," 38.

[81] Leidner, Bernhard and Emanuele Castano. 2012. "Morality Shifting in the Context of Intergroup Violence." *European Journal of Social Psychology* 42(1):82–91.

security and safety from harm, whose violation triggers moral condemnation, is simply projected into the foreign policy realm. As Walzer notes, perceived rights of sovereignty and territorial integrity are a "palpable feature of our moral world," the "collective form" of expectations "entailed by our sense of what it means to be a human being."[82]

Protecting the group sometimes requires violence, and this is morally justified, indeed celebrated, from the binding perspective. Because the adversary is morally blameworthy, violence is virtuous as opposed to merely instrumental.[83] There is a strong connection between virtuous violence and group morality. "[W]hen humans violently defend their children, spouses, family buddies, or allies, this defense is virtuous violence.... It is a moral obligation to protect one's partners, and throughout history humans have accorded great honor to heroes who aggressively defend themselves, their families or their communities."[84] Without moral condemnation, mobilizing collective action might be impossible, as even a structural realist like Mearsheimer realizes: "It is difficult to imagine a modern political leader openly asking the public to fight and die to improve the balance of power. No European or American leader did so during either world war or the Cold War. Most people prefer to think of fights between their own state and rival states as clashes between good and evil, where they are on the side of the angels and their opponents are aligned with the devil."[85] Importantly, for binders the threats society faces are from other humans who lack morality, not from falling trees or faulty electrical wiring or, apparently, deadly pandemic diseases.

In foreign policy, binding morality goes hand in hand with a "deterrence model" mindset, the mental model whose "central argument [is] that great dangers arise if an aggressor believes that the status quo powers are weak in capability or resolve."[86] This mindset creates a preoccupation with generating a reputation for toughness. Even small acts of weakness might, it is feared, create the impression that one is weak.[87] Any rapprochement or effort to avoid spiraling conflicts will

---

[82] Walzer, *Just and Unjust Wars*, 54.
[83] Fiske and Rai, *Virtuous Violence*, 5.   [84] Ibid, 36.
[85] Mearsheimer, John J. 2001. *The Tragedy of Great Power Politics*. New York: WW Norton & Company, 25.
[86] Jervis, Robert. 1979. *Perception and Misperception in International Politics*. Princeton: Princeton University Press, 58.
[87] Schelling, Thomas. 1966. *Arms and Influence*. New Haven: Yale University Press.

not only go unreciprocated; it will also be exploited. Central to the deterrence model, as Tetlock has argued, is an image of the adversary as immoral and intent on doing harm – that is, moral condemnation.[88]

If there were no moral condemnation between groups, then binding morality would be the attractive force holding the atoms of the billiard ball together, but the interactions of those billiard balls would be in an amoral sphere of the kind often assumed in international relations. Binding morality would merely provide the unobserved and presumed microfoundation of the units interacting in anarchy. Ethics would stop at the water's edge, a situation of pure outgroup indifference. However, to morally condemn those in other nation-states or countries for their actions toward our group requires that the condemner believes that there is something more to morality than the binding foundations; there must be moral expectations for how those outside of our borders treat us.

Strength of Character: The Virtue of Resolve in Binding Morality

In situations of threat, resolve becomes a virtue for the binding moralist, an expression of sacrifice and commitment to the group. If a group is thought to be under constant threat, it needs as many members as possible to do their bit and refuse to give up. Conversely, a lack of determination indicates selfishness and free-riding. To the extent that such lack of resolve is observable to the adversary, it is doubly wrong for sending signals of weakness. Service to the ingroup deserves special moral praise and cowardice special moral censure.[89]

Just as individuals are keen to defend their moral reputation for honesty and generosity, they also want to be seen as good members of a community. A set of virtuous traits that convey honor emerges out of the binding moral foundations.[90] In places that stress these

[88] Tetlock, Philip E. 1983. "Policy-Makers' Images of International Conflict." *Journal of Social Issues* 39(1): 67–86.

[89] Rodriguez Mosquera, Patricia M., Antony S. R. Manstead, and Agneta H. Fischer. 2002. "The Role of Honour Concerns in Emotional Reactions to Offences." *Cognition & Emotion* 16(1): 143–163; LaVaque-Manty, Mika. 2006. "Dueling for Equality: Masculine Honor and the Modern Politics of Dignity." *Political Theory* 34(6): 715–740.

[90] LaVaque-Manty, "Dueling for Equality."

"traditional" or "conservative" values, individuals are defined primarily by the social roles they play in the larger community.[91] Honor is conferred based on how well they fulfill those duties, which often involve preserving hierarchy and protecting the reputation of the family. These honor expectations vary substantially across the sexes.[92] Bravery, courage, and toughness are held in high esteem particularly among men. Martial prowess is celebrated as an honorable characteristic since it is the expression of courage.[93] These virtues contribute to the ability of a community to act collectively and decisively against external threats. Lebow writes that "in warrior societies, the spirit," that is honor, "finds expression in bravery and selflessness, from which the society as a whole profits."[94] International relations scholars have identified honor concerns as an important element of individual resolve[95] and that cultures of honor predict aggressive behavior.[96]

Those who do not demonstrate such perseverance are liable to moral condemnation from inside the group, even (actually, as we will see in Chapter 7, *especially*) leaders. Not only do states castigate each other, but citizens castigate their own leaders and vice versa. Elites can be lambasted for their weakness in crises, which in threatening situations is equivalent to a moral judgment. Once the public is aroused, self-serving leaders can face accusations of a lack of resolve and even betrayal, a violation of binding morality. Just as the public must do their part as good moral citizens, leaders must also demonstrate a commitment to stand up for their country. This dynamic, most familiar to readers from the literature on audience costs, is actually a moral one.[97] Colaresi finds that in rivalry contexts leaders who attempt to

---

[91] Berger, Thomas. 1970. "On the Obsolescence of the Concept of Honor." *European Journal of Sociology* 11(2): 339–347; Lebow, *Why Nations Fight*.

[92] Rodriguez Mosquera et al., "The Role of Honour Concerns."

[93] Kaufman, Whitley. 2011. "Understanding Honor: Beyond the Shame/Guilt Dichotomy." *Social Theory and Practice* 37(4): 557–573.

[94] Lebow, *Why Nations Fight*, 67.

[95] Kertzer, Joshua D. 2017. *Resolve in International Politics*. Princeton: Princeton University Press.

[96] Dafoe, Allan and Devin Caughey. 2016. "Honor and War: Southern US Presidents and the Effects of Concern for Reputation." *World Politics* 68(2): 341–381.

[97] Fearon, James D. 1994. "Domestic Political Audiences and the Escalation of International Disputes." *American Political Science Review* 88(3): 577–592.

de-escalate tensions are removed from office at higher rates than those that do not. "As the public, and potentially elites, becomes more insecure and distrustful of a rival ... any leader that attempts to offer concessions to a rival could be attacked as being weak, or accommodating a dangerous enemy."[98]

As a moral universal, group loyalty becomes a potent ethical weapon in internal moral duels based on rhetorical coercion. Krebs and Jackson argue that the Israeli government was compelled to grant citizenship rights to Druze Arabs who argued that their service in the military entitled them to equal treatment. The universality of the binding foundations makes it quite understandable why such a strategy would be highly effective.[99]

Impartiality and the Partiality of Liberal Morality in International Relations Theory

Curiously, given the centrality of group interaction to international relations, which is embedded in the very name of the discipline, the binding foundations generally go neglected in IR. Nations are after all groups. Excessive nationalism (although not necessarily patriotism) is thought to contribute to international conflict,[100] but nationalism is not generally understood as a *moral* phenomenon. I suspect that this empirical neglect of the binding foundations reflects the liberal ethical standards that inform the study of morality in international relations, both positive and normative. As a system of moral thought, liberalism is hostile both to excessive deference to authority and to unchecked ingroup favoritism. Normative liberal scholars tend to deny the ethical status of hierarchical authority because this binding foundation entails the subordination of individual rights, the basis of moral value in Western thought, to group welfare. In the conflict between conformity and obedience on the one hand and individual choice and autonomy on

---

[98] Colaresi, Michael. 2004. "When Doves Cry: International Rivalry, Unreciprocated Cooperation, and Leadership Turnover." *American Journal of Political Science* 48(3): 552.

[99] Krebs and Jackson, "Twisting Tongues and Twisting Arms."

[100] Bertoli, Andrew D. 2017. "Nationalism and Conflict: Lessons from International Sports." *International Studies Quarterly* 61(4): 835–849; Van Evera, Stephen. 1999. *Causes of War: Power and the Roots of Conflict.* Ithaca: Cornell University Press.

the other, liberals favor the former.[101] Pinker writes, "Autonomy, the ethic we recognize in the modern West, assumes that the social world is composed of individuals and that the purpose of morality is to allow them to exercise their choices and to protect them from harm. The ethics of community, in contrast, sees the social world as a collection of tribes, clans, families, institutions, guilds and other coalitions, and equates morality with duty, respect, loyalty and interdependence."[102]

Liberal normative theory utilizes an "impartialist" perspective to derive ethical principles, making it dismissive of special obligations to specific ingroups.[103] To establish what is right or wrong, one must consciously remove oneself from the particularities of her position so as to avoid the prejudice and bias that might color her moral conclusions. It is through this "view from nowhere"[104] behind the "veil of ignorance"[105] that we can be sure that morality is not simply self-serving justification; after all, selfishness is what morality regulates. Group membership biases our moral conclusions, leading us to favor those with whom we have associations. As a result, the individualizing foundations are by nature cosmopolitan.[106] If all human beings have inherent and equal worth and are thereby bound by moral principles

---

[101] Feldman, "Enforcing Social Conformity."

[102] Pinker, *The Better Angels of Our Nature*, 625.

[103] Shapcott, Richard. 2010. *International Ethics: A Critical Introduction.* Polity; Erskine, Toni. 2012. *Embedded Cosmopolitanism.* Oxford: Oxford University Press, 43–72.

[104] Nagel, Thomas. 1989. *The View from Nowhere.* Oxford: Oxford University Press.

[105] Rawls, John. 2009. *A Theory of Justice.* Cambridge: Harvard University Press.

[106] There are alternative, non-liberal traditions in political theory whose implications for international relations have been considered from a normative point of view – most notably, communitarianism. However, these have not been incorporated into the empirical literature on morality in international relations. Erskine, Toni. 2012. "Whose Progress, Which Morals? Constructivism, Normative IR Theory and the Limits and Possibilities of Studying Ethics in World Politics." *International Theory* 4(3): 449–468, complains that Price, "Moral Limit and Possibility in World Politics," for instance, notes how communitarianism offers a different approach to ethics but quickly sidelines it, a move he feels justified because "such projects tend to struggle with the difficulty of how to deal with *transcommunity* morality such as international norms." Erskine, "Whose Progress, Which Morals?" Yet why must the empirical study of ethics define morality in such a way that transcends communities except for the fact that one is bringing in one's own conceptualization of ethics to define the legitimate scope of inquiry?

to care for others' well-being (or least avoid doing them harm), then we are linked in a global community of humankind that has ethical force beyond national borders.[107] This call for impartiality is at the heart of the liberal focus on "reasoned dialogue" as the preferred way by which individuals, and nation-states, might resolve their differences.[108] Ironically, however, in utilizing the standard of impartiality, we become oblivious to how such a standard is inherently partial in terms of the way we are defining morality itself. It favors liberal ethics and thereby obscures the ethics of community.

Is Consequentialism Consequential?: Realism and the Moral Necessity of "Evil"

The attentive reader will have noticed that I have not yet mentioned a key concept that has featured in both the normative literature on morality and the international relations literature on norms – consequentialism. In a previous article, I have made the case that the norms literature fundamentally mischaracterizes the distinction between consequentialism and other types of ethical decision-making, such as the "logic of appropriateness" and "deonotological" reasoning.[109] In terms of the former, Goldmann persuasively contends that March and Olsen, those most responsible for the popularization of the former distinction, confuse the form of an argument with its content: "In their approach, consequentialist reasoning – a method – is associated with the pursuit of self-interest – a substantive feature – and non-consequentialist reasoning with the application of rules grounded in socially constructed identities."[110] In other words, rather than a type of ethical reasoning, consequentialism is equated to egoism, which is judged to be inherently less moral. "Appropriate action is action that is virtuous."[111] March and Olsen write: "Scholars committed to a

---

[107] Barnett, "Evolution without Progress," 622.
[108] Risse, Thomas. 2000. "'Let's Argue!': Communicative Action in World Politics." *International Organization* 54(1): 1–39.
[109] Rathbun, Brian C. and Rachel Stein. 2020. "Greater Goods: Morality and Attitudes toward the Use of Nuclear Weapons." *Journal of Conflict Resolution* 64(5): 787–816.
[110] Goldmann, Kjell. 2005. "Appropriateness and Consequences: The Logic of Neo-Institutionalism." *Governance* 18(1): 40.
[111] March, James G. and Johan P. Olsen. 1998. "The Institutional Dynamics of International Political Orders." *International Organization* 52(4): 951.

consequentialist position tend to see an international system of interacting autonomous, egoistic, self-interested maximizers.... Scholars
committed to an identity position ... see political actors are acting in
accordance with rules and practices that are socially constructed. They
portray an international society as a community of rule followers and
role players with distinctive sociocultural ties, cultural connections,
intersubjective understandings and senses of belonging."[112]

Consequentialism, however, is a type of ethical reasoning that might
be entirely altruistic in character. To sacrifice five of our own compatriots to save fifty of another is both consequentialist and altruistic,
even if it might be empirically rare. March and Olsen are confusing
the weights applied to the inputs into a utilitarian decision-making
process with the process itself. There are altruistic consequentialists
and non-consequentialist egoists.

Consequentialism properly conceived is often compared to deontological reasoning, in which moral judgments are made independently
of the anticipation of their effects by virtue of the inherent morality
of an act. Deontological judgments are evident if decision-makers rule
out particular actions as simply unthinkable, regardless of the good
they might do. In practice, however, it is extremely difficult to distinguish consequentialism from deontological reasoning. If American
foreign policymakers feel a taboo against the use of nuclear weapons,
is this because it is simply wrong to incinerate instantly hundreds of
thousands of people, as is maintained in the "taboo" literature, or is it
because the advantages can never outweigh the sheer scale of such an
atrocity when benefits and costs are weighed? If I say, "my country,
right or wrong," that sounds like a categorical rule of the deontological variety; yet it might also indicate that when compared, national
interests always have more utility for me than humanitarian interests.

Moreover, the scenarios invented by moral philosophers to distinguish between these types of reasoning, such as trolley car dilem-
mas, have no real parallel in politics, especially international politics.
If we will not divert a trolley car, killing one person so as to save
five, we can say that we have made a deontological judgment. In foreign policy, those who are not willing to trade the lives of foreigners
for one's own compatriots might be making a deontological choice
that violence is never justified. Or they might simply demonstrate a

[112] March and Olsen, "The Institutional Dynamics," 952.

different utility function to a more nationalist individual, whose binding morality makes her more willing to make such a tradeoff because compatriots have more moral value to her. Ingroup favoritism is part of binding morality.

More useful, I argue, is the distinction between emotionally driven moral decision-making and more deliberate, thoughtful and cool ethical judgment, of which consequentialism is an example. This is the difference between System I and System II thinking I explored in my last book, *Reasoning of State*. As I will argue in the next chapter, morality is inextricably tied up in our emotions; that is one way we know it has a biological basis. It might be possible to make a true consequentialist judgment in which we coolly and phlegmatically evaluate the costs and benefits of alternative courses of actions while trying to keep our emotions at bay, but it is hard. Consequentialism is almost by definition emotionally painful since to justify an act by its consequences implies that there is a downside to the choice, a tradeoff of values. For this reason, I believe it is empirically rare.[113]

More common it seems is not deontological thinking but rather "motivated consequentialism," in which human beings align their beliefs to avoid the admission of conflicting ends. For instance, as Liu and Ditto find, those who believe in the death penalty also believe that it is not painful for those who are condemned to it.[114] Those who believe torture is wrong also believe it is unlikely to yield actionable intelligence. The true consequentialist would be one who believes that torture is wrong but in particular instances might be justified because it provides information that serves the greater good. Yet, such a position is empirically rare.

The exception is realists. Typically in discussions of ethics in international relations, liberal morality is contrasted with realist morality. To the extent that realists argue for the existence of an autonomous moral sphere, this is correct. But upon closer examination, many

---

[113] I should stress, however, that certain types of consequentialist choices are intuitive and automatic, such as "white lies." Not all consequentialist choices are deliberative. See Kahane, G., K. Wiech, N. Shackel, M. Farias, J. Savulescu, and I. Tracey. 2012. The Neural Basis of Intuitive and Counterintuitive Moral Judgment. *Social Cognitive and Affective Neuroscience*, 7(4): 393–402.

[114] Liu, Brittany S. and Peter H. Ditto. 2013. "What Dilemma? Moral Evaluation Shapes Factual Belief." *Social Psychological and Personality Science* 4(3): 316–323.

classical realists and Realpolitik practitioners reject such a distinction between private and public ethics and are instead best understood as consequentialists, frustrated liberals who settle on ingroup favoritism through a sense of sober necessity rather than moral condemnation. Although rare, realist practitioners are important for this book, particularly Chapters 8 and 9 on World War I.

Realist ethics are actually based on a liberal standard of morality. Morgenthau explicitly invokes Kant's categorical imperative, a liberal standard, in defining morality: "The test of a morally good action is the degree to which it is capable of treating others not as means to the actor's ends but as ends in themselves." Meinecke and Morgenthau both use the language of "sin" and "evil"[115] in describing the use of violence against one's "fellow men."[116] "It is the most frightful and staggering fact of world history, that there is no hope of making radically moral the human community itself which encloses and comprehends all other communities," laments Meinecke.[117] According to Morgenthau, "we are inevitably involved in sin and guilt. We want peace among nations and harmony among individuals, yet our actions end in conflict and war. We want to see all men free, but our actions put others in chains as others do to us. We believe in the equality of all men, yet our very demands on society make others unequal."[118]

Realists differ from liberals not as to what is morally ideal but what is morally possible given some combination of egoistic human nature and the anarchical structure of international politics. Morgenthau writes, "The demands which life in society makes on our good intentions surpass our faculty to satisfy them all." Tough choices are necessary. "Political realism does not require, nor does it condone, indifferaence to political ideals and moral principles, but it requires indeed a sharp distinction ... between what is desirable everywhere and at all times and what is possible under the concrete circumstances of time and place," writes Morgenthau.[119] Realists are not morally indifferent but rather

---

[115] Meinecke, Friederich. 1957. *Machiavellianism: The Doctrine of Raison D'État and Its Place in Modern History*. New Haven, CT: Yale University Press, 6, 12, Morgenthau, Hans. 1946. *Scientific Man vs. Power Politics*. Chicago: University of Chicago Press, 202.

[116] Morgenthau, *Scientific Man vs. Power Politics*, 202.

[117] Meinecke, *Machiavellianism*, 12; Morgenthau, "The Evil of Politics," 11.

[118] Morgenthau, "The Evil of Politics," 11.

[119] Morgenthau, *Politics among Nations*, 7.

realistic, willing to admit truths unpleasant not just to liberals but to them. There is an "ineluctable tension between the moral command and the requirements of successful political action. And it is unwilling to gloss over and obliterate that tension and thus to obfuscate both the moral and the political issue by making it appear as though the stark facts of politics were morally more satisfying than they actually are."[120] This incompatibility between desirability and possibility and the liberal refusal to admit it is an old theme in realism, the central point of Carr's canonical takedown of utopianism.[121] Realism both "condemns politics as the domain of evil par excellence" and "reconciles itself to the enduring presence of evil in all political action."[122]

The most salient tradeoff is between the demands of one's group, country, or nation, and those of others with which it is interacting. Morality "compels us to choose between different equally legitimate demands. Loyalty to the nation comes into conflict with our duties to humanity."[123] Because no leader is capable of providing for all humanity and can only directly control what happens to his or her own country, the country often comes first. However, Morgenthau rejects a "dual morality," in which decision-makers take into account how any choice might affect his or her own country with no regard to those outside.[124] It is unacceptable because under this metric "the welfare of the group, for the sake of which the welfare of another group is sacrificed, is an end with a positive ethical quality only for the members of that group and its apologists."[125] He rejects a WTR of 0.

In light of the limitations posed by the realities of international politics, Morgenthau advocates for a Weberian ethics of responsibility based on a consequentialist logic.[126] Actions are judged by their outcomes, and a comparison to what would have happened had someone done something else. He offers a "practical morality which emphasizes the continued application of cosmopolitan imperatives to action, mitigated by a consequentialist orientation which demands that they be applied cautiously and always adapted to circumstances."[127] The best that one can hope for is a lesser evil. "Man cannot hope to be too good but must be content with not being too evil."[128]

---

[120] Ibid, 19.   [121] Carr, *The Twenty Years' Crisis, 1919–1939*.
[122] Morgenthau, "The Evil of Politics," 17.   [123] Ibid, 11.
[124] Ibid, 7.   [125] Ibid, 8.   [126] Ibid, 10.
[127] Murray, "The Moral Politics of Hans Morgenthau," 81.
[128] Morgenthau, "The Evil of Politics," 13.

To speak of evil at all is to acknowledge the moral conflict inherent in state decision-making. A consequentialist is someone who must justify the costs associated with his or her actions based on the ends achieved. If those harmed have no value or deserve such punishment – in other words, if there were no humanitarianism in realism – no such justification would be necessary at all. The realist must feel conflicted, even if ultimately deciding on using force and violence. Morgenthau writes, "To know with despair that the political act is inevitably evil, is moral courage."[129] The very fact that realist morality is consequentialist is an indication that it uses a liberal benchmark for morality. Were it only concerned with the nation-state, no apologies would be necessary. This is the proper understanding of the logic of consequences, not the way by which it has been used in the 'norms' literature – as synonymous with egoism.[130]

The ultimate virtue for a realist is therefore not loyalty to the group or resolve, as it is to the binding moralist, but prudence. "There can be no political morality without prudence; that is, without consideration of the political consequences of seemingly moral action. Realism ... considers prudence – the weighing of the consequences of alternative political actions – to be the supreme virtue in politics."[131] Prudence might mean not acting on humanitarian impulses for fears of making situations worse, seen for instance in the realist position on military intervention and international criminal justice.[132] As we will see, prudence might also mean the emotionally painful choice to stop fighting when one's situation is increasingly hopeless since persistence threatens to add more casualties, throwing good money after bad. Wolfers and Morgenthau both distinguish realist from "nationalistic ethics," which "place what are called vital national interests – and not national survival only – at the very pinnacle of the hierarchy of values," which are "assumed to justify the sacrifice of almost every other value."[133]

---

[129] For Morgenthau, it is not that private morality is different from public morality (a position that he explicitly rejects), but that public life puts leaders in positions where they are forced into these types of difficult tradeoffs.

[130] Rathbun and Stein, "Greater Goods."

[131] Morgenthau, *Politics among Nations*, 10.

[132] Michael C. Desch. 2003. "It Is Kind to Be Cruel: The Humanity of American Realism." *Review of International Studies* 29(3): 415–426; Snyder, Jack and Leslie Vinjamuri. 2004. "Trials and Errors: Principle and Pragmatism in Strategies of International Justice." *International Security* 28(3): 5–44.

[133] Wolfers, "Statesmanship and Moral Choice," 188.

What distinguishes the realist therefore is the willingness to engage issues objectively and to be honest with the inherently tragic nature of many political issues and decisions. As I argued in *Reasoning of State*, realists are "System II" thinkers who base their judgments on a deliberative and objective consideration of the situation.[134] Realist thinkers explicitly warn against allowing emotions and wishful thinking to intrude into decision-making.[135] Meinecke writes that the realist "should rule himself strictly that he should suppress his emotions and his personal inclinations and aversions, and completely lose himself in the practical task of securing the common good. He should also seek, quite coolly and rationally, to ascertain the practical interest of the State, and to separate these from any emotional overtones – for hatred and revenge ... are bad counsellors in politics."[136] He cautions that "raison d'état demands ... an ice-cold temperature."[137] Morgenthau equates moral prudence with utilitarian rationality: "[P]olitical realism considers a rational foreign policy to be good foreign policy; for only a rational foreign policy minimizes risks and maximizes benefits and hence, complies both with the moral precept of prudence and the political requirement of success."[138] Recent neuroscience demonstrates that consequentialist judgment is associated with System II thinking, both in longer decision-making times and neural activation in parts of the brain implicated in complex and self-conscious reasoning.[139] Realist morality is therefore different from both humanitarian and binding morality, which are more emotional in character, as I argue in the next chapter.

As deliberative thinkers, realists are better able to follow Morgenthau's "second rule" of diplomacy, that they "must look at the political scene from the point of view of other nations."[140]

---

[134] Rathbun, Brian C. 2019. *Reasoning of State: Realists, Romantics and Rationality in International Politics.* Cambridge: Cambridge University Press.
[135] Rathbun, Brian C. 2018. "The Rarity of Realpolitik: What Bismarck's Rationality Reveals about International Politics." *International Security* 43(1): 7–55.
[136] Meinecke, *Machiavellianism*, 6. [137] Ibid, 7.
[138] Morgenthau, *Politics among Nations*, 8.
[139] Greene, Joshua D., R. Brian Sommerville, Leigh E. Nystrom, John M. Darley, and Jonathan D. Cohen. 2001. "An fMRI Investigation of Emotional Engagement in Moral Judgment." *Science* 293(5537): 2105–2108; Greene, Joshua D., Sylvia A. Morelli, Kelly Lowenberg, Leigh E. Nystrom, and Jonathan D. Cohen. 2008. "Cognitive Load Selectively Interferes with Utilitarian Moral Judgment." *Cognition* 107(3): 1144–1154.
[140] Morgenthau, *Politics among Nations*, 553.

Such perspective-taking requires a cool head and cognitive work. In this way, realist pragmatism and liberal "reason" are partially overlapping, even if realists argue that the necessities of international politics ultimately and unfortunately require a narrow fixation on the national interest.

This rational thinking works against moral condemnation. Morgenthau warns of the dangers of such feelings of moral superiority. His first rule of diplomacy is that it "must be divested of the crusading spirit."[141] This "moral excess ... destroys nations and civilizations."[142] During the Cold War, he was extremely concerned about "nationalistic universalism" leading to a nuclear war that both sides would lose. Neoclassical realists show empirically that leaders can dramatize conflicts using moral frames, which arouses the public and causes threat inflation and overbalancing.[143] Realists are, quite strikingly, more inclined to write about the evil one must do oneself than the evil done to them by others. As we will see in the German chapters that follow, the political opponent of the realist when it comes to foreign policy is more often the nationalist than the liberal. Morality makes strange bedfellows. However, because System II processing requires cognitive work and entails a head-on confrontation with emotionally painful choices, realism is rare empirically and most useful in establishing a baseline by which to compare other types of ethical judgment.

---

[141] Ibid, 550.   [142] Ibid, 10.
[143] Christensen, Thomas J. 1996. *Useful Adversaries: Grand Strategy, Domestic Mobilization, and Sino-American Conflict, 1947–1958*. Princeton: Princeton University Press.

3 | Mankind Is What Anarchy Makes of It
The Material Origins of Ethics

Moral condemnation and the binding foundations (and altruism as well) are so universal that there is now a strong consensus among evolutionary biologists that morality emerged through a process of selection as a way to promote the survival of individuals' genetic material. Morality creates bonds and regulates disputes, allowing for greater cooperation among individuals that improves their chances of their survival or at least that of their close kin. Our moral evolution, at least biologically, is thought to have ended about 45,000 years ago, in the late Pleistocene era.[1] "Today, even though we live in cities and write and read books about morality, our actual morals are little more than a continuation of theirs," writes Boehm.[2]

There are two primary reasons for believing that morality has a material foundation. The first is its universality.[3] We can always find immoral individuals. There is significant cultural variation in terms of what constitutes right and wrong. Yet despite these individual-level and intergroup differences, we cannot find any human society entirely devoid of ethics, historical or contemporary, and there is a significant degree of fundamental similarity. Boehm writes that "even though certain types of moral belief can vary considerably (and sometimes dramatically) between cultures, all human groups frown on, make pronouncements against, and punish the following: murder, undue use of authority, cheating that harms group cooperation, major lying, theft and socially disruptive sexual behavior."[4] This universality "is

---

[1] Boehm, Christopher. 2012. *Moral Origins: The Evolution of Virtue, Altruism, and Shame.* New York: Basic Books, 14–15; Bowles, Samuel and Herbert Gintis. 2013. *A Cooperative Species: Human Reciprocity and Its Evolution.* Princeton: Princeton University Press, 3.
[2] Boehm, *Moral Origins*, 17.
[3] Wrangham, Richard. 2019. *The Goodness Paradox: The Strange Relationship between Virtue and Violence in Human Evolution.* New York: Pantheon, 8; Bowles and Gintis, *A Cooperative Species*, 17.
[4] Boehm, *Moral Origins*, 34.

why, for all their superficial differences of language and custom, foreign cultures are still immediately comprehensible at the deeper level of motives, emotions and social habits," writes Ridley.[5] Anthropologists and archaeologists find that the same moral themes that preoccupy us today are the same that we find in hunter-gatherer tribes "whose lifestyles are similar to those of the prehistoric foragers who basically had evolved our modern set of genes for us by 45,000 years ago."[6] We find "such strictures in favor of extrafamilial generosity to be both prominent and probably universal in these mobile band-level cultures."[7] If something is rooted in our very species, it likely has evolutionary origins.

The second strong indication that morality has evolutionary origins is that "the building blocks of human morality are emotional."[8] When something is right or wrong, we literally feel it, and those feelings motivate us to act. We have a sense, literally, of right and wrong. As Skitka writes, "All major theories of morality predict that there should be strong associations between moral concerns and emotion. Consistent with this idea, there are strong connections between having moral convictions about issues and having correspondingly strong emotional reactions to these issues."[9] We experience sympathy in response to suffering, which leads us toward altruism. We experience anger at injustice, which inclines us toward defiance. We feel gratitude for generosity, which leads us to repay favors. We feel affection and pride for our ingroups, however narrowly or broadly they are conceived.[10] There are not many stoic freedom fighters.

Since moral judgments are accompanied by physical sensations and feelings, which are the realm of biology, and evolution is our best explanation of biological design, it stands to reason that our morality has evolutionary origins. Haidt calls this a "moral intuitionist"

---

[5] Ridley, Matt. 1997. *The Origins of Virtue*. New York: Viking Press, 6; see also Boehm, *Moral Origins*, 11, 34.

[6] Boehm, *Moral Origins*, 11.   [7] Ibid, 34.

[8] Haidt, Jonathan. 2007. "The New Synthesis in Moral Psychology." *Science* 316(5827): 998.

[9] Skitka, Linda J. 2010. "The Psychology of Moral Conviction." *Social and Personality Psychology Compass* 4(4): 276.

[10] Haidt, "The New Synthesis in Moral Psychology"; Wright, *The Moral Animal*, 198; Boehm, *Moral Origins*, 19; Wrangham, *The Goodness Paradox*, 218.

model so as to capture the automatic nature of moral feelings, which are beyond our control, even if we can reason our way toward or away from ethical injunctions. "[E]volution shaped human brains to have structures that enable us to experience moral emotions, and these emotional reactions provide the basis for intuitions about right and wrong."[11] Wright explains: "Animals, including people, often execute evolutionary logic not via conscious calculation, but by following their feelings, which were designed as logic executers" leading people to act morally "without giving much thought to the fact that that's what they're doing."[12]

The notion of morality as based in feelings and intuition is not new. It was at the heart of Hume's theory of moral sentiments, a critique of reason-based approaches that dominated philosophy during the Enlightenment.[13] As Jeffery explains, "[W]hile reason can assist us in modifying our sentimental judgments, it cannot, by itself, motivate ethical action in response to the moral judgments we make."[14] We determine what is right and wrong by how it makes us feel, not by adding factual information. Telling us that we should not punch others because it causes pain to others might change our behavior, but only if we already have an intrinsic desire not to harm them. We cannot entirely reason our way to this concern. We have to feel it. We do not refer to a "sense" of right and wrong by accident. What is right is what feels right; what is wrong is what feels wrong. To denounce doing harm to others merely because we know it causes them pain is to commit what in moral philosophy is called the "naturalistic fallacy," deriving an "ought" from an "is."

This might strike readers as hopelessly tautological, yet the same is true with so many of our fundamental human tendencies. One cannot define pleasure separate from the feeling of being pleased, for instance. We have enough commonalities with all other human beings that we can speak meaningfully of pleasure because all others have experienced it, not because we have deduced the definition of pleasure by reason independent of the experience of pleasure itself. The same is

---

[11] Haidt, "Morality," 68.

[12] Wright, *The Moral Animal*, 190; also Frank, *Passions within Reason*, 12.

[13] See in particular Book III, Part I, Sections II–III in David Hume, *Treatise on Human Nature*.

[14] Jeffery, Renée. 2014. *Reason and Emotion in International Ethics*. Cambridge: Cambridge University Press, 89.

equally true of the concept of beauty. We are then left with an obvious charge: to work backward from our feelings of right and wrong and provide a framework for what induces them.

If morality has a biological foundation, it must have played a role in enhancing the survival of our genes.[15] Evolutionary psychology accounts "presume that the structure of the human brain has been designed by natural selection to respond reliably and efficiently to adaptive problems. An 'adaptive problem' is any challenge, threat, or opportunity faced by an organism in its environment that is evolutionarily recurrent … and affects reproductive success."[16] As Frank wryly puts it, "We can't eat moral sentiments. For them to be viable in competitive environments, they must have a material payoff."[17] Evolutionary accounts are functional in character.

Why Don't Nice Humans Finish Last? Moral Condemnation as the Solution to the Evolutionary Paradox

This creates a puzzle, however. If morality is a set of feelings about right and wrong that suppress selfish desires, how can moral concern for anyone beyond our immediate family be anything other than dangerous for our genes and therefore a mutation destined to disappear in competition with others who do not have it?[18] Frank calls this the "fundamental paradox of the Darwinian model."[19] Crudely understood, "The inexorable logic of the evolutionary model is that we should end up with only such [self-interested] people. Yet this has not happened." This is, I believe, the flawed understanding of evolutionary logic that prevails in international relations.

The key insight is that human beings are of little use, and generally in greater danger, when they are on their own. They need others

---

[15] This is not always the same thing as ourselves. Successful genes contribute to "fitness," which we must recognize as "inclusive" in that we will gladly sacrifice for our closest relatives because they share some of our genetic material, just as many other animals do. For this revolutionary realization, see Hamilton, William D. 1964. "The Genetical Evolution of Social Behaviour. II." *Journal of Theoretical Biology* 7(1): 17–52.

[16] Lopez, Anthony C., Rose McDermott, and Michael Bang Petersen. 2011. "States in Mind, Coalitional Psychology, and International Politics." *International Security* 36(2): 50.

[17] Frank, *Passions within Reason*, 54.   [18] Ridley, *The Origins of Virtue*, 38–39.

[19] Frank, *Passions within Reason*, 41–42.

to help them survive and prosper.[20] Evolutionary scholars surmise that morality is a genetic product of the need to meet the recurrent social challenges faced by early humans, such as protection against threats, the collection of food, and the guarantee of mutually beneficial exchange, struggles they could not have coped with effectively alone.[21] Brewer observes that "human beings are characterized by obligatory interdependence. For long-term survival, we must be willing to rely on others for information, aid, and shared resources, and we must be willing to give information and aid and to share resources with others."[22] We do better together than alone, and our genetic makeup reflects that fact. "Group living represents the fundamental survival strategy that characterizes the human species. In the case of our evolutionary history, humans abandoned most of the physical characteristics and instincts that make possible survival and reproduction as isolated individuals or pairs of individuals, in favor of other advantages that require cooperative interdependence with others in order to survive in a broad range of physical environments." Humans are a social species, "evolved to rely on cooperation rather than strength, and on social learning rather than instinct as basic adaptation."[23] De Waal writes, "Universally, human communities are moral communities; a morally neutral existence is as impossible for us as a completely solitary existence."[24]

Humans need to cooperate both to provide and to protect, which is facilitated by the combination of moral conscience and moral condemnation. The former creates the impulse to aid others, the latter to punish their excessively egoistic actions so as not to be a doormat. Unless accompanied by and coupled with moralistic punishment, moral concern of the harm/care variety is "genetically reckless" if "generosity extends beyond nepotism to nonkin."[25] As De Waal writes, "Reciprocity can exist without morality; there can be no morality without reciprocity."[26] It is not an "evolutionarily stable

[20] Alexander, The Biology of Moral Systems, 82; Boehm, *Moral Origins*, 8; Bowles and Gintis, *A Cooperative Species*, 3.

[21] Brewer, Marilynn B. 1999. "The Psychology of Prejudice: Ingroup Love and Outgroup Hate?" *Journal of Social Issues* 55(3): 429–444; also Wright, *The Moral Animal*, 186.

[22] Brewer, "The Psychology of Prejudice," 433.   [23] Ibid.

[24] De Waal, *Good Natured*, 10.   [25] Boehm, *Moral Origins*, 11.

[26] De Waal, *Good Natured*, 136.

strategy," or ESS.[27] The gains of cooperation are familiar to international relations scholars,[28] but evolutionary psychologists argue that morality is essential to guaranteeing cooperation in large groups where we cannot be assured of interacting with the same partners repeatedly. Pure, conscious egoism does not work.

The impulse toward moral condemnation is an evolved system designed to minimize the costs that others impose on us and is therefore self-interested in origin (although, as we will see, not always in outcome and implementation). It serves to deter opportunism and was favored by natural selection for its ability to resolve recurrent social problems humans encountered in their earliest days.[29]

We are led toward retaliation not by a conscious strategy of inducing better behavior for self-interested purposes but rather by a sense of moral indignation and outrage.[30] Scholars have long recognized that moral indignation is associated with the emotion of anger.[31] When others injure us, we do not object merely because our interests have been harmed. We morally judge others for violating an ethical principle. "Much of human aggression has moral overtones. Injustice, unfairness, and lack of reciprocity often motivate human aggression and indignation," writes Trivers.[32]

There is an evolutionary reason for this: It motivates us to act and serves as the ultimate costly signal of credibility. The automaticity of emotions can have an advantage. Those who developed this tendency to retaliate and convey that fact to others were more likely to prosper and pass along their genes. If others think that we will judiciously think twice before striking back, our credibility will be in doubt. If instead our response is emotional and automatic, this is a signal of

---

[27] Smith, J. Maynard. 1974. "The Theory of Games and the Evolution of Animal Conflicts." *Journal of Theoretical Biology* 47(1): 209–222; also Boehm, *Moral Origins*, 11.

[28] Beginning with Keohane, Robert. 1984. *After Hegemony*. Princeton University Press.

[29] McCullough, Michael E., Robert Kurzban, and Benjamin A. Tabak. 2013. "Cognitive Systems for Revenge and Forgiveness." *Behavioral and Brain Sciences* 36(1): 1–15.

[30] McDermott et al., "Blunt Not the Heart, Enrage It," 71.

[31] Wright, *The Moral Animal*, 205; Sell, "The Recalibrational Theory and Violent Anger."

[32] Trivers, Ronald L. 1971. "The Evolution of Reciprocal Altruism." *The Quarterly Review of Biology* 46(1): 49; Sell 2008.

resolve to others.[33] McDermott et al. remind us that when it comes to retribution, "not to confuse the conscious or 'proximate' goals of the actors (revenge) with the evolutionary or 'ultimate' function of the evolved psychology behind it (deterrence)."[34] In addition to deterrence, retaliation promotes fairness. As Wright explains, "exploitation should be discouraged ... emphatically. Hence, the fury of our moral indignation, the visceral certainty that we've been treated unfairly, that the culprit deserves punishment. The intuitively obvious idea of just deserts, the very core of the human sense of justice, is, in this view, a by-product of evolution, a simple genetic stratagem."[35]

Sell hypothesizes that the purpose of anger is to force others to revise their welfare tradeoff ratios (WTRs), a concept introduced earlier, in our favor. Low WTRs on the part of others induce outrage on our part, which serves as a signal to others to treat us better. Empirically, Sell finds that our anger increases as a function of how skewed others' ratios are, although we automatically take into account other factors as well, such as physical formidability.[36]

This automatic tendency toward retaliation and condemnation, driven by anger, is fundamentally different from a rationalist deterrence account, in which political actors engage in conscious and deliberative reasoning, investing in reputation for resolve so as to prevent future challenges. While difficult to distinguish empirically in international relations, in which interactions tend to be iterated, behavioral economists have shown that in single-shot interactions, such as ultimatum games, players will still punish those who take advantage of them, even if it comes at a personal cost that leaves them worse off.[37] The universality of such findings suggests an evolved mechanism that likely served self-interest unconsciously in our evolutionary past. Of course, political actors do sometimes actively think about deterring future challenges by standing firm, although this behavior itself might be less deliberative and more intuitive than we believe.

---

[33] Ridley, *The Origins of Virtue*, 135.
[34] McDermott et al., "Blunt Not the Heart, Enrage It," 71.
[35] Wright, *The Moral Animal*, 205 (emphasis added).
[36] Sell, "The Recalibrational Theory and Violent Anger."
[37] Henrich, Joseph, Robert Boyd, Samuel Bowles, Colin Camerer, Ernst Fehr, Herbert Gintis, and Richard McElreath. 2001. "Cooperation, Reciprocity and Punishment in Fifteen Small-Scale Societies." *American Economic Review* 91(2): 73–78.

However, condemnation and moralistic punishment are most unique in that even bystanders take an ethical stand against selfish individuals.[38] This "third-party punishment" is altruistic in the sense that intervention does not directly affect their interests or payoffs and they actually pay a cost for doing so, whether it be in the form of effort, risk, or susceptibility to potential retaliation.[39] Experimental studies show how third parties punish unfair offers in ultimatum games.[40]

Third-party punishment is particularly important for explaining the origins and maintenance of cooperation in large groups, where the problem of policing bad behavior becomes particularly difficult because the mechanisms of repeated games among the same individuals no longer function effectively.[41] Second-party punishment strategies (in which we only punish those who harm us directly) are not evolutionarily stable for enforcing norms of reciprocity.[42] Of course, at some point, groups become so large as to require formal institutions to provide these functions, which supplement our evolved moral sense. Some scholars note that cultures that develop religions in which all-seeing gods that see all and punish bad behavior fare particularly well, a cultural selection process.[43] Nevertheless, our moral sense is still with us and provides the very motivation to create these governance mechanisms in the first place.

Wrong Makes Right: Condemnation Creates Conscience

Moral condemnation is so important that evolutionary thinkers believe that moral conscience could not have developed without it. Indeed the latter likely developed because of it.[44] Scholars argue that conscience is an evolutionary adaptation to the threat of moralistic

---

[38] DeScioli and Kurzban, "Mysteries of Morality."

[39] Bowles and Gintis, *A Cooperative Species*; Fehr and Fischbacher, "Why Social Preferences Matter," 3.

[40] Fehr, E., and Fischbacher, U., 2004. "Third-Party Punishment and Social Norms." *Evolution and Human Behavior* 25(2): 63–87.

[41] Bowles and Gintis, "The Evolution of Strong Reciprocity"; Fehr and Fischbacher, "Third-Party Punishment and Social Norms."

[42] Fehr and Fischbacher, "Third-Party Punishment and Social Norms."

[43] Norenzayan, Ara, Azim F. Shariff, Will M. Gervais, Aiyana K. Willard, Rita A. McNamara, Edward Slingerland, and Joseph Henrich. 2016. "The Cultural Evolution of Prosocial Religions." *Behavioral and Brain Sciences* 39.

[44] DeScioli and Kurzban, "Mysteries of Morality," 282; Boehm, *Moral Origins*, 19.

punishment, particularly group punishment. Conscience leads us to internalize a commitment to moral norm adherence so as to avoid the moral condemnation of others. Our conscience acts as an intuitive reputation monitor, a "social mirror ... to keep track of shameful pitfalls that threaten our reputational status and ... are likely to land us in trouble with our groups."[45] De Scioli and Kurzban maintain that "through natural selection humans became equipped with an increasingly sophisticated moral conscience for steering clear of moral mobs," so as to "avoid actions that could trigger coordinated condemnation by third parties."[46]

In order to avoid moral condemnation and punishment, the evolutionary pressure is not only to act altruistically but to actually be altruistic – that is, take the welfare of others into account, at least to some non-trivial degree. We speak of good people and bad people, not just people who do good and bad things, because we understand this intuitively. Conscience is a moral attribute, a dispositional trait leading us to do the right thing not based on a conscious expectation of reward or fear of punishment but because it is just the right thing to do.[47] This is the key to unraveling the paradox of the evolutionary model. By checking our selfishness, we can maximize the possibility of genetic success.[48]

Just as anger attends moral condemnation, guilt and gratitude guide conscience. Trivers writes that "the emotion of guilt has been selected for in humans partly in order to motivate the cheater to compensate his misdeed and to behave reciprocally in the future, and thus to prevent the

---

[45] Boehm, *Moral Origins*, 172.
[46] DeScioli and Kurzban, "Mysteries of Morality," 492.
[47] Gintis et al., "Strong Reciprocity and the Roots of Human Morality."
[48] Johnson makes the case that in addition to this internal voice, there is an external eye for much of humankind: the all-seeing and angry God who is necessary for explaining this human tendency. Johnson, Dominic. 2016. *God Is Watching You: How the Fear of God Makes Us Human*. Oxford University Press. Henrich et al. (2001) are critical of this individual-level evolutionary perspective, noting that human beings do not have any innate tendency toward believing in "Big Gods," even if there does seem to be a universal propensity toward attributing causality to the supernatural that may or may not have contributed to human's adaptive success (see Atran, Scott. 2002. *In Gods We Trust: The Evolutionary Landscape of Religion*. Oxford University Press). For our purposes, an omniscient and judging God can supplement conscience but only if there is something to judge, a prosocial code of right and wrong that must have already developed.

rupture of reciprocal relationships."[49] When others do good by us, not only do we feel the need to return the favor, we instinctively calibrate the gesture, rewarding more significant acts of kindness to a greater degree.

Moral conscience not only keeps you out of trouble, however. It opens up opportunities by signaling that you are a reliable partner, both to those with whom you are directly interacting and to others observing, what Alexander calls "indirect reciprocity."[50] Moral systems in which "the return is expected from someone other than the recipient of the beneficence"[51] are made possible by the "presence of interested audiences – groups of individuals who continually evaluate the members of their society as possible future interactants from whom they would like to gain more than they lose."[52] Over a very long period of time, evolution will therefore have favored those who possess the moral virtues of selflessness and honesty precisely because others will have seen, talked about, and rewarded those traits.

Participation in third-party punishment, because it is an indication of conscience, also likely promotes fitness by (again, unconsciously) creating opportunities for gain. Precisely because of the lack of direct stakes in the outcome, third-party punishment is a particularly costly signal of virtue. Kurzban et al. find that third-party punishment increases substantially when there is an audience.[53] Conservatives now derogatorily call this "virtue signaling," but it is often sincere and likely as old as *Homo sapiens*. Conversely, of course, we are judged – that is, morally condemned – when we refrain from helping others, being a mere bystander.[54]

This internal sense of the need to do the right thing, guided by our emotional intuitions, separates an evolutionary account from a standard rationalist theory of cooperation of the kind we have seen applied to international relations, for instance, in neoliberal accounts.[55]

---

[49] Trivers, "The Evolution of Reciprocal Altruism," 49.
[50] Alexander, *The Biology of Moral Systems*, 85. See also Wright, *The Moral Animal*, 273; Frank, *Passions within Reason*, xi; Trivers, "The Evolution of Reciprocal Altruism," 49; Boehm, *Moral Origins*, 187.
[51] Alexander, *The Biology of Moral Systems*, 85.   [52] Ibid, 94.
[53] Kurzban, Robert, Peter De Scioli, and Erin O'Brien. 2007. "Audience Effects on Moralistic Punishment." *Evolution and Human behavior* 28(2): 75–84.
[54] Alexander, *The Biology of Moral Systems*, 100.
[55] Keohane (1984), who popularized the concept, explicitly seeks to see how extensively self-interested based on reciprocity can induce cooperation without introducing morality, which he layers only in the concluding chapter.

Our moral sense of conscience does not operate solely on the basis of calculated and self-conscious self-interest and would not be nearly as effective if it did. It is our "selfish genes" acting without our knowledge, a term popularized by Richard Dawkins based on the landmark insights of George Williams, who made genes the central element of evolutionary theory.[56] Neural studies show that reciprocating cooperation in a prisoner's dilemma is associated with consistent activation in brain areas linked with reward processing. Reciprocity feels better than cheating. This is the biological manifestation of the moral norm of reciprocity.[57]

We find the same when it comes to participation in third-party punishment. Scholars again stress the good *feeling* we have in standing up to bad guys doing harm to others. Bowles and Gintis write that the "most parsimonious proximal explanation of cooperation, one that is supported by extensive experimental and other evidence, is that people gain pleasure from or feel morally obligated to cooperate with like-minded people. People also enjoy punishing those who exploit the cooperation of others, or feel morally obligated to do so."[58] After Fehr and Fischbacher, they call these feelings *social preferences,* which "include a concern, positive or negative, for the well-being of others, as well as a desire to uphold ethical norms."[59] Neural studies show that enforcing norms altruistically on behalf of others actually activates pleasure centers in our brain.[60] This suggests an evolved system to encourage good behavior automatically in the service of selfish genes.

Therefore, in neglecting moralistic punishment, or confining it to the condemnation of ethical transgressions by the international community as a whole rather than the targets of bad behavior themselves, the ethics literature in international relations is overlooking not only one of the most central moral impulses of humans but also the one that is necessary

---

[56] Williams, George Christopher. 2018. *Adaptation and Natural Selection: A Critique of Some Current Evolutionary Thought.* Vol. 75. Princeton University Press; Dawkins, Richard. 2016. *The Selfish Gene.* Oxford University Press.

[57] Rilling, James K., David A. Gutman, Thorsten R. Zeh, Giuseppe Pagnoni, Gregory S. Berns, and Clinton D. Kilts. 2002. "A Neural Basis for Social Cooperation." *Neuron* 35(2): 395–405.

[58] Bowles and Gintis, *A Cooperative Species,* 3.

[59] Ibid; Fehr and Fischbacher, "Why Social Preferences Matter."

[60] De Quervain, J. F. Dominique, Urs Fischbacher, Valerie Treyer, and Melanie Schellhammer. 2004. "The Neural Basis of Altruistic Punishment." *Science* 305(5688): 1254–1258.

for the very moral conscience whose expanding scope that scholarship documents. In order to understand why people do good, we need to know that they condemn the bad. There is no right without wrong.

For Shame: Egoists under an Ethical Shadow

To say that human beings have an evolved moral sense is not to claim that moral behavior is universal across individuals, nor even that everyone has a conscience. If everyone were always ethical, we would not even have the concept of morality. Bull notes, "If men in their wants of material things were wholly egotistical, the stabilization of possession by rules of property or ownership would be impossible – just as if men were wholly altruistic in relation to these wants, such stabilization would be unnecessary."[61] As the phenomenon of moral condemnation makes clear, much of what ethical behavior entails is chastising others for their lack of ethics. Evolutionary game theorists work with models of "frequency dependent selection," in which multiple different types interact and rise and fall in numbers based on how well they perform.[62] They find there are ecological niches for pure altruists, pure egoists, and conditional cooperators, and every human society will consist of a combination of different types.[63]

Nevertheless, the presence of moralistic condemnation, both second and third party in nature, strongly encourages egoists to mimic those with moral conscience in order to avoid moralistic punishment.[64] Fehr and Fischbacher find that "even a minority of strong reciprocators suffices to discipline a majority of selfish individuals when direct punishment is possible."[65] And "[o]nce friendship,

---

[61] Bull, *The Anarchical Society*, 5.   [62] Smith, "The Theory of Games."

[63] Frank, *Passions within Reason*, 54–63; Bowles and Gintis, "The Evolution of Strong Reciprocity," 18; Ridley, *The Origins of Virtue*, 61.

[64] Trivers, "The Evolution of Reciprocal Altruism," 50; Alexander, *The Biology of Moral Systems*, 105.

[65] Fehr, Ernst and Urs Fischbacher. 2003. "The Nature of Human Altruism." *Nature* 425(6960): 785. However, given that cooperation for reciprocators is predicated on good behavior, if reciprocators believe this is not likely to be forthcoming, cooperation in a group can collapse as well (Fehr and Fischbacher, "The Nature of Human Altruism"; Fehr, Ernst and Klaus M. Schmidt. 1999. "A Theory of Fairness, Competition, and Cooperation." *The Quarterly Journal of Economics* 114(3): 817–868; Frank, *Passions within Reason*, 54; Gintis et al., "Strong Reciprocity and the Roots of Human Morality."

moralistic aggression, guilt, sympathy, and gratitude have evolved to regulate the altruistic system," Trivers writes, "[S]election will favor mimicking these traits in order to influence the behavior of others to one's own advantage."[66] The "inevitable result is an uneasy balance between people who really possess the underlying emotions and others who merely seem to."[67] Pinker concurs: "A social group is a marketplace of cooperators of differing degrees of generosity and trustworthiness, and people advertise themselves as being as generous and trustworthy as they can get away with, which may be a bit more generous and trustworthy than they are."[68]

In ultimatum games, most do not make stingy offers, partially based on a commitment to fairness but also an expectation that others will expect an equal split. In dictator games, when the recipient must simply accept an offer, individuals behave less generously, indicating that part of beneficence is a rational calculation that others will act based on a self-defeating sense of fairness.[69] Even though it makes no self-interested sense for recipients to punish a stingy offer, humans have an intuitive sense that others might nevertheless do so, and this induces them to be more generous. When that constraint is removed, self-interest increases.

In other words, even pure egoists must find their way in the *shadow of morality*. If they do not, they will not prosper, which is bad for their inclusive fitness. Frank explains: "The ecological balance between more and less opportunistic strategies is at once in harmony with the view that self-interest underlies all action and with the opposing view that people often transcend their selfish tendencies. The key to resolving the tension between these views is to understand that the ruthless pursuit of self-interest is often self-defeating."[70] With moral condemnation in place, blatantly egoistic behavior becomes the puzzle to explain, not moral behavior that places bounds on self-interest. It is narcissism that becomes genetically reckless. As Lopez et al., who also apply an evolutionary framework to international relations, write, "An individual who is universally egoistic or altruistic (i.e., invariant

---

[66] Trivers, "The Evolution of Reciprocal Altruism," 50.
[67] Frank, *Passions within Reason*, 10.
[68] Pinker, *The Better Angels of Our Nature*, 490–491.
[69] Fehr and Fischbacher, "The Nature of Human Altruism"; Ridley, *The Origins of Virtue*, 140.
[70] Frank, *Passions within Reason*, 11.

egoism or altruism across contextual domains, or, what evolutionary
game theorists would refer to as an 'unconditional strategy') would
likely have been at a fitness disadvantage relative to peers entrained
with contextually dependent strategies."[71]

Therefore, when I write that morality is everywhere, I do not mean
that everyone is moral all the time, but that this shadow of morality –
that is, the possibility of moral condemnation and judgment – hangs
over virtually all human interaction. Even if there is a lot of moral
performance in the world, such hypocrisy and disingenuousness speak
for the importance and ubiquity of morality rather than skepticism
and dismissal. It is because the expectations of moral behavior are
so strong, enforced by third-party and second-party punishment and
incentivized by the potential gains from having a virtuous reputation,
that egoists cannot simply reveal their egoism. Ridley writes, "[E]ven
if you dismiss charitable giving as ultimately selfish – saying that people only give to charity in order to enhance their reputation, then you
have to explain why it does enhance their reputations. Why do other
people applaud charitable activity? We are immersed so deeply in a
sea of moral assumptions that it takes an effort to imagine a world
without them. A world without obligations to reciprocate, deal fairly,
and trust other people would be simply inconceivable."[72]

This shadow explains why human beings care deeply about how
others view them. Gossip is a human universal, found even in hunter-
gatherer societies,[73] and evolutionary theorists attribute it to its ability
to improve our fitness.[74] Almost fifty years ago, Trivers hypothesized,
"Selection should favor learning about the altruistic and cheating tendencies of others indirectly, both through observing interactions of
others and, once linguistic abilities have evolved, by hearing about
such interactions or hearing characterizations of individuals (e.g.,
dirty, hypocritical, dishonest, untrustworthy, cheating louse)."[75] By
sharing information about the moral failings – and gossip is predominantly negative in nature – of others, individuals avoid those who
would harm them but also coordinate their collective punishment.[76]
In a now famous experiment, the mere presence of a picture of eyes

[71] Lopez et al, "States in Mind," 57.   [72] Ridley, *The Origins of Virtue*, 143.
[73] Boehm, *Moral Origins*, 239.
[74] Alexander, *The Biology of Moral Systems*, 85.
[75] Trivers, "The Evolution of Reciprocal Altruism," 52.
[76] Wright, *The Moral Animal*, 266; De Waal, *Good Natured*, 10.

increases contributions to an honor system coffee fund.[77] This human tendency also requires and makes use of our large brains, capable of remembering the actions of many others over time. Spite helps too. "Spreading the word that someone cheated you is potent retaliation, since it leads people to withhold altruism from that person for fear of getting burned."[78]

Concern for our standing in front of peers is so ingrained that there are automatic emotions that attend the discovery of our moral failings: shame and embarrassment. Whereas guilt can be private, shame only occurs in front of an audience. As was the case with anger, shame acts as a costly signal of commitment to the very moral norms we violate. In order to show our genuine rather than feigned embarrassment, evolution has given us the involuntary physiological response of the blush.[79] Darwin himself had this intuition and corresponded with colonial administrators and missionaries all over the world to ask whether indigenous peoples in the British Empire blushed with shame. He found, of course, that blushing was universal.[80]

Unsurprisingly, humans are committed to defending their moral reputation since it is such a valuable currency. Honor is ethical prestige, the external recognition of one's internal virtue.[81] In the previous chapter, we noted a number of virtues, such as determination, resolve, and bravery, that are venerated under binding morality. However, many of the virtues on which honor is based can be traced to maintaining a reputation for valuing the welfare of others more generally regardless of group membership, an inherent commitment to a high WTR. Rodriguez Mosquera et al. group these under the category of "social interdependence," the "group of values that focus on the strengthening of social bonds and the maintenance of interpersonal harmony."[82] This is the "honor code" that we expect of students, the moral integrity that comes from conscience keeping them from cheating while no one

[77] Bateson, Melissa, Daniel Nettle, and Gilbert Roberts. 2006. "Cues of Being Watched Enhance Cooperation in a Real-World Setting." *Biology Letters* 2(3): 412–414.

[78] Wright, *The Moral Animal*, 208.   [79] Boehm, *Moral Origins*, 20.

[80] Ibid, 14.

[81] Kaufman, "Understanding Honor"; Cross, Susan E., Ayse K. Uskul, Berna Gerçek-Swing, Zeynep Sunbay, Cansu Alözkan, Ceren Günsoy, Bilge Ataca, and Zahide Karakitapoğlu-Aygün. 2014. "Cultural Prototypes and Dimensions of Honor." *Personality and Social Psychology Bulletin* 40(2): 246.

[82] Rodriguez Mosquera et al., "The Role of Honour Concerns."

is watching. Those with honor are honest and generous. They do not steal or cheat.[83] They keep their promises. Actions by others that call into question one's commitment to the particular qualities defined as virtuous provoke outrage and anger.[84] Honor is highly emotional, as morality generally is.[85] This is particularly true when those slights and insults are public in nature. Honor functions largely on the basis of shame; humans aim to avoid a fall in their moral reputation.[86] While seemingly trivial, in our evolutionary past, it was anything but. This is why words do hurt as much as sticks and stones.

Putting this all together, armed with the knowledge that an ethical compass is not situational but rather an attribute that some have and others do not, humans are on the lookout for those who do good and punish bad relatively *indiscriminately*, as a general rule of right and wrong.[87] We will be looking for the goodies who derive pleasure from acting morally. It is precisely those who do not care as much about material payoffs and individual gains who can be entrusted with our welfare without constant monitoring.[88] Good people can be trusted without having to literally keep an eye on them, a particularly important factor in early human societies that lacked security cameras and police forces. Those who only help their friends or when they have something directly to gain are of much less use. This explains why morality is the key attribute we use in forming impressions of others, more so than other key attributes such as competence or warmth.[89]

[83] Cross et al., "Cultural Prototypes and Dimensions of Honor"; Kaufman, "Understanding Honor"; Rodriguez Mosquera et al., "The Role of Honour Concerns."

[84] Rodriguez Mosquera et al., "The Role of Honour Concerns"; Lebow, *Why Nations Fight*.

[85] Dolan, Thomas. 2015. "Demanding the Impossible: War, Bargaining, and Honor." *Security Studies* 24(3): 528–562; Lanoszka, Alexander and Michael A. Hunzeker. 2015. "Rage of Honor: Entente Indignation and the Lost Chance for Peace in the First World War." *Security Studies* 24(4): 662–695.

[86] Wyatt-Brown, Bertram. 1982. *Southern Honor: Ethics and Behavior in the Old South*. New York, NY: Oxford University Press.

[87] Alexander, *The Biology of Moral Systems*, 77.

[88] Frank, *Passions within Reason*, 54; Trivers, "The Evolution of Reciprocal Altruism," 51.

[89] Goodwin, Geoffrey P., Jared Piazza, and Paul Rozin. 2014. "Moral Character Predominates in Person Perception and Evaluation." *Journal of Personality and Social Psychology* 106(1): 148–168; Wojciszke, Bogdan, Roza Bazinska, and Marcin Jaworski. 1998. "On the Dominance of Moral Categories in Impression Formation." *Personality and Social Psychology Bulletin* 24(12): 1251–1263.

I call this *moral screening,* and in the next chapter, I demonstrate that a similar phenomenon is evident in international relations, indicating an evolutionary underpinning to even modern state behavior.

War Made Man and Man Made War: The Origins of Binding Morality

Just as moralistic punishment is a universal phenomenon, suggesting an evolutionary origin, so too is the human tendency to join groups and favor insiders over outsiders. Everett et al. write, "One of the most enduring findings in social psychology is intergroup bias: the powerful tendency to evaluate and treat in-group members more favorably than out-group members."[90] In a recent review, Balliet et al. summarize, "People evaluate ingroup members more positively than outgroup members, tend to reward ingroup members more than outgroup members, and work harder to accomplish ingroup goals."[91]

If the binding foundations have evolutionary origins, then they must also have helped human beings to solve recurrent challenges in their ancestral past, offering fitness advantages. Yet why would parochial altruism have emerged as a moral impulse separate from more generic altruism? Evolutionary scholars have provided two answers, both of which likely contribute to the ethics of community.

First, ingroup favoritism emerges as a solution to the problems of policing opportunism. By confining altruism to smaller groups, individuals run less risk of exploitation.[92] Ingroup identity, marked by symbols or behaviors that differentiate from outgroups, is a marker of greater trustworthiness. "Such positive bias toward one's ingroup may promote the functioning and performance of one's ingroup, which may provide the individual with long-term benefits and increased survival probability," explain Balliet et al.[93]

---

[90] Everett, Jim AC, Zach Ingbretsen, Fiery Cushman, and Mina Cikara. 2017. "Deliberation Erodes Cooperative Behavior – Even towards Competitive Out-Groups, Even When Using a Control Condition, and Even When Eliminating Selection Bias." *Journal of Experimental Social Psychology* 73: 76.

[91] Balliet, Daniel, Junhui Wu, and Carsten KW De Dreu. 2014. "Ingroup Favoritism in Cooperation: A Meta-Analysis." *Psychological Bulletin* 140(6): 1556.

[92] Brewer, "The Psychology of Prejudice," 434.

[93] Balliet et al., "Ingroup Favoritism in Cooperation," 1556.

This "bounded generalized reciprocity" (BGR) model argues "that because of generalized trust in ingroup members and the need to build a positive reputation among ingroup members, people cooperate with ingroup members more than with outgroup members and unclassified strangers."[94] Research shows that human beings are remarkably but unconsciously perceptive of signals that delineate coalitional membership, even as these markers can take virtually any form. The color of one's t-shirt can be as potent a signal as race.[95] The BGR model claims that individuals strive for a reputation as a cooperator to secure indirect benefits from members of the group. They want to be seen as loyal.

Other theorists trace the origins of ingroup favoritism to intergroup competition. Human beings face not only the dangers of cheating from within but also the threat of physical aggression from without. When engaged in struggles over material resources, groups will do better vis-à-vis other groups if their members are loyal rather than universally altruistic or entirely selfish.[96]

However, individuals have an incentive to free ride on the parochial altruists in their group, making it hard to explain how loyalty could have developed in the first place. In fact, the tendency to cheat and avoid this social burden might be particularly pronounced in situations of extreme danger. Sharing meat is one thing; dying for others is another.[97]

Third-party moralistic punishment and costly signaling provide some of the answers. We punish others, whether it be through ostracism or physical violence, for acting unfairly, but we also punish them for disloyalty. Humans have a particular vocabulary for the violation of binding morality; betrayal is a particularly grave sin. In the modern intergroup context of international relations, betrayal is treason. Those who avoided the temptation to figuratively draft dodge likely also reaped gains that would have encouraged the biological evolution of ingroup loyalty and deference to authority. Humans love their heroes, and being a hero has

---

[94] Ibid, 1559.
[95] Kurzban, Robert, John Tooby, and Leda Cosmides. 2001. "Can Race Be Erased? Coalitional Computation and Social Categorization." *Proceedings of the National Academy of Sciences* 98(26): 15387–15392.
[96] Alexander, *The Biology of Moral Systems*; Choi and Bowles, "The Co-Evolution of Parochial Altruism and War."
[97] Wrangham, *The Goodness Paradox*, 134; Wright, *The Moral Animal*, 187.

likely always come with material perks. Those who did not do their duty would have faced costly social derision, just as they do today.[98]

"Multi-level" evolutionary theorists supplement this individual-level account with a concurrent group-level dynamic.[99] In the past, whether and how long individuals and their genes survived was partly a function of the attributes of the groups to which they belonged, most importantly how many group loyalists were in the community.[100] Our moral instincts emerged during a time of extreme material peril in which human beings were living subsistence lives, threatened by both environmental catastrophes and animal predation, but more importantly, the threat of other humans.[101] Whether groups had significant numbers of parochial altruists might have literally been the difference between life and death for the group as a whole.[102]

When group extinction was possible, even small advantages in the proportion of parochial altruists in a group might have been decisive, and the genetic advantages of free-riding would have disappeared.[103] An individual's interests become identical to the group "whenever the group [is] threatened externally in such fashion that complete cooperation by its members would be necessary to dissipate the threat, and when failure of the group to dissipate the threat would more severely penalize any remaining individuals than would the group's

---

[98] Pinker, *The Better Angels of Our Nature*, 522; Fiske and Rai 2015: 73.

[99] Bowles and Gintis, *A Cooperative Species*. Proponents of this view call it "multi-level" selection so as to distinguish it from discredited group-level selection theories. The unit of selection is the individual, as it is in other approaches, although misunderstandings of this fact persist. The debate between multi-level and purely individualist approaches resembles in many ways that between paradigmatic adherents in international relations – misrepresentations of the other side and vitriolic polemics, all without enough evidence to mediate. In my mind, multi-level approaches seem to do a better job at explaining the human propensity toward ingroup loyalty and deference to authority figures in those communities. Individual-level theorists, for instance, are forced toward explanations of solidarity in war by reference to factors that must surely be incomplete, such as the bond felt by soldiers for the other soldiers who fight with them side by side.

[100] Choi and Bowles, "The Co-Evolution of Parochial Altruism and War."

[101] McDermott et al., "Blunt Not the Heart, Enrage It," 76; Alexander, *The Biology of Moral Systems*, 78.

[102] Alexander, *The Biology of Moral Systems*, 79.

[103] Gintis et al., "Strong Reciprocity and the Roots of Human Morality": 242; also Ridley, *The Origins of Virtue*, 40; Bowles and Gintis, *A Cooperative Species*, 76.

survival after that individual had used all of its effort to support the group."[104] This explains how between-group differences could have outrun the "within-group" selection encouraging free-riding and allowed individual-level dispositions toward costly group favoritism to emerge, survive, and proliferate. De Waal writes that the "moral underpinnings of the community, on the one hand, and warfare and ethnic strife, on the other, are two sides of the very same coin."[105] To paraphrase Tilly,[106] war made man and man made war.

A Bias toward Bias: Humanitarian and Binding Morality Are Not Opposites

What is the relationship between ingroup morality and humanitarianism, between the binding and the individualizing foundations? Some of the literature on intergroup bias implies that the two are opposites. Much is made, including in international relations, of the findings of the "minimal group paradigm" and social identity theory (SIT).[107] The finding that human beings are easily led to identify with ingroups, even on trivial criteria, and favor those ingroups over outgroups is thought to provide a microfoundation for the assumptions of national egoism in international relations that makes competition rather than cooperation the norm. Mercer summarizes, "The more we identify with our group, the more we will differentiate our group from other groups. This leads to between-group competition, perceived conflicts of interest, and preference for relative over absolute gains."[108]

However, intergroup bias is an empirical regularity in search of an explanation, and social identity theory has not fared well in coming

---

[104] Alexander, *The Biology of Moral Systems*, 102.

[105] De Waal, *Good Natured*, 30.

[106] Tilly, Charles. 1975. *The Formation of National States in Western Europe.* Princeton University Press.

[107] Turner, John C., Rupert J. Brown, and Henri Tajfel. 1979. "Social Comparison and Group Interest in Ingroup Favouritism." *European Journal of Social Psychology* 9(2):187–204; Tajfel, Henri. 1970. "Experiments in Intergroup Discrimination." *Scientific American* 223(5): 96–102; Tajfel, Henri, Michael G. Billig, Robert P. Bundy, and Claude Flament. 1971. "Social Categorization and Intergroup Behaviour." *European Journal of Social Psychology* 1(2): 149–178.

[108] Mercer, Jonathan. 1995. "Anarchy and Identity." *International Organization* 49(2): 247.

to grips with the phenomenon. The central issue is the distinction between ingroup love and outgroup hate, between ingroup favoritism and outgroup derogation. In a recent review of the literature, Balliet et al. conclude that "decades of research consistently revealed that variations in bias in intergroup perceptions, attitudes, and evaluations emerge because of variation in ingroup favoritism more than because of variations in outgroup derogation." As Brewer notes, favoritism in the contexts constructed by social identity theory (SIT) researchers is easily explainable even "in the absence of any negative affect or hostile intent towards outgroups."[109] If I have only one slice of pizza, giving it to my friend does not mean I have any enemies. In other words, positive identity, the warm feeling of belonging that comes from group membership, does not necessitate negative identity. A second generation of studies has found consistent evidence of what has become known as the "positive–negative asymmetry effect."[110] Whereas experimental participants favor ingroup members in their allocations of positive benefits, when they are tasked with distributing costs, they do not indicate such ingroup favoritism, doling out negative outcomes in a fair fashion. They do the same when it comes to categorizing groups based on traits, describing their own group in more positive terms but not describing the outgroup in more negative terms.[111]

Bowles and Gintis conducted an experiment among the "famously bellicose highlands of Papau New Guinea" so as to test whether individuals make more stingy offers in ultimatum games to outgroups

---

[109] Brewer, "The Psychology of Prejudice," 432.

[110] Mummendey, Amélie, Bernd Simon, Carsten Dietze, Melanie Grünert, Gabi Haeger, Sabine Kessler, Stephan Lettgen, and Stefanie Schäferhoff. 1992. "Categorization Is Not Enough: Intergroup Discrimination in Negative Outcome Allocation." *Journal of Experimental Social Psychology* 28(2): 125–144; Mummendey, Amélie and Sabine Otten. 1998. "Positive–Negative Asymmetry in Social Discrimination." *European Review of Social Psychology* 9(1): 107–143; Brown, Rupert. 2000. "Social Identity Theory: Past Achievements, Current Problems and Future Challenges." *European Journal of Social Psychology* 30(6): 745–778; Wenzel, Michael and Amélie Mummendey. 1996. "Positive–Negative Asymmetry of Social Discrimination: A Normative Analysis of Differential Evaluations of In-Group and Out-Group on Positive and Negative Attributes." *British Journal of Social Psychology* 35(4): 493–507.

[111] Brewer, Marilynn B. 1979. "In-Group Bias in the Minimal Intergroup Situation: A Cognitive-Motivational Analysis." *Psychological Bulletin* 86(2): 307; Brewer, Marilynn B. and Donald T. Campbell. 1976. *Ethnocentrism and Intergroup Attitudes: East African Evidence.* Oxford: SAGE Publications.

as opposed to ingroups but also whether third parties punish their ingroup members less than outgroup members for being cheap. They found that participants exhibited ingroup favoritism but also significant generosity vis-à-vis outgroups. Third parties punished most severely stingy outgroup members playing with a fellow ingroup member, but they also punished ungenerous offers from their own group to outgroup members.[112]

Both ingroup favoritism and cooperation with others, even outgroups, are automatic and intuitive human tendencies. One of the ways by which researchers uncover our gut instincts, called System I processing, is by having experimental participants make decisions while under time pressure, precluding the use of the reflective, calculating, and rational part of our cognition, called System II.[113] Not only do individuals demonstrate greater tendencies toward cooperation in prisoner dilemma and trust games when under time pressure compared to when they are not, they do this with both ingroups and outgroups. This is the case even when the situation is competitively framed. Cooperation with ingroups is higher relative to outgroups, but intuition always produces more cooperation. The authors conclude that "while we might be intuitive cooperators, we are not intuitively impartial."[114] I would reframe this: We are not inherently impartial, but we are intuitive cooperators, nevertheless.

Pessimistic findings about ingroup bias are often based on research designs that do not allow us to distinguish between outgroup hate and outgroup fear.[115] Research to date overwhelmingly suggest that ingroup favoritism is driven by the perception of threat, emerging in the context of perceived defense against other's aggression. This includes studies that I review in the conclusion, which manipulate oxytocin levels in respondents' bodies.[116]

---

[112] Bowles and Gintis, *A Cooperative Species*, 134.

[113] For a summary, see Rathbun, "The Rarity of Realpolitik," and Rathbun, *Reasoning of State*.

[114] Everett et al., "Deliberation Erodes Cooperative Behavior," 80.

[115] Halevy, Nir, Ori Weisel, and Gary Bornstein. 2012. "'In-Group Love' and 'Out-Group Hate' in Repeated Interaction between Groups." *Journal of Behavioral Decision Making* 25(2): 188–195.

[116] De Dreu, Carsten K. W., Lindred L. Greer, Michel J. J. Handgraaf, Shaul Shalvi, Gerben A. Van Kleef, Matthijs Baas, Femke S. Ten Velden, Eric Van Dijk, and Sander W. W. Feith. 2010. "The Neuropeptide Oxytocin Regulates Parochial Altruism in Intergroup Conflict among Humans." *Science* 328(5984): 1408–1411.

Therefore, the preponderance of the evidence suggests instead that human beings have humanitarian inclinations, but also exhibit ingroup favoritism, and that the two are not direct opposites. Dislike or ill feeling toward outgroups is activated by threat, suggesting that we begin with an encompassing moral circle that becomes restricted to the degree that defense becomes salient.[117] Binders do not generally hate outsiders or wish them harm; they are instead highly attuned to how outsiders might harm them. We will see, when we discuss the dual-process model, that binding morality and humanitarianism are separate dimensions by which we determine what is right and wrong, not poles of a single continuum. This has crucial normative implications I discuss in the conclusion.

There is an evolutionary reason for this as well. To deny the possibility of mutually beneficial exchange with outsiders poses opportunity costs. Indeed research shows that those who trust more generally do better in experiments since they do not restrict their interactions to just a few known participants.[118] As Bowles and Gintis (who, remember, are advocates of the idea that parochial altruism emerged in the context of war) conclude from their experiment, "These results are hardly surprising when one recalls that members of ancestral human groups not only fought one another, they also depended on one another for help in times of need, for information, mates and trade goods. When we say that altruism is sometimes parochial, we mean that it recognizes group boundaries, not that it always stops at the border."[119]

Not Immaterial: The Ubiquity of Morality in Power Politics

Once we have incorporated moral condemnation and binding ethics into our study of international relations, we begin to see how morality is actually everywhere, the rule rather than the exception. There is a reason for this: Morality is literally embodied; it is a part of our physiology based on a process of evolution. An evolutionary-based account

---

[117] Hewstone, Miles, Mark Rubin, and Hazel Willis. 2002. "Intergroup Bias." *Annual Review of Psychology* 53(1): 575–604.

[118] Orbell, John M. and Robyn M. Dawes. 1993. Social Welfare, Cooperators' Advantage, and the Option of Not Playing the Game. *American Sociological Review* 58(6):787–800; for a review, see Rathbun, *Trust in International Cooperation.*

[119] Bowles and Gintis, *A Cooperative Species*, 134.

therefore contrasts with all the major schools of thought not just on ethics, but on the very nature of international relations.

Contrary to the typical materialist approaches of international relations, we see that our moral psychology is an evolved mechanism to cope with material needs in an environment of anarchy, not a luxury we only enjoy once we have transcended it. The Pleistocene era in which these traits evolved looked much like the anarchy described in theory by security scholars. Johnson and Thayer write, "Our ancestors not only lived in a state of anarchy for millions of years, but they also evolved in that state of anarchy and consequently developed cognitive and behavioral adaptations specifically to survive and reproduce effectively under conditions of anarchy."[120] Morality is one such adaptation, but one that has received scant attention from IR scholars, even those interested in evolutionary insights.

Since morality is an intrinsic part of the human experience (and the human body), there is no realm of human interaction where morality is absent (although there might be specific situations, of course). Even many classical realists have had this realization. Wolfers concludes, "[T]he ethic of politics is but a part of general ethics."[121] Morgenthau observes of the public/private distinction, "The importance of this conception has been literary rather than practical. Mankind has at all times refused to forego the ethical evaluation of political action.... Whatever some philosophers may have asserted about the amorality of political action, philosophic tradition, historic judgment and public opinion alike refuse to withhold ethical valuation from the political sphere."[122] Evolutionary psychologists therefore offer the basis for a "first imaged reverse" argument, one which "inverts the analytic focus of the subfield from micro-micro causation to macro-micro causation: from the effects of actor-level characteristics or individual differences on attitudes and behaviors, to the effects of environmental forces on actor-level characteristics."[123]

What differentiates private and public life is not moral standards but the situations in which the individual typically finds himself or herself. However, if the private individual were to face, as a country's

---

[120] Johnson and Thayer, "The Evolution of Offensive Realism."
[121] Wolfers, "Statesmanship and Moral Choice," 180; also Morgenthau, "The Evil of Politics," 14.
[122] Morgenthau, "The Evil of Politics," 5.
[123] Kertzer and Tingley, "Political Psychology in International Relations," 330.

leaders sometimes do, some enemy with no one else to protect her, such as in a home invasion, she would be morally justified in using force for self-defense as the lesser evil. And within the borders of our country, just as outside, we morally authorize the deadly use of force in certain instances to protect the broader community. While the frequency of such situations is lower in private life, the moral standards are not different.

The notion of the autonomy of the political sphere plays a greater role in the writings of structural realists who try unsuccessfully to extricate considerations of human nature from their approaches. However, as mentioned previously, this notion also persists, largely implicitly, in rationalist approaches that utilize elements central to evolutionary theory such as reciprocity, deterrence, and reputation while stripping them of their moral nature. Whereas structural realists explicitly disavow the moralized nature of international politics, rationalists demoralize it by avoidance and inattention.

By virtue of their truncated set of moral motivations, liberal scholars tend to conceive of morality's role in international relations as moving us past the traditional power politics of international relations. They point to the "considerable body of constructivist scholarship [that] tracks the steady evolution and institutionalization of 'good' norms that countermand power politics."[124] I would agree, yet juxtaposing moral behavior with the amoral application of force creates a false framing. What we generally regard as the most striking manifestations of the lack of ethics, the use of violence for political purposes, are more often the very expression of moral principles, just different ones. The question is not whether international politics have become *more* moral but rather whether they have become *differently* moral. The controversy over whether international relations have experienced moral progress is better characterized as a debate over whether international relations have experienced *liberal* moral progress.

Most articles on international norms juxtapose a materialist pursuit of self-interest against a more enlightened pursuit of the ethical good. Ethics constitute what we might consider a "post-material" realm in which nation-states, particularly great powers, have risen above the

---

[124] Barnett, "Evolution without Progress," 622; also Price, "Moral Limit and Possibility," 520.

grubby business of dividing up and exploiting the world.[125] However, I will argue in this book, morality is omnipresent in the material realm since ethics are partly biological and remain so even after we enter the post-material world.

This biological position is a departure from the conventional way that constructivist international relations scholars approach morality: as a social product without any material moorings. If social reality is "ideas all the way down,"[126] then human beings are free to construct any ethical system they might devise. There are no material limits on intersubjectivity. Constructivism essentially takes the same position as anthropologists typically do: The "distinction between right and wrong is made by people on the basis of how they would like their society to function. It arises from interpersonal negotiation in a particular environment, and derives its sense of obligation and guilt from the internalization of these processes. Moral reasoning is done by *us*, not by natural selection."[127] Tooby and Cosmides call this approach, which privileges culture, as the "Standard Social Science Model": "According to this view, all of the specific content of the human mind originally derives from the 'outside' – from the environment and the social world – and the evolved architecture of the mind consists solely or predominantly of a small number of general-purpose mechanisms that are *content-independent,* and which sail under names such as 'learning', 'induction', 'intelligence', 'imitation', 'rationality', 'the capacity for culture', or, simply, 'culture'."[128]

Evolutionary psychology indicates that morality is not merely what we make of it. While morality in international relations is more varied than liberals in particular commonly recognize, there is a limited set of universal moral foundations. Wright explains that evolutionary psychologists "focus less on surface differences among cultures than on deep unities. Beneath the global crazy quilt of rituals and

[125] Inglehart, Ronald. 1981. "Post-Materialism in an Environment of Insecurity." *American Political Science Review* 75(4): 880–900.
[126] Wendt, Alexander. 2000. *Social Theory of International Politics.* Cambridge: Cambridge University Press.
[127] De Waal, *Good Natured,* 39.
[128] Cosmides, Leda and John Tooby. 1992. "Cognitive Adaptations for Social Exchange." In: Barkow, Jerome H., Leda Cosmides, and John Tooby (eds.). *The Adapted Mind: Evolutionary Psychology and the Generation of Culture.* Oxford: Oxford University Press, 164.

customs, they see recurring patterns ... people in all cultures worry about social status ... people in all cultures not only gossip, but gossip about the same kinds of things. People everywhere feel guilt, and feel it in broadly predictable circumstances; people everywhere have a deep sense of justice, so that the axioms 'One good turn deserves another' and 'An eye for an eye, a tooth for a tooth' shape human life everywhere on this planet."[129] Therefore, we cannot simply invent a morality to justify anything we please and expect it to last or for others to accept it. An evolutionary approach that conceives of ethics as moral intuitions is different from constructivist accounts in that it does not think of humans as a blank slate. As it is for those who stress the logic of habit or internalized norms, our moral sense is intuitive and non-representational. However, it is not produced solely by practice or socialization.[130]

The evolutionary basis of morality is part of the "rump materialism"[131] with which social theories must come to terms. Morality is not the transcendence of material reality; it is material reality. It helps us navigate challenges posed by our material environment; it is embodied in our physiology precisely for that purpose. Morality emerged to help us divide resources, deter threats, and promote and police cooperation, the recurrent challenges of our evolutionary past.[132] When nation-states issue and interpret threats or bargain hard over trade today, they are engaged in the same sorts of interactions that human beings have engaged in since their origins and with the same moral concepts.

However, the evolutionary position is not deterministic or incompatible with a constructivist position focused on the importance of social influences. Culture, socialization, and other external influences are still crucial. Graham et al. speculate that where the first draft of the human mind is genetically determined, it is rewritten in light of early formative experiences on the basis of cultural influences: "If there were no first draft of the psyche," they write, "then groups would be free to invent utopian moralities ... and they'd be able to pass them on to

[129] Wright, *The Moral Animal*, 7–8.
[130] Pouliot, Vincent. 2008. "The Logic of Practicality: A Theory of Practice of Security Communities," *International Organization* 62(2): 257–288.
[131] Wendt, *Social Theory of International Politics*, 98.
[132] Alexander, *The Biology of Moral Systems*, 77.

their children because all moral ideas would be equally learnable. This is clearly not the case. Conversely, if cultural learning played no formative role, then the first draft would be the final draft, and there'd be no variation across cultures."[133] Haidt and Joseph use the analogy of taste.[134] The tongue has discrete taste receptors that diverse and wildly varying cuisines are capable of satisfying. Yet there are things that no one will eat. De Waal uses the metaphor of language. Our brains are preprogrammed to be receptive to morality just as they are prepared for language. Morality is like language in that it is "too complex to be learned through trial and error and too variable to be genetically programmed."[135] Like language, our genetic systems do not determine but make morality "exceptionally easy to learn."[136]

Socialization is a key variable. Evolutionary psychologists suggest an early window in which we are more morally malleable.[137] At these points, "Our goodness can be intensified or corrupted, just as our selfishness can be exaggerated or reduced."[138] However, this window itself might be an evolutionary adaptation. In our early days, we soak up the moral norms that define our cultural context and will therefore serve us best in our particular situation. For a species that lives in every imaginable environment, this flexibility was a key to survival.[139] Even Trivers, a forefather of modern evolutionary psychology, expects "selection to favor developmental plasticity of those traits regulating altruistic and cheating tendencies."[140]

Nevertheless, it is important to stress that we are not entirely free to invent moralities at will. Even infants have prosocial inclinations.[141] A menu, while providing choice, is still a limited selection of items. Social influences seem to have two primary impacts.

First, they determine the relative weighting of different moral principles when they come into conflict, and these tradeoffs occur all the

---

[133] Graham et al., "Moral Foundations Theory," 63.
[134] Haidt, Jonathan and Craig Joseph. 2004. "Intuitive Ethics: How Innately Prepared Intuitions Generate Culturally Variable Virtues." *Daedalus* 133(4): 55–66.
[135] De Waal, *Good Natured*, 39.   [136] Boehm, *Moral Origins*, 10.
[137] Ibid, 35; Wright, *The Moral Animal*, 9.
[138] Bowles and Gintis, *A Cooperative Species*, 6.
[139] Wrangham, *The Goodness Paradox*, 112; Bowles and Gintis, *A Cooperative Species*, 15.
[140] Trivers, "The Evolution of Reciprocal Altruism," 51.
[141] Wrangham, *The Goodness Paradox*, 204; Boehm, *Moral Origins*, 98.

time. There is nothing in the evolutionary literature that suggests a total convergence toward one particular ethical foundation, particularly since different moral standards are designed to solve different problems. There will be significant "phenotypic" variation, as the biologist puts it, as evident in the above mentioned discussion of frequency-dependent selection. As seen in the chapters that follow, the political right is defined largely by its commitment to binding morality, and cultural expressions of ingroup loyalty such as nationalism ebb and flow. The liberal literature on the evolution of humanitarian norms seems to demonstrate such a process, in which the behaviors of power politics and the assertion of egoistic interests, even if morally justified, have been increasingly inhibited by an understanding of a broader obligation to humanity. Wright conceives of morality as "knobs of human nature" present in all human beings but whose exact tuning varies from person to person.[142] The knobs themselves, such as for fairness or altruistic concern, are present in all of us but their volume, so to speak, is partially a function of cultural circumstances. Our biology gives us a moral repertoire not a moral map. "Society influences what we care about, but evolution has produced the fact that we care."[143] Those who develop inventories of the fundamental moral impulses in human beings, on which the earlier parts of this book are based, all stress that different cultures and individuals place different emphases on them.

Second, social influences translate moral principles into discrete norms of behavior. "[Moral] sentiments," writes Frank, "are almost surely not inherited in any very specific form. Definitions of honesty, notions of fairness, even the conditions that trigger anger, all differ widely from culture to culture."[144] Thomas' distinction between norms and principles is useful. Norms are specific applications of an underlying moral principle. As Thomas explains, "Ethical norms ... are specifically concerned with moral notions of right and wrong and therefore prescribe or prohibit behavior that is subject to moral praise or blame.... It is difficult to account for the existence of certain norms without reference to some prior and independent moral principle. Norms protecting human rights, for example, reflect fundamental

---

[142] Wright, *The Moral Animal*, 9.
[143] Wrangham, *The Goodness Paradox*, 205.
[144] Frank, *Passions within Reason*, 93.

beliefs concerning the proper treatment of individuals and would not exist but for those beliefs."[145] The principles, essentially moral foundations, of societies are roughly similar across societies. Yet, the application of those principles and the specific way by which they are operationalized in a given time and place in the form of specific injunctions for behavior vary. "Our cultures are not random collections of arbitrary habits. They are canalized expressions of our instincts," writes Ridley.[146]

A key theme of this book is how wildly the applications of the binding values can vary, even within short periods of time (blinks of an eye in evolutionary terms). Culture defines the very definition of the group to whom we owe loyalty. Is it a family unit? A linguistic and cultural construct that unifies strangers? Those who look like us physically? Biology will not tell us this. The same is true of authority. To whom do we defer? Those duly elected? Our elders? Our spiritual leaders? Even the basis of legitimate authority varies. For some cultures, it is given by God. For others, it is based on service to the community. Reus-Smit has documented the very different ways by which the "moral purpose" of the state is constituted and the diffusion of those forms across the international system. This is certainly a cultural process; evolutionary psychologists have been almost entirely silent on the subject.[147] Yet the feelings of deference owed to some authority and of greater obligation to some group is a human universal. King and country are just the latest cultural iterations of an innate moral intuition.

Consider again the phenomenon of honor, observed to vary in intensity and definition across different cultures. In "honor cultures," those which "promote a view of manhood in which expressions of toughness, strength, and status in public behaviour are even more desirable than is the case in individualistic cultures,"[148] "face" is particularly important. Losing face means looking weak in an environment in which courage, determination, and strength are socially esteemed. Since in individualistic societies, members are less expected to fill specific social roles, these more traditional markers of honor

[145] Thomas, *The Ethics of Destruction*, 28.
[146] Ridley, *The Origins of Virtue*, 6.
[147] Reus-Smit, Christian. 2009. *The Moral Purpose of the State*. Princeton University Press; Reus-Smit, Christian. 2013. *Individual Rights and the Making of the International System*. Cambridge: Cambridge University Press.
[148] Rodriguez Mosquera et al., "The Role of Honour Concerns," 145.

have faded in significance, although they are still powerful in non-Western societies. "Appraisal respect" has been supplanted by "recognition respect," the dignity that we feel a right to rather than a need to earn.[149] Recognition is an egalitarian concept and can be seen as the actualization of the liberal, individualistic project.

Yet, as much as these honor cultures are social constructions, some theorists nevertheless argue that they might ultimately have material origins. Cohen and Nisbett, for instance, attribute the emergence of an honor culture in the American South to the largely lawless environment that once prevailed. They quote Fischer: "In the absence of any strong sense of order as unity, hierarchy, or social peace, back-settlers shared an idea of order as a system of retributive justice. The prevailing principle was ... the rule of retaliation. It held that a good man must seek to do right in the world, but when wrong was done to him, he must punish the wrongdoer himself by an act of retribution that restored order and justice in the world."[150] Morality serves the protection of interests, motivating individuals to take actions that indicate they will not be exploited. Cohen and Nisbett write that "where self-protection is essential, a culture of honor will develop."[151] Empirical studies show that such intra-group dynamics can also emerge between groups.[152]

A biological approach that puts morality front and center is also an improvement on crude applications of Darwinism previously applied to international relations, which make no mention of human beings' unique ethical sense.[153] Most notably, Thayer argues that evolutionary

---

[149] Darwall, Stephen L. 1977. "Two Kinds of Respect." *Ethics* 88(1): 36–49.

[150] Cohen, Dov, Richard E. Nisbett, Brian F. Bowdle, and Norbert Schwarz. 1996. "Insult, Aggression, and the Southern Culture of Honor: An 'Experimental Ethnography'." *Journal of Personality and Social Psychology* 70(5): 946.

[151] Cohen, Dov and Richard E. Nisbett. 1994. "Self-Protection and the Culture of Honor: Explaining Southern Violence." *Personality and Social Psychology Bulletin* 20(5): 552.

[152] Lebow, *Why Nations Fight*; Dafoe and Caughey, "Honor and War."

[153] Gat, Azar 2000. "So Why Do People Fight? Evolutionary Theory and the Causes of War." *European Journal of International Relations* 15(4): 571–599. Morality is not all there is to biology of course, and evolution is useful for explaining phenomena like negativity bias (Johnson and Tierney 2018) or territoriality (Johnson and Toft 2013). My complaint is with evolutionary accounts that try to paint a picture of international relations as a whole without mention of ethics. See Johnson, Dominic and Dominic

theory provides a microfoundation to classical realist theory by providing a scientific explanation for human egoism and the will to power and dominance. Simply put, he argues: "In times of danger or great stress, an organism usually places its life – its survival – before that of other members of its group, be it pack, herd, or tribe. For these reasons, egoistic behavior contributes to fitness."[154] Thayer falls back on to the too common use of human nature as synonymous with resignation to instrumental egoism.

However, human beings, as all evolutionary theorists stress, are no typical organism. It is their tendencies toward other-regarding behavior – that is, their lack of constant egoism, monitored by moral condemnation and conscience – that sets them apart. No other organism extends generosity beyond immediate kin.[155] "Human societies represent a huge anomaly in the animal world," write Fehr and Fischbacher. "They are based on a detailed division of labour and cooperation between genetically unrelated individuals in large groups.... In contrast, most animal species exhibit little division of labour and cooperation is limited to small groups.... Exceptions are social insects such as ants and bees, or the naked mole rat; however, their cooperation is based on a substantial amount of genetic relatedness."[156] The "core problem" for evolutionary psychology is to explain "why, in a dog-eat-dog world, humans' sense of virtue has developed beyond the level seen in other animals."[157] The world is indeed marked by the constant quest for material resources highlighted by Thayer, but humans have solved this problem more often than not by repressing selfish impulses rather than by sharpening them. Indeed "the conscious pursuit of self-interest is incompatible with its attainment ... someone who always pursues self-interest is doomed to fail."[158] We live "in the thrall of a

Tierney. 2018. "Bad World: The Negativity Bias in International Politics." *International Security* 43(3): 96–140; Johnson, Dominic and Monica Duffy Toft. 2013. "Grounds for War: The Evolution of Territorial Conflict." *International Security* 38(3): 7–38.

[154] Thayer, Bradley. 2000. "Bringing in Darwin: Evolutionary Theory, Realism, and International Politics." *International Security* 25(2): 132.

[155] Bowles and Gintis, *A Cooperative Species*, 2; Ridley, *The Origins of Virtue*, 38–39; Alexander, *The Biology of Moral Systems*, 97.

[156] Fehr and Fischbacher, "The Nature of Human Altruism," 785.

[157] Wrangham, *The Goodness Paradox*, 135.

[158] Frank, *Passions within Reason*, ix.

logical absurdity"[159]: Our genes are selfish, but we are moral. Without moral condemnation and conscience, humans could never have come to dominate the planet.

Indeed, without morality, the very groups that feature so centrally in realism could not have come to exist in the first place. In other words, no binding foundations, no nation-states. They are a necessary, although insufficient, condition. In an effort to explain group solidarity absent ethics, Thayer makes reference to "inclusive fitness," the idea that when we sacrifice for close kin we are caring for the preservation of our own genetic material.[160] However, once groups approach even a few hundred, inclusive fitness arguments break down completely, as evolutionary game theorists note. Something else is necessary to preserve solidarity. As argued earlier, if severe enough, threats can provide that stimulus but some moral sense of loyalty is also necessary to prevent free-riding on the defense efforts of others. Yet neither Thayer nor Gat[161] – another prominent advocate of applying evolutionary theory to international relations – makes any mention of ethics in human societies, despite the fact that Thayer relies extensively on Richard Alexander, one of the first to make the case for the importance of ethics to evolution. Lopez et al. only imply the importance of morality in noting that assumptions of pure egoism cannot explain humans' "coalitional psychology."[162] The binding foundations seem to be a central part of that story.

A biological approach that takes morality seriously expects neither 100% egoism nor 100% altruism in order to classify behavior as moral. It paints a more realistic picture – not of a world of all against all, which does not capture the human experience at all, but rather a mix of egoism and other-regarding behavior of different types (loyalty, fairness, and retribution), all under the shadow of others' expectations that we will restrain our self-interest and judge us if we do not. This is true even in the "power politics" that have long preoccupied IR scholars. This book tries to really understand and reclaim human nature, not treat it as equivalent to pessimism about human cooperation.

---

[159] Wright, *The Moral Animal*, 338.   [160] Thayer, "Bringing in Darwin," 122.
[161] Gat, "So Why Do People Fight?"
[162] Lopez et al., "States in Mind, Coalitional Psychology, and International Politics."

4 | *See No Evil, Speak No Evil?*
Cross-National Micro- and
Macrofoundational Evidence
of Morality's Ubiquity

When others harm us or others, we react with condemnation, passing moral judgments and sometimes retaliating; we *speak evil*. Moral condemnation encouraged the development of moral conscience to avoid the outrage and often violent group punishment by those who were wronged. This attribute in turn acted as a credible signal of cooperativeness that unwittingly and unconsciously paid material dividends and promoted, rather than detracted from, fitness. The presence of conscience allows individuals to use morality as a marker – indeed, the most important factor – by which to judge whether another individual is threatening. To protect themselves, individuals *see evil*, forming judgments by assessing others' morality. I call this phenomenon "moral screening." As reviewed in the last chapter, evolutionary theorists think this all to be a part of our very nature.

Yet, this is not at all how so many understand the nature of international relations. While we might not be surprised to see that states do not place the same restraint on the pursuit of their self-interest as ordinary individuals do, it is striking that states and their leaders are thought to respond phlegmatically when others lack such inhibitions, without any sense of outrage. International relations is "just business"; it isn't personal. There is nothing to be upset about. War resembles an athletic competition in which beating the other is part of, indeed the very point, of the game. Just as we cannot presume that others will not try to score, there is nothing to judge if another state desires a piece of your territory. There is simply a divergence of interests.

What does this phrase, "just business," even mean? It is associated with excuses offered by dastardly mafiosos as a way of avoiding moral condemnation from others. It presumes that within the transactional world of business, there is a different set of moral standards. The instrumentalization of others and pure self-interest are appropriate, even commendatory. The hostile takeover of one business by another is perfectly acceptable, whereas the hostile takeover of our neighbor's yard is not. Taking an offer to work for a competing firm is legitimate, not a betrayal of one's team. In the world of organized crime, this moral absolution even extends to the use of violence. As individuals, international relations scholars might find this shocking, yet they extend the same logic to their object of study.

I find all of this highly dubious. While plenty of international relations scholars whose work has inspired me have pointed out cases of outrage, justice-seeking, and retribution, we do not yet have a sense of how ubiquitous moralistic violence and its precursor, moral condemnation, are. Considering the evolutionary origins of morality and the centrality accorded to moral judgments about the unacceptable behavior and traits of excessively egoistic others, we should find an international environment saturated with moralizing.

Yet, how do we show that something is everywhere, central or ubiquitous? In this chapter, I throw the kitchen sink at the problem, utilizing word-embeddings analyses of massive textual corpora of three different kinds – public speeches at the United Nations, private foreign policy documents of American decision-makers, and quotidian text scraped from among other sources the universe of Wikipedia pages – and surveys of the Russian, Chinese, and American publics. The former establishes the macro-foundational evidence for the claims, and the latter allows us to observe the microfoundations at work. If ethics are part of our evolutionary past, they should be present in the attitudes and behavior of ordinary Josefs as well as the elites who lead them. And we must remember that even if the latter are fundamentally different ethically, they operate in a context moralized by the presence of domestic and international audiences that will constrain them to some extent. Knowing what the masses think about morality is a necessary component of understanding even high politics. I also believe that the distinction between the psychology of masses and elites is overstated, something being demonstrated by actual tests of this well-worn but unproven conventional wisdom.[1] The similarities are borne out in the text analysis presented in the following text. Of course, this is consistent with an evolutionary account, which stresses the commonalities across individuals given our common biological origins. All of the analyses in this chapter were conducted in collaboration with Caleb Pomeroy, my partner in justice

---

[1] Kertzer, Joshua D. 2020. "Re-Assessing Elite-Public Gaps in Political Behavior." *American Journal of Political Science* 66(3): 539–553.

Textual Corpora and the International Body Politic

My argument implies that when humans, even the leaders of nation-states, talk about security, they cannot help but talk about moral-ity, since the evolution of ethics, humankind and physical security are intertwined. Some of this is undoubtedly intentional; we castigate to create support for our cause, draw attention to our plight and recruit allies. However, I suspect that much of this is also simply natural, unconscious, and intuitive given the inextricability of morality from the material needs of social life in human evolution. In any case, we should be able to detect the moralized nature of international security through the analysis of text.

We first analyze a corpus of 8,640 speeches by heads of state dur-ing the annual United Nations General Debate (UNGD) from 1965 to 2018.[2] Second, we examine almost 16,000 private documents con-tained in the Foreign Relations of the United States (FRUS) collection – internal diplomatic cables, and communications curated by the State Department's historian's office for importance and frequently used in qualitative research.[3] Our FRUS corpus includes all documents in the FRUS over the period of 1964–1966[4] as well as all documents avail-able in Katagiri and Min,[5] which includes volumes "centered on the Soviet Union and the Eastern Bloc" from 1952 to 1977.[6] While not the universal set of documents, which has not yet been compiled, our cor-pus contains one portion that is truly comprehensive, albeit for a lim-ited period of time and another which is less global but includes texts over several decades. We combine the corpora for the analysis pre-sented here.[7] Because my argument maintains that morality is a basic

---

[2] Baturo, Alexander, Niheer Dasandi, and Slava J. Mikhaylov. 2017. "Understanding State Preferences with Text as Data: Introducing the UN General Debate Corpus." *Research & Politics* 4(2).

[3] For information about the FRUS, see history.state.gov/historicaldocuments/about-frus.

[4] Lauretig, Adam M. 2019. "Identification, Interpretability, and Bayesian Word Embeddings." In *Proceedings of the Third Workshop on NLP and Computational Social Science*. Minneapolis: Association for Computational Linguistics.

[5] Katagiri, Azusa and Eric Min. 2015. *Identifying Threats: Using Machine Learning in International Relations* (Unpublished Manuscript). We thank the authors for access to their data.

[6] We thank Azusa Katagiri and Eric Min for making the latter data available to us.

[7] Online Appendix 1.2.1 shows that the results are robust to analyzing the two collections separately.

feature of international political life, I expect to see the moralization of harm and threat in both public speeches and private communications. The UN corpus has the advantage of being truly global, including speeches from leaders across the world; the FRUS serves as a more difficult test for my argument since it is private. A fuller description of the corpora and pre-processing is offered in Online Appendix 1.1.

We locally train word embeddings on these two corpora using the global vectors for word representation (GloVe) model.[8] Word embeddings operationalize the intuition that we can know a word by the company it keeps. As Kozlowski et al. explain, "[I]n word embedding models, words are assigned a position in a vector space based on the context that word shares with other words in the corpus. Words that share many contexts are positioned near one another, while words that inhabit very different contexts locate farther apart."[9] Word embeddings depart from count-based "bag-of-word" representations of textual data traditionally used in political science, which rely on frequencies of word occurrence, often to compare documents. Instead, word embeddings – or vector space representations of text – preserve far richer semantic context, providing unique leverage on the question of even implicit associations. Words do not need to co-occur for their vectors to be positioned close to one another so long as they co-occur with the same words. Distance between words in this high-dimensional space is assessed using the cosine of the angle between word vectors.

Using word embeddings, we can construct dimensions composed of antonyms (such as male–female) and then estimate the placement of moral terms on "harm" and "threat" dimensions. We take the average vector space locations of harm-related and threat-related words and subtract off the average locations of harm and threat antonyms, respectively. Caliskan et al. show that this technique can yield similar results to implicit association tests that capture unconscious prejudice.[10]

[8] Pennington, Jeffrey, Richard Socher, and Christopher D. Manning. 2014. "Glove: Global Vectors for Word Representation." In *Proceedings of the 2014 Conference on Empirical Methods in Natural Language Processing (EMNLP)*, 1532–1543.

[9] Kozlowski, Austin C., Matt Taddy, and James A. Evans. 2019. "The Geometry of Culture: Analyzing the Meanings of Class Through Word Embeddings." *American Sociological Review* 84(5): 905–949.

[10] Caliskan, Aylin, Joanna J. Bryson, and Arvind Narayanan. 2017. "Semantics Derived Automatically from Language Corpora Contain Human-like Biases." *Science* 356(6334): 183–186.

Comparisons of the vector space locations of harm, threat, and morality terms allow us to assess whether harm and morality, as well as threat and morality, really do go hand in hand in speech. As Schein and Gray write, "[H]arm and morality are naturally fused together in the human mind because harm is the biggest threat to genetic survival. Given its evolutionary importance, it follows that harm should be the most developmentally basic and universal psychological cause of moral judgments."[11] With the word embeddings in hand, we average the differences between antonym pairs of harm-related words, as well as threat-related words, to construct "harm" and "threat" dimensions, respectively. Our dictionary of harm words includes "harm," damage," "violent," "suffer," "kill," and "attack." To estimate the harm dimension, we contrast these words with "help," "benefit," "aid," "protect," "safe," and "safeguard." Our dictionary of threat words includes "threat," "danger," "advers," "aggress," "invas," "assault," "injur," "damag," and "enemi." To estimate the threat dimension, we contrast "threat," "enemi," "advers," and "danger" with "secur," "alli," and "safe." Our moral dictionary derives from the twenty-six traits found by survey respondents to be most useful in determining the morality of others, which notably are caring terms and others identified as central for cooperation, both within and between groups, such as honesty and fairness.[12] We excluded "violent" due to endogeneity issues (although its presence on this list indicates the very point we are trying to make) as well as un/prejudiced, since this is a more modern, liberal value and our aim is more universal. We supplement this list with attributes from Lapsley and Lasky's investigation of "prototypic moral character" and Walker and Hennig's study of "moral exemplarity."[13]

Since the vector space is multidimensional, to present the data visually, we project each word onto the underlying dimension (either harm or threat), essentially by drawing a line from the word in the vector space to the nearest point on the underlying dimensions. If harm and threat are unrelated to morality, induced dimensions will be orthogonal to our moral words and ethical terms will project at zero on the continuum.

---

[11] Schein and Gray, "The Theory of Dyadic Morality," 36.
[12] Goodwin et al., "Moral Character Predominate," 148.
[13] Lapsley, Daniel K. and Benjamin Lasky. 2001. "Prototypic Moral Character." *Identity: An International Journal of Theory and Research* 1(4): 345–363; Walker, Lawrence J. and Karl H. Hennig. 2004. "Differing Conceptions of Moral Exemplarity: Just, Brave, and Caring." *Journal of Personality and Social Psychology* 86(4): 629.

Harm and threat will be morally neutral, as we would expect if ethical considerations were removed from this sphere of human interaction.

We apply this same procedure to GloVe word vectors that were pre-trained on a corpus of Wikipedia and Gigaword 5 data, with a total of 6 billion tokens (essentially, words) and a 400,000-word vocabulary. Because these data represent encyclopedic entries and newswire text data, these data represent quotidian, non-political speech. Whereas stemming the terms in the UN corpus improves the quality of the embeddings, the size of the underlying GloVe corpus permits more precise identification of the full-length terms. If we see similar patterns to the UN and FRUS data, it is evidence that the political sphere is not autonomous but rather simply another realm of human activity, one in which morality functions similarly.

Figure 4.1A presents the harm results for all three corpora. We find that each moral word occupies a position that is non-orthogonal to the harm dimension, which suggests that "harm speech" contains moral content. Further, positively and negatively valenced moral words tend to cluster on opposite sides of the dimension, as expected. We note that only a subset of our moral dictionary appears in the UN and FRUS embeddings because these corpora are much smaller than the corpus underlying the pre-trained GloVe vectors. Figure 4.1B presents the threat results. Again, we find that each moral word occupies a position that is non-orthogonal to the threat dimension, with positively and negatively valenced morals clustering on opposite sides, which suggests that "threat speech" contains moral content. Overall, 87.8% and 81.3% of the moral terms fall on the expected sides of the harm and threat dimensions, respectively. These classification rates are surprisingly strong given the simplicity of the approach (namely, cosine similarities between word vectors) and are comparable to the rates found in Kozlowski et al.'s gender, race, and class analyses. In a separate analysis not presented here, we find that democracies and non-democracies do not differ in the frequency of moral language when discussing threats, and autocracies are slightly more likely to use negative moral terms when discussing harm. This is not a product of Western, liberal moralizing that we might expect in the human rights era.

In Online Appendix 1.2, we report non-parametric confidence intervals for the political corporate and a permutation test for the quotidian corpus to show that significant proportions of the words fall reliably far from zero. We do not misclassify any of these more robust terms

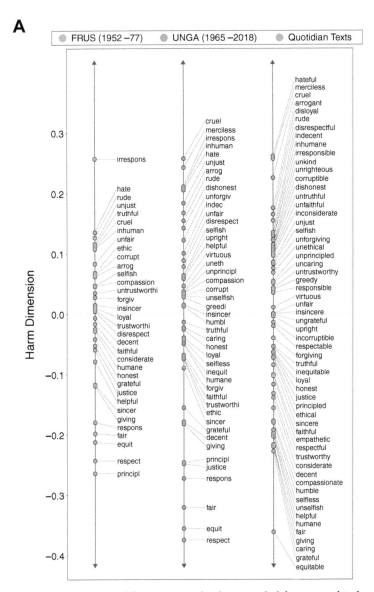

Figure 4.1 *Threat and harm cannot be disentangled from moral judgment.* In (A), moral terms projected onto a "harm" dimension in vector space suggest that negative moral terms are semantically nearer to pronouncements of harm, whereas positive moral terms are more distant from harm terms, in both political and quotidian texts. In (B), the same procedure and similar results, but with moral terms projected onto a "threat" dimension.

B

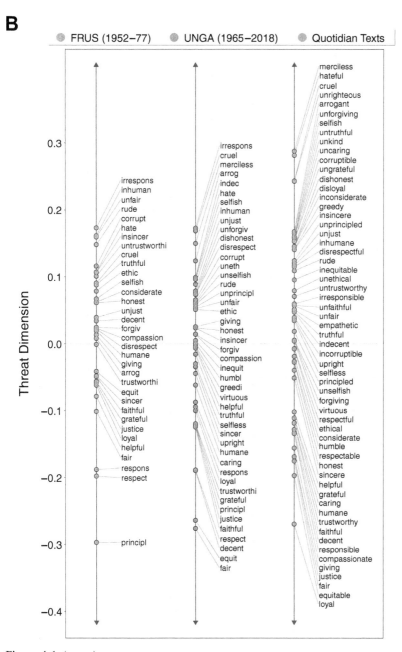

Figure 4.1 (cont.)

in the quotidian corpus and only three terms in the political corpus. In sum, harm and threat seem to be inherently moralized concepts regardless of the context. Whether it is masses or elites, or in public or private, makes little difference. In this way, the FRUS results are particularly striking in that these documents are records of private conversations among practitioners away from the preying and judging eyes of the public. There simply is no amoral sphere of international politics in public or in private, even for elite decision-makers.

Build-a-Threat: Morality as the Central Characteristic for Judging Threat

One concrete implication of my argument is that state leaders and the public will use moral judgments as a basis, indeed the most important factor, for assessing international threats, just as research shows they do at the interpersonal level. This latter finding emerged out of stereotype research, most importantly Fiske's warmth/competence model, which identified two primary, and generally orthogonal, dimensions by which humans categorize others.[14] Subsequent research indicates that the warmth dimension has a number of different subcomponents, of which morality is the most important in determining how we evaluate others.[15]

Humans are on the lookout for those who do good and punish bad relatively indiscriminately, as a general rule of right and wrong.[16] Those who only help their friends or when they have something directly to gain are of much less use. In other words, we use the fact of moral conscience to help us judge those around us. For instance, two-thirds of respondents in one study regarded the moral character as the most important thing to know about a person.[17] When selecting information about an unknown ingroup or outgroup member, individuals seek out data more relevant to trustworthiness and honesty than sociability and friendliness.[18] As Goodwin et al. write, the "goodness of another person's character

---

[14] Fiske et al., "Universal Dimensions of Social Cognition."
[15] Wojciszke et al., "On the Dominance of Moral Categories."
[16] Alexander, *The Biology of Moral Systems*, 177.
[17] Goodwin et al., "Moral Character Predominates."
[18] Brambilla, Marco, Patrice Rusconi, Simona Sacchi, and Paolo Cherubini. 2011. "Looking for Honesty: The Primary Role of Morality (vs. Sociability and Competence) in Information Gathering." *European Journal of Social Psychology* 41(2): 135–143.

determines whether they are likely to be harmful or helpful to the self....
A person of good moral character is likely at the very least to not be
harmful, and in some circumstances, to be actively helpful."[19]

These findings about the centrality of morality in the impression formation literature are grounded in a functional, evolutionary explanation. Fiske et al. write, "Like all perception, social perception reflects
evolutionary pressures. In encounters ... social animals must determine, immediately, whether the 'other' is friend or foe (i.e. intends
good or ill) and, then, whether the 'other' has the ability to enact those
intentions.... Dark alleys and battle zones approximate the survival
settings of ancestral encounters with strangers."[20] Whether someone
is honest and fair is more important to our safety and prosperity than
if they are funny or polite. Brambilla et al. explain, "These findings
might be interpreted from a functionalist perspective. Indeed, knowing another's intentions for good or ill ... turns out to be essential
for survival even more than knowing whether a person can act on
those intentions."[21] Fifty years ago, Trivers had already hypothesized:
"Selection should favor learning about the altruistic and cheating tendencies of others indirectly, both through observing interactions of
others and, once linguistic abilities have evolved, by hearing about
such interactions or hearing characterizations of individuals (e.g.,
'dirty, hypocritical, dishonest, untrustworthy, cheating louse')."[22]

In other words, morality and threat perception are intertwined. Yet,
despite the centrality of morality for how humans make judgments
about others, the literature on threat perception makes virtually no
mention of morality. In IR terms, morality helps us assess "aggressive
intentions," which, in addition to capability, are the key elements of
threat.[23] Although "balance of threat" theory makes no mention of
morality, ordinary humans think otherwise. In a review of the valence
of 170 traits, respondents in one study ranked "violent" as the eighth
most important of 150 traits in judging whether someone was moral
or not, following only honest, trustworthy, dishonest, respectful, just,
forgiving, and principled.[24]

[19] Goodwin et al., "Moral Character Predominates."
[20] Fiske et al., "Universal Dimensions of Social Cognition," 77.
[21] Brambilla et al., "Looking for Honesty," 136.
[22] Trivers, "The Evolution of Reciprocal Altruism."
[23] Walt, Stephen M. 1987. *The Origins of Alliances.* Ithaca: Cornell University Press.
[24] Goodwin et al., "Moral Character Predominates."

Research indicates that morality becomes more important to us the more that others can affect or control us. We care more about whether our surgeon, long-term romantic partner, or close friend is ethical than a cashier at a store or a social acquaintance.[25] Since nothing is more central to us than physical harm, this research is extremely relevant to international relations.

I hypothesize that moral traits will be the most important ones that individuals use to judge threats, both from other individuals and from collectivities such as nation-states. In early March 2020, I surveyed 1,245 Russian respondents recruited through the survey firm Anketolog to create a sample extremely similar to the general population in terms of age, gender, and region of residence. The study was fielded before the COVID-19 pandemic became widespread in Russia. For such a central test of the evolutionary argument, I did not want to conduct the survey in the United States since Americans, and particularly the American public, are sometimes accused of moralizing conflicts in a way that is not true of other countries that have a more Realpolitik understanding of IR.[26] Russia, known for a much more power-political foreign policy approach, serves as a hard test for my argument. My instrument was translated by a native speaker,[27] piloted on a small sample for difficulties in comprehension, and also evaluated by another, non-native, Russian speaker. Online Appendix 1.3 includes sample demographics (compared to the national population) and instrumentation in both languages.[28]

In a variant of the previous research situated at the interpersonal level, I asked subjects to identify attributes that subjects deem most important in judging whether others might harm us (as opposed to

---

[25] Ibid.   [26] Krebs and Lobasz, "Fixing the Meaning of 9/11."

[27] Thank you, Evgeniia Iakhnis!

[28] All participants in our Russia survey were asked to consent to participate in research. The study received relevant Institutional Review Board approval or exemption. In the text that follows, we provide the English version of the statement, which was translated into Russian for our Russian respondents, who were recruited by the survey firm Anketolog. Our respondents were compensated directly by Anketolog at market rates. All respondents had to consent in order to move forward with the survey. No identifying information was collected other than basic demographic data. Anketolog merely recruited subjects, who were directed to our Qualtrics platform. The firm has no access to the data. The Russian survey instrument contained no politically sensitive questions such as party identification or support for political leaders, only questions on hypothetical foreign policy scenarios.

merely an overall impression or evaluation, the basis of previous studies). Individuals were randomized into two conditions. In the interpersonal condition, they were asked to think about harm from other individuals; in the international condition, they were asked to think about harm from other countries. I provided respondents with a list of the most important attributes identified in previous stereotype work,[29] including sociability, competence, and morality-related attributes, as well as attributes that IR scholars traditionally use as predictors of threat, such as power.[30]

The English translation for the prompt is as follows:

In [our lives/foreign policy], [we/our leaders] must form impressions of [others/other countries] and whether they might harm us or not. We never know for sure, but if you were asked to form a judgment about [someone/another country] and were offered reliable information about the following traits, which would you find to be most relevant and most important? In other words, which would you want to know?

The full list of attributes is as follows: Fair and just; Generous and compassionate; Honest and trustworthy; Powerful and strong; Friendly and considerate; Culturally similar, such as sharing a language, religion, or home town; Resolute and determined; Organized and competent; and Intelligent.

Respondents were instructed to drag at least two attributes to a box to the right and to rank those selected attributes according to importance. Attributes were listed randomly to avoid order effects. This relatively inductive appoach provided subjects with the chance to "build their own threat" as it were, rather thran simply asking subjects to identify whether a particular attribute is threatening or not. Importantly, it allows us, based on the country versus person randomization, to compare whether subjects' conceptions of threats differ at the individual versus country level, a type of group that has not been included in previous stereotype research. My argument expects that morality will be the most important factor for both the judgments of individuals and other countries because moral screening is an evolved mechanism individuals use to make threat assessments. Moreover, we do not expect large differences in the ordering of attributes across conditions, since humans tend to make similar moral attributions across the individual and group levels.

---

[29] Fiske et al., "Universal Dimensions of Social Cognition."
[30] Walt, *The Origins of Alliances.*

Figure 4.2A reports the rank importance for individual and country threat traits, with D statistics and significance levels for each person-country distribution comparison printed in the top-right corner according to a Kolmogorov–Smirnov (K–S) test. The figure presents traits in descending order of overall mean importance, with honesty/trustworthiness ranked first. The results are striking. First, the overall distributions are broadly similar, with very few statistically significant differences across treatments. Second, the moral attributes of honesty/trustworthiness and fair/just are by far the most important characteristics that individuals use to judge threats from both other individuals and other countries. This indicates that humans use morality to screen for threats at both the interpersonal and the international levels and in similar ways. Third, determinants of threat perception traditionally considered central to IR theory, such as power, resolve, and cultural similarity, lag significantly behind. Power and resolve are competence traits and, as the psychological research suggests, are secondary in making judgments about others, even in the ostensibly different autonomous sphere of international politics where might is supposed to make right. Only two distributions significantly differ; intuitively, subjects place more emphasis on intelligence when evaluating individuals and more emphasis on organization/competence when evaluating states.[31]

Finally, I asked my respondents to, in essence, construct a composite image of a threat. Figure 4.2B presents the trait co-occurrence network for individual traits, with darker ties representing more frequent co-occurrences. Honesty and fairness tend to cluster, and subjects tend to place emphasis on a third trait: either intelligence or friendliness, but not necessarily both. In Figure 4.2C, the trait co-occurrence network for country traits shows that honesty, fairness, and friendliness tend to cluster, which in turn link to competence traits, like intelligence and organizational competence. Overall, the networks look very similar. These results provide evidence that humans tend to weigh moral attributes most heavily when assessing whether a generic "other" could potentially pose harm to the self, whether that "other" is an individual or a country.

---

[31] The exact rankings for individuals are, in descending order: honesty, intelligence, fairness, friendliness, resolve, competence, power, cultural similarity, and generosity. The exact rankings for countries are: honesty, fairness, friendliness, intelligence, competence, power, resolve, cultural similarity, and generosity.

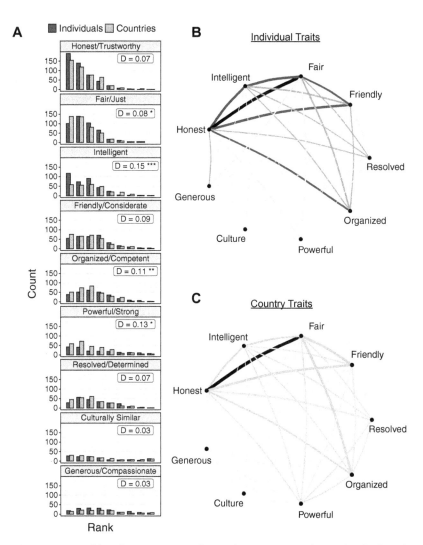

Figure 4.2 *Build-a-threat.* In (A), the rank importance for individual and country threat traits, plotted in descending order of overall mean importance with individual versus country distribution differences assessed using a Kolmogorov–Smirnov test. $^{\wedge}p < .10$, $^{*}p < .05$, $^{**}p < .01$. In (B), the trait co-occurrence network for individual traits shows that honesty and fairness tend to cluster, followed by either intelligence or friendliness. In (C), the trait co-occurrence network for country traits shows that honesty, fairness, and friendliness tend to cluster, which in turn links to intelligence and organizational competence.

My Russia survey has the advantage of having respondents choose from a carefully selected set of potentially threat-relevant traits but arguably suffers from external validity problems. In order to judge respondents' use of different traits at the interpersonal and international levels, I posed the problem generally, without specific country names. Do we find observational evidence of those same tendencies in a population of significance to IR researchers on real-world issues mentioning particular threats? Here, I present convergent evidence from two different surveys of the Chinese public: the Beijing Area Study (BAS) survey and the US-Chinese Security Perceptions Project of the Carnegie Foundation (USCSPP). The BAS is a random sample survey of opinion in the Beijing municipality administered by the Research Center for Contemporary China at Peking University ($N = 1,410$). The USCSPP survey was conducted May 2–July 5, 2012, among 2,597 adults in urban areas and used the same sampling technique as the BAS. Appendices 1.4 and 1.5 describe the data sources in detail and present the instrumentation's original text as well as the translation.

The 2007 version of the BAS asked respondents to characterize the United States, Japan, and China itself along continua that present a forced choice between contrasting end points central to my theoretical arguments: peace-loving or warlike, moral or immoral, modest or arrogant, sincere or insincere, and civilized or barbaric.[32] If the text analysis results generalize to humans' views of IR, and if the results from the Russia screening experiment extend to named countries, then perceptions of immorality should correlate with perceptions of threat. Figure 4.3A presents correlations between perceptions that a country is "warlike" and negative moral attributions. Each correlation is significant ($p < .001$) and substantively large (ranging between $\rho = .53$ and $\rho = .78$), including for the perception of China by the Chinese themselves.

The USCSPP project asked members of the Chinese mass public whether they associate a number of traits with Americans – being greedy, selfish, deceitful, honest, generous, and tolerant – each response gathered on a "yes/no" dichotomous scale. Furthermore, the survey collected respondents' perceptions of the importance of a host of security issues, gathered on four-point scales that range from "very

---

[32] Johnston, Alastair Iain. 2017. "Is Chinese Nationalism Rising? Evidence from Beijing." *International Security* 41(3): 7–43.

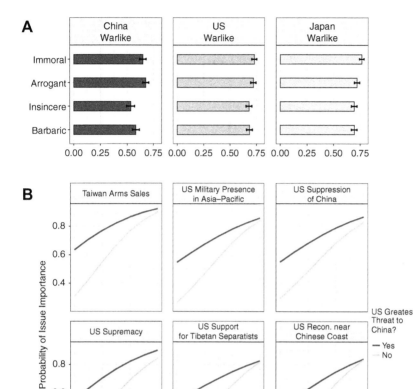

Figure 4.3 *The Chinese judge like everyone else.* In (A), negative moral attributions correlate positively with the perception that a given country is "warlike." In (B), fitted probabilities from logistic regressions show that perceptions of American immorality and perceptions of American threat correlate with a higher likelihood that subjects attach importance to a host of US–China security issues. The slight negative immorality by threat interaction suggests that subjects concerned with threats other than the United States, but that view Americans as immoral, more quickly attach importance to US–China security issues.

important" to "not at all important." Here, we use responses to these attribute questions to construct an immorality scale by summing the number of negative ethical traits subjects associate with Americans, as well as the reverse-coded positive traits. We also control for whether the United States is China's largest security threat to establish whether, even if a respondent does not believe the United States poses the greatest danger to China, immorality can provide an independent pathway to explain variance in security issue importance.

Figure 4.3B displays the results of logistic regressions that estimate the relationship between the importance respondents attach to a host of security issues (the DVs, with responses of "very serious problem" and "somewhat serious problem" coded as 1, and "not a serious problem" or "not a problem at all" coded as 0) and perceptions of US threat, immorality, and a threat–immorality interaction.[33] Across issues, we naturally find that respondents who believe the United States presents the greatest danger to China also attach greater importance to security issues that involve the United States. In addition, however, subjects who believe the United States is not China's greatest security threat – but do believe the United States is immoral – eventually settle at security positions nearly identical to those respondents who do believe that the United States represents China's greatest threat. In fact, the slight negative interactive relationship suggests that those respondents concerned with threats other than the United States are precisely the population most affected by the moderating effects of perceived American immorality; those subjects are quicker to attach importance to US security issues by virtue of perceived American immorality.[34]

Trigger Feelings: Intuitive Condemnation

If moral condemnation is based on evolution, it should be intuitive, automatic, and therefore easy to invoke. Another likely evolved and therefore intuitive and ubiquitous tendency thought to have implications for international relations, ingroup favoritism, has been studied with a "minimal group paradigm," in which participants are given very sparse and trivial information about group membership, which proves sufficient

---

[33] Online Appendix 1.5.3 presents a table with full regression results, including controls.

[34] Because we also show that moral attributions undergird threat perception, we recognize the potential for post-treatment bias in these models. Thus, Online Appendix 1.5.4 presents a mediation analysis, which demonstrates that moral attributions provide an extremely large independent explanatory source of security issue importance. Those analyses also demonstrate that the results are robust to representing the DVs on a continuous, rather than dichotomized, scale.

to develop ingroup favoritism.[35] Because such favoritism is so easy to invoke, it is presumed to be universal and relevant for international relations even though the findings are at the micro-level and in the mass public. I use a similar type of logic in the two experiments presented here, hypothesizing that individuals do not need substantial amounts of information about others to draw negative moral judgments and that such condemnation is difficult to shake, even with exculpatory evidence.

In this way, moral condemnation is different from "image theory," which has long maintained that the "pictures people have of other countries become central building blocks in their identification of the threats and opportunities their country faces. These images of others can become assumptions that are so taken for granted that they produce routinized habits that define basic parameters of what is seen as in a country's interest or contrary to it."[36] While images are frequently negative and moralistic – degenerate or evil, for instance[37] – and are heuristics used to simplify decision-making, they are typically pictures formed of particular countries based on historical interactions. I am sure these are important but imagine that it is considerably easier to generate negative moral attributions.

Where There Is a Centrifuge, There Is Fire: Threat and Moral Judgment

While revenge and self-defense are clear-cut cases of virtuous violence against those who have already harmed us, I suspect that even the possibility of violence – that is, the perception of threat – is likely to generate moral condemnation and negative moral attributions. In a survey experiment, I presented respondents with a hypothetical country developing nuclear weapons to examine whether the factors that typically generate perceptions of threat also lead to negative moral attributions, whereas a more instrumental account would not. In the latter, threats are threats; it is not personal. Someone else simply has

---

[35] Turner et al., "Social Comparison and Group Interest in Group Favouritism."

[36] Herrmann, Richard K. 2013. "Perceptions and Image Theory in International Relations." In: Leonie Huddy, David O. Sears, and Jack S. Levy (eds.). *The Oxford Handbook of Political Psychology*, 2nd ed. Oxford University Press, 5.

[37] Herrmann, Richard K. and Michael P. Fischerkeller. 1995. "Beyond the Enemy Image and Spiral Model: Cognitive–Strategic Research after the Cold War." *International Organization* 49(3): 415–450.

designs on you. This is an adaptation of Tomz and Weeks's study demonstrating that those who violate basic moral principles, such as the violation of human rights, are regarded as more threatening and also more deserving of moralistic punishment.[38] I test whether the very presence of a potential threat induces moral condemnation. In our own daily lives, we fear others with guns not just because the weapon will harm us but because we think that having a gun is an indication of being a bad person. Where there is smoke, there is fire.

I fielded the experiment on 1,022 respondents recruited through Amazon Mechanical Turk in May 2018.[39] I asked respondents to "imagine a country with a major regional rival" that is "dramatically increasing the size of its military, including a nuclear weapons program." The survey manipulates three elements of the scenario, yielding a fully crossed 2 × 2 × 2 design. The first factor varies offensive and defensive abilities. Respondents are presented with a country for which "there is a fear that its nuclear weapons could be used offensively since its main adversary does not have nuclear weapons," or one in which "it is thought that its nuclear weapons cannot be used offensively since its main adversary also has nuclear weapons." Offensive capability is a primary element in Walt's balance-of-threat theory.[40] The second factor varies the country's "past actions," a key element in models of credibility and threat assessment.[41] Respondents are randomly told either that "this country has been engaged in conflicts with that rival in the past and has taken part of its rival's territory" or that "this country has never fought its rival in the past." The third factor varies the country's past relations with the United States, namely whether the country has historically had good *or* poor relations with the United States, in order to assess how interest conflicts factor into threat assessment. Online Appendix 1.6 presents the full instrument as well as the demographic characteristics of the sample.

After treatment, subjects were asked to assess the morality of the state in question at two levels: (1) the second image – an estimation of a country's human rights record and level of democracy and (2) the first image: judgments about the leaders of the country in question in

---

[38] Tomz, Michael R. and Jessica L. P. Weeks. 2020. "Human Rights and Public Support for War." *The Journal of Politics* 82(1): 182–194.
[39] Online Appendix 1.6.1 presents the sample characteristics.
[40] Walt, *The Origins of Alliances*.
[41] Press, D. G. 2005. *Calculating Credibility: How Leaders Assess Military Threats*. Ithaca: Cornell University Press.

terms of three central moral attributes (trustworthiness, aggressiveness, and greediness) and a non-moral attribute thought to be central for threat assessment (resolve). Each DV was based on a ten-point scale. This mix of first- and second-image DVs allows us to establish whether individuals make not only personal but also more essentialist attributions about the actors in question with the assumption that American respondents regard democracy and human rights as indicators of a society's moral essence. We then estimate how these moral attributions in turn affect judgments about the extent to which the state poses a threat, again on a ten-point scale.

Figure 4.4A displays OLS estimates of the effect of the treatments (the y-axis) on subjects' perceptions of our first- and second-image attributes (the x-axis). Standard predictors of threat – namely offensive capability, past conflict, and poor US relations – decrease perceptions that the hypothetical state is a democracy or respects human rights and also affect perceptions of leaders' moral attributes.[42] Participants believe that states with offensive capability, bad relations with the United States, and a history of past conflict are not only less likely to be a democracy or respect human rights, but also believe that their leaders must be untrustworthy, greedy, and aggressive. Mere offensive capability has the weakest effect of the treatments, affecting significantly only trustworthiness and human rights respect, although in the expected direction. Notably, past conflict and poor US relations have a more consistent effect on leader attributions of immorality than institutional attributions.

None of the treatments, however, affects the non-moral attribute: resolve. Judgments about leaders derived from my treatments are confined to moral attributes. This is a remarkable finding. Resolve features heavily in the international security literature, much more so than morality.[43] Yet my experimental treatments on power, past actions, and interest divergence have effects on ethical characterizations but not assessments of others' determination.

While these results suggest that standard predictors of threat significantly influence subjects' moral attributions, a natural question is the extent to which these moral attributions mediate between the treatments and threat perception. Figure 4.4B displays a non-parametric

---

[42] The full regression table is available in Online Appendix 1.6.3.
[43] Kertzer, Joshua. 2017. *Resolve in International Politics.* Princeton: Princeton University Press.

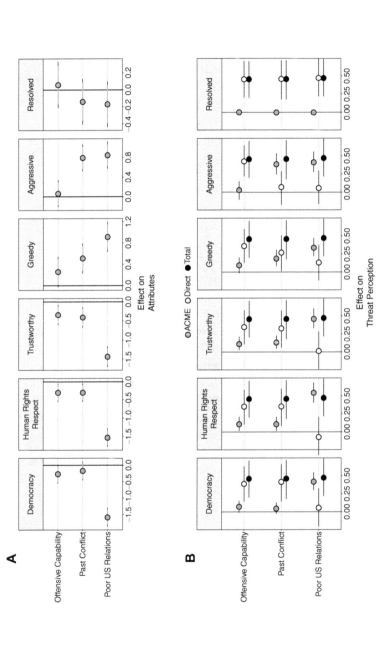

Figure 4.4 *Americans judge nuclear proliferators.* In (A), OLS estimates of the effect of our three treatments – offensive capability, past conflict, and nature of US relations – on perceptions of state and leader attributes. Note the x-axis scales vary. Ninety-five percent confidence intervals are plotted in red, and 90% confidence intervals are plotted in gray. In (B), mediation analysis of the effect of our treatments on threat perception, using the first- and second-image attributes as mediators. We use N = 1,500 simulations to produce 95% non-parametric bootstrapped confidence intervals. All models include controls for gender, race, age, political ideology, and party identification.

mediation analysis between the treatments (the y-axis) and threat perception (the x-axis), with each of the first- and second-image attributes serving as possible causal pathways between the two.[44] The "direct" effect represents the amount of the treatment effect that flows through all other pathways apart from these first- and second-image attributes. Each treatment significantly increases threat perception – the "total" effect – as expected, given that the treatments draw from standard predictors of threat. But, substantial variation exists in the mechanisms through which these treatments flow, the "average causal mediation effect" (ACME).

American respondents form threat perceptions about the state partially as a function of beliefs induced by the treatments that the other state is undemocratic or disrespects human rights, in line with recent research that suggests that human rights respect informs perceptions of threat.[45] But, importantly, so too does the effect of these standard predictors of threat flow through negative moral attributions about leaders. Most notably, subjects told that the hypothetical state has a history of poor relations with the United States do not seem to discount this information as a matter-of-fact divergence of interests. Rather, subjects use their moral attributions about that state – as untrustworthy, greedy, and aggressive – to make sense of and form beliefs about the other state as threatening. Indeed, these three moral attributes mediate between 71.5% and 97.7% of the "poor US relations" effect. Together, these results suggest that typical predictors of threat in IR theory lead to negative moral attributions, and these moral attributions in turn explain threat perception.[46] The leader trait of resolve, however, does not mediate between state action and threat perception at all.

---

[44] Imai, Kosuke, Luke Keele, Dustin Tingley, and Teppei Yamamoto. 2011. "Unpacking the Black Box of Causality: Learning about Causal Mechanisms from Experimental and Observational Studies." *American Political Science Review* 105(4): 765–789.

[45] Tomz and Weeks, "Human Rights and Public Support for War."

[46] We also conduct sensitivity analyses on these mediation effects to probe their robustness, particularly potential violations of the sequential ignorability assumption. To do so, we analyze the mediation effects against the correlation (ρ) between residuals of the mediator and outcome models, and report the ρ at which the ACME would be zero. We find that our mediation results are relatively robust (democracy: $\rho = -.29$; human rights respect: $\rho = -.34$; trustworthy: $\rho = -.33$; greedy: $\rho = .41$; aggressive: $\rho = .52$), with the obvious exception of resolve ($\rho = .01$), which did not significantly mediate.

Oil and Water: Resource Conflicts and Moral Condemnation

The results of my nuclear proliferation experiment suggest that subjects morally condemn states that are developing nuclear weapons, despite no harm having yet been done, and in turn use those moral judgments to form images of the other state as threatening. I, therefore, expect that survey respondents will automatically draw inferences about the moral qualities of leaders who use force. However, I am also interested in whether there are circumstances in which we might morally excuse predatory behavior. The most likely case would be in a situation of great scarcity in which we must literally choose between life and death and can escape moral condemnation even if we choose to prioritize our own welfare. Hardin famously calls this "lifeboat ethics." Hardin asks us to imagine a scenario:

So here we sit, say 50 people in our lifeboat. To be generous, let us assume it has room for 10 more, making a total capacity of 60. Suppose the 50 of us in the lifeboat see 100 others swimming in the water outside, begging for admission to our boat or for handouts. We have several options: we may be tempted to try to live by the Christian ideal of being "our brother's keeper," or by the Marxist ideal of "to each according to his needs." Since the needs of all in the water are the same, and since they can all be seen as 'our brothers,' we could take them all into our boat, making a total of 150 in a boat designed for 60. The boat swamps, everyone drowns. Complete justice, complete catastrophe.[47]

The implication of lifeboat ethics is that it is morally justifiable in situations of life-and-death to prioritize one's own interest. As mentioned previously, this is an example of a welfare trade-off ratio that would not provoke as much moral outrage. Greed and survival are not morally equal. However, the less this matters to our respondents in international relations, the more that we can conclude that moral condemnation is inescapable since this is the most excusable example for aggression we can think of.

It is hard to imagine a life-and-death like this in international relations. However, I approach this intuition by distinguishing between conflict over the pursuit of water, a necessary ingredient for life, and oil, only necessary for our material welfare. I constructed a resource conflict

---

[47] Hardin, Garrett. 1974. "Commentary: Living on a LIFEBOAT." *BioScience* 24(10): 561–568.

scenario, asking respondents to make inferences about the moral attributes of leaders in response to a set of hypothetical actions. I test this scenario, with slight variations, on both a Russian and an American sample.

US Sample and Results

My first resource conflict experiment was fielded on 1,022 respondents recruited through Amazon Mechanical Turk in May 2018.[48] All participants were given the following prompt: "Imagine a country that is having a dispute with its neighbor over who owns a particular piece of territory." Participants were subsequently randomly assigned to a cell in a 2 × 3 fully crossed factorial, which randomized the resource type (water or oil) and the outcome of the action (US casualties, other casualties, or demand for a 50–50 split).

The first randomized factor was the resource type, namely water or oil, corresponding to one of the two following prompts:

- This territory is considered of vital importance because it contains significant amounts of freshwater that the country desperately needs for its people.
- This territory is very economically valuable because it contains a significant amount of oil.

The text for the second randomized factor – outcome of the action – corresponded to one of the following prompts, with increasing severity of harm:

- Suppose that the country demands that its neighbor split the territory 50/50.
- Suppose that the country seizes 50% of the territory from its neighbor in a military operation that leads to the death of civilians.
- Suppose that the country seizes 50% of the territory from its neighbor in a military operation that leads to the death of American citizens who were in the region.

After treatment, subjects responded to the same set of questions used in the nuclear proliferation experiment mentioned previously, again gathered on ten-point scales: perceptions of democracy, human rights

---

[48] Online Appendix 1.6.1 presents the sample characteristics and Online Appendix 1.6.2 the instrumentation.

respect, trustworthiness, greed, aggressiveness, and resolve, as well as overall threat perception.

I manipulate the type of casualties in order to establish whether respondents are more likely to morally condemn those who do violence to their own citizens or the citizens of other countries, comparing each to a scenario in which no forceful action is taken. I expect that military actions will evoke greater moral condemnation by my respondents than simple demands, even though in all three manipulations the state is seeking the same ends. The use of force tells us not only about the other states' interests but also about their ethical character. The less that respondents distinguish between foreign and civilian casualties, the more that the results indicate third-party moral outrage.

Figure 4.5A reports the moral condemnation results, estimated via linear regression, with results plotted for the oil condition (holding the water condition as the baseline), as well as the effects of the seizure conditions in comparison to the demand for a 50–50 split (that serves as the baseline condition).[49] As expected, subjects perceive countries that use violence to be less moral, both in terms of the country's characteristics and attributions about their leaders. States using force are judged to be less democratic and committed to human rights. Their leaders are less trustworthy, more greedy, and more aggressive. Further, the effects are substantively large, about 20% of the scale.

Notably, respondents do not seem to respond differently to American as opposed to foreign casualties in terms of their moral inferences. We find scant evidence of statistically or substantively significant differences between the perceptions of subjects assigned to the "other casualties" or "US casualties" conditions, both at the levels of the second image (democracy: $t = -1.91$, p = .06; human rights respect: $t = -.96$, p = .34) and the first image (trustworthy: $t = -.93$, p = .35; greedy: $t = -.04$, p = .97; aggressive: $t = .13$, p < .9; resolved: $t = -1.41$, p = .16). Bad guys are bad guys.

Casualty manipulations lead to substantially larger effects on perceptions of democracy and human rights commitment than oil/water manipulation. When it comes to leaders, there is a slight effect of the oil condition on trustworthiness and aggressiveness and a substantially larger effect on greediness, as we might expect. In general, however, Americans give little benefit of the doubt to countries trying to

---

[49] The full regression table is available in Online Appendix 1.7.1.

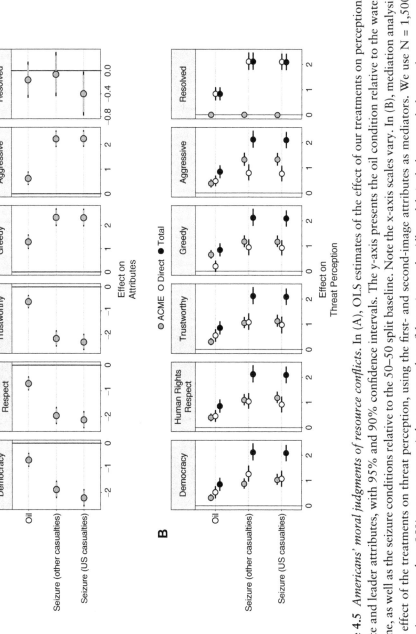

Figure 4.5 *Americans' moral judgments of resource conflicts.* In (A), OLS estimates of the effect of our treatments on perceptions of state and leader attributes, with 95% and 90% confidence intervals. The y-axis presents the oil condition relative to the water baseline, as well as the seizure conditions relative to the 50–50 split baseline. Note the x-axis scales vary. In (B), mediation analysis of the effect of the treatments on threat perception, using the first- and second-image attributes as mediators. We use N = 1,500 simulations to produce 95% non-parametric bootstrapped confidence intervals. All models include controls for gender, race, age, political ideology, and party identification.

provide for the basic essentials of life. That is, subjects do not forgive situational constraints, operationalized here by water instead of oil. The same is largely true of the second-image DVs.

Figure 4.4B displays the mediation analysis, the extent to which the effect of these treatments on threat perception flows through these attributes. The results suggest that these moral assessments are an important part of the causal process leading to threat evaluation; there are considerably larger coefficients for ACME than was the case in the previous experiment. Beliefs about the country's respect for human rights, leader greed, leader trustworthiness, and leader aggression all seem to be invoked by the violent action of the imaginary state, which in turn affect threat perception. The larger mediation effects likely reflect the difference between the actions taken by the fictional countries in question. The largest ACME coefficients appear in the casualty conditions.

Russia Sample and Results

In March 2020, I reran the resource conflict experiment on a Russian sample in order to address a number of potential concerns with the US experiment.[50] First, the US instrument could be accused of being double-barreled when it comes to the actions taken by the hypothetical state. The casualty treatment differ from the diplomatic treatment in two ways: the state both takes military action and kills others, preventing us from disentangling the morally condemnable use of force from the morally condemnable effects of that force. Therefore, in my Russian experiment, I changed the three actions our state could take to a (1) a diplomatic demand for 50% of the territory, (2) a military action seizing 50% of the territory without any casualties, and (3) a military action seizing 50% of the territory in which there were civilian casualties.

Second, I was concerned that some might be skeptical that the first-image DVs, such as aggressiveness and trustworthiness, have a moral valence. For instance, some in the rationalist tradition interpret trust in an entirely amoral manner, and the premise that aggressiveness is neither immoral nor moral in international relations is the

---

[50] The study was fielded just before the COVID-19 pandemic became widespread in Russia.

very claim that I am trying to test. I therefore removed aggressiveness and enhanced the understanding of trustworthiness as a moral concept. Here, the four first-image attributes include reliable and honest (Надёжность и честность), just and objective (Справедливость и объективность), greedy and selfish (Жадность и эгоистичность), and resolved (Решительность), again measured on ten-point scales. However, I leave out second-image attributions since human rights commitment and democracy do not necessarily have the same positive moral connotations in a semi-authoritarian state. Third, as mentioned previously, there are a number of reasons why an American sample might be an outlier.

The Russian sample was the same that completed the build-a-threat experiment (see Online Appendix 1.3.2 for a description of Russian sample #1). The experimental ordering was randomized to mitigate against order effects. I used the same resource conflict scenario described earlier, in which an unidentified state "is having a dispute with its neighbor over who owns a particular piece of territory." I again assigned participants to a cell in a 2 × 3 fully crossed factorial design, in which the first factor randomized resource type: oil that is simply economically valuable versus water desperately needed for the country's people. The second factor – the action taken by the hypothetical state – was adjusted as I described earlier. As in the US version of the experiment, I expect that respondents will draw inferences about the moral character of other countries based on the extent to which they took aggressive action and caused harm to the hypothetical country. The instrument and its translation are found in Online Appendix 1.8.1.

Figure 4.5A reports the moral condemnation results, estimated via linear regression, with results plotted for the oil versus water condition, as well as the effects of the seizure conditions above and beyond the 50–50 split baseline condition.[51] As expected, subjects perceive the leaders of countries that use violence to be less reliable/honest and just/objective, and more greedy/selfish. Further, many of the effects are substantively large, about 20% of the ten-point scale. The results are extremely similar to the American survey. Although the two samples are not directly comparable given the slight change in treatments, in general, Americans do not appear to be any more moralistic than Russians. Just like Americans, Russians also give little benefit of the

---

[51] The full regression table is available in Online Appendix 1.8.2.

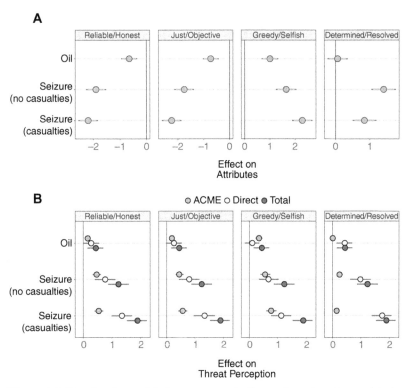

Figure 4.6 *Russians' moral judgments are similar to Americans' moral judgments.* In (A), OLS estimates of the effect of our treatments on perceptions of leader attributes, with 95% and 90% confidence intervals. The y-axis presents the oil condition relative to the water baseline, as well as the seizure conditions relative to the 50–50 split baseline. Note the x-axis scales vary. In (B), mediation analysis of the effect of the treatments on threat perception, using the first image attributes as mediators. We use $N = 1,500$ simulations to produce 95% nonparametric bootstrapped confidence intervals. All models include controls for gender, age, education, and income.

doubt to countries trying to provide for the basic essentials of life. That is, subjects do not forgive situational constraints, operationalized here by water instead of oil. Moral condemnation is easy to elicit and hard to avoid.

Beyond the comparisons to the 50–50 split baseline, subjects assigned to the seizure-with-casualties condition reported significantly different perceptions in comparison to subjects assigned to the seizure-without-casualties condition. The former believed that the leaders of the more violent state were less just ($t = -2.66$, p < .01), more greedy ($t = 3.17$, p < .01), and, surprisingly, less resolved ($t = -3.19$, p < .01). We find only a marginal difference for honesty, however ($t = -1.59$, p = .11). When people get hurt, moral condemnation increases. While this might strike us as intuitive, that is precisely the point. It is phlegmatic IR theory that lacks this intuition.

Figure 4.6B displays the mediation analysis, the extent to which the effect of these treatments on threat perception flows through these attributes. Moral attributions mediate less between fictional country behavior and threat perception than is the case with Americans. However, there is nevertheless substantial mediation, again in those treatments in which forceful action is taken.[52] The fact that such radically different populations with very different foreign policy histories and cultures react similarly to the same scenarios makes me more confident in my claim that moral condemnation is an intuitive process generalizable across populations.

Unlike in the American sample, forceful action by the imaginary state increases perceptions of resolve when compared to a mere diplomatic demand in the Russian sample. However, the attribution of resolve does not mediate at all between those treatments and overall threat perception, whereas moral judgments do. I would stress again that whereas resolve is a central element of international security studies, ethical attributions are largely absent suggesting that the study of threat must be moralized.

---

[52] Here, the ACMEs would be zero at the following values of ρ: reliable/honest: $\rho = -.26$; just/objective: $\rho = -.27$; greedy/selfish: $\rho = .39$; and determined/resolved: $\rho = .18$. These values suggest that the mediation effects are relatively robust, albeit slightly weaker than in the US version of the resource conflict experiment.

5 | To Provide and to Protect
A Dual-Process Model of Foreign
Policy Ideology for a Dangerous
or Competitive World

Recent advances in moral and social psychology have made clear that political ideology has ethical underpinnings, the same moral foundations thought to have evolutionary roots. While the emotional feeling of concern for others in need is so common in the species that it seems to be universal, this does not mean that it is felt to the same degree across individuals; indeed, some might lack this impulse entirely. The same is also true of the binding foundations. Not everyone feels the same allegiance to the larger group, however it might be defined. Also, these moral foundations are often in tension with one another. Our most bitter political conflicts tend to be those in which each side emphasizes a different moral principle. Foreign policy should be no exception. Indeed, the question of war always places humanitarianism and group identity in conflict, and individual-level commitments to different ethical values, likely conditioned by their cultural context, explain how those tradeoffs are resolved.

In this chapter, I will explain how morality marks not just the interactions among states but also the divides within them. I introduce a "dual-process model" of foreign policy, derived from Duckitt's synthesis of findings on ideology, moral values, and prejudice. He posits the existence of two fundamental dimensions of ideological conflict, one which corresponds to humanitarian morality and the ethical motivation to provide for others, and the other to binding morality and the ethical motivation to protect from threats. Primarily applied so far to domestic politics, his framework, which is consistent with the research in moral psychology reviewed in the previous chapters, illuminates foreign policy as well.

The centrality of ethics to human behavior is evident in the "structure" of foreign policy belief systems. Questions of foreign affairs are so complicated that it seems that every issue requires a unique response following careful consideration. However, we know that not even elites approach foreign policy issues on a case-by-case basis. They deduce their positions from underlying predispositions and postures that provide a general response to any number of challenges, often intuitively and unconsciously. When we describe some politician as a foreign policy "hawk," this means that more often than not he or she believes that coercion and force must be a part of achieving aims in the international arena.

The most widely used framework for explaining the structure of foreign policy beliefs reduces divides over foreign policy issues to two underlying dimensions: cooperative internationalism (CI) and militant internationalism (MI). I argue that these predispositions and postures likely arise from underlying moral foundations highlighted by the dual-process model. CI emerges from a motivational goal of providing for others and creating equality. MI is the expression of a motivational goal of protecting the group from harm, particularly physical threats. Given the grounding of dual-process models in ethics and in evolution and the centrality of underlying foreign policy dispositions in guiding decision-making and attitude formation, we see again how biology and morality are essential and unavoidable elements of international affairs.[1] And since these same moral foundations inform positions on domestic politics, we are again reminded that foreign policy is hardly a separate domain of human interaction.

Duckitt argues that broad ideological worldviews are associated with the motivational goals of providing and protecting. Dangerous world beliefs (DWB) depict the social world as one in which malicious actors threaten the virtuous. Competitive world beliefs (CWB) understand the social environment as a dog-eat-dog struggle for survival in which basic ethical principles know no place. DWB create a felt need for security and lead to hostility against those who undermine group safety and cohesion. CWB create a need for domination and winning and lead to prejudice against low-status groups. These

---

[1] Of course, I am not arguing that we are biologically predisposed to build intercontinental ballistic missiles or organize ourselves into nation-states as opposed to some other form of political organization. However, given the existence of armaments and nation-states, binders are more inclined to identify with co-nationals and use the available means to protect them. As we will see in Chapters 7 and 9, the basis on which we form communities to bind together is a larger cultural process.

worldviews contain second-order moral beliefs, judgments about the ethical character of others, including whether there is such a thing as ethics at all.

This chapter both builds out the dual-process model for foreign policy purposes, particularly the second-order moral beliefs that will feature centrally in subsequent chapters on German foreign policy, and tests my claims on public opinion data. Following a theoretical review, I present findings from two original surveys indicating that CI and MI are the foreign policy manifestations of fundamental motivational goals identified in dual-process models. Among Americans, CI is mostly predicted by individuals' commitment to the individualizing foundations, harm/care in particular – that is, the desire to provide. MI, in contrast, is predicted most strongly by the binding foundations of ingroup, authority, and purity – that is, the desire to protect. We find convergent evidence when examining the relationship of CI and MI with the values identified in the Schwartz value framework, the most prominent in social psychology. Among Americans, MI is highly predicted by the commitment to conservation values of conformity, tradition, and security, those values that hold communities together. CI is associated with the "self-transcendence" value of universalism in particular. Benevolence, although generally encompassed under self-transcendence, generates support for MI. However, since benevolence measures concern for others in one's immediate surroundings, this is consistent with a dual-process model, since narrower ingroup identification accompanies the motivational goal of stability and threat neutralization.

First-Order Moral Beliefs: Do I Provide or Protect?

There has been remarkable convergence in recent years on what Duckitt calls a "dual-process" model of social, political, and cultural attitudes, the basis of which are alternative moral foundations familiar to us from previous chapters – humanitarianism and binding morality.[2] Each different author offers slightly different taxonomies and underlying constructs – values, motivational goals, schemas, or ideology, for our purposes, these distinctions are not important. Duckitt identifies the unmistakable overlap in findings that allows us to extend

---

[2] Duckitt, "A Dual-Process Cognitive-Motivational Theory."

the dual-process model to international relations, thereby showing the way that morality structures foreign policy postures.

The first dimension captures a motivation to *provide* for others' welfare[3] – in essence, humanitarianism. It is associated with the "individualizing" moral foundations of harm/care and fairness/reciprocity and the Schwarz values of self-transcendence[4] defining virtue as taking care of others. Those driven by the goal of providing for others indicate greater egalitarianism and are committed to caring for the most vulnerable so as to level out those social, economic, and political inequities. Providing for others is most often associated with the left since the right consistently endorses a more hierarchical vision for society.[5] In politics, this is the morality underlying the welfare state as well as efforts to counter discrimination against marginalized groups. As a motivation, it is more universalist and tolerant than group-centric and exclusive. However, its true antithesis is moral indifference to others.

The second dimension captures a motivation to *protect* from dangers and threats.[6] Associated with a narrower ingroup identity, the motivational goal of protection is associated with moral foundations that bind groups together in order to meet challenges from inside and outside. If individuals subordinate their personal desires, authority figures can police threats both symbolic and material. The values of conformity and tradition, by reducing change over time and diversity across individuals, promote cohesion. This "existential" motivation[7] is critical to conservativism and political right. In policy, this finds expression in strong law and order to preserve social stability and in an insistence on strong moral norms that repress individualistic, libertine behavior.

Whether it be Janoff-Bulman's Model of Moral Values, Haidt and Graham's Moral Foundations Theory, or Schwartz's Universal Theory of Human Values, all ground dual-process models in the same requirements of group living – that is, in the conditions in which humankind evolved.[8] Janoff-Bulman explains: "We are

---

[3] Janoff-Bulman, "To Provide or Protect."
[4] Schwartz, "Universals in the Content and Structure of Values."
[5] Jost et al., "Political Conservatism."
[6] Janoff-Bulman, "To Provide or Protect."
[7] Jost et al., "Political Conservatism."   [8] Haidt, "The New Synthesis."

fundamentally social animals; from day one we are socially dependent, and over time we grow socially interdependent, in that our individual survival is generally tied to the success of our group. At the smallest group level, the family, the primary parental responsibilities are to protect and provide for the child; more specifically parents protect their children from threats and danger (i.e., keep children safe from harm) and provide for their welfare and wellbeing (e.g., give food, shelter, physical comfort).... As we move to a far broader level – that of society – these same two responsibilities continue to define group living. A successful society protects members from danger and provides them with the means to subsist and thrive."[9] Schwartz writes that "values represent ... responses to three universal requirements with which all individuals and societies must cope: needs of individuals as biological organisms, requisites of coordinated social interaction, and requirements for the smooth functioning and survival of groups."[10]

Beliefs about Other's Morality: Competitive and Dangerous Worldviews as Second-Order Beliefs

Duckitt finds that the moral motivations to provide and to protect have corresponding sociocultural schemas that are "chronically accessible," in other words intuitive and natural in such a way that is consistent with an evolutionary account. Positions on the protection dimension are a product of "dangerous world beliefs," based on a core understanding that the "social world is a dangerous and threatening place in which good, decent people's values and way of life are threatened by bad people." DWB are measured through agreement or disagreement with survey statements such as "there are many dangerous people in our society who will attack someone out of pure meanness, for no reason at all." If the world is a precarious place, individuals must bind together in tight groups to face common enemies. For those who perceive the world as safer and more secure, more leeway can be given to individuals to define their own destinies. DWB are threat-centric and fear-driven. They are associated with strong tendencies toward

---

[9] Janoff-Bulman, "To Provide or Protect," 12.
[10] Schwartz, Shalom. 1994. "Are There Universal Aspects in the Structure and Contents of Human Values?" *Journal of Social Issues* 50(4): 21.

right-wing authoritarianism (RWA), in which individuals endorse strong law-and-order principles as well as rigid adherence to conventional social norms to police personal behavior and generate conformity.[11] This is what we now call "conservative" morality.

Importantly, differences along this dimension revolve around the degree to which there are wrongdoers who want to do good people harm – second-order moral beliefs. The central social problem of those who embrace binding values and DWB is distinguishing the good from the bad – that is, moral screening. Protection-based morality emphasizes "blameworthiness"; it is "condemnatory and strict."[12] DWB are the basis of the morality of RWA, which is not morally indifferent although it is non-liberal. As Alteyemer describes, right-wing authoritarians "tend to be highly self-righteous. They think themselves much more moral and upstanding than others."[13]

Even humanitarians, of course, might morally condemn. If evolutionary theorists are right, altruism could not have emerged were it not for moralistic punishment. We can shame and guilt both the greedy billionaire who will not help the poor and the cowardly draft dodger who lets others go and fight for the country. Humanitarians are distinguished not only by their care beyond the parochial community but also by their egalitarianism within it. They will condemn those hostile to either. However, adherents of binding morality, highly attuned to threats as they are, will always be more actively searching for bad guys and define them in a particular way – those who threaten the stability and safety of society.

DWB are different from CWB, a schema based on an understanding of the world "as a competitive jungle characterized by a ruthless and amoral struggle for resources and power in which the fittest and most powerful succeed and the unfit and weak fail." If the world is a dog-eat-dog place where everyone is on their own, little attention can be given to caring for others or creating social equality by lifting up the weakest and most vulnerable. The antithesis of the CWB schema is a "social world as a place of cooperative and altruistic harmony in which people care for, help, and share with each other."[14]

---

[11] Duckitt, "A Dual-Process Cognitive-Motivational Theory," provides the most extensive statement of his conceptual framework.
[12] Janoff-Bulman and Carnes, "Surveying the Moral Landscape."
[13] Altemeyer, "The Other 'Authoritarian Personality,'" 52.
[14] Duckitt, "A Dual-Process Cognitive-Motivational Theory," 15.

CWB are power-centric and dominance-driven. They are anti-humanitarian, defined primarily by what they lack. Unlike DWB, CWB do not distinguish between good and bad or recognize inhibitions on personal interest on behalf of the greater good. It is every man for himself. In this mindset, the social world is marked by the "amoral struggle for resources and power in which might is right, and winning everything." CWB underlie "social dominance orientation (SDO)," another right-wing orientation characterized by the "traits of being hard, tough, ruthless and unfeeling to others, as opposed to compassionate, generous, caring and altruistic."[15] In contrast to right-wing authoritarians, social dominators demonstrate little concern for binding morality, either the ingroup or authority foundations. They instead embrace the Schwartz values of hedonism, power, and achievement, all individualistically egoistic tendencies suppressed by binding morality for the good of the group.[16] SDO is highly predicted by belief in such "Machiavellian" sentiments: "One of the most useful skills a person should develop is how to look someone straight in the eye and lie convincingly"; "Basically people are objects to be quietly and cooly manipulated for your own benefit"; and "Deceit and cheating can be justified if they get you what you really want."[17] As Altemeyer writes of those with CWB, "Righteousness itself means little to someone who rejects being guided by moral laws, who instead believes ... there really is no such thing as 'right' and 'wrong'."[18]

As Duckitt notes, there is likely a causal link flowing from CWB to DWB, but not the reverse.[19] If one assumes that all have the goal of maximizing power, then the world becomes a dangerous place indeed. Just ask John Mearsheimer.[20] This makes it hard to distinguish the two tendencies, one of the reasons why I believe political scientists (and even historians) get Hitler so wrong.

Those who embrace CWB are the most likely culprits of that indifference to our most basic humanitarian morality thought to be so

---

[15] Ibid, 51.

[16] Federico, Christopher M., Christopher R. Weber, Damla Ergun, and Corrie Hunt. 2013. "Mapping the Connections between Politics and Morality: The Multiple Sociopolitical Orientations Involved in Moral Intuition." *Political Psychology* 34(4): 589–561.

[17] Altemeyer, "The Other 'Authoritarian Personality,'" 73.

[18] Ibid, 76.   [19] Duckitt, "A Dual-Process Cognitive-Motivational Theory," 59.

[20] Mearsheimer, *The Tragedy of Great Power Politics*.

common in international relations, but which I maintain is the exception, not the rule. The dual-process model indicates where we should look. Even though evolutionary findings tell us morality is endemic to the human species, there is no reason to expect that all individuals have a moral compass. Indeed, it is this very fact that makes morality something we look for in others and which gives the phenomenon of ethics any meaning. There can be no morality without immorality.

It bears repeating that the dual-process model posits two separate dimensions of moral thinking, not a single continuum between humanitarians on one end and binders on the other. Indeed, binders are not indifferent to humanitarian considerations. Rather they believe that bad things, such as coercion and violence, are sometimes necessary to achieve group ends. RWAs consider themselves to be benevolent, in a way not true of social dominators.[21] RWA, for instance, is *positively* correlated with harm/care and the fairness/reciprocity foundations, even if somewhat weakly when compared to the binding foundations.[22]

Yet there are surely tensions between humanitarian and binding morality, conflicts between providing and protecting. Binding moralists draw a line between ingroup and outgroup, and while not indifferent or hostile to outsiders, do give preference to insiders. To the extent that all social life is marked by some degree of material scarcity, this tradeoff will always exist. And protecting the group, if it calls for violence, also goes against humanitarian principles. If our moral duty is to care for others, harming them is a violation of that obligation. It is at these friction points, where welfare tradeoffs become necessary and unavoidable, where we see the moral politics of foreign policy both within and between countries most clearly.

Providing and Protecting in the Foreign Policy Sphere: The Two-Dimensional Structure of Foreign Policy Beliefs

The analysis of American foreign policy attitudes consistently reveals a two-dimensional structure that is common to both masses and the elites. Largely inductively derived through factor analysis of survey responses in the United States, these dimensions are called "cooperative

---

[21] Altemeyer, "The Other 'Authoritarian Personality,'" 61.
[22] Federico et al., "Mapping the Connections between Politics and Morality."

internationalism" (CI) and "militant internationalism" (MI)[23] and have been found to organize the beliefs of those in other countries as well, both Global South and North and in both elite and mass public samples.[24] This widely used framework is described as the "gold standard"[25] for conceptualizing the structure of foreign policy thinking.

CI and MI are general orientations, predispositions, or postures that not only allow ordinary individuals but also elites, to formulate their attitudes on more specific policy questions. In psychological terms, they act as schemas and heuristics.[26] Neither masses nor elites are, or need to be, informed about each issue they confront. Rather they can consult their core intuitions about foreign affairs. This explains why attitudes tend to cluster in predictable ways, giving them a structure. Hawkish individuals, for instance, are consistently more inclined to think that force can settle international matters.

CI is an orientation toward international affairs that stresses concern for others abroad, with whom we should work toward common goals. Chittick et al. write, "What all these [cooperative internationalism] questions seem to have in common is a concern for the wider community. We believe that those who emphasize the importance of these goals have a more inclusive identity than those who deemphasize these same goals."[27] Similarly, Nincic and Ramos write of

[23] Wittkopf, Eugene R. 1990. *Faces of Internationalism: Public Opinion and American Foreign Policy*. Durham, NC: Duke University Press; Holsti, Ole R. 1998. "The Domestic and Foreign-Policy beliefs of American Leaders." *Journal of Conflict Resolution* 32(2): 248–294.

[24] Ganguly, S. and T. Hellwig. 2016. "Thompson WR: The Foreign Policy Attitudes of Indian Elites: Variance, Structure, and Common Denominators." *Foreign Policy Analysis* 13(2): 416–438; Gravelle, T. B., J. Reifler, and T. J. Scotto. 2017. "The Structure of Foreign Policy Attitudes in Transatlantic Perspective: Comparing the United States, United Kingdom, France and Germany." *European Journal of Political Research* 56(4): 757–776; Bjereld, U., and A. Ekengren. 1999. "Foreign Policy Dimensions: A Comparison between the United States and Sweden." *International Studies Quarterly* 43(3): 503–518; Reifler, J., T. J. Scotto, and H. D. Clarke. 2011. "Foreign Policy Beliefs in Contemporary Britain: Structure and Relevance." *International Studies Quarterly* 55(1): 245–266.

[25] Nincic, Miroslav and Jennifer M. Ramos. 201. "Ideological Structure and Foreign Policy Preferences." *Journal of Political Ideologies* 15(2): 122.

[26] Hurwitz, Jon and Mark Peffley. 1987. "How Are Foreign Policy Attitudes Structured?" *American Political Science Review* 81(4): 1099–1112.

[27] Chittick, William O., Keith R. Billingsley, and Rick Travis. 1995. "A Three-Dimensional Model of American Foreign Policy Beliefs." *International Studies Quarterly* 39(3): 318.

"other-regarding" objectives.[28] Global solidarity constitutes a key element of CI, but cosmopolitanism concerns more than just self-sacrifice and service to others. Cooperative internationalists also believe that cooperation leads to mutual gains. Accordingly, previous work finds that support for humanitarianism, multilateralism, and international collaboration all load on the same CI dimension.[29]

MI, on the other hand, generally captures the familiar division between hawks and doves over the importance, effectiveness, and desirability of using force to reach foreign-policy objectives. Hurwitz and Peffley posit a "dimension of militarism ... anchored, on the one end, by a desire that the government assume an assertive, militant foreign-policy posture through military strength and on the other by a desire for a more flexible and accommodating stance through negotiations."[30] The MI posture rests on a particular cognitive model about the effectiveness of force.[31] Hawks embraces the "deterrence model," in which strength and the demonstration of resolve best achieve peace. In this worldview, lack of credibility and signs of weakness invite challenges by aggressive foes in a dangerous environment.

The CI and MI dimensions of foreign policy attitudes are inductively derived, yet findings strongly suggest that they are the expressions of more fundamental motivational goals and schemas thought to structure ideology across situations, ranging from interpersonal to international, and which emerge out of moral intuitions highlighted in the dual-process model. CI is defined by its multilateralism and humanitarianism. The same individuals who identify as being on the left andsupport the social welfare state and egalitarianism at home also show greater support for CI.[32] The deterrence model mindset underlying MI indicates more than a surface similarity with the schema of binding morality that strong law and order and strict

[28] Nincic and Ramos, "Ideological Structure and Foreign Policy Preferences," 201.

[29] Rathbun, Brian C. 2007. "Hierarchy and Community at Home and Abroad: Evidence of a Common Structure of Domestic and Foreign Policy Beliefs in American Elites." *Journal of Conflict Resolution* 51(3): 379–407; Wittkopf, *Faces of Internationalism*; Holsti and Rosenau, "The Domestic and Foreign-Policy."

[30] Hurwitz and Peffley, "How Are Foreign Policy Attitudes Structured?," 1107.

[31] Jervis, *Perception and Misperception in International Politics*; Tetlock, "Policy-Makers' Images of International Conflict."

[32] Holsti and Rosenau, "The Domestic and Foreign-Policy"; Rathbun, "Hierarchy and Community at Home and Abroad."

adherence to moral norms are necessary to generate social stability in a dangerous world.[33] Those high in MI tend to identify as more conservative and favor authoritarian policies that restrict individual choice at home.[34]

I hypothesize that CI is the foreign policy manifestation of humanitarian morality: Janoff-Bulman's motivation to provide, Haidt and Graham's "individualizing foundations" of harm/care and fairness/reciprocity, and Schwartz's "self-transcendence." MI is the foreign policy expression of binding morality, Janoff-Bulman's protection motivation, and Schwartz's conservation values with DWB at its core. However, lower support for MI might also be a product of humanitarianism given that protecting the group, if it entails violence, means doing harm to other human beings. And lower support for CI might emerge out of the natural inclination of binding moralists to favor ingroups. Nevertheless, I expect these effects to be smaller since the function of binding morality is to protect the group, not to harm the outgroup.[35]

Moral Foundations Survey (with Joshua Kertzer, Kathleen Powers, and Ravi Iyer)

With my co-authors, I gathered data from 2,000 respondents in the spring of 2012 on yourmorals.org, an online platform created to collect data on moral foundations, where participants register to complete a variety of questionnaires that shed light on a range of personality traits, moral values, and individual differences. The website featured an inventory of questions on foreign policy attitudes so as to allow us to estimate the association of moral values with foreign policy dispositions and to make inferences about the underlying structure.

---

[33] Altemeyer, Bob. 1988. *Enemies of Freedom: Understanding Right-Wing Authoritarianism*. San Francisco: Jossey-Bass.

[34] Holsti and Rosenau, "The Domestic and Foreign-Policy"; Rathbun, "Hierarchy and Community at Home and Abroad."

[35] It is important to note that CI and MI, while generally inversely correlated, are not reducible to a single dimension so that combinations of high CI and high MI, for instance, are quite possible. Indeed this is the phenomenon of the "humanitarian hawk" committed to using force to compel respect for human rights. See Rathbun, Brian C. 2004. *Partisan Interventions: European Party Politics and Peace Enforcement in the Balkans*. Ithaca: Cornell University Press."Hierarchy and Community at Home and Abroad."

The foreign policy instrumentation consisted of twenty questions, listed in Online Appendix 2.1. A six-item scale measuring MI and a five-item scale measuring CI contained standard items from Wittkopf,[36] dropping those specific Cold War policy items that may no longer be relevant to present-day respondents. The six MI items ($\alpha = .84$) tap into participants' views about the use of American military might abroad, asking generally whether war and the use of force are potentially beneficial and whether the United States needs to demonstrate its might and resolve. The five CI items ($\alpha = .88$) ask participants about the importance of working with other countries or organizations like the United Nations to solve transnational problems (including human rights violations, poverty, and protecting the global environment). A standard five-item isolationism scale ($\alpha = .78$) assessed participants' impressions of whether the United States should concentrate on domestic problems, scale back its global leadership, and generally stay out of other countries' problems. Isolationism has been found to be an important, although somewhat distant third, dimension in American foreign policy attitudes.[37]

The moral foundations were measured using the moral foundations questionnaire (MFQ) developed by Haidt and his colleagues, presented in Online Appendix 2.1.2. Participants record how relevant certain considerations are to their judgments of right and wrong (on a six-point scale from "not at all relevant" to "extremely relevant") and the extent to which they agree with statements about the importance of each value on a six-point scale from "strongly disagree" to "strongly agree." Haidt specifies five moral foundations, two of which fall under the category of "individualizing foundations" (harm/care and fairness/reciprocity) and three of which fall under the category of binding foundations (authority/respect, ingroup/loyalty, and purity/sanctity). The way by which the MFQ measures fairness is akin to the equality understanding in which all should be guaranteed basic rights rather than the equity understanding in which individuals should be rewarded for their contributions. Therefore, I consider it part of liberal humanitarianism, the "provide" motivation of Janoff-Bulman.

[36] Wittkopf, *Faces of Internationalism.*
[37] Chittick et al., "A Three-Dimensional Model"; Rathbun, "Hierarchy and Community at Home and Abrod."

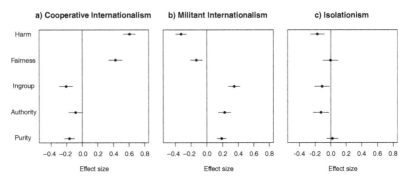

Figure 5.1 *Moral foundations strongly predict foreign policy dispositions.*
The point estimates and 95% confidence intervals for the effects of the moral
foundations on foreign policy orientations. The models also control for demographic characteristics, omitted from the figures for presentational purposes.
All variables are scaled from 0 to 1, so the point estimates represent the effect
of moving from the minimum to the maximum value of each moral foundation.

In Online Appendix 2.1.3, I report the full regression which estimates the impact of the five moral foundations on CI, MI, and isolationism, operationalized using factor scores to obtain more precise
estimates of the constructs of interest.[38] Principal axis factoring was
used to generate the scores for each of the three foreign policy orientation scales, which were then normalized to range from 0 to 1 to facilitate substantive interpretation of the results. Here, I convey the results
more simply using a coefficient plot in Figure 5.1.

We see that CI and MI have strong moral foundations, while isolationism does not. Harm/care has a strong positive relationship
with CI: a 1 unit increase (moving from the minimum to the maximum value) in harm/care is associated with a .60 unit increase in
CI. Fairness/reciprocity is similarly related: a 1 unit increase in fairness is associated with a .42 unit increase in CI. Thus, the more an
individual's moral foundations emphasize relieving harm and caring about the welfare of others, Janoff-Bulman's *providing* motive,
the more likely she is to support working with the international

[38] See Kertzer et al., "Moral Support" appendix, which demonstrates that
weighting the survey to more closely resemble the broader American population
does not change the results. Factor score regression is frequently used in survey
research in political science. By allowing researchers to extract solely the
dimension of interest, factor scoring allows for less noisy estimates that would
arise from the use of additive scores that simply average across survey items.

community to tackle issues like hunger and global warming and support promoting human rights.

The negative effect of these two moral foundations on MI is consistent with the notion that coercive force comes at the expense of humanitarian concern. However, the relationship between these individualizing foundations and CI is substantively stronger.

Conversely, the largest substantive predictor of support for MI is ingroup/loyalty: individuals who emphasize patriotism and group loyalty are .35 units more supportive of hawkish foreign policies. Authority/respect has a similar effect: individuals who emphasize obedience, duty, and tradition are .23 units more supportive of MI. This brings home a central theme of the book, that morality in foreign policy is not the exclusive preserve of cosmopolitan liberals who advocate humanitarianism and multilateralism. Binders are *differently* moral.

The binding foundations have negative effects on CI but these are substantively smaller than those of the individualizing foundations. Individuals who venerate the ingroup are .19 units less supportive of CI. Those individuals whose morals depend greatly on authority/respect are .08 units less supportive of CI, an effect that misses statistical significance.[39]

[39] Since Graham et al. (2009) find that liberals are high in the individualizing moral foundations while conservatives are high in both individualizing and binding foundations – and liberalism is associated with high levels of CI and low levels of MI – this pattern of results raises the specter that political ideology is driving the results. In Kertzer et al., "Moral Support," we perform a series of non-parametric mediation analyses, in which each of the five moral foundations' effects on CI, MI, and isolationism are mediated by political ideology. Mediation analyses show that for CI, it is the individualizing foundations that are more likely to exert effects independent of ideology, while for MI, it is the binding foundations that are more likely to exert effects independent of ideology. This is in keeping with our theoretical predictions that the links between the binding foundations and MI on the one hand and the individualizing foundations and CI on the other would be the most direct. The two individualizing foundations have significant positive direct and indirect effects on CI: fairness and harm's effects on support for dovish foreign policies are partially transmitted by political ideology, but not exclusively so; 34.2% of fairness' effect on CI, and 59.6% of harm's effect, come through other mechanisms. In contrast, the binding foundations' negative effects on CI are largely mediated through ideology: they all have significant mediation effects on CI, but only ingroup has a significant direct effect. The effects of both ingroup and authority on MI are more direct than indirect, whereas the opposite is true for harm/care and fairness. Indeed, the latter has no direct effect on MI, being entirely mediated by political ideology. Kertzer et al., "Moral Support."

Table 5.1 *Moral foundations structure foreign policy orientations in Russia just as they do in the United States*

	CI	MI
Harm/care	.26***	−.17***
	(.03)	(.03)
Fairness/reciprocity	.10***	−.04
	(.03)	(.03)
Ingroup/loyalty	−.09**	.20***
	(.03)	(.03)
Authority/respect	.06#	.23***
	(.04)	(.04)

Table entries are OLS regression coefficients, with standard errors in parentheses. Variables are based on additive scales, rescaled to vary between 0 and 1 to ease comparisons. Coefficients for demographic controls are not reported. ***$p < 001$, **$p < .01$, *$p < .05$, #$p < .10$. N = 1,112

As mentioned earlier, studies have shown that the CI/MI framework captures the structure of political ideology in other countries as well, which we would expect if these dimensions are indeed expressions of basic human moral tendencies grounded in evolution. Table 5.1 shows a replication of these same associations in the Russian sample examined earlier in the chapter. CI is positively associated with harm/care and fairness, whereas ingroup loyalty and authority are better predictors of MI. Again, the positive effects of the individualizing foundations on CI are larger than the negative effects of the binding foundations. The positive effects of the binding foundations on MI are larger than the negative effects of the individualizing foundations. In the German case chapters, we will see significant evidence of the dual-process model at work in major foreign policy events of the twentieth century.

Schwartz Values Survey (with Joshua Kertzer, Jason Reifler, Paul Goren and Tom Scotto)

If CI and MI are indeed expressions of underlying moral foundations, then we should see a similar structure and set of associations between core ethical systems and other dual-process models, such as

Schwartz's theory of universal values, "the most widely employed model of values[40] in social psychology" and "the standard model in values research."[41] Over the past 25 years, Shalom Schwartz and others working with his framework have collected data from over 400 independent samples covering some 80 countries.[42] Given the number of independent samples and the fact that they have been drawn from diverse cultures, linguistic traditions, age groupings, probability, and non-probability samples, and at different points in time, it seems fair to conclude this model of value content and structures rests on a strong and universal empirical foundation.

Values are not identical to moral principles but are closely related and partially overlapping. Schwartz conceptualizes personal values as (i) abstract beliefs, (ii) about desirable end states or behaviors that (iii) transcend specific circumstances and contexts, (iv) guide evaluation and behavior, and (v) can be rank-ordered in terms of relative importance.[43] Schwartz has identified ten broad value domains: benevolence, universalism, self-direction, stimulation, hedonism, achievement, power, security, conformity, and tradition. The content and structure of personal values can be illustrated using the circumplex shown in Figure 5.2, which arrays the value types along a circular motivational continuum. Adjacent values share similar motivations (and should be positively correlated with one another), and opposed values across the circumplex share conflicting motivations (and should be weakly or negatively correlated with one another). Values should have the highest positive correlations with those directly next to them

[40] Hitlin, Steven, and Kevin Pinkston. 2013. "Values, Attitudes, and Ideologies: Explicit and Implicit Constructs Shaping Perception and Action." In *Handbook of Social Psychology*, edited by John Delamater, and Amanda Ward. 2nd ed. New York: Springer, 322.

[41] Gollan, Tobias, and Erich H. Witte. 2014. "From the Interindividual to the Intraindividual Level: Is the Circumplex Model of Values Applicable to Intraindividual Value Profiles?" *Journal of Cross-Cultural Psychology* 45(3): 452–467.

[42] Schwartz, "Universals in the Content and Structure of Values"; Spini, Dario. 2003. "Measurement Equivalence of 10 Value Types from the Schwartz Value Survey Across 21 Countries." *Journal of Cross-Cultural Psychology* 34(1): 3–23. Davidov, Eldad, Peter Schmidt, and Shalom H. Schwartz. 2008. "Bringing Values Back In: The Adequacy of the European Social Survey to Measure Values in 20 Countries." *Public Opinion Quarterly* 72(3): 420–445.

[43] Schwartz, "Are There Universal Aspects," 20.

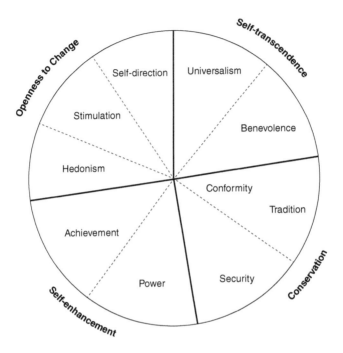

Figure 5.2 *Behold the circumplex.* May the Schwartz be with you.

in the circumplex, so that, for instance, achievement and power have a stronger positive association than achievement and security.

When the motivational bases underpinning the identified universe of personal values are considered en masse, four superordinate values emerge. As indicated in Figure 5.2, the capstone principles are (1) self-transcendence values, which emphasize the acceptance of and concern for other individuals (known and unknown), groups, society writ large, and even the global community; (2) self-enhancement values, which call for the pursuit of one's own self-interest, success, satisfaction, and dominance, over others if necessary; (3) openness values, which privilege independent feeling, thought, creativity, and action; and (4) conservation values, which emphasize self-restraint, social stability, resistance to change, and deference to established traditions and cultural dictates.

To illustrate, tradition values call for deference to established familial, cultural, and religious norms and practices. They are compatible with adjacent conformity values that prioritize the goals of impulse control, self-restraint, and submission to social expectations. Together as conservation values, they stand opposed to stimulation values, which prioritize excitement and novelty, and self-direction values, which emphasize thought and action free of socially imposed norms or internally imposed restraints. Hence, the realization of one value (e.g., self-direction) can obstruct the attainment of another (e.g., tradition or conformity).

Conservation values are the Schwartz equivalent to the binding values. When it comes to harm/care, Schwartz's framework is more fine-grained, distinguishing between benevolence, which is caring for those in one's local community, and universalism, marked by "understanding, appreciation, tolerance, and protection for the welfare of all people and for nature." Benevolence is therefore akin to parochial altruism, while universalism indicates a more general humanitarianism.

In late January 2011, a national representative sample of 1,200 American adults was given the "Core Values Project" (CVP) survey through the polling firm YouGov/Polimetrix of which I was an organizer. We measured our dependent variables of interest – participants' foreign policy orientations rather than specific issue attitudes – by asking participants about the extent to which they agree or disagree with a series of ten statements taken from the CI/MI literature (see Online Appendix 2.2.1). Four of the items measure MI (sample item: "The United States must demonstrate its resolve so that others do not take advantage of it"), four capture CI (sample item: "The United States needs to cooperate more with the United Nations"), and two reflect support for isolationism (sample item: "The United States should mind its own business internationally and let other countries get along the best they can on their own.").

To measure our independent variables of interest – participants' personal values – we employed a twenty-item version of the Schwartz Portrait Value Questionnaire (PVQ, see Online Appendix 2.2.2) in which respondents are presented with verbal "portraits" of individuals (sample item for universalism: "She thinks it is important that every person in the world should be treated equally. She believes everyone should have equal opportunities in life") gender-matched with each respondent, and asked to indicate "how much each person is or is not like you." We used principal axis factoring with varimax rotation to generate factor scores from a six-factor solution, in which two of the factors correspond to superordinate value categories discussed previously (conservation and openness to change), and the remaining factors refer to the two self-transcendence values (universalism and benevolence) and two self-enhancement values (achievement and power).

The empirical strategy is straightforward: We estimate the underlying trans-situational values people hold and use them to explain foreign policy outlooks while controlling for other political values. I report the full model in Online Appendix 2.2.3 and restrict the presentation to a plot of the Schwartz values. As is standard in this type of survey research, we also include the usual demographic controls, measuring age, race, gender, and so on.

The top panel of Figure 5.3 presents a set of coefficient plots from a series of regression models regressing foreign policy orientations on the Schwartz values, while the bottom panel presents the same results another way, comparing each variable's statistical significance and contribution to the model's in-sample predictive power. As we would expect, universalism is the primary driver of CI. Indeed, in terms of substantive significance, it has a dramatically stronger effect than any of the other values. Conservation, capturing the same attitudes as Haidt and Graham's authority foundation, is the strongest predictor of MI. Benevolence, akin to ingroup identification, is also highly positively associated with MI. In sum, we find convergent evidence for the dual-process model using a different conceptual framework.

Just as we saw a negative relationship between harm/care and MI, when using the Schwarz framework we see that hawks score low on universalism. However, the negative effect of universalism on MI is not as large as universalism's positive effect on CI. The results also indicate that binding morality is not synonymous with hostility to outgroups. While benevolence and conservation are positive predictors of MI, they are not negative predictors of CI. This brings home the important point that the dual-process model posits two separate dimensions of moral thinking. Instead, it is power, which captures a fundamentally self-interested approach to life likely capturing a moral callousness in opposition to harm/care, that predicts lower scores on CI.

We illustrate these results another way in the bottom panel of Figure 5.3, which replicates the regression results presented in the top panel, but this time plotting the effects of each of the personal

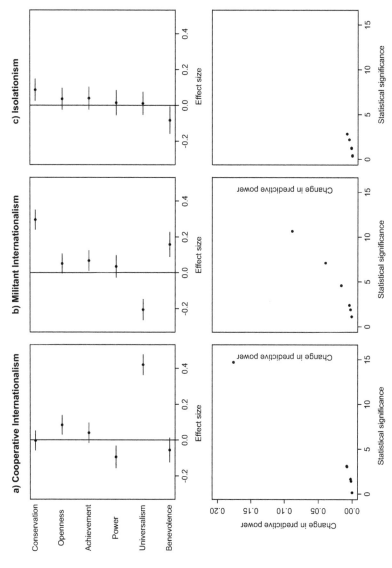

Figure 5.3 *Personal values predict foreign policy orientations.*

values as a function of their statistical significance (on the x-axis, represented here as the absolute value of its z-statistic), and the change in in-sample predictive power (on the y-axis, represented here by the change in the R^2 statistic) incurred by dropping the personal value from the model. These results reconfirm the intuitions from the previous sets of results: Universalism is the driving value behind CI (explaining almost 20% of the variance), while conservation – and to a lesser extent, low universalism – underpins MI. The Schwartz values have relatively little impact on isolationism. The substantive effects of universalism on CI and conservation on MI are substantively large: holding all other variables at their means, a change from the 5th to the 95th percentile in universalism is associated with a change from the 17th to the 70th percentile in CI, while a change from the 5th to the 95th percentile in conservation is associated with a change from the 29th to the 67th percentile in MI.

6 Just Desserts in the Desert
Fairness, Status, and Wilhelmine Foreign Policy during the Moroccan Crises

When we think of Wilhelmine Germany, morality is not what comes to mind. Germany after Bismarck is instead seen as the *enfant terrible* of world politics, the spoiled child demanding ever more and even threatening violence to get it. Its adversaries regarded it as an extortionist and a bully. A quote from Eyre Crowe, the British diplomat, during the second Moroccan crisis captures the general feeling of Germany's adversaries and subsequent academic treatments of German foreign policy: "The actions of German governments, sovereigns, princes, ambassadors, and committees have time and again been shown to be the contrary of straightforward and ingenuous. Germany may now be counted upon to continue her well-tried policy of blackmailing. [France] has twice before (at Algeciras and in 1909) paid a price for 'German good-will' in Morocco.... I am afraid France is not in a position now to refuse payment. But it is quite certain that whatever price she pays now, it will not prevent Germany from further extortions of exactly the same nature before long."[1]

Byman and Pollack make it more personal, comparing the German emperor unfavorably to Bismarck: "Where Bismarck had tried to downplay the image of German power, the Kaiser swaggered.... Germany under Bismarck had sought to promote peace among the European powers and demonstrate that Germany was a satiated power. Wilhelm II, on the other hand, was an incorrigible jingoist who, rather than reassure other capitals, regularly frightened them by rattling Germany's saber and demanding more 'respect' for Berlin."[2]

Scholars today and decision-makers at the time frequently remark that Germany was the status-seeker par excellence, evident by the way in which it provoked crises to secure largely symbolic concessions that

---

[1] *British Documents on the Origins of the War*, Vol. III. London: His Majesty's Stationery Office, 1928, no. 369 (hereafter BD III).
[2] Byman, Daniel L., and Kenneth M. Pollack. 2001. "Let Us Now Praise Great Men: Bringing the Statesman Back In." *International Security* 25(4): 124–125.

conferred rank and prestige on the country. Status-seekers are not just spoiled egoists; they aim for relative gains. And status-seekers value these comparative advantages not for what instrumental uses they might put them but simply because they indicate a higher position or rank. They intrinsically value being seen as better than others. If morality always serves as a constraint on egoism, and status-seeking is egoism run amok, it seems safe to conclude that there is no worse candidate for moral behavior than Germany before World War I (except of course, Germany after World War I, a case we explore in Chapters 9–10). Renshon argues, "A common theme throughout this time period is Germany's tendency to instigate crises (or use them once they appear) in order to bargain over status. And because of the positional nature of status, Germany could not gain more unless it came at the expense of those above it in the hierarchy that it cared most about: the small, exclusive club of major European powers.... [T]here is abundant evidence that Germany's pattern of crisis provocation is linked closely to its desire to gain international standing."[3]

Germany does not come out looking any better, through the lens of liberal morality, to the extent that its status ambitions largely concerned obtaining a more extensive imperial portfolio. Germany's pursuit of a global role, known by the phrase *Weltpolitik* (or global policy/politics), was synonymous with a greater territorial and military footprint abroad that would safeguard and expand its trading opportunities.[4] A significant driver of this, goes the argument, was status. As Murray writes, the "special rights and duties" that confer status "have historically included being able to exclusively determine their own affairs as well as playing a leading role in determining the direction and shape of international affairs, but beyond this, they have varied over time as constitutive norms that define this identity have changed. At the turn of the twentieth century, when Germany made its bid to join the ranks of the great powers, this leadership role included direct control over and exploitation of much of the world through colonial empires."[5]

---

[3] Renshon, Jonathan. 2017. *Fighting for Status: Hierarchy and Conflict in World Politics*. Princeton: Princeton University Press, 198.

[4] On *Weltpolitik*, see Smith, Woodruff D. 1986. *The Ideological Origins of Nazi Imperialism*. Oxford: Oxford University Press.

[5] Murray, Michelle. 2015. "Recognition, Disrespect and the Struggle for Morocco: Rethinking Imperial Germany's Security Dilemma." In: Thomas Lindemann and Erik Ringmar (eds.). *International Politics of Recognition*. Routledge, 134.

I will argue in this chapter instead that German foreign policy was highly – indeed, excessively – moralistic during the Wilhelmine period, something obscured by the overly truncated way in which we think about morality in international relations but also as a consequence of conceptual confusion in which scholars mistake the pursuit of fairness for the pursuit of status. Germany's pursuit of just treatment and just desserts, to which German leaders and the public felt entitled by virtue of its position in the world, was incredibly myopic and biased. German decision-makers fixated on the injustices done to them far more than those done to others. German behavior is best described as *self*-righteous, but that should not distract us from its moralism, especially because the character of German action proved self-defeating at several points in the crises reviewed in this chapter. Its moralism mattered.

Status-seeking behavior, the pursuit of a higher position on an international social hierarchy as perceived and defined by members of a community, has received considerable attention in recent years. Yet much of what this recent literature calls status-seeking is difficult to distinguish from something else: the pursuit of fairness. This is particularly true of a series of arguments about how states behave when they do not receive the respect, treatment, and spoils they feel they deserve. Indeed, one proponent of such a model argues that a "belief in status immobility is equivalent to a belief that the rules are hopelessly unfair."[6] Yet, intuitively, fairness and status seem strikingly different. Status-seeking is rarely considered principled but instead connotes pettiness, self-serving behavior, and superficiality. Rich men in sports cars are not held up as moral models, at least to most of us. Fairness has a moral connotation that status does not. I disentangle status-seeking from fairness-seeking by identifying where a pure status-seeking and a fairness-seeking argument diverge – in the degree to which state actors demand *exclusive* rights and privileges. Status-seekers have a desire for ever greater rank, and status is diminished by the degree to which others share their position on the social hierarchy. Fairness-seekers simply want their rank to reflect their achievements; otherwise, they are content for others to share that rank. They want what they deserve, a conception of fairness as equity seen in Chapter 2.

---

[6] Ward, Steven. 2017. *Status and the Challenge of Rising Powers*. Cambridge: Cambridge University Press, 50.

Consistent with previous research, however, we see that conceptions of fairness are biased; individuals are more likely to see and
respond to injustices done to them than the equivalent injustice done
to others. This puts the "self" in self-righteous. I call this *myopic*
fairness.

Fairness, however, can also serve as an instrumental justification
for purely self-interested and material-driven behavior of the kind
typically explored in international relations scholarship, behavior
that has nothing to do with status-seeking at all. Previous accounts
gloss over and understate the interests at stake in Germany's bid
for a colonial empire so as to make the case for how status-seeking
can overcome and even obstruct the pursuit of more tangible interests. By virtue of its universal nature, fairness is also a more useful means by which to justify the pursuit of selfish interests to an
international audience. Because it is so understandable, it emerges
as one of the more natural ways by which to rhetorically coerce
others into acceding to our claims. Status-seeking, because it is so
exclusive and self-serving, is unlikely to resonate outside of one's
borders. In other words, not only is our conception of fairness egoistically subjective, but it is also even used by those with little concern
for fairness to achieve the egoistic aims often downgraded in status
accounts, another indication of the shadow of morality. This can
have unintended consequences. As we will see, Germany's transparent manipulation of ethical principles, felt necessary to justify its
claims, actually encumbered its pursuit of selfish advantage by trig-
gering moral outrage and denying it the use of alternative arguments
to legitimate its demands.

Any analyst can cherry-pick evidence from German behavior in this
period indicating either status or fairness considerations. Instead, I
focus on two historical events thought to be emblematic of German
status-seeking – the two Moroccan crises of the early twentieth century
that set the scene for World War I. Murray claims, "By 1890 Germany
was the strongest power on the European continent; however, its
power beyond Europe was insignificant.... One part of German strategy to achieve world-power status involved instigating a series of crises
over the independent status of Morocco."[7] Renshon's main case study
of status-seeking is Wilhelmine Germany, with a significant portion

---

[7] Murray, "Recognition, Disrespect and the Struggle for Morocco," 132.

dedicated to the two Moroccan crises.[8] These, therefore, serve as critical case studies and discipline the analysis by requiring more than just a few, perhaps unrepresentative pull quotes.

I instead claim that Germany wanted its just desserts in the desert. A more nuanced consideration of the case shows that Germany felt unfairly treated by France as the latter came to terms with other European powers so as to gain a freer hand in Morocco. Its leaders demanded the convocation of an inclusive international conference in an effort to deny their rival a major foreign policy coup, the rounding off of its North African empire. German leaders reasoned that by positioning the country as the defender of third-party rights writ large, not just for Germany, it could more effectively isolate France. Germany actually turned down offers by France to negotiate a separate deal that would have been more most status enhancing.

In the second Moroccan crisis, Germany insisted on adequate compensation for France's further penetration of the country. As security in the Sharifian empire deteriorated, the Moroccan Sultan asked French troops to quell disturbances in the interior, creating a de facto protectorate. The Germans were looking for tangible gains, not mere face-saving baubles as the status argument suggests. The German foreign minister, Kiderlen-Wächter, sought the French Congo, so as to join German imperial possessions on opposite shores of Africa. Yet, even as Germany had tangible interests in mind, France and Britain recognized that fairness demanded German compensation. Of course, no one had any concern at all for the wishes of Moroccans themselves. This would require a moral revolution of a different kind, more familiar to us from the works of liberal scholars. Yet, as stressed, I am approaching morality phenomenologically in this book, from the point of view of those under study.

Morality had major consequences for the outcome of both crises. At the conference convened in Algeciras at Germany's insistence to settle the first crisis, Germany became a prisoner of its own efforts at rhetorical coercion. As other countries were not similarly outraged, they did not back the German position. And since that position hinged on making Germany the defender of fair treatment of the collectivity, this left the country without diplomatic options, save a war it did not want to fight. Morality had tied its hands.

---

[8] Renshon, *Fighting for Status*, ch. 6.

In the second Moroccan crisis, in a premeditated move, the Germans dispatched a gunboat to a closed port off the Atlantic Coast, Agadir, to show the French that they meant business. However, they refused to admit as much, instead coming up with transparently disingenuous rationales for the *Panthersprung* ("Panther leap," after the name of the ship). This had the primary effect of alienating the English, who justifiably found German behavior untrustworthy even as it was, in their eyes, ultimately unthreatening to English interests. A speech implicitly condemning German behavior at London's Mansion House triggered a full-scale crisis between the two countries that consisted almost exclusively of each side trying to affix moral blame to the other for disturbing the peace. Yet despite the lack of tangible conflicts of interest between the two, the second Moroccan crisis led to a dramatic decline in Anglo-German relations and solidified the Entente Cordiale between England and France, hardening the fault lines between countries that would soon find themselves at war.

I supplement the German case studies with an analysis of two survey experiments conducted on the Russian public. These survey experiments get at the most difficult aspects of the problem to measure and observe in the case studies. Like Germany, Russia is a crucial case for status dissatisfaction models since contemporary Russia is considered a modern-day exemplar of status-seeking.[9] My survey experimental designs allow me to distinguish between fairness-seeking and status-seeking as well as between a self-serving, biased definition of fairness and a more objective, neutral one. My experiments demonstrate that publics thought to be status-seeking are more interested in fairness. Being deliberately excluded provokes not status concerns, but fairness concerns. Provided that Russia is included in an institution like the G8, the Russian public actually prefers an outcome with many other members rather than an exclusive club in which Russia is one of the few cardholders. Respondents base decisions about who to include, even their own country, on whether or not they meet the criteria for membership – that is, on equity. Rather than insisting on a status prerogative, Russians aim at keeping up with the Joneses.

[9] Clunan, Anne L. 2014. "Historical Aspirations and the Domestic Politics of Russia's Pursuit of International Status." *Communist and Post-Communist Studies* 47(3–4): 281–290.

No Fair: Questioning the Status Quo on Status in International Relations

So as to distinguish between fairness and status, we begin with a discussion of the latter. Recent literature has converged on a conception of status as perceptual, positional, and social[10] based on intersubjective beliefs about others' beliefs about another state's relative position – perceptual in that it is not based on some objective standard but rather socially constructed criteria that change over time; positional in that it implies rank; and social in that it is conferred by others.[11] Larson, Paul, and Wohlforth use the same three characteristics of status, simply using different words: "collective, subjective and relative."[12]

Countries that are not granted the status that they deserve are particularly dangerous and are the subject of considerable recent attention. Renshon offers a "status dissatisfaction" theory showing that states are inclined to use force when expectations about the status they "deserve" are inconsistent with the deference showed to them in the international system, operationalized for instance in the form of diplomatic missions.[13] Ward builds an argument about "status immobility," what results when a country "deserves membership, but other states seem fundamentally unwilling to treat it as a full member of the club."[14] Barnhart uncovers the destabilizing force of humiliation, "the emotional response to the perceived undeserved decline of one's status in the eyes of others."[15] Humiliated states are inclined to initiate conflicts at much higher rates. Wolf writes of "disrespect," which "challenges an actor's self-respect or self-esteem by denying her the degree of esteem or attention she feels entitled to."[16] It is usually experienced as an unacceptable mismatch between the social position one is assigned by the other and the position one expects according to prevailing standards or

---

[10] Renshon, Jonathan. 2016. "Status Deficits and War." *International Organization*: 520.
[11] Ward, *Status and the Challenge of Rising Powers*; Lebow, *Why Nations Fight*.
[12] Larson, Deborah Welch, Tarzha Varkey Paul, William C. Wohlforth, et al. 2014. "Status and World Order." In *Status in World Politics*. Cambridge: Cambridge University Press, 8.
[13] Renshon, "Status Deficits and War," 516, 524.
[14] Ward, *Status and the Challenge of Rising Powers*, 42.
[15] Barnhart, Joslyn. 2020. *The Consequences of Humiliation: Anger and Status in World Politics*. Ithaca and London: Cornell University Press.
[16] Wolf, Reinhard. 2011. "Respect and Disrespect in International Politics: The Significance of Status Recognition." *International Theory* 3(1): 106.

norms. Indeed Ward argues that a "belief in status immobility is equivalent to a belief that the rules are hopelessly unfair."[17] Barnhart says the same, that "humiliation involves a strong sense of other-directed outrage at the party deemed responsible for treating one unfairly."[18]

Notice that in all of these conceptions of status, another key factor is at work: concern for fairness. There is a disjuncture between what a state is getting out as compared to what it has put in. In other words, states are responding to a lack of equity, one of the main ways in which human beings define fairness.[19] Welch calls this same phenomenon the "justice motive," the "reaction to a perceived discrepancy between entitlements and benefits."[20] We do not want to split the pie evenly if it means that those who did not contribute to the cooking get to eat it.

In all of these "status" studies, states feel they "deserve" status. Deservingness implies that someone has a right to something, and to deny rights is unfair. Rights, particularly to deference and respect, are a large part of what status confers. Great power identity, the most important status in international relations, comes with an expectation of being consulted on the important international issues of the day and also of maintaining a sphere of influence within at least a state's immediate geographic area.[21] Just what great powers deserve and what confers status, these observers note, changes over time as a process of shifting international norms.[22] Great powers in the past felt they deserved colonial territories.

Deservingness typically implies that someone has done something to earn something.[23] Achievement differentiates individuals and groups

[17] Ward, *Status and the Challenge of Rising Powers*, 50.

[18] Barnhart, *The Consequences of Humiliation*, 19.

[19] Adams, "Inequity in Social Exchange"; Anderson, William D., and Miles L. Patterson. 2008. "Effects of Social Value Orientations on Fairness Judgments." *The Journal of Social Psychology* 148(2): 223–246; Deutsch, "Equity, Equality, and Need."

[20] Welch, David A. 1995. *Justice and the Genesis of War*. Cambridge: Cambridge University Press, 19.

[21] Ward, *Status and the Challenge of Rising Powers*; Larson et al., "*Status and World Order*"; Barnhart, *The Consequences of Humiliation*.

[22] Duque, Marina G. 2018. "Recognizing International Status: A Relational Approach." *International Studies Quarterly* 62(3): 578.

[23] However, it may not always be. Status based on ascriptive characteristics not in our control, such as race or gender, are not achievement based. Naylor, Tristen. 2018. *Social Closure and International Society: Status Groups from the Family of Civilised Nations to the G20*. London: Routledge. The privileged status of kings and queens, bestowed through the divine right of sovereigns, is not achievement based, for instance.

from one another – in other words, establishes a ranking – but on the basis of their excellence. To deny these achievements and their just rewards is therefore unfair. The achievement itself is not necessarily moral – for instance, running fast. In international relations, the achievement that confers status has historically been the accumulation of material power and prosperity, which is not ethical in and of itself. Status is therefore different from honor, since honor is conferred based on adherence to a particular code of moral behavior.[24] However, if achievements are socially appraised highly enough, accomplished individuals or states feel ethically entitled to certain treatment in light of it.

Therefore, "status-seeking" in international relations on the part of rising powers might be the quest for fair treatment in light of state achievements, the desire for "appraisal respect."[25] This is different from "recognition respect," taking others into consideration regardless of their status or other characteristics. Appraisal respect establishes a hierarchy, whereas recognition respect is based on equality.[26]

How might we begin to conceptually and empirically distinguish fairness from status motivations in international relations considering that the former seems to be baked into the status literature? A careful consideration of the empirical record, armed with a more nuanced conceptual understanding, is important. Status-seeking is the pursuit of rank. Status-seekers value this socially privileged position. Larson and Schevchenko's[27] theory, by Ward's estimate[28] the most prominent model of status in international relations, posits an underlying motivation of esteem rather than fairness, grounded as it is in social identity theory. Renshon argues that at the individual level, social dominance orientation, the desire to be at the top of a hierarchy, predicts status-seeking.[29]

Fairness-seeking entails expectations in light of one's rank and achievements, but fairness-seekers need not be motivated first and foremost by the pursuit of a privileged position in a social hierarchy. The distinction is subtle but important. A student who wants to be the only one with an "A" is a status-seeker; a student who merely

---

[24] Dolan, "Demanding the Impossible."   [25] Darwall, "Two Kinds of Respect."
[26] Lebow, *Why Nations Fight*.
[27] Larson, Deborah Welch, and Alexei Shevchenko. 2010. "Status Seekers: Chinese and Russian Responses to US Primacy." *International Security* 34(4): 63–95.
[28] Ward, *Status and the Challenge of Rising Powers*.
[29] Renshon, *Fighting for Status*.

wants to be rewarded for studying hard, indifferent to how many others achieve this rank, is a fairness-seeker.

The current muddle in the status literature is partially an indication of the difficultly of disentangling the concepts. Is there a way to empirically distinguish between the two? This requires an understanding of the ways by which status-seeking and fairness-seeking might diverge. The key, I argue, is in another characteristic of status, often equated to rank and position, but conceptually and potentially empirically distinct – status's exclusivity. Status' draw is its exclusiveness, membership in a highly regarded and highly restrictive group or category of actors. Status is zero-sum in nature: "If everyone has high status, then no one does.... Elite groups restrict membership to avoid diluting their status and privileges."[30] To have status is to be part of a select few; the more that others have status, the less one has. "[S]ocial closure – the establishment of a boundary between the group and outsiders – shapes status relations."[31]

While appraisal respect based on achievement necessarily creates a hierarchy, that rank can be more or less exclusive. Hierarchy only implies a lack of equality, that not all individuals are of the same rank. It tells us nothing about the distribution of individuals into various ranks. Hierarchy can be bottom heavy or top heavy or something in between, whereas exclusivity implies a bottom-heavy system. Larson et al. explain that in "international politics, status manifests itself in two distinct but related ways: as membership in defined club of actors, and as relative standing within such a club."[32] Similarly, Naylor differentiates between stratification and exclusion.[33] Yet all fail to consider the differences between exclusivity and hierarchy and the conceptual implications, particularly as regards fairness. To the extent that not everyone has the same rank, the upper ranks are exclusive when compared to the lower. However, this misses a lot of other possibilities.

The desire for exclusivity distinguishes status-seeking from fairness-seeking more than the pursuit of rank does, the wish to be behind the velvet rope or to have the island to oneself. The search for appraisal respect does not imply exclusivity, only the deference and benefits that one has achieved and to which others are perfectly entitled. Pure

---

[30] Larson et al., "Status and World Order," 19.
[31] Duque, "Recognizing International Status," 578.
[32] Larson et al., "Status and World Order," 7.
[33] Naylor, *Social Closure and International Society.*

status-seekers want to be on the top rung of the ladder alone with as few others as possible; pure fairness-seekers want to be on the rung they deserve and are perfectly happy with others being there too, provided they also deserve it. Pure status has no fairness in it at all.

Putting the Self in Self-Righteous: Biased Fairness and Inequity Aversion

My expectations about the fairness we might see in international relations are drawn from behavioral economics. Inequity aversion models distinguish between two types of inequality.[34] Individuals exhibit strong aversion to "disadvantageous inequality," that is outcomes that leave them relatively behind. However, they are not more supportive of "advantageous inequality," that is outcomes that leave them ahead, than equality. In experiments that manipulate the gains from allocative games, Loewenstein et al. find the highest support for the equal outcome, which is also judged the fairest.[35] However, peoples' distaste for outcomes that leave them relatively worse off is much stronger than their distaste for outcomes that leave them relatively better off. If individuals applied the rule of fairness impartially, this would not be the case. When we proclaim "no fair!," we are generally doing this on our own behalf.

This is a biased conception of fairness – one that is subjective and particularly sensitive to injustices done to oneself, but not so biased as to simply judge fairness after the fact based on whether one came out ahead.[36] In this conception, individuals are self-involved but not purely self-interested. They are not blind to fairness, but near-sighted. In this vein, Gottfried and Trager find that American respondents prefer an equal distribution of territory in a hypothetical dispute with Russia but express less dissatisfaction with an outcome tilted to the United States' advantage than with an outcome tilted to Russian advantage.[37]

---

[34] Fehr and Fischbacher, "Why Social Preferences Matter."

[35] Loewenstein, George F., Leigh Thompson, and Max H. Bazerman. 1989. "Social Utility and Decision Making in Interpersonal Contexts." *Journal of Personality and Social Psychology* 57(3): 426.

[36] Babcock, Linda, George Loewenstein, Samuel Issacharoff, and Colin Camerer. 1995. "Biased Judgments of Fairness in Bargaining." *The American Economic Review* 85(5): 1337–1343.

[37] Gottfried, Matthew S., and Robert F. Trager. 2016. "A Preference for War: How Fairness and Rhetoric Influence Leadership Incentives in Crises." *International Studies Quarterly* 60(2): 243–257.

Inequity aversion models are actually inappropriately named. They are based on the equality sense of fairness, which makes sense in that they are typically tested in games among peers in which there is no real input on the part of equal participants into the process and thereby no way to judge what one deserves by virtue of their contributions. Ultimatum games are conducted with someone else's money. Where this is not true, participants typically interpret fairness in a manner that serves their interests.[38] Given that international relations occurs between unequal states who feel deserving of outcomes that reflect their accomplishments, I expect that equity will matter more, and I adjust the behavioral economic models accordingly. I anticipate leaders and publics will expect outcomes and treatment (substantive and procedural fairness, respectively) that take into account their accomplishments and contributions, what we have called "appraisal respect." And being biased, leaders and publics will fixate more on their own inequity than those suffering a similar injustice.

The key difference from pure status-seeking actors is that fairness-seeking actors do not begrudge others the same rank that they have so long as the self is justly compensated. In the terms of aversion models, fairness-seekers will oppose disadvantageous inequity but will not demand or seek the advantageous inequity that would make their rank more rarified. In contrast, status-seeking, taken to its logical conclusion, involves making the club as exclusive as possible.

The First Moroccan Crisis

The first Moroccan crisis began when the German Kaiser, Wilhelm II, traveled personally to Tangier on March 31, 1905, where he stressed Germany's commitment to the independence of the Sultan of Morocco and the continued openness of the Sharifian empire to "peaceful competition of all nations without monopoly or exclusion," by which the emperor meant the maintenance of the open door to economic trade.[39]

---

[38] DeScioli, Peter, Maxim Massenkoff, Alex Shaw, Michael Bang Petersen, and Robert Kurzban. 2014. "Equity or Equality? Moral Judgments Follow the Money." *Proceedings of the Royal Society B: Biological Sciences* 281(1797): 2112.

[39] *Die große Politik der europäischen Kabinette 1871–1914.* 1927, Vol. XX. Berlin: Deutsche Verlagsgesellschaft für Politik und Geschichte, no. 6589. Hereafter GP.

The Madrid Treaty of 1880 had guaranteed that all countries would have most favored nation status in regard to trade with Morocco. These principles had been called into question by the conclusion of the Franco-British agreement in 1904, a settlement of outstanding difference between the historic rivals that signaled a fundamental realignment of great power politics. As part of that deal, British recognized France's special interests in Morocco and France did the same for the British in Egypt, amounting to an exchange of spheres of influence. In the wake of what became known as the Entente Cordiale, France pressured the Sultan for reforms of his empire that threatened to make it into a French protectorate, as it had done recently in Tunisia. Reports from Morocco indicated that in doing so, the French representative claimed to speak for all Europeans. French foreign policy strategy was directed by Théophile Delcassé, who the Germans believed aimed at their diplomatic and military isolation and the creation of an eventual Anglo-Franco alliance.

So as to resist Delcassé's designs, high-ranking German officials convinced a reluctant Kaiser to add a stop in Tangier to his Mediterranean pleasure tour as a symbolic act of defiance. On land, the Emperor snubbed the French representative sent to greet him and in spontaneous comments proclaimed that Germany would enter into direct relations with the Sultan and ensure that his just claims were respected by France.[40] "Although the whole event smacked of a comic opera, it none the less threw down the gauntlet to M. Delcassé and French policy in Morocco and ushered in a long period of crisis in international relations. The echoes which the Emperor's speeches aroused in Europe reverberated like the distant rumblings of cannons."[41]

What exactly did Germany expect to accomplish with this provocation? What were its ultimate aims? The Germans were concerned about their future economic interests in Morocco, particularly the granting of contracts on major projects such as the constructions of railroads. They believed this process would inevitably favor French firms were France to control the security and bureaucracy of the country, regardless of any treaty protections.[42] They also wanted to separate Britain from France and prevent a consolidation of the Entente

---

[40] Ibid.
[41] Anderson, Eugene Newton. 1930. *The First Moroccan Crisis, 1904–1906.* Chicago: University of Chicago Press, 195.
[42] GP XX, no. 6515.

Cordiale into an alliance. German motives were defensive as well, preventing further French influence over Morocco. The empire was one of the few remaining territories in Africa that had not been colonized by the European powers and its absorption by France (this was called "Tunisification," after the process that had occurred there) would complete its domination of North Africa. There was also the prospect of obtaining a share of Morocco for Germany itself; a port along the Atlantic coast would bolster its economic and military reach. The stakes were not nearly as trivial as often maintained.

Nevertheless, more than interests were at stake, something less tangible that others call status. Murray claims that "allowing the French intrusion into Morocco to go unchallenged would be tantamount to relinquishing its status as a great power."[43] Renshon argues that the first Moroccan crisis "had a significant status component.... Its main goal was to force other powers to take account of Germany.... [S]tatus and prestige were the causes of the crisis from the beginning."[44] Germany certainly felt anger at being excluded from deliberations of Morocco, both as a function of the Entente Cordiale and in French efforts to pursue internal Sharifian reforms without consulting the empire. By this logic, Germany's exclusion was a status snub against a country that had a particularly high degree of status dissatisfaction. The chancellor wrote the Kaiser, "It is not in Germany's interests to support the gradual incorporation of Morocco into France.... Apart from the fact that the systematic exclusion of all non-French merchants and enterprises from Morocco according to the model used in Tunis would signify an important economic loss for Germany, it is also an underappreciation of our power position if M. Delcassé has not considered it worth the effort to negotiate with Germany over his Moroccan plans. M. Delcassé has completely ignored us in this affair."[45] Rich concludes that at least for Theodore von Holstein, the long-standing head of the political department of the German Foreign Office, the primary purpose was to make Britain and France realize that they could not make far-reaching colonial settlements without German consent.[46] "We don't want to achieve anything in particular.

---

[43] Murray, "Recognition, Disrespect and the Struggle for Morocco," 138.
[44] Renshon, *Fighting for Status*, 200–201. [45] GP XX, no. 6565.
[46] Rich, Norman. 1965. *Friedrich von Holstein, Politics and Diplomacy in the Era of Bismarck and Wilhelm II*. Cambridge: Cambridge University Press, 700.

Our action was intended to demonstrate that things can't be done without us."[47] German officials complained to the French premier and Delcassé that not only had the empire been left out of negotiations, but Germany also had never even been formally notified of the Entente Cordiale, having to read about it in the government publication, *les Livres Jaunes*.

These quotes imply status considerations in that they evoke issues of disrespect given Germany's power position. However, reading more closely, it becomes clear that German leaders believed this involved a question of moral principle concerning how in general third countries with interests in regions affected by agreements between particular countries could expect to be treated. Germany was due the same treatment that France had accorded other countries, including those significantly weaker, such as Spain, with whom France had also come to terms regarding Morocco. Chancellor Bernhard von Bülow explained to a French envoy, "Germany could not allow France to keep it outside the Moroccan question. It considers that the French Government should have negotiated with it as with the other Powers, and it will pursue its policy in this sense so that the interests of Germany are respected."[48] Germany was asking for similar treatment as other interested parties. This was a matter of principle. "Germany would be astonished," Bülow stressed, "if a third party made decisions affecting its interests without asking us ... [t]he material worth of the threatened interests is secondary to considerations of these other type."[49]

Even when invoking concerns about "prestige," Germans moralized the question. Holstein wrote in an internal memorandum, "Even more alarming would be the injury to Germany's prestige, if we sat still whilst German interests were being dealt with without our taking a part. It is the duty of a Great Power not merely to protect its territorial frontiers, but also the interests lying outside them. In this sense all interests are to be held justified, which are not opposed by another and stronger right.... German government intends to oppose the wrong involved when one Power injures the interest of another in neutral territory without that Power's consent." At least in Holstein's mind, this was different from the pursuit of selfish gains or changes to the status quo. "That there may

[47] Ibid, 709.   [48] GP XX, no. 6658.   [49] GP XX, no. 6637.

be no doubts as to its motives, the German Government declares that the position taken up is only intended to prevent injury to its legitimate interests and dignity."[50]

Putting France in the Wrong: Germany's Insistence on an International Conference

The key to distinguishing status-driven motivations from fairness or honor concerns is whether or not Germany was making exclusive claims to treatment that it would not afford to others that shared its rank, or even those who did not. A purely status-driven Germany would want to receive better treatment than as many others as possible. Subsequent aspects of the crisis, beyond the mere precipitation, better allow us to tease apart its driving forces.

Germany framed its resistance to French moves not as a snub to German status but rather as an affront to all parties with an interest in the maintenance of the open door in Morocco, which included not only the United States but also many smaller powers who were parties to the Madrid Convention. Holstein wrote after the conclusion of the Anglo-French convention:"England is the gaining party in Egypt, and France in Morocco. England sought and obtained an understanding with the Powers who have legitimate interests in Egypt, whilst in acquiring Morocco France entirely ignored the justified interests of *third parties*, with the exception of Spain," and even then, only at the insistence of England. "It is undeniable that the losses which third Powers would suffer through the gradual absorption of Morocco by France would be immensely greater than any injury or loss caused by the new arrangements in Egypt.... France's evident scheme to absorb Morocco finishes the free competition of foreign countries and involves sensible injury to the interests of third Powers."[51] Bülow wrote the emperor that Germany "seeks no special advantages" but instead demands "equal commercial rights for all States to include not merely freedom of trade or even formal most-favored-nation treatment, but the 'open door' in the fullest sense."[52] He explained to the German envoy to Tangier, "The security of our position is that we do not demand any special advantages but only insist on the maintenance

[50] GP XX, no. 6521.   [51] Ibid.   [52] GP XX, no. 6599.

of the status quo, that is the equal treatment of all nations."[53] The German position, Bülow explained, was that "the fact that France, in not discussing the April 8 convention with us, could ignore our dignity, but it could not change our legal position, which is or should be the same for us and for all contractual powers, namely that the status of Morocco cannot be changed not through special agreements of individual powers but only with the involvement of all contracting countries."[54] Germany also continually stressed that it had no territorial ambitions in Morocco, a suspicion common in France and Britain, by referring to the emperor's declaration to this effect the previous year.[55] Even as the chancellor stressed the injury to Germany's dignity, Germany simultaneously emphasized to the French that other countries were in a similar position.[56]

This framing affected German behavior, not just German complaints. The German urged the Sultan to call for an international conference open to all the signatories of the Madrid treaty, and therefore affected by French action, to jointly approve any alterations to the status quo. Germany was to stress that it was not looking for special prerogatives or concessions. Were this its goal, the chancellor explained, it would have insisted on participation in negotiations like the French had conducted with the Spanish.[57] The Germans emphasized from the beginning that they would not consider such an "exclusive agreement" (*Sonderabkommen*). This was a fear of the British, who thought such an agreement might come at their expense.[58] Holstein instructed the press to convey as the basic principle of German policy: "Moroccan matters are, to repeat, to be settled through a conference, by which the collective powers including the United States, jointly participate. The German government would not participate in any exclusive agreement over Moroccan matters in which the Moroccan government and the collective powers are not in the discussion."[59] The Germans underlined to the British that the calling of a conference indicated that Germany had asked for no special advantages for herself, and any improvement that might take place in Morocco would be to the advantage not only of Germany, but of all the nations who had commercial interests there. As for the proposed Conference he regarded it as a piece of

[53] GP XX, no. 6582; also no. 6576.   [54] GP XX, no. 6604.
[55] GP XX, no. 6590.   [56] GP XX, no. 6637.
[57] GP XX, no. 6613.   [58] BD III, no. 94.   [59] GP XX, no. 6597.

diplomatic etiquette that the Powers who had acquired certain rights in Morocco in virtue of the Madrid Convention should have their say as to the reforms which would benefit them all. This at all events was a proof that Germany was not pursuing a selfish policy, and that she did not wish for any territorial acquisition, although certain articles in the English press seemed calculated to force her to ask for a port."[60]

German strategy was certainly at least partially instrumental. Holstein recognized that such a position, given the moral weight that came with its more disinterested quality, was superior to one stressing how France had not consulted Germany, which he called a policy of "sensitivity and pouting"[61] that made Germany look weak.[62] Fairness was a natural means of rhetorical coercion. "To avoid the suspicion of pursuing, like France, a profit-seeking policy," Germany should "refer France to the collectivity of the treaty powers."[63] Holstein noted that in a memo that "our standpoint, that the [Madrid] treaty powers have a right to be heard, is unassailable," to which the chancellor responded "correct" in the margins.[64] The diplomat cautioned that "in addition to this main question, but only in addition, can be mentioned that Germany belongs to those great powers, whose dignity is injured when legally-recognized, justified interests are disposed of without agreement or even consultation."[65] Holstein wanted to downplay status and play up equal treatment. Holstein believed that if the Germans "say that the absorption of Morocco by France injures us materially, that the injury is done without consulting us and wounds our dignity as a Great Power, then it must be admitted that that we are acting for Germany alone."[66]

This suggests that even if genuinely aggrieved by what was perceived as France's unjust actions, the Germans were tailoring their response to an audience. Fairness would work better than status, placing more pressure on the French to make concessions to German interests. The chancellor called the conference a "trump card" that would apply significant moral pressure on France, making it difficult for it to refuse.[67] Holstein believed that if France were to refuse such a conference, "it would be in the wrong. In international law, right and wrong are only of consequence when the lawbreaker is not strong enough to override everything. In this situation, France would hardly be able to do so."[68]

---

[60] BD III, no. 98.   [61] GP XX, no. 6606.   [62] GP XX, no. 6597.   [63] Ibid.
[64] GP XX, no. 6601; also nos. 6597, 6611.   [65] GP XX, no. 6597.
[66] GP XX, no. 6521.   [67] GP XX, no. 6599.   [68] GP XX, no. 6604.

By "putting itself in the wrong," France might give England, Spain, and Italy "a perhaps welcome pretext to remove themselves."[69] Holstein believed in the power of moral coercion: "Contractual collectivity is a principle on which we can take a firm stand without ourselves appearing to harbor aggressive intentions. Moreover this idea has the advantage that while affecting French interests, it does not affect French pride.... If France refuses the Conference, she puts herself in the wrong, shows that she has a bad conscience and evil intentions."[70]

In using fairness, however, Germany was consciously ruling out what would have been the most obvious redress for any German concerns about status: a separate agreement with France in which it was compensated for French moves in the same way that other great powers had been, notably Britain. This would have conveyed status as well as offered tangible gains. The conference idea, by its very inclusive nature, could not boost German status. Murray recognizes that "Germany's claims at the conference were based on the idea of equality" but interprets this equivalent to status-seeking. "Germany, as a signatory to the Madrid Convention, deserved the *same rights* as the other *great powers* involved in Morocco."[71] Beyond the fact that such a conception of status is indistinguishable from fairness, Germany's strategy was to keep Morocco open to all third parties that had been a party to the Madrid Convention. It was much more inclusive than a pure status-seeking motivation would have been. The Germans' main goal was to prevent French absorption of Morocco, even for Holstein: "If the conference is held it will, whatever the result, definitely not hand Morocco over to the French."[72] One might attribute this to an effort to undermine French status, but German officials were under explicit instructions not to humiliate the French.[73]

"Reserving the Future": German Morally Entraps Itself

As the Germans predicted, the French tried to thwart the convocation of a conference they feared would impede on their Moroccan designs by offering to negotiate a separate agreement. The French premier

[69] GP XX, no. 6601.
[70] Holstein, Friedrich. 1955. *The Holstein Papers*, Vol. 4. Cambridge: Cambridge University Press, 882.
[71] Murray, "Recognition, Disrespect and the Struggle for Morocco," 140.
[72] Holstein, *The Holstein Papers*, 882.   [73] GP XXI, nos. 6914, 6916.

Rouvier offered Germany a deal resolving any outstanding issues, including Morocco, directly comparing this to the recent accord with England.[74] Even Delcassé approached Germany to resolve the "misunderstanding" arising from its snub.[75] In an effort at compromise, Rouvier suggested that France accept an invitation to a conference provided that the two countries could work out a conference agenda and set of principles guiding negotiations in advance, in other words a fait accompli for the conference over the heads of the Moroccans.

Yet German officials anticipated and stressed from the very beginning it would not negotiate such a buy-out and resisted every overture[76] even though its envoys to Morocco[77] and Paris[78] advised them to do so. "We are not alone but rather one of the states of the Madrid convention," Prince Radolin, German ambassador to France, told Paris. To do so would be hypocritical, the German envoy to Tangier told his English equivalent. "We cannot do what we are reproaching the French for; we must and want to remain honest in the matter.... What would the other signatory powers say if we negotiated with France behind their back?"[79] The Germans insisted on "first acceptance, then negotiation."[80]

The Germans seem to have become morally implicated by their own efforts at rhetorical coercion, trapped by their own scheme of entrapment. After the country made its advocacy of a conference known to the other powers,[81] it became impossible to back out since no appropriate excuse could be found.[82] Germany's hands were tied morally. Germany had made a commitment to the Sultan that it could not simply "change from one day to another."[83] "I cannot settle with France on Morocco and leave the Sultan in the lurch because it would go against my word," Bülow explained to the emperor.[84] "I cannot do that because I explained to the Sultan that I regard him as an independent sovereign and he rejected Declassé's proposal trusting my word. I cannot let him down because the French show a friendly face."[85] Bülow told the French that such a reversal would give credence to claims in the English press that Germany simply sought special advantages.[86]

---

[74] GP XX, no. 6642. [75] GP XX, no. 6623. [76] GP XX, no. 6621.
[77] GP XX, no. 6642. [78] GP XX, no. 6622. [79] GP XX, no. 6642.
[80] GP XX, no. 6746. [81] GP XX, no. 6646. [82] GP XX, no. 6649.
[83] GP XX, no. 6725. [84] GP XX, no. 6732. [85] Ibid.
[86] GP XX, no. 6702. German officials blamed Delcassé, who remarkably, after coming under criticism at home for having soured relations with Germany, had been dismissed by the French premier largely due to German

However, Germany could consider such a path in the future. Bülow told the French: "A temporary pause is now necessary, with which one could win time for reassurance and eventually new combinations. There is no better means than a conference to allow for this temporary pause and the unavoidable standstill that is not injurious to either side."[87] The conference was merely a question of "etiquette and respite."[88] Once this "formal obstacle is cleared, I see no obstacle to an appropriate discussion of these questions" in which he saw much commonality.[89] After the conference was convened, Germany could claim that it fulfilled its obligations to the Sultan.[90] If, as expected, any reforms of Morocco were to fail,[91] then a new situation would arise and Germany would be released from its moral pledges and able to negotiate with France.[92] The key was to slow down the pace so that Germany could climb down from its commitments.[93] The two should "keep the future open" (in German, *die Zukunft reservieren;* in French, *réserver l'avenir*).[94] The chancellor put it baldly: "If these reforms, instead of bringing about an improvement, brought new crises ... we would be in the presence of a new situation, not foreseen by previous engagements. So the future is free. In this future which is perhaps not so far away, we could once again become opportunists. But today we are constrained.... The difference between France and us is this: France can act as an opportunist today, while we cannot, but we may be able to do so at some point that I suspect is not to be too far away. The only question really in dispute between us and France is therefore the question of time, the question of the opportune moment. It seems to me that it is not worth a war."[95]

Any disingenuousness though masked a pursuit of interests rather than status. The chancellor used the same logic internally in correspondence with Tattenbach, the German representative in Fez, who

---

complaints. Things might have been different had France approached Germany the previous year, before it had made a commitment to Moroccan independence (GP XX, no. 6646), they said. "A year ago and a day ago," the chancellor wrote on the anniversary of the Entente Cordiale and the day after Delcassé was let go, "we were free to place relations with France on a different foundation.... Since then Mr. Delcassé required us to seek another foundation. We cannot desert the Sultan at the moment in which he stuck his neck out by calling a conference based on our advice" (GP XX, no. 6683).

[87] GP XX, no. 6683.   [88] GP XX, no. 6702.   [89] GP XX, no. 6706.
[90] GP XX, nos. 6750, 6753.   [91] GP XX, no. 6740.   [92] GP XX, no. 6650.
[93] Ibid.   [94] GP XX, nos. 6673, 6725.   [95] GP XX, no. 6740.

had urged a simple pursuit of a territorial piece of Morocco. "In reality, we are confronted with the alternative either of relinquishing Morocco now to France without adequate compensation to Germany or of working for the extension of life of the Sharifian Empire in the expectation of a turn of events favorable to us. Thus, I perceive your important task to be in holding the future free for the profit of German interests."[96] He wrote the German ambassador in the United States, "When the collectivity proves itself illusory and we are released, we are required to make exclusively German policy."[97]

No Ulterior Motives? Germany Morally Entraps Itself Again

The French finally acquiesced to a conference in July 1905 after the Germans conceded in advance France's overwhelming interest in securing the Moroccan border with Algeria. The two also agreed that the two main issues for conference consideration were the creation of a Moroccan state bank and the reform of the Moroccan police on the coastal areas to create more security for international trade interests.

Germany's goal for the conference, convened in Algeciras, Spain in January 1906, was to block the creation of a French protectorate.[98] Were the French to obtain the general mandate for organizing the police in the country's coastal areas, it would establish a political predominance and effective occupation that would inevitably result in unequal treatment when it came to commercial interests, thereby paving the way for an eventual absorption of the country.[99] Economic power followed political power. In his instructions, the chancellor stressed that he did not want to humiliate France, as would have been the case if Morocco were primarily about status.[100]

The Germans settled on a strategy that portrayed them as the principled defender of collective interests, that is as the voice of fairness in the crisis. Responsibility for the police might be (1) divided among the conference participates, with each receiving certain ports and hinterlands, (2) given exclusively to small powers, or (3) left to the Sultan to allocate mandates. Germany looked to the United States for diplomatic help at the conference, believing that President's Roosevelt commitment to the Open Door in other parts of the world would

---

[96] GP XX, no. 6643.   [97] GP XX, no. 6667.   [98] GP XXI, no. 6914.
[99] GP XXI, no. 6922.   [100] GP XXI, nos. 6914, 6916.

make him a naturally ally in Algeciras. In keeping with its strategy of disinterestedness, Bülow wanted proposals to come from friendly countries, rather than Germany itself, and suggested three alternatives to the Americans, the common denominator of which was the internationalization of the Moroccan police.[101] German representatives told the Americans to choose the option they found best.[102]

Internationalization had the advantage of precluding French predominance without appearing as if the Germans sought some sort of special position for themselves. The chancellor instructed his delegates to Morocco that "seeking special benefits of any kind in Morocco was not part of German foreign policy. On the contrary [German policy] accords with the most noble intentions, that the principle of the open door must be fully preserved for the economic development of Morocco."[103] The country was not looking for anything else, "otherwise we will be suspected of seeking special political advantages."[104] The country had no "ulterior motives" (*Hintergedanken*), it emphasized; its interests were identical to all of the other parties to the conference.[105] The Germans did stress that any such arrangement would be provisional, consistent with their pledge to keep the future open if circumstances changed.

Germany aimed to use the moral high ground to pressure and isolate France at the conference, something the British recognized in the days before the conference began. Arthur Nicolson, the British representative to the proceedings, wrote presciently to the English foreign secretary, Edward Grey, "[I]t would be most unfortunate if the Conference were to break down on the police question, and that it would be still more unfortunate if it were made to appear that France was to blame for the miscarriage. To speak quite frankly the situation seemed to me as follows. Germany or possibly the Moorish delegates would propose that some of the minor Powers should undertake the police organization : France would object; we should follow suit : no agreement would be reached, the Conference would break up, and it would be published abroad that Germany had asked nothing for herself, that she had been actuated by the disinterested and humane desire that the necessary protection should be accorded to the foreigners at the ports, and that the task should be entrusted to Powers of whom

---

[101] GP XXI, no. 6922.   [102] GP XXI, no. 6956.   [103] GP XXI, no. 6922.
[104] Ibid.   [105] GP XXI, no. 6988.

no one could be jealous or suspicious; and that, for her own selfish aims, France had opposed the proposal, and had thus prolonged an intolerable situation in Morocco, subjecting the lives and property of foreigners to a continued reign of terror. It was essential that if the Conference did fail, it should not be on account of the opposition of France."[106] The English and French were trying to avoid moral condemnation by the international audience.

Therefore, the French needed a rationale other than pure self-interest for their pursuit of a police mandate. The British suggested a practical justification. All countries needed more effective security to protect their nationals and commercial interests. The French and Spanish had experience in policing in Islamic states, knew the customs and the language, and were already present in the country.[107] The French seized on this strategy, stressing that "if we take the practical point of view, we will recognize that France and with it Spain are the only ones capable of providing this help with promptness and efficiency."[108] By drawing in Spain, they claimed that the question was properly internationalized and refused to budge.[109]

The German strategy had a vulnerability. By claiming to speak for collective interests, it would find itself isolated at the conference if the participants tended to side with France. The Germans identified avoiding blame for any breakdown as the highest priority and

---

[106] BD III, no. 224.   [107] BD III, nos. 244, 239, 249, 285.

[108] BD III, no. 330.

[109] GP XXI, no. 7010. The French also justified their position by reference to a different, equity conception of fairness, one that served their interests. The French had, in comparison with the other powers, much greater economic interest in Morocco, which entitled them to a preponderant influence on the maintenance of security. This also justified a greater percentage of the capital shares in a new Moroccan bank (GP XXI, nos. 6976, 7010))."The open door does not signify that those who are in the house must leave it," they maintained (GP XXI, no. 6974). The British embraced their moral argumentation (BD III, nos. 285, 295, 296). "It had to be borne in mind that France had a great deal at stake in Morocco," Grey told the German ambassador. "As a neighbouring Power she was politically very much affected by what went on in Morocco. She had the greatest share of the trade in Morocco, and owing to the unsettled state of the country, which had diminished the trade on the Algerian frontier" (BD III, no. 285). Germany countered by basing fairness in equality, claiming that French proposals "completely depart from the open door principles and equal treatment of nations adopted by the conference" (GP XXI, no. 6976). The conference had the character of a moral duel.

"chief object."[110] If they lost the support of others "after all that has occurred, our situation would be almost ludicrous," recognized the chancellor.[111] In this way, an argument based on fairness disarmed Germany in a way that a status-driven argument based on exclusivity would not have.

This is exactly what happened. Grey noted in early February, as the negotiations dragged on, "it does not appear that proposals as to Bank or Police, which would be made or accepted by France are objected to on their merits by any Power except Germany."[112] He pressured the German ambassador to England, Metternich, asking "as the other Powers did not object to the police being entrusted to France and Spain, why should Germany raise objection to it, seeing that her trade interests were analogous to the trade interests of the other Powers, being at any rate much nearer to those of the other Powers than they were to those of France and Great Britain, which were much the largest of all? If, therefore, the Powers other than France and Great Britain did not think their trade interests would be endangered by the police at the ports being entrusted to France and Spain, why should Germany object?"[113]

This kink in the German's moral armor was exploited in an identical manner by Russia. The German ambassador was told, "It is difficult to understand why [Germany] is so stubbornly committed at the conference to stand up for rights that all other powers are willing to give up in view of the practical solution that the French propose."[114] The Russian ambassador to Berlin told the Germans that "in answer to [the German] contention [to be] acting in the interests of Europe, that he considered the powers of Europe the best judges of their own interests, and that Germany could not speak for them without their authority.... [I]f the Representatives of the Powers at the Conference which met in deference to the wishes of Germany declared themselves satisfied with French proposals he did not believe it possible for Germany on her own motion to break up the Conference. If she did so, her aggressive policy would be plain to the whole world."[115] The Russian chargé d'affaires predicted to Grey that if Germany went to war as a result of a failed conference, "she would have against her the moral opinion of the whole of Europe."[116]

---

[110] GP XXI, no. 6922; GP XXI, no. 6900.   [111] GP XXI, no. 6900.
[112] BD III, no. 195.   [113] BD III, no. 285.
[114] GP XXI, no. 7037.   [115] BD III, no. 274.   [116] BD III, no. 297.

The Germans even lost the confidence of the Americans. Roosevelt told the emperor he would lose "credit" and "moral power" if the conference failed.[117] Germany was being a "big bully."[118] Its behavior was "petty and unworthy of a great nation."[119] The country's diplomatic failures were a function of having "created an impression of German insincerity and dishonesty. The German threats in particular awoke fears that Germany had profoundly sinister intentions, and it is understandable that every nation should have found it difficult to believe that Germany had stirred up the entire crisis over Morocco simply to give disinterested aid to the Sultan and to preserve the principle of the Open Door for a few minor German economic interests."[120]

Entirely isolated, the Germans eventually conceded to a shared organization of the Moroccan police by the French and Spanish with a Swiss inspector general. Its self-righteous policy had backfired. Anderson writes, "Germany could have placed herself on the same basis with reference to France that Great Britain occupied, both in regard to European and to colonial affairs. Instead, however, of weakening the Entente Cordiale, instead of making a valuable colonial accord by accepting the French offers, the German government had preferred both to keep its promises to the Sultan and to free itself from those promises by forcing a conference upon an unwilling world. Caught in the toils of its own tangled policy ... it had refused present offers of colonial gain with the hope of bringing about their renewal in the future. *Its virtue, not appreciated by any other Power, was greater than its common sense.*"[121]

Second Moroccan Crisis

Following the conclusion of the Algeciras Act, the internal situation in Morocco deteriorated as the Germans had expected. Tribal uprisings in the interior of the country threatened the Sultan's rule, and he called in French troops to relieve the capital city of Fez. The Germans asserted that this was a violation of the Algeciras agreement, which

[117] Anderson, *The First Moroccan Crisis, 1904–1906*, 385.
[118] Ibid, 360.   [119] Ibid, 388–389.
[120] Rich, *Friedrich von Holstein: Politics and Diplomacy in the Era of Bismarck and Wilhelm II*, 735.
[121] Anderson, *The First Moroccan Crisis, 1904–1906*, 256.

limited the international presence to coastal areas. The foreign minister told the French ambassador that "if French troops remained at Fez with the result that the Sultan can only govern with the help of French bayonets, for our part we could no longer regard him as the Sultan who was confirmed under the Act of Algeciras. In this case we would consider that the Act as lapsed 'et reprendre entièrement notre liberté d'action (regain entirely our freedom of action)."[122] The French stressed that their actions came at the request of the Sultan, were temporary in nature, and were necessary to protect European settlements in the region.[123] Privately the Germans doubted these assertions, claiming the situation was not as bad as the French represented.[124] In communication with the French, they predicted that the force of events would keep them in Fez.[125] Once in, they would never leave. The French ambassador admitted as much, telling the German foreign minister, Kiderlen-Wächter: "[N]o one can prevent the fruit to mature, nor Morocco to fall under our influence one day."[126] In other words, a French protectorate was inevitable.

However, even before the French entered Fez, German officials were strategizing about how to acquire adequate compensation for German acquiescence to the rounding off of France's north African empire. Kiderlen-Wächter developed a scheme for when the French entered the city, after which

we might ask a friendly question in Paris ... how long they consider it essential to keep the troops there.... [T]he return march will naturally be put off on some pretext or another. Then would be the moment for us to declare to the Signatory Powers that we fully comprehend the reasons obliging the French to remain at Fez, but that we cannot any longer regard a Sultan who can only govern with the aid of French troops as the independent sovereign ruler contemplated by the Act of Algeciras; the Act has been torn up by the force of circumstances, and entire freedom of action has been restored to all the Signatory Powers. For us then the question would be what use to make of this freedom. The occupation of Fez would pave the way for the absorption of Morocco by France. We should gain nothing by protesting

---

[122] GP XXIX, no. 10545.
[123] GP XXIX, nos. 10532, 10537, 10542, 15044, 10545.
[124] GP XXIX, nos. 10527, 10532.   [125] GP XXIX, nos. 15044, 15049, 10563.
[126] Ministère des Affaires Étrangères, 1912. *Documents Diplomatique: Affaires du Maroc*, Vol. 6. Paris: Imprimerie Nationale, no. 366, subsequently referred to as DD; GP XXIX, no. 10575.

and it would mean a moral defeat hard to bear. We must therefore look for an objective for the ensuing negotiations, which shall induce the French to compensate us.[127]

German officials did not believe that France would offer them appropriate compensation spontaneously, however.[128] The country had to send a signal. On July 1, 1911, the German gunboat, the Panther, arrived off the coast of Tangier, a port in southern Morocco closed to international trade. The goal was to create a bargaining chip (in German, a *Faustpfand*) that would increase German leverage, as Kiderlen-Wächter described already in May. "In possession of such a Faustpfand, we should look confidently at the further development of affairs in Morocco and see whether France will offer us proper compensation in her own colonial possessions, in return for which we could abandon" the port.[129] He explained his reasoning to the chancellor. "The French will only make an acceptable offer if they are convinced that we are willing to go to extremes."[130] The Kaiser, as had been the case during the previous crisis, was initially reluctant, arguing that the creation of law and order in Morocco was in Germany's interest and the plan was likely to suck it into a quagmire costing the country blood and treasure.[131] Yet at some point in May he approved the *Panthersprung* – the Panther leap, named after the gunboat dispatched. For the second time in less than a decade, the Germans provoked a crisis by sea in Morocco.[132]

Renshon and Murray again claim that Germany was driven by status motivations and had little tangible in mind as they provoked the crisis. Renshon claims that Kiderlen-Wächter reveals Germany's "true motivations in writing, 'One must remind the French that Germany is still there,' that its 'position in the world depended on the outcome of the Morocco crisis,' and that 'its rights could not be trampled on.'"[133] The goals that it sought, he claims, were materially trivial, so it must have been after status. Murray claims that just by provoking the crisis, Germany improved its status; either France would return to the status

---

[127] GP XXIX, no. 10549.   [128] GP XXIX, no. 10572.
[129] GP XXIX, no. 10549.
[130] Kiderlen-Wächter. Alfred von.1925. *Der Staatsman und Mensch: Briefwechsel und Nachlass*, Vol. 2. Stuttgart: Deutsche Verlags-Anstalt, 128.
[131] GP XXIX, nos. 10543, 10548.
[132] Ibid, 122.   [133] Renshon, *Fighting for Status*, 204–205.

quo or offer compensation. Either way "it would affirm Germany's status as great power."[134]

This interpretation falls apart when we carefully consider German documents. The foreign minister's goal was to link existing German colonies in the west and east of the continent, what was known as the *Mittelafrika* strategy endorsed by many German colonialists.[135] Were Germany to obtain the French Congo, only the Belgian Congo, thought to be vulnerable, would remain in between German territory on the coasts.[136] Correspondence indicates Kiderlen-Wächter setting straight a National Liberal leader who visited him in July 1911 "to congratulate us for the securing of an annexation in Morocco. I had to make it clear to him that we really did not want to establish ourselves in Morocco. But the idiot just did not believe me."[137] This was the last chance, he emphasized, to "obtain something useful in Africa ... [L]ittle pieces of the Congo with minerals are not useful. We have to have territory up to the Belgian Congo so that we can connect it to East Africa."[138] He later noted that only one of the press articles speculating on his intentions accurately judged his goals.[139]

While Kiderlen-Wächter might have thought the final outcome after Germany backed down to be paltry, this is not the same as claiming that at least the foreign minister, the mastermind behind the Panthersprung, sought something other than status at the beginning. He aimed, as noted, for the whole French Congo. "Every other solution would mean a defeat for us," he proclaimed, and twice resigned in an effort to keep the government resolved.[140] The chancellor did not accept and persuaded him to stay. Renshon is therefore technically correct when he writes that "German leaders never had any interest in the territory that was purportedly the object of dispute."[141] Instead they sought to trade that against compensation elsewhere thought to be of more value. By missing this point, Renshon downplays the potential gains for Germany in the crisis, leading him to overstate the role of status.

However, in Germany's eyes, this was not the naked pursuit of egoistic interests but only fair. In speaking of compensation, the Germans were invoking fairness and reciprocity. If the France were

---

[134] Murray, "Recognition, Disrespect and the Struggle for Morocco," 142.
[135] Kiderlen-Wächter, *Der Staatsman und Mensch*, 127, 137.
[136] Smith, "*The Ideological Origins of Nazi Imperialism*," 133–136.
[137] Ibid, 123. [138] Ibid, 128ff. [139] Ibid, 139. [140] Ibid, 128ff.
[141] Renshon, *Fighting for Status*, 204.

to gain, Germany should as well. Kiderlen-Wächter wrote of obtaining an "equivalent" for Germany's removal of claims to influence in Morocco.[142] They were making a concession of great value to France, so they were deserving of an equally great sacrifice on France's part. Full control of Morocco was "such a great bite, that its compensation-bite would cost the French a hell of a piece of flesh from their body," wrote the foreign minister in marginalia of a memo.[143] It was "such a great service that that France must be convinced that it required a great service in return," Bethmann-Hollweg explained to the chancellor.[144] "Only when France is itself convinced of its obligation to compensate [Germany] will it enter into negotiations over our demands."[145] He wanted a "fair settlement with France, which would settle their differences over the Morocco question once for all."[146] Germany was "clearly entitled [to compensation]." It was "justified in asking for some colonial advantages," the foreign minister stressed.[147] The Kaiser wrote of what the French "should graciously grant us."[148]

Leaders stressed again, as they had in the first crisis, that France had come to terms with other powers but Germany had been excluded. Kiderlen-Wächter complained to the French ambassador to Germany that "France had made arrangements with England and Spain and even Italy to compensate them for their concurrence in French designs in Morocco. Germany, who had interests in Morocco, got nothing."[149] "Surely the acquisition of this enormous advantage was worth some considerable sacrifice on the part of France," he told the English ambassador. "Besides, other Powers interested in Morocco had been paid for leaving France alone. Why therefore should not Germany also receive compensation?"[150] Metternich told Lord Grey that if France wanted that Germany, like England, take a backset in Morocco they must offer a compensation equivalent in value with the great goal they were pursuing.[151] They used the same argument against the English. The Emperor complained during a May visit that England had struck deals with France and Russia without consulting Germany, which

---

[142] Ibid, 128ff.   [143] GP XXIX, no. 10572.
[144] GP XXIX, no. 10613.   [145] Ibid.
[146] *British Documents on the Origins of the War: The Agadir Crisis*, Vol. VII. London: His Majesty's Stationary Office, 1932, no. 410, hereafter BD VII.
[147] BD VII, no. 373.   [148] GP XXIX, no. 10600.
[149] BD VII, no. 392; DD, no. 455.   [150] BD VII, no. 424.
[151] GP XXIX, no. 10617.

would not put up with "unequal treatment."[152] England could not be allowed to "measure with two different rulers, one for France, another for Germany," the German ambassador told Lord Grey.[153]

The Germans also argued that the distribution of colonial territory was inequitable, not in keeping with Germany's position in the world. Grey wrote that the German ambassador "remarked that forty years ago Germany waged a successful war, since when she had attained her unity and developed enormously her force and power. In that time France, the vanquished country, had added greatly to her colonial possessions, and England had added hundreds of thousands of square miles to her vast Empire. Germany had merely received a few small portions practically of little value. If the matter were looked at impartially it was clear that Germany had a right to more, and if she received more, this would not mean the break-up of the British Empire."[154] Metternich argued that "no one could with justice dispute her receiving large concessions."[155] Germany wants "to have its share in dividing up the world," stressed Kiderlen-Wächter.[156] "One speaks here a lot of the balance of power," Metternich said to Grey, "but there is also a colonial balance. We do not understand it as France receiving everything and us nothing. I cannot admit that our claims are immoderate. One look at the map proves the opposite."[157]

Fairness claims might appear as an obvious pretext. However, the French and English actually agreed with Germans about both its right to compensation and a more equitable colonial balance. Before the Panthersprung, in the same breath as noting that Morocco would fall like a ripe fruit into French hands, the French ambassador to Germany admitted that his country "realized that Germany could not put up with this without compensation," mentioned "provisionally the possibility in the colonial area" and asked Germany to consider what it would regard as fair compensation.[158] In doing so, Cambon invoked an agreement like that negotiated with the British in 1904, the Entente Cordiale.[159] France could not make any territorial concessions in Morocco, but "[we] can look elsewhere."[160]

The English, who backed the French during the crisis, felt the same. Foreign Secretary Grey repeated Metternich's arguments, admitting

[152] GP XXIX, no. 10562.   [153] GP XXIX, no. 10617.   [154] BD VII, no. 388.
[155] BD VII, no. 395.   [156] DD, no. 366.   [157] GP XXIX, no. 10617.
[158] GP XXIX, no. 10575; also 10554.   [159] DD, no. 366.   [160] DD, no. 399.

that Germany "should concede to France the same position in Morocco as we had conceded, but she could not be expected to do this without some compensation. Germany's argument had always been that we had received compensation for conceding this position to France, and that as Germany also had interests in Morocco she should also receive something."[161] He telegrammed the English ambassador to France, "Neither France, nor we can reasonably expect to increase what we have and keep Germany who has much less out of everything."[162] "If one looks at a map of Africa and considers the large amount coloured British and coloured French," he wrote, "much larger each of them than all that Germany has, it is obvious that neither France nor we can put more of our own colour on the map without Germany getting some substantial addition to her share."[163] The German ambassador to England reported back to Berlin: "It is understood in the relevant circles here, that as a consequence of Agadir, our retreat will not be possible without satisfactory compensations."[164]

The Panther Pretext: Germany's Justification Goes Wrong

Where the Germans went wrong, quite literally, was in their justification of the *Panthersprung*. The country's leaders did not declare that its interests could not be overlooked and demand compensation or else. Instead they erected a pretext they believed would ethically justify their actions. This seems to indicate that they believed such a bald-faced declaration of Germany's egoistic interests was morally unacceptable to the international audience. Even self-righteous Germany recognized a broader shadow of morality. Extortion, though justified in German minds, needed a cloak. However, the justification was so transparently disingenuous that it actually exacerbated the crisis and undermined German diplomacy.

Kiderlen-Wächter reasoned: "If the French," he explained, "out of 'anxiety' for their compatriots, settle themselves at Fez, it is our right, too, to protect our compatriots in danger. We have larger German firms at Mogador and Agadir. German ships could go to those ports to protect the firms.... The importance of choosing those ports, the great distance of which from the Mediterranean should make it unlikely

---

[161] BD VII, no. 368.   [162] BD VII, no. 402.
[163] BD VII, no. 405.   [164] GP XXIX, no. 10615.

that England would raise objections, lies in the fact that they possess a very fertile hinterland, which ought to contain important mineral wealth as well."[165] Germany tried to insulate itself from accusations of opportunism and naked coercion through moral equivalence, by claiming that it was merely doing what France had done – protect its interests and people in the region.[166] Germany had a "natural right" and a "national duty" to do so, its ambassador to France declared.[167] The Germans claimed in their official notification that the troubles among the tribes that led the French into Fez had spread to the area near Agadir and a warship was sent to be ready in case it was necessary to secure subjects, protégés, and German interests.[168]

However, this pretext was extremely flimsy. As the British quickly noted, Agadir was a closed support so no German firms nor citizens should have been in the region at all.[169] Nicolson drolly noted, "I was unaware that any German or foreign subjected resided there or in its neighborhood."[170] Indeed, there had been no spontaneous call for protection from any German commercial interests; the government generated these after they dispatched the ship.[171] "So far" as the French foreign minister knew, "there were no disturbances or excitement" in Agadir.[172] The Germans then supplemented their original justification, claiming that the "German public could no longer bear that the imperial Government disinterests itself from Moroccan affairs at the moment where France and Spain appear to no longer comply with the Algeciras Act."[173] It did not help convince the entente when their official justification was immediately followed by a willingness to negotiate outstanding disagreements between France and Germany in the same text.[174]

The British could tell that German officials were being dishonest. Metternich was "extremely nervous during [the] delivery" of the German justification.[175] Upon being pressed, he admitted that there were no German citizens, only German interests in the region.[176] The French observed that the German ambassador was "embarrassed" to deliver a communication that the foreign minister "might not think

---

[165] GP XXIX, no. 10549. [166] DD, no. 444; BD VII, no. 339.
[167] GP XXIX, no. 10602. [168] GP XXIX, no. 10578.
[169] BD VII, nos. 339, 356. [170] BD VII, no. 339.
[171] BD VII, no. 356. [172] BD VII, no. 366.
[173] DD, no. 419; also GP XXIX, no. 10590; BD VII, nos. 340; 369.
[174] GP XXIX, no. 10579. [175] BD VII, no. 359. [176] BD VII, no. 388.

quite agreeable."[177] Even Kiderlen-Wächter was "naturally somewhat embarrassed and ill at ease."[178]

The obviously disingenuous pretext served only to generate distrust of German motives; the country might have been better off trying to openly extract concessions for the removal of its gunboat. Somewhat remarkably, the French bore the insult with equanimity, even though they did not buy the German argument.[179] This was less true of the English, who continued to dwell on the issue for the next two months, during which time the Germans made things worse by continually changing their story. Even the Kaiser changed his justification mid-meeting.[180] The hapless Metternich told Grey that there had been an attack on a German farm,[181] to which Grey responded, "I had understood that the dispatch of the ship had been due to apprehension as to what might happen, not to what had actually happened. Count Metternich remarked that he had not been told of it before." When told Germany would only intervene to save German lives, "I observed that I thought there were no Germans in this region, and that I supposed, therefore, the term German must mean German protected persons. Count Metternich said that he had no information on this point."[182] By August, German officials claimed that the Panther was meant to make it easier for French to accede to German demands![183] Grey sarcastically noted that the Germans should have asked the French ambassador beforehand if such a step would be helpful to him.

German behavior drew the British into the crisis in a way that the Germans had not anticipated. The breaking point for the English came when it heard of Germany's negotiating posture in Franco-German

---

[177] BD VII, no. 366.   [178] BD VII, no. 373.

[179] Kiderlen-Wächter observed in his first meeting with the French ambassador after the Panthersprung that he "expressed through his facial expressions and gestures unmistakable doubts about our interests and their endangerment" (GP XXIX, no. 10598). Yet the French foreign minister de Selves merely ribbed the German ambassador that he was "of the old school who salutes before fighting" (GP XXIX, no. 10586) and that "in a duel the adversaries began by saluting each other and not by one giving the other a sword thrust in the stomach, nor when one person desired a conversation with another did one generally begin by a blow with the fist" (BD VII, no. 366). After expressing his personal feeling of disappointment and slight, the French ambassador to Berlin quickly turned to picking up negotiations where they had left off (BD VII, no. 373).

[180] BD VII, no. 483.   [181] GP XXIX, no. 10618.
[182] BD VII, no. 417.   [183] BD VII, no. 518.

discussions. Kiderlen-Wächter told Cambon on July 15 that Germany would require the entire French Congo in return for relinquishing control of Morocco to France. The French ambassador, according to the German foreign minister, almost fell off his chair.[184] Not only did Germany not offer satisfactory counter-concessions, but the proposal would have cut off French access to the Western coast of Africa.[185] Germany's excessive demands seemed to indicate that they had no real desire to settle and therefore aimed to remain in southern Morocco, where they could build a German colonial presence.[186] The English and French suspected that the Germans were aiming at constructing a naval base there, even though there is no indication this was actually the case in German documents.[187]

Grey, however, indicated (to French annoyance) that he was not terribly concerned about German efforts to establish a naval base on the Atlantic coast of Morocco since the British navy could easily prevent it from fortifying the port.[188] Instead, the Foreign Secretary was outraged that Germany had not bothered to adequately consult England.[189] In other words, Germany was guilty of the same disregard and disrespect of which it was accusing France. Grey literally counted the days that the British cabinet response to the Panthersprung, in which the government declared that it could not be disinterested regarding any new settlement on Morocco,[190] went unanswered by the German government.[191]

The English thought a public warning was necessary, resulting in Lloyd George's famous Mansion House speech. The chancellor of the exchequer used the occasion of an annual address typically confined to economic matters to read from a prepared statement:

[It] is essential in the highest interests, not merely of this country, but of the world, that Britain should at all hazards maintain her place and her prestige amongst the Great Powers of the world.... I would make great sacrifices to preserve peace.... But if a situation were to be forced upon us in which peace could only be preserved by the surrender of the great and beneficent position Britain has won by centuries of heroism and achievement, by allowing Britain to be treated where her interests were vitally affected as if she were

---

[184] GP XXIX, no. 10607.   [185] BD VII, no. 392.
[186] GP XXIX, no. 10617; BD VII, no. 392; BD VII, no. 395.
[187] BD VII, nos. 395, 430.   [188] BD VII, nos. 397, 408.   [189] BD VII, no. 399.
[190] BD VII, no. 356; also no. 430.   [191] BD VII, no. 399.

of no account in the Cabinet of nations, then I say emphatically that peace at that price would be a humiliation intolerable for a great country like ours to endure.... [T]he peace of the world is much more likely to be secured if all nations realize fairly what the conditions of peace must be.[192]

Germany, although never mentioned explicitly by Lloyd George, had made the Moroccan issue into a matter of fairness and honor for England and introduced a third party to the crisis. The Mansion House speech, given its public nature, excited the press in both countries as well as France.

The Blame Game: Mutual Recrimination in Anglo-German Relations

Anglo-German relations during this period are marked by what one can only call a moral duel, in which each government tried to convince the other that it was to blame for exacerbating the crisis and complained that the other side's press was making unfair accusations. This, each side claimed, made it impossible for them to compromise. This was a crisis entirely moral in character, in which what was at stake was who was in the wrong. Yet this put the two countries on the brink of war.

   While the public aspect raised the stakes (see the next chapter), what is remarkable is the effort and energy each expended in trying to convince the other in private. Grey complained to Germany's ambassador that "Germany had opened the question in the worst possible way. After giving it to be understood that her interests were only commercial, she had gone to a port which was commercially closed. She had thus made it clear that commercial interests were only a pretext. Agadir happened also to be the port most suitable for a naval base. Germany had thus at the outset mobilised the whole of British public opinion, and if she had been in any doubt as to what our attitude would be she had by her own action removed that doubt, and made it certain that our interest would be engaged on the side of France. If Germany wished conversations to be easy, it was now for her, having charged the atmosphere with electricity, to do something to calm it."[193] What else, asked Grey, did they think was going to happen?[194] In other words,

---

[192] BD VII, no. 411.   [193] BD VII, no. 394; also no. 404.   [194] BD VII, no. 430.

the Germans started it, the key element in assigning blame in negative reciprocity. Grey was still stewing about it months later.[195]

For their part, the Germans were outraged at being accused of making excessive demands and at French and English reproaches of "marchandage" and "chantage" (haggling and blackmail).[196] Kiderlen-Wächter was offended by the insinuation that his demands were inflated and disingenuous.[197] The Germans argued that if the English wanted to inflame the situation, there was no better means than the speech given by Lloyd George, which they regarded as a threat.[198] The speech "came upon us like a thunderbolt,"[199] "aroused the animosity of the German press" and was to blame for the "ill-feeling" between the two countries.[200] German dignity would not allow them to compromise in that context.[201] Every time the Germans mentioned the Mansion House speech; however, the English noted that the Panthersprung came first.[202] In essence, the Germans started it. In response, the Kaiser asked why the British were so upset about "his sending a little ship with only two or three little pop guns on board to the coast of Morocco?"[203] What is one warship among friends?

As the crisis dragged on, each side complained that the other country's press was misrepresenting the situation and engaging in unfair criticism. Grey complained about the "extraordinary outburst of animosity against this country which has found almost daily expression in the columns of the German press for the last three months," which "appears to be an organized campaign to mislead public opinion in Germany for the purpose of prejudicing it against England and of exciting animosity in one country against the other."[204] The Germans also complained about the tone of the English and French press,[205] refusing responsibility for their own.[206] At one point the German foreign minister and the English ambassador had an extended conversation over whose press was most to blame, each referring to specific misleading articles on the other side. Herr von Kiderlen said: "When, I should like to know, has any English newspaper expressed regret

[195] BD VII, no. 529.   [196] BD VII, nonos. 406, 407.
[197] BD VII, no. 406; also GP XXIX, no. 10617.   [198] GP XXIX, no. 10623.
[199] BD VII, no. 518.   [200] BD VII, no. 661; also 483.
[201] BD VII, no. 438.   [202] BD VII, nos. 476, 518, 661, 658.
[203] BD VII, no. 476.   [204] BD VII, no. 657; also 661, 659.
[205] BD VII, nonos. 457, 555, 660.   [206] BD VII, no. 659.

for its false statements with regard to Germany?" To which I replied: 'When has any English newspaper published a false report of a speech by a German statesman, and then grossly abused him for what he did not say?'"[207] This was a battle of holier than thou. Both had a point.[208] In the following chapters, we will turn our attention to the domestic politics of the second Moroccan crisis in Germany and the internal effect of its unsatisfying resolution.

Surveys of the Russian Public

The Moroccan case studies give us reason to believe that what is often taken for status-seeking is better understood as fairness-seeking of a particular sort, driven by appraisal respect and the demand for equity. However, case studies have weaknesses in terms of generalizability, causal identification, and measurement. Therefore, I supplement the historical analysis with two survey experiments conducted on a sample of the Russian public. Are the status or fairness concerns of ordinary people relevant? I believe so for two reasons. First, we have grounds to believe, based on the instrumental nature of some of the German rhetoric seen earlier that even in semi-authoritarian states, fairness frames are chosen so as to resonate with audiences both domestic and international. Second, even if mass publics were entirely powerless, they can still provide insight into the motivations of elites. If only as passive observers regurgitating state propaganda, ordinary Russians are still a mirror of their government's (official) aspirations, particularly considering Russia's highly state-controlled news media. The status immobility models with which I am engaging also see leaders as performing before an audience whose desires and aspirations both constrain and reflect elite behavior.

In early March 2020, I surveyed respondents recruited through the survey firm Anketolog, chosen to create a sample similar to the general population in terms of age, gender, and region of residence. The Russian public is an ideal place to gauge status-seeking considering that it is frequently maintained that Russian foreign policy behavior historically and in recent years, particularly under President Putin, is driven by status concerns. Forsberg writes, "Status and honor have often been regarded as motivations for Russia either to go to war, or

[207] BD VII, no. 661.   [208] BD VII, no. 602.

to cooperate with the Western partners and also explain why their relationships were difficult. Prominent scholars claim that the key problem in the mutual relationships is not about security, but rather about how Russia receives the status and respect from the West that she expects."[209] Urnov claims, "The expression 'greatpowerness' ('velikoderzhavnost') denotes one of the most important components of Russian self-consciousness: a belief that Russia is or has to be a great power."[210] Clunan makes a more nuanced argument, maintaining that the importance of status was contested in post-Soviet domestic politics; the country eventually "settled on a statist national identity that focused on retaining Russia's historical status as a Western great power and hegemon in the former Soviet Union."[211] Larson and Chevenko attribute recent Russian assertiveness to the same status immobility frustrations highlighted in the models I critique as indistinguishable from fairness, making it an ideal case: "When a state loses status, the emotions experienced depend on the perceived cause of this loss. When a state perceives that others are responsible for its loss, it shows anger. The belief that others have *unjustly* used their power to deny the state its appropriate position arouses vengefulness."[212]

I conducted two separate survey experiments, each on a different sample, revolving around the question of Russian participation in the G8, from which Russia was uninvited in 2014 following the annexation of the Crimea (returning it to the G7). Membership in exclusive institutions, like the United Nations Security Council, are considered by theorists as modern-day status symbols.[213] Paul and Shankar argue that rising powers' status ambitions can be accommodated through membership in "elite clubs."[214] Larson et al. mention the G8 explicitly

[209] Forsberg, Tuomas. 2014. "Status Conflicts between Russia and the West: Perceptions and Emotional Biases." *Communist and Post-Communist Studies* 47(3–4): 323.

[210] Urnov, Mark. 2014. "'Greatpowerness' as the Key Element of Russian Self-Consciousness under Erosion." *Communist and Post-Communist Studies* 47(3–4): 305.

[211] Clunan, "Historical Aspirations."

[212] Larson and Shevchenko, "Status Seekers," 269.

[213] Larson et al., "Status and World Order."

[214] Paul, T. V. and Mahesh Shankar. 2014. "Status Accommodation through Institutional Means: India's Rise and the Global Order." In *Status in World Politics*. Cambridge: Cambridge University Press, 176.

and Naylor uses it as an example of a "status group."[215] Participating in the G8 can be considered an indication of respect and socially recognized rank. Based on my theoretical argument and the findings of the German case, we have reason to believe, however, that any dissatisfaction arising from exclusion from the G8 is fairness based rather than status based. The full translations and instrumentation are included in Online Appendix 3.

Survey Experiment #1: In da Club

In the first survey experiment presented here (using Russian sample #2, see Online Appendix 3.1 for demographic data, N = 962), respondents were introduced to the question of Russian involvement with the G8 but randomized into two different treatments. The first stressed Russia's deliberate exclusion and highlighted the status aspects of the institutions, whereas the second downplayed those status aspects. The treatments were as follows:

Since 2014, Russia has not been allowed to participate in the G8, a prestigious and influential association of the world's leading powers (the United States, Britain, France, Japan, Germany, Italy and Canada), whose goal is to coordinate policy lines in accordance with the common interests of the member countries of the group. Meetings of the group attract wide media attention and demonstrate membership in an elite club of the world's leading countries.

The second treatment downplayed those aspects:

Since 2014, Russia has not participated in the G8, an association of countries (the United States, Britain, France, Japan, Germany, Italy, and Canada) whose goal is to agree on policy lines in accordance with the common interests of the member countries of the group. Russian authorities have stated that participation in this informal and purely deliberative group is of no particular importance to them.[216]

---

[215] Naylor, *Social Closure and International Society*; Larson et al., "Status and World Order."

[216] I recognize that by stressing both the publicity and prestige of the organization, I am using something of a "double-barreled" status treatment. My purpose is not to show which element of status-seeking matters to respondents but rather to assess whether this is really status-seeking at all.

Then, respondents were randomized into three additional groups: subjects received either no further information or one of two supplemental statements priming fairness in different ways. Of these two supplemental statements, one emphasized the objective fairness of Russia's non-participation or exclusion:

Although frustrating to many Russians, Russia's exit is objectively consistent with the country's actual influence in the world. Membership in the G8 is largely based on the size of the members' economies and Russia is not one of the world's eight largest economies by most measures. No country with a gross domestic product smaller than Russia is included in the organization.

If respondents care about fairness in an objective manner, this treatment should lead to greater dissatisfaction. My biased fairness argument, however, expects that respondents will not respond to such a treatment. So long as Russia is not a part of the group, this will be perceived as unfair. This is disadvantageous inequity.

The second supplemental treatment instead stressed the lack of fairness of Russia's "exit" given its rank, which according to status inconsistency arguments should be more likely to invoke fairness concerns and greater dissatisfaction.

Russia's exit is not consistent with its real influence in the world as a permanent member of the United Nations Security Council with a history as a great power and outstanding cultural achievements.

To avoid mentioning Russia's expulsion from the G8 for those who received the non-participation treatment, in these additional treatments I utilize the neutral Russian term "exit" (Выход). There is actually no direct translation of the term "exclusion" in Russian.

Having randomized respondents into one of eight conditions in this 2 × 4 survey experimental design, I then presented all respondents with three questions: How satisfied they were with the state of affairs, whether the current membership of the organization was fair, and how concerned they were that "Russia does not rank in the eyes of the world as among a select group of great countries." If pure status concerns are driving attitudes, respondents primed with the first treatment should indicate greater dissatisfaction and do so as a function of concern about Russian status rather than fairness. This is the advantage of the survey method: I can directly measure respondent motivations.

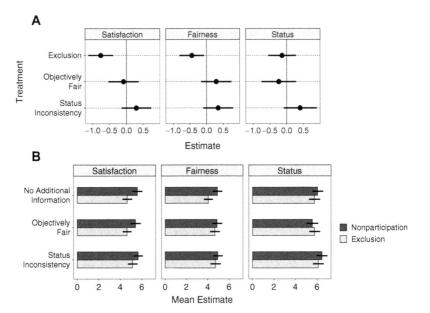

Figure 6.1 *G8 vignette experiment results.* In (A), OLS estimates of the effect of treatment on the DVs with 95% confidence intervals. The DVs (listed at the top of each panel) include levels of satisfaction with the state of affairs, fairness of the current G8 membership, and concerns about Russia's status in the world. The "Exclusion" estimate uses the non-participation assignment as the baseline. The "Objectively Fair" and "Status Inconsistency" estimates use the no additional information condition as the baseline, that is, no further text beyond the exclusion/non-participation manipulation. In (B), mean estimates for each treatment condition with 95% confidence intervals, which provide a sense of the substantive effect sizes.

Figure 6.1A displays the effects of the treatments on the three DVs, estimated via ordinary least squares regression, and Figure 6.1B plots the mean estimates for each condition, which provides a sense of the substantive effect sizes.[217] Only deliberate exclusion (relative to non-participation) significantly affects respondents' attitudes. However, and crucially, respondents experience exclusion as lacking in fairness.

Even if fairness matters to the respondents, however, they are not judging equity objectively, as indicated by the lack of any effect of the

---

[217] Online Appendix 3.3 provides the full regression table and demonstrates that the results are robust to inclusion of control variables.

objective fairness treatment. As suggested by inequity aversion models of fairness, if one is falling relatively behind, outcomes are judged unfair.

Overall, however, Russian respondents do have status concerns, as indicated by the mean score on the status scale. These simply are not affected by the exclusion or other treatments. However, as I have noted, what status entails might be more or less exclusive. This survey does not attend to that question, which I take up in a second experiment.

Survey Experiment #2: Design a Group of X

The above mentioned results provide evidence that Russian exclusion from the G8 generates concerns about fairness more than status. However, inequity aversion arguments suggest that provided Russia is included, respondents will not begrudge the inclusion of others. As argued previously, this is the best way to distinguish pure status-seeking, which aims at maximum exclusivity, from fairness, even if the latter is myopic and asymmetrical. My second survey experiment directly examines this phenomenon using Russian sample #1 (N = 1249), whose demographics are presented in Online Appendix 1. Online Appendix 3.4 provides the original Russian and English translations for these prompts.

All subjects again received information about Russian exclusion from the G8, specifying that the basis of membership was economic with an achievement-based equity frame:

Russia has been excluded since 2014 from the G8. Membership is based primarily on the size of countries' economies, but other prominent countries with large economies, like China, have also been excluded and there are different ways of measuring economic activity.

All respondents were then asked to "design your own organization of this type in which you decide both the size of the organization and the specific members." They were also told to "consider the following information about 15 countries' economies and please categorize them as inside or outside of your preferred organization," with a minimum of four countries but no maximum.

However, subjects were randomly assigned one of two sets of economic data about the same fifteen countries – the United States, China, Japan, Germany, India, France, the United Kingdom, Italy, Brazil, Canada, Russia, South Korea, Spain, Mexico, and Indonesia. In the first condition, subjects were assigned aggregate GDP figures, "a measure of the total value of economic activity in the country in a year calculated in US dollars, which is how international organizations generally calculate this number." In the second condition, subjects were instead given cost-adjusted GDP figures, namely, figures that take "into account the cost of living in each country so that, for instance, China's GDP is larger than the United States." These were based on realistic figures at the time of the survey. In both conditions, countries were listed from the largest economy to the smallest by their assigned economic figures, and subjects were asked to drag icons with country flags into a box representing their institution, with a minimum of four countries included.

An objective fairness argument would expect that the likelihood of inclusion into the Group of X will reflect the objective size of the economies, which vary across the two treatments. Russia will be much more likely to be included in the adjusted GDP condition than the aggregate GDP condition and considerably less likely to be included than the countries with larger economies in both treatments. A pure status motivation would be evident in preferences that Russia be included regardless of the treatment, with a preference for very few other countries so as to make the organization as exclusive as possible. My biased fairness argument also expects that subjects not only will tend to include Russia in their organization but will also apply equity considerations to other countries, content to admit others into their organization based on economic size.

The results indicate support for both the biased and the objective fairness arguments. Figure 6.2 ranks all countries by the number of times they were included in the Group of X by treatment condition, with the objective ranking for each treatment in parentheses next to the name of the nation. While Russia ranks only eleventh in aggregate GDP and sixth in adjusted GDP, it is the country most included in both treatments. As found in behavioral economics, evaluations of fairness are biased toward oneself.

Nevertheless, there is a large and significant effect of the treatment on Russian inclusion. Figure 6.3 displays logistic regression results for the effect of the adjusted GDP condition (holding the aggregate GDP condition as the baseline) on subjects' inclusion of each country. Subjects in the adjusted GDP condition are approximately 2.25 times more likely to include Russia in their organization than subjects in the aggregate GDP condition ($p < .001$). Said differently, 93% of

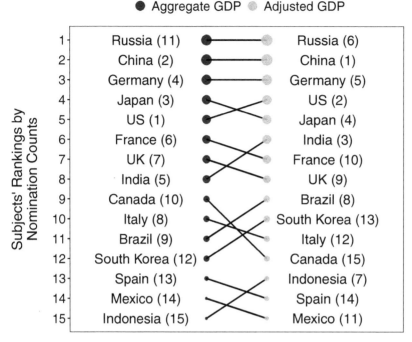

Figure 6.2 *Design-a-GX results.* Ranks of the total number of times a country is included in an organization according to treatment condition (i.e., GDP vs. cost-adjusted GDP). Countries in each condition are ranked by total number of nominations received, and dots are sized according to that number of nominations. Lines indicate the similarity or differences in country inclusion according to condition. Numbers in parentheses indicate the actual rank of that country according to the country's GDP or cost-adjusted GDP, respectively.

subjects who are told that Russia has the sixth largest GDP in the world include it in the Group of X of their choice, but this drops to 84% among those told that Russia ranks eleventh. This result, which is the largest effect of the treatment on any country's inclusion, is evidence of an objective fairness effect and is remarkable from a status point of view.

The treatments have an effect on the inclusion of other countries, as well. Figure 6.3 shows respondents are more likely to include countries as they move up the economic hierarchy, namely, India ($p < .001$), Indonesia ($p < .01$), and China ($p < .05$). Similarly, subjects

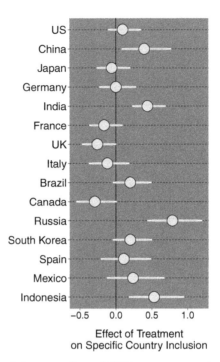

Figure 6.3 *Effect of the cost-adjusted GDP treatment on inclusion of specific countries, using the GDP condition as the baseline and estimated via logistic regression.* Countries listed in order of GDP size.

are less likely to include states as they move down the economic hierarchy, though these effects are less pronounced and only significant at the p < .10$ level (e.g., Canada, p = .059; United Kingdom, p = .053). Of course, beyond mere fairness considerations, geopolitical alignments and historical antagonisms matter as well, evidenced by the low ranking of the United States relative to GDP calculations of any kind. Nonetheless, consistent with inequity aversion models of fairness, Russians tend to include themselves and, once this is assured, bring in those more deserving.

Finally, in the first experiment, Russians reported non-trivial concerns about Russian status. Collapsing responses across experimental conditions to arrive at an observational measure, subjects in the first experiment reported a mean status concern of 5.98 (95% CI [5.77, 6.18]) on a ten-point scale. However, the findings from the current experiment suggest that this result requires contextualization.

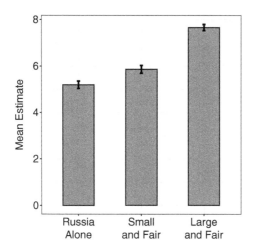

Figure 6.4 *Mean satisfaction with various organizational arrangements.*

Specifically, I asked respondents to report their satisfaction with the following three outcomes with respect to the G8, gathered on ten-point scales:

- Russia added back into the organization with no other new members (Russia alone).
- Russia added back into the organization as well as a number of powerful others like China so that the organization truly represents international influence but is larger than eight members (small and fair).
- Russia added back into the organization as well as a number of powerful others like China but others should be excluded who are less powerful so the organization remains the same size of eight (large and fair).

Figure 6.4 displays the descriptive responses to these questions. The outcome highest in exclusivity, "Russia alone," receives the lowest satisfaction scores. By far, respondents prefer the "large and fair" outcome, by almost three points on the ten-point scale. Even compared to the "small and fair" outcome, the most inclusive option scores almost two points higher on average. As we found in the sorting exercise mentioned previously, so long as Russia plays a part, Russians do not insist on exclusivity. Respondents first ensure that Russia is included in the organization, then add in countries largely based on equity considerations, with larger economies more likely to be included.

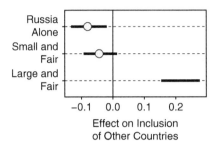

Figure 6.5 *Arrangement satisfaction levels on number of countries included.* Subjects who are more satisfied with the addition of Russia alone to the organization included fewer countries in their own organizational design. Subjects who prefer larger and fairer criteria for country inclusion included more countries in their organizational design. Estimates from OLS regressions with number of countries included by each subject as the DV.

To add inferential precision to these descriptive findings, Figure 6.5 plots OLS estimates of the effect of these preferences on the number of countries included in each participant's organization, controlling for treatment group and demographic factors.[218] Consistent with their beliefs, respondents more satisfied with "Russia alone" included fewer countries. Those more satisfied with "large and fair" outcomes included more countries in their organization.

Since this survey was conducted, Russia has invaded a sovereign country. Does the Ukraine conflict make these findings irrelevant? To the contrary, I would argue, when we consider how President Vladimir Putin justified the attack, which shows again the shadow of morality. He, like all other politicians, appears to have felt the need to justify Russian actions in a way that is consistent with universal moral principles. In this particular case, it is again the principle of fairness, albeit a likely biased application as I would expect. As the Russian leader announced Russian recognition of the independence of eastern Ukrainian provinces and forces began their assault on the country, Putin morally condemned NATO, blaming it for provoking the conflict through its unwillingness to take into account Russian needs and legitimate interests. NATO acted excessively egoistically. In his words, "the attempts to use us in their own interests never ceased …"; the West

---

[218] Online Appendix 3.5 displays the full regression results.

"pushed through decisions that suited only themselves." In locating the justification for Russian action in NATO expansion, Putin explicitly disavows an amoral conception of international politics as a way of morally judging the West: "To reiterate, they have deceived us or, to put it simply, they have played us. Sure, one often hears that politics is a dirty business. It could be, but it shouldn't be as dirty as it is now, not to such an extent. This type of con-artist behaviour is contrary not only to the principles of international relations but also and above all to the generally accepted norms of morality and ethics. Where is justice and truth here? Just lies and hypocrisy all around." Unsurprisingly for my dual-process moral framework, Putin simultaneously makes a commitment to traditional, binding values: "[T]hey sought to destroy our traditional values and force on us their false values that would erode us, our people from within, the attitudes they have been aggressively imposing on their countries, attitudes that are directly leading to degradation and degeneration, because they are contrary to human nature."[219] We have every reason not to take these statements at face value. Yet, this still begs the question as to why they had to be made at all.

---

[219] For quotes, see the transcript: "Putin Orders 'Special Military Operation' for Ukraine," *Bloomberg News* (February 24, 2022).

7 | Barking Dogs and Beating Drums
Nationalism as Moral Revolution
in German Foreign Policy

Status-seeking is not the only explanation for Germany's assertive foreign policy during the reign of Wilhelm II. Arguably more prominent, especially in the political science literature, are accounts rooted in the domestic politics of the country at the time, captured under the broad label of "social imperialism." In these *Primat der Innenpolitik* (primacy of domestic politics) arguments, German assertiveness abroad, whether it be the construction of a powerful navy or the pursuit of colonial possessions, were efforts to cover the ever widening cracks in a rapidly changing society. *Weltpolitik* was an attempt to deal with Germany's social problem at home, the lack of unity and solidarity not only between elites and the mass public but also among the elites themselves. Eley identifies the "central contradiction of Wilhelmine politics: the persistence of a state structure which guaranteed the historic privileges of a landowning interest, at a time when the capitalist transformation of German society, the diminishing role of agriculture in the economy and the antagonism of capital and labour were all demanding an adaptation of that state to entirely novel situations."[1]

The social imperialist argument maintains that foreign policy was the way by which elites tried to square this circle, distracting the masses away from their material, class interests by emphasizing the importance of national cohesion, solidarity, and loyalty to a young nation pursuing its destiny in international relations. The more that ordinary citizens thought of themselves as Germans rather than workers or any other narrow section of German society, the safer elite prerogatives. Crudely stated, imperialism was the political response of threatened elites to domestic class conflict.[2] Weltpolitik

---

[1] Eley, Geoff. 1991. *Reshaping the German Right: Radical Nationalism and Political Change after Bismarck.* Ann Arbor: University of Michigan Press, 8.
[2] Smith, 1986. *The Ideological Origins of Nazi Imperialism,* 6.

was the "red herring of the ruling classes," an "enterprise of national demagogy."[3] To this end, the government used national-istic *Verbände* (leagues) like the Pan-German League (PGL),instead of political parties, to mobilize public opinion behind foreign policy enterprises of national assertiveness outside of the formal political process. Bergahn writes, for instance, that naval construction was "to act as a focus for divergent social forces which the government hoped to bribe into a conservative *Sammlung* (collection or asso-ciation) against the 'Revolution'."[4] Whereas status-seeking accounts diagnose Wilhelmine Germany with a surfeit of national egoism, social imperialist accounts see the problem as excessively egoistic elites. Morality, in any case, is nowhere to be seen.

While a lens on domestic politics is absolutely necessary to account for the direction of German foreign policy during the Wilhelmine period, the social imperialist and logrolling arguments have severe limitations, particularly in their overly materialist and simplistic, uni-directional, top-down account of politics. In reality, efforts to create national solidarity in a fractured German society were from the begin-ning a bottom-up process in German politics spearheaded by true-believing elements of German society outside of upper elite circles.[5] Nationalist groups, the most important being the PGL, were evange-lists of a new binding morality that reordered and reconfigured ethical priorities, placing loyalty to the German nation at the top, even if it came at the expense of deference to the Kaiser's authority. As argued, binding morality is so common as to be universal, yet our instincts toward ingroup identification can take any number of socially con-structed shapes. The nationalist Verbände was trying to create some-thing that social imperialist accounts, arguing backward in time and presuming the new moral terrain constituted by this very movement, assume was already in existence. This was a moral revolution in Germany with profound consequences, generating dynamics familiar to modern-day foreign policy but which at the time were without prec-edent. However, when one looks at the Wilhelmine period, one cannot avoid the importance of morality.

[3] Blackbourn, David. 1987. *Populists and Patricians: Essays in Modern German History*. London: Allen & Unwin, 221.
[4] Berghahn, Volker. 1973. *Germany and the Approach of War*. New York: St. Martins, 26.
[5] Smith, *The Ideological Origins of Nazi Imperialism*, 9.

In social imperialist accounts, nationalist "myths of empire" were part of an effort to rally the country around the flag, one that culminated in the outbreak of the Great War. Nationalist groups were the ultimate sorcerer's apprentices, created to undergird the traditional institutions of the Reich but ultimately proving uncontrollable. Snyder describes a process of "ideological blowback," in which the very ideas instrumentalized to support the regime come back to haunt them.[6] In this view, "The cracks in the fabric could only be papered over by a fresh diversionary emphasis on foreign affairs, and this 'social-imperialism' mechanism led to the ultimate gamble of July 1914."[7]

However, nationalist ideas, rather than bolstering the regime, had for over a century been seen as threats to conservative forces in that they presumed that the emperor's and other elites' right to rule rested in their service to the nation's people. A uniquely German nationalism arose not through an act of elite manipulation but, as scholars have long maintained, out of ideological tendencies in nineteenth-century German romanticism articulated before Germany was even unified. While it would be preposterous to assert that elites never made instrumental use of nationalist ideology to preserve traditional hierarchies in German society, it is equally fatuous to assert that the aggressive German foreign policy of the Wilhelmine period was not based on fundamentally new moral ideas that had a force of their own.

For German nationalists, the divisions within German society that emerged in the late nineteenth century were symptoms of a moral crisis. In order for the nation to assert itself in a dangerous world, it was necessary that all Germans, from the lowly factory worker up to the Kaiser, dedicate themselves to the national cause in the field of foreign affairs and beat the national drum. Class, religious, and regional cleavages all inhibited the creation of such unity. Unlike the proponents of German unification during the revolution of 1848, radical nationalists like the Pan-Germans were anti-democratic and therefore unsympathetic to socialist and liberal demands for greater reform. The latter all indicated narrower, individually selfish concerns indicative of a lack of national feeling and deserving of moral contempt. This anti-liberal sentiment made them part of the political right in Germany.

---

[6] Snyder, Jack. 1991. *Myths of Empire*. Ithaca: Cornell University Press.
[7] Eley, *Reshaping the German Right*, 7.

However, nationalist ideas were also highly subversive in that they located the monarch's legitimacy in his service to the people. Frustrated with the lack of resolve and determination in post-Bismarckian foreign policy, they increasingly questioned the emperor's authority. This led to something very new in Germany: moral condemnation of leaders for being insufficiently committed to the nation's interest and welfare. This was moral condemnation *internal* to the state based on binding morality. As argued previously, a lack of resolve and determination is taken to be, in a dangerous world, a moral failing. Loyalty to the German nation required nationalists to openly criticize Wilhelm II and his ministers in a way that the German right never had. This culminated in the formation of a "national opposition," long thought to be a contradiction in terms, which was in essence a severing and reordering of the binding moral foundations of obedience and loyalty. The disappointment following the outcome of the second Moroccan crisis was a decisive step in this process.

Even this semi-authoritarian regime had to concern itself with public opinion and accusations of weakness from nationalist pressure groups. Wilhelmine elites tried at times to harness and direct this national energy for their benefit, but they did not create it. They were more opportunistic than instrumental. The German foreign minister spoke of letting the dogs bark to suit the government's purposes, but he had not started them up and had no real control over how long they would howl.

The dynamics seen in Germany in the early 1900s are familiar to international relations scholars. They underlie many rationalist models such as modern theories of audience costs. Governments can feel compelled to undertake bellicose foreign policy behavior, whether it be the threat or use of violence, so as not to appear irresolute in front of their domestic audiences[8] (and, at least theoretically, use such knowledge on the part of others to more credible signal resolve, although this is highly disputed).[9] I argue that this literature misses two important substantive elements embedded in its own arguments. First, such dynamics are only possible when the public believes it has the right to criticize authority and when it feels it has a moral investment in

---

[8] Snyder, Jack, and Erica D. Borghard. 2011. "The Cost of Empty Threats: A Penny, Not a Pound." *American Political Science Review* 105(3): 437–456.
[9] Fearon, "Domestic Political Audiences."

the fate of the nation. If there is no national feeling, then there can be no national betrayal. In other words, audience models rely on an implicit, ethical foundation. Second, disapproval of weakness is an act of *moral* condemnation. The shadow of morality, this time the specter of domestic ethical censure, is again everywhere. The "inconsistency costs" that leaders pay, or anticipate, in crises if they do not stand firm are the attribution of moral failing.[10]

In the following sections, I briefly lay out the central claims of social imperialist arguments and how they miss the ways in which nationalist ideas had historically threatened, rather than bolstered, the *ancien régime* that German elites are thought to have so desperately wanted to save. I then explore the content of those ideas showing that German nationalism was the articulation of a new set of moral foundations with profound implications for foreign policy. I rely heavily on the views of the PGL, the most important voice of German nationals and ideological innovator in the Wilhelmine period, and in particular a book by its leader, Heinrich Class, entitled *Wenn ich der Kaiser wäre* (If I were the Kaiser), published under a pseudonym given its pointed criticism of the emperor.[11] These new moral foundations put the nationalists on a collision course with the emperor. An investigation of the domestic politics of the second Moroccan crisis shows how the government tried to harness the power of the nationalists, only to make the situation worse by not demonstrating the moral attributes of resolve, determination, and will venerated by these binding moralists. This culminated in the creation of a national opposition eager to hold the government's feet to the flame on matters of foreign policy, unburdened any longer by the traditional need for deference to the government, just before the Great War broke out.

A final section tests the microfoundations of my claim that resolve and determination are considered virtues with moral connotations, particularly on the part of those who hold beliefs in a dangerous world. A survey experiment on the American public indicates that the four virtues of being disciplined and hardworking, strong-willed

[10] Kertzer, Joshua D., and Ryan Brutger. 2016. "Decomposing Audience Costs: Bringing the Audience Back into Audience Cost Theory." *American Journal of Political Science* 60(1): 234–249.

[11] Class, Heinrich. 1912. *Wenn ich der Kaiser wäre: Politische Wahrheiten und Notwendigkeiten*. Leipzig: Dieterichschen Verlagsbuchhandlung.

and determined, tough and strong, and persistent and resolute – which are generally understood as indicators of "competence" rather than morality – are judged as ethical traits by those who have a more threatening view of the social environment. Respondents as a whole think of these as particularly virtuous traits for leaders as compared to ordinary people. In other words, we hold our leaders to ethical standards judged by difficult benchmarks than we apply to our peers. This provides a moral microfoundation both for historical accounts like the second Moroccan crisis, in which German nationalists morally condemned government officials not only for their lack of resolution and for more general audience models premised on "inconsistency costs."

From Staatsnation to Nationalstaat

The year 1890 saw not only Bismarck's departure but also the expiration of the ban on the Social Democrat Party in Germany. Political participation in elections was increasing dramatically, rising from just about 50% in Bismarck's time to 85% in the 1907 and 1912 Reichstag elections.[12] "[T]he masses have come of age (through elementary schooling, mass conscription, universal suffrage and the cheap oil lamp)," wrote an observer at the time.[13] "The challenge of mobilizing previously unenfranchised or politically passive social groups was *the* central dilemma facing all parties that were trying to adapt to a new political age."[14] This posed a particular problem for political conservatives: Prussian elites benefitted from a restrictive franchise in regional elections, which systematically depressed the influence of unpropertied Prussian voters and translated into underrepresentation of their voices in the upper house of the German parliament, the Bundesrat, in which Prussia had the largest say. Large industrialists, however, also feared growing working-class mobilization since any new social benefits would come at the expense of their bottom line, not to mention the threat of expropriation in the event of revolution.

Denied any longer a direct ban on working-class participation, these "parties of order" (as Bismarck had called them) had to find new tools

---

[12] Blackbourn, *Populists and Patricians*, 222–223.   [13] Ibid, 224.
[14] Retallack, James. 2006. *The German Right, 1860–1920: Political Limits of the Authoritarian Imagination.* Toronto: University of Toronto Press, 8.

of political neutralization. "As classic defenders of throne and altar, politically powerful members of the Right hoped that their ranks would be supplemented in number, but not supplanted in influence, by lower-middle-class and even working-class recruits. They attempted to reconcile mass infusion and political exclusivity."[15] The solution, goes the argument, was a shift from "repressive to propagandist anti-socialism" in which nationalism and assertive foreign policy would distract away from social, political, and economic inequality and unify classes behind a common purpose.[16]

Others in this tradition focus more on the intra-elite log-rolling made necessary by the conflicting material demands of different privileged groups. A naval program that economically benefited the large industrialists, for instance, required significant financial outlays that necessitated a reform of the German taxation system. The most obvious untapped resource was the agricultural estates of the Prussian elites, the Junker, whose protectionist preferences kept food prices high for workers, requiring in turn higher wages from industrial producers. The government's response was to give all elite sections what they wanted the most. As Kehr writes, "for industry the fleet, Weltpolitik and expansion, for the agrarians the tariffs and the upolding of the social supremacy of the Conservatives."[17] Even so, such a logroll also needed a public rationale, provided by the "myths of empire." Germany was encircled by hostile foreign adversaries seeking to deny the country its rightful place in the sun and its ability to secure its economic future through the acquisition of valuable colonial territories, lands that would also contribute to the nation's security.[18]

These accounts are Marxist in origin, explaining Germany's aggressive foreign policy as the inevitable outgrowth of internal contradictions in capitalism. Kehr's account became the "cornerstone of Marxist-Leninist historiography."[19] Chickering notes the extensive use of passive voice in this literature; monopoly capitalism is assumed to have a will of its own, consistent with the structural

---

[15] Ibid, 6.   [16] Eley, *Reshaping the German Right*, 166.
[17] Kehr, Eckhart. 1975. *Battleship Building and Party Politics in Germany, 1894–1901*. Chicago: University of Chicago Press.
[18] Snyder, *Myths of Empire*.
[19] Chickering, Roger. 1984. *We Men Who Feel Most German: A Cultural Study of the Pan-German League, 1886–1914*. London: Allen & Unwin, 11.

and teleological nature of capitalism.[20] Nor is there much documentary evidence suggesting a conscious effort at manipulation of the masses in service of narrow, material interests.[21] Moreover, those who embrace nationalist propaganda are seen as hopeless tools of powerful elites against whom they are powerless.[22] "Tied up with this is a tendency to concentrate far too much on the manipulative genius of the politicians at the top."[23]

When we consider the historical context in which the social imperialist argument is applied, a number of obvious problems stand out. Germany was a very young nation, unified only in 1870 across numerous cleavages, the most important of which at the time was confessional. The structure of the empire was highly decentralized and encompassed not only numerous diverse states but also a number of different kingdoms. Germany had not just an emperor; it had a number of other sovereigns such as the Bavarian and Saxon kings who maintained significant autonomy in their realms. There simply was no widespread feeling of nationalism on which to draw. Even for an account like that offered in this book, which regards binding morality as an intuitively natural ethical impulse based on human evolution, it must be recognized that nationalism could not be created out of whole cloth overnight.

More importantly, national consciousness was long considered a threat to the legitimist basis of the German emperor and his Prussian forebearers. Historically, in Germany as in other places, nationalism was not a conservative force but rather a progressive and liberal one in that it located sovereignty in the people rather than the monarch. Bismarck initially rose to prominence on the basis of a speech he made in the Prussian Landtag that explicitly denigrated the portrayal of German resistance to the Napoleonic invasion as an indication of a spontaneous surge in German national feeling. It was only in the face of significant resistance (and ridicule) from elements of the ancien régime that the Iron Chancellor had used the promise of universal male suffrage to rally allies for the creation of a new German nation and empire during the wars of unification.[24]

---

[20] Ibid, 10.   [21] Smith, *The Ideological Origins of Nazi Imperialism*, 7.

[22] Eley, *Reshaping the German Right*, 11, 41; Blackbourn, *Populists and Patricians*, 222.

[23] Eley, *Reshaping the German Right*, 207.

[24] See my discussion in chapters 4 and 5 of Brian C. Rathbun. 2019. *Reasoning of State: Rationality, Realists and Romantics in International Relations*. Cambridge: Cambridge University Press.

Bismarck pragmatically sought to recruit those nationalists who had unsuccessfully tried to unite Germany in 1848 behind his cause, but he was never a real nationalist. German nationalism was historically anti-absolutist. Bismarck's conception of the nation was as identical to the state, a *Staatsnation* (state nation), rather than a culturally and ethnically defined people. The Kaiser ruled over subjects in a defined territorial space.[25] Wilhelm II's own conception of the nation was predicated on dynastic loyalty. He was the "symbol of the nation and of the imperial monarchy by the grace of God."[26] The nation was him.

Where the traditional conservative elites saw a *Staatsnation*, German nationalists sought to create a *Nationalstaat* (national state), one defined by, and which was comprised of, the German *Volk*, which at the end of the nineteenth century was understood in cultural and linguistic terms. As Hasse, an early Pan-German leader, explained it: "[T]he only thing that possesses stability in the flux of a thousand years of development is the Volk…. States, as conglomerations of ethnic groups, come and go; and even more transitory are political constitutions and social conditions."[27] Political perfection was an identity between Volk and Staat. For this reason, German nationalists were preoccupied with the fate of Germans abroad, while Bismarck and his peers were indifferent. "[T]he nation comprehended people who spoke German and carried German culture everywhere in the world…. The official nationalism seemed to do violence to the most compelling of all symbols of national unity. Millions of people whose first language was German lived outside Imperial Germany."[28]

The national feeling ostensibly created and manipulated by powerful conservative elites to manage an unruly mass public actually emerged out of ideological currents in nineteenth-century Germany, particularly the Counterenlightenment tradition of German romanticists such as Herder and Moeser. It was bottom-up rather than top-down. As Mosse explains, "[T]o the German thinkers ever since the birth of German romanticism in the late eighteenth century, 'Volk' signified the union of a group of people with a transcendental 'essence' … fused to man's innermost nature, and represented the

---

[25] Chickering, *We Men Who Feel Most German*, 26.
[26] Frankel, Richard E. 2005. *Bismarck's Shadow*. Oxford: Berg, 54.
[27] Chickering, *We Men Who Feel Most German*, 77.   [28] Ibid, 26.

source of his creativity, his depth of feeling, his individuality, *and his unity with other members of the Volk.*"[29] This is an expression of what we have called binding morality, although a particular version in which the basis for group identity is the nation,defined in largely cultural terms.[30]

This romantic nationalism amounted to a critique of the Enlightenment's atomistic individualism, thought to sever the links between members of the community, leaving them socially untethered to anything bigger. Nationalists sought instead to fold members of society into a larger collective whole, the "mythical Deutschtum."[31] "Rather than viewing society as a collection of distinct individuals held together by rational norms and abstract laws," German romanticists "regarded it as an organic whole joined by the ties of tradition, custom and sentiment," writes Beiser. "The identity of the individual is not fixed by nature independent of society ... but is determined by society itself, by factors such as custom, education and law. The individual develops a sense of identity and self-respect by living in the group, not by seeking self-interest apart from it. Like the young romantics, then, the conservatives laid great stress on the value of community."[32] In contrast to the cosmopolitanism of liberal morality, "The individual linked himself with every other member of the Volk in a common feeling of belonging, in a shared emotional experience ... the Volk did not have universal dimensions but was limited to a particular national unity."[33]

Given the fundamentally new way in which German nationalists, most notably the PGL, defined the political community and the implicit threat it posed to the powers-that-be, we should not be surprised that these nationalist forces were largely spontaneous in origin, even defining themselves in opposition to the type of politics that the old elites practiced. While efforts like the Naval League began as

---

[29] Mosse, George. 1964. *The Crisis of German Ideology: Intellectual Origins of the Third Reich.* New York: Grossett and Dunlap, 4.

[30] Beiser, Frederick. 1992. *The Genesis of Modern German Political Thought, 1790–1800.* Cambridge: Harvard University Press, 238; Stern, Fritz. 1974. *The Politics of Cultural Despair: A Study in the Rise of the Germanic Ideology.* Berkeley: University of California Press, xii.

[31] Stern, *The Politics of Cultural Despair,* xiii; also Beiser, *The Genesis of Modern German Political,* 235.

[32] Beiser, *The Genesis of Modern German Political Thought,* 287.

[33] Mosse, *The Crisis of German Ideology,* 15.

attempts by the government to harness the power of German nationalism for purposes that benefited entrenched elites, even these groups
were quickly penetrated by true believers; they were "riddled from
the start with dissatisfaction with the governmental orientation of
their highly connected leaders."[34] Social imperialist arguments miss
the anti-establishment tendency and character of groups like the PGL
and thereby misconstrue their role, seeing them as hopeless and loyal
government pawns. Nationalism was the "political ideology of a
marginal generation"[35] that was denied political access to the elit-
ist, notable-driven style of politics that prevailed at the time but was
beginning to fray as political success dependent more and more on
mass mobilization.[36]

Nationalist leagues like the PGL saw themselves as opponents of
the type of horse trading that characterized politics in the Wilhelmine
regime and which distracted from the true national interest, which
could only be successfully pursued with true national unity. They
wanted a new form of politics in which they stood above politics.[37]
The PGL, for instance, had no formal ties to any political party. Its
members resisted assimilation and "on the contrary claimed a separate existence, patrolling the nation's conscience and proclaiming their
own higher virtue, asserting their independence of the parties and their
moral superiority."[38] They were the guardians of binding morality,
castigating the very type of politics for which they are said to be an
instrument in social imperialist accounts. Nationalists saw themselves
as holier than the traditional right. Mosse writes that for nationalists,
"politics was seen as exemplifying the worst aspect of the world in
which they lived. They rejected political parties as artificial, and representative government was swept aside in favor of an elitism which
derived from their semi-mystical concepts of nature and men."[39] For
a movement that claimed the Volk as the ultimate source of value in
politics, this populism was only natural.

---

[34] Eley, *Reshaping the German Right*, 44.   [35] Ibid, 184.
[36] Smith, *The Ideological Origins of Nazi Imperialism*, 9; Blackbourn, *Populists
and Patricians*, 225.
[37] Blackbourn, *Populists and Patricians*, 224; Eley, *Reshaping the German
Right*, 190.
[38] Eley, *Reshaping the German Right*, 57; also Retallack, *The German Right,
1860–1920*, 88.
[39] Mosse, *The Crisis of German Ideology*, 2.

The Primacy of Foreign Policy in Binding Morality: National Cohesion in a Dangerous World

While potentially threatening the established order, nationalism's embrace of the ethics of community appealed to the German right. Völkisch thinkers had a vision of a hierarchical society in which individuals played particular roles for the good of the community, rather than an egalitarian one in which all men were created equal.[40] The völkisch tradition looked back on the corporatist social structure of the Middle Ages with admiration. Völkisch advocates were "moralists and guardians of what they thought was an ancient tradition."[41] The nation was "not a family in which all members were supposedly equal, but a patriarchial family in which the factory owner played the same role which the master craftsman had played in the past."[42] In other words, völkisch ideology offered a new basis for group loyalty but retained a commitment to and justification of social hierarchy. This explains how it began to ideologically penetrate the German right following unification.

So as to maintain national order, it was imperative to maintain a social order in which everyone knew his or her place, which justifiably privileged those with *Bildung* (cultivation and education) and *Besitz* (property ownership).[43] These were the natural leaders of the country. This was an "ethical necessity," Class wrote.[44] "Universal equal suffrage has always been a falsehood because it requires an equality of men that will never be realized. It is immoral in that it treats the worthy, capable, and mature identically as the unworthy, incapable and immature. Ultimately it is unjust in that in reality it deprives the rights of the educated and the propertied through the force of the masses."[45]

Socialist class politics or liberal demands for greater individual rights and democratization threatened the cohesion of German society. Class wrote of the "immorality and injustice of universal equal suffrage" that "permanently splits the people into ... groups."[46] Democracy was only safe if the masses were sufficiently patriotic and accepted natural

---

[40] Beiser, *The Genesis of Modern German Political Thought*, 238.
[41] Stern, *The Politics of Cultural Despair*, xi.
[42] Mosse, *The Crisis of German Ideology*, 21.
[43] Chickering, *We Men Who Feel Most German*, 89.
[44] Class, *Wenn ich der Kaiser wäre*, 4.   [45] Ibid, 43.   [46] Ibid, 52.

hierarchies. "[T]his democratic right to vote is politically only possible if the totality of the voters is infused with the same national and state sentiments, if everyone agreed on the foundations of civic life such as nationality, monarchy and property."[47] The Reichstag lost its "moral weight" to the extent that the leaders of the masses merely "represent their interests, which threaten national development."[48]

The German patriotic societies wanted to make loyal nationalists of the working class. Class wrote, "In the political sense, we are all the people, from the Kaiser down to the lowest men, and the national community reaches its borders when it encounters foreign peoples – in the sense of the highest ethical and political values and the final responsibility a people is only at its best if it recognize those willing to make sacrifices, who are free from selfishness, the servants of the whole."[49] As Eley notes, radical nationalists might have been deluded into thinking that ideas and propaganda alone could "conjure material want, social inequality political repression and class conflict out of existence," but that does not mean that they were disingenuous. This was a "retreat into ideology."[50]

For Germany to act as a unified whole, there must be deference to authority. "There is still a need today for the best of our people to follow a strong, capable leader. All of those who have not been seduced by the teachings of anti-German democracy long for this, not because they are servile or weak in character, but because they know that great things can only be achieved by the combining of individual forces, which in turn must be subordinated to a leader."[51] This is a pure statement of binding morality.

The nationalist movement genuinely believed that national solidarity was necessary for an effective foreign policy, a sentiment that social imperialist arguments dismiss as lip service disguising the material interests of narrow interest groups profiting from an assertive course abroad. The German nationalist saw domestic politics through the lens of *inter*-national interactions. Whereas social imperialist arguments claim the primacy of domestic politics in which narrow class and material interests drive foreign policy preferences, a proper understanding of German nationalism is as an ideology with a primacy of

---

[47] Ibid, 40.   [48] Ibid, 44.   [49] Ibid, 230.
[50] Eley, *Reshaping the German Right*, 266.
[51] Class, *Wenn ich der Kaiser wäre*, 227.

foreign policy vision that in turn makes demands of domestic politics. Petty sectional concerns that distract from the national interest are morally condemnable; domestic politics are subservient to foreign policy, not the reverse.

The Pan-Germans had a highly moralized conception of international politics premised on a dangerous world. Class wrote, "To pursue German power politics means to secure the future of our people by doing what is absolutely necessary; not to gain advantages, not to deprive the weak, not to bow to the stronger, but to walk upright through the world of nations; conscious of the accomplishments of our people and their values, openly demanding what is our right and not evading the struggle offered."[52] Chickering's review of the ideology of the PGL, the most important of the national leagues, notes how for the group "history and politics were a morality play, which pitted Germans against everyone else and whose denouement would come to war.... Their search for intellectual order led them to divide the world rigidly into categories of friends and enemies."[53] There were "Feinde ringsum," enemies all around us, justifying national egoism and a fixation on national resolve, which we will consider later.[54] "Consumed with hatred, these omnipresent enemies shied from nothing in their attack: they were fanatical, shameless, unscrupulous, perseverant, ruthless, given to violence and saw conciliation as a sign of weakness."[55] The common denominator was a "vivid vision of fear. The symbolism of the flood, the premonitions of catastrophe, the obsession with enemies, the anxieties about disorder."[56] This was a belief in a dangerous world.

War therefore could have the positive effect of expunging unpatriotic ideas and inculcating binding values of loyalty and sacrifice to the ingroup. "Everyone should love peace – everyone should also honor war," Class wrote.[57] "War is holy to us ... because it will awaken in our people everything great and prepared for sacrifice – that is, selflessness – in our people and wash clean its soul of the cinder of selfish smallness."[58] Analysts like Snyder claim that this process began

---

[52] Ibid, 227.   [53] Chickering, *We Men Who Feel Most German*, 124.
[54] Class, *Wenn ich der Kaiser wäre*, 123.
[55] Chickering, *We Men Who Feel Most German*, 85–86.   [56] Ibid, 122.
[57] Class, *Wenn ich der Kaiser wäre*, 182.   [58] Ibid, 183.

disingenously but nationalist myths, in a process of ideological "blow-back," came to construct the visions of subsequent generations.[59] However, the timing of such a progression – that is just when instrumental beliefs become convincing and persuasive – is never identified. More importantly, the historical record indicates that elites neither could nor did originate an ideological vision that was in tension with the very basis of the regime. True believers were present at the creation. The PGL and others were not sorcerer's apprentices. They were tails that wagged the dog.

Unsurprisingly, the Pan-Germans rejected liberal morality explicitly. Heinrich Class compared his father's liberalism of patriotism, tolerance, humanity, and equality before the law with his ideology: "[W]e were national pure and simple. We wanted nothing to do with tolerance if it sheltered the enemies of the people and the state. Humanity in the sense of that liberal idea we spurned, for our own people were bound to come off worse."[60] The Pan-German newspaper, the *Alldeutscher Blätter*, proclaimed that "when we call the entirety of Germandom to unification and warn it, in consideration of its world power position, to hold back everything divisive before the great feeling of common blood; when we let the national thoughts shine high over the petty goings-on of the parties; his spirit is with us when we declare war on spineless cosmopolitanism and set our German sense of self with quiet pride against all other peoples when we demand German interest-politics, which knows absolutely no other guidelines than the well-being of our people."[61]

More Patriotic than Thou: Nationalists and the Emperor's Resolve

German nationalism contained an internal tension that even the Pan-Germans were reluctant to admit. They were committed monarchists, not republicans, which distinguished them from the liberal nationalists of the recent German past. However, by defining their locus of moral concern as the German nation, they indirectly challenged the legitimist basis of the Emperor's rule, at least as it had been understood up to that point. As Chickering explains:

---

[59] Snyder, *Myths of Empire*.   [60] Eley, *Reshaping the German Right*, 185.
[61] Frankel, *Bismarck's Shadow*, 60.

The League had long claimed to speak in the name of the German nation. This claim rested on the proposition that as 'cultivated' Germans, the League's members enjoyed a special, prior, and creative relationship to German culture, which was the supreme and most essential expression of German ethnicity and national will. This special relationship entitled culti-vated Germans to precedence in the structure of authority.... It reflected a modified theory of popular sovereignty: an immediate tie to German culture made Pan-Germans the most genuine expression of the collective *Volkswille* (will of the people).[62]

By situating the emperor's legitimacy in his service to his people, German nationalism opened him up to the prospect of criticism for not representing the national interest adequately, as the nationalists saw it. This was a moral revolution in German society, one whose implications even the Pan-Germans resisted as long as they could. Yet given Wilhelm II's erratic and pusillanimous leadership, an open break seems to have been inevitable.

In the moral terms used in this book, the rise of German nationalism was a reconfiguring of the foundations of ingroup loyalty and defer-ence to authority. So long as the monarchy was the ingroup because the state was the monarchy, respect for the emperor was equivalent to faithful allegiance to Germany. As Germans became "citizens not sub-jects,"[63] the relationship between loyalty and authority was renegoti-ated. In the words of one nationalist, "above the person must stand the dynasty, and above the dynasty the welfare of the people."[64] Class wrote of the "reciprocal influence of the people and the statesman ... necessary for a great national policy" and stressed how important it was that "the rulers and the general public, the statesmen and public opinion" to all be "filled with the breath of great national will."[65] The "basic moral principle" of the German state was "to serve the most loyal, the bravest, the most willing to sacrifice. Those who have the highest rights have the highest obligations; whoever has the highest freedom is the most bound to duty; whoever possesses the highest command must obey himself the most."[66] Class pointed out that in the Prussian past, the king had been selected not on the basis of hereditary

---

[62] Chickering, *We Men Who Feel Most German*, 231.
[63] Blackbourn, *Populists and Patricians*, 226.
[64] Eley, *Reshaping the German Right*, 191.
[65] Class, *Wenn ich der Kaiser wäre*, 181.   [66] Ibid, 221.

principles but by achievement and sacrifice, his status conferred by the "voluntary recognition of the people,"[67] "the conviction of the people that with his whole being he takes most seriously that he should be the first in concern and striving, the most tirelessly serving, the most willing to sacrifice."[68] In other words, the emperor must represent binding values.

Foreign policy was the main focus of the Pan-Germans since the measure of a community's cohesion and achievement was in the arena in which it acted as a whole. "The deed of an entire people is a fine foreign policy. A proud, independent policy that safeguards the future of our people will deliver glory and warmth into the hearts of the Germans and awaken what is not lost but only fallen asleep, a real love of country," Class wrote.[69] In 1903, Class published an influential PGL pamphlet excoriating the direction of German foreign policy since Bismarck's departure. Class declared: "We must free up the moral forces in our people for a national policy that puts the people above the state when both come into conflict.... How absurd and unworthy it is to expect all salvation, all help from above.... [E]very national comrade is responsible before history and our grandchildren for what happens today."[70] Class was calling for a replacement of a Staatsnation with a Nationalstaat, indicating how the forces thought to provide a firmer foundation for an anachronistic German state structure by the social imperialist account were actually destabilizing. "For every simple affirmative impulse which deferred to the government's tactical needs, there was a disruptive radical-nationalist counterpart which deliberately repudiated them," Eley explains. "It suggests the political diversity of nationalist initiatives in public life, nationalism's disruptive as well as its integrative potential, its ability to divide as well as unite the nation, even within the limited spectrum of the right."[71]

The Pan-Germans and their sympathizers faced criticism from the right for disloyalty as understood traditionally in the country.[72] "It is irresponsible ... for an organization like the Pan-German League, which professes in its statutes to be patriotic, to hurl such unworthy and groundless charges at the authorities," remarked the German

---

[67] Ibid, 219.   [68] Ibid, 224.   [69] Ibid, 184.
[70] Frankel, *Bismarck's Shadow*, 66.   [71] Eley, *Reshaping the German Right*, 184.
[72] Blackbourn, *Populists and Patricians*, 229.

Chancellor, Bethmann-Hollweg in 1910.[73] A few years before, the emperor had told Class to love it or leave it: "I will not tolerate pessimistic alarmists and whoever is not suited to work, let him leave and seek, if he wants, a better country."[74] The Prussian Minister of the Interior, von Loebell, asked rhetorically, "Is it loyal, conservative policy to speak of washing away sins, to excite popular passions ... and to bellow for the applause of the rabble?" He complained that nationalists were "tearing down the authority that, according to tradition ... one should protect."[75] The traditional right made the worst possible accusation: the nationalists were democrats!

Mindful and perhaps sensitive to these critiques, the Pan-Germans directed their ire at first at the emperor's ministers and the government as a whole.[76] However, the League broke even this taboo after the Kaiser gave what he expected to be an innocuous interview with the British newspaper, the *Daily Telegraph,* in October 1908. In a self-pitying effort to get in the good graces of the British public, the emperor revealed the ways by which he had refrained from helping the Boer cause in South Africa to British advantage. For the Pan-Germans, this was a betrayal of the Afrikaans population, which for them was a part of the German cultural community. Yet the outrage reached across a wide section of the German right, including the Conservatives, and triggered a political crisis. The Alldeutscher Blätter proclaimed, "The words fail us to express the depths of our despondency, bitterness and shame."[77] Class demanded for the League to "subject foreign policy to the strictest control of the public."[78] At the group's annual convention, he declared: "The Kaiser must learn from recent events that a gulf has opened between him and the German people, that it is not the people's business to make that gulf disappear, but that every bond of loyalty has two sides, and that the bond between Kaiser and people depends on mutual respect."[79] Not even the emperor was German enough for the Pan-Germans.

What was the critique of German foreign policy offered by the nationalists? On what did they base their accusation of not representing

---

[73] Chickering, *We Men Who Feel Most German*, 263.   [74] Ibid, 221.
[75] Retallack, *The German Right, 1860–1920*, 392.
[76] Chickering, *We Men Who Feel Most German*, 62.   [77] Ibid, 222.
[78] Class, *Wenn ich der Kaiser wäre*, 223.   [79] Ibid, 289.

the German national interest, defined in terms of the people's will? Believing as they did in a dangerous world, it was necessary for the government to be assertive and forceful in its dealings with other countries. Strength and resolve were moral virtues, and weakness and indecisiveness were moral vices.[80] Class' speech before the League's 1903 convention shows the connection between ingroup loyalty and an insistence on resolve. "Where is the German citizen who dares to say when abroad, 'I am a German!' without being viewed as a nuisance or falling prey to the curse of ridicule. We flatter everyone and turn them all into enemies, *since no one believes any longer in our reliability and persistence.*"[81] Chickering argues, "It was self-evident to Pan-Germans that certain collective traits defined the essence of any ethnic unit and were central features of any nation's culture. In speaking of their own essential national characteristics, these writers isolated a long list of traits" that included "daring, German bravery, ... German honor, Germany loyalty, German courage ... and German conscientiousness."[82] These are all reducible to binding morality. To ensure social order, especially in a dangerous international environment, one needed "strength, masculinity and self-assertion." "Moral strength, toughness, vigilance, purposefulness" were all "public virtues."[83] Resolve was a "commandment." Nothing could be allowed to "distract the one who fights for the future of a fine people" who must push forward "with an indomitable will, with an iron nerve."[84]

German foreign policy of the Wilhelmine period never lived up to these standards. Class complained about this lack of leadership and action: "Do we even have an imperial government? We have authorities, more than enough. But do we have a government? We are administered, properly and benevolently – but governed?"[85] The Kaiser lacked determination and decisiveness.[86]

Consistent with a morally driven movement, the Pan-Germans are consistently described as emotional.[87] Morality has an affective basis, which we know by its biological basis. As such it provided energy that the government and political establishment on the right tried to

---

[80] Ibid, 93; Frankel, *Bismarck's Shadow*, 38.
[81] Chickering, *We Men Who Feel Most German*, 215.   [82] Ibid, 94.
[83] Ibid, 94–95.   [84] Ibid, 232.   [85] Class, *Wenn ich der Kaiser wäre*, 16.
[86] Ibid, 222.
[87] Chickering, *We Men Who Feel Most German*, 15; Mosse, *The Crisis of German Ideology*, 15.

harness at times (most notably in the second Moroccan crisis as we will review in the following text). Chancellor von Bülow talked of "beating the national drum."[88] A Foreign Office official flippantly remarked, "If the Pan German League did not exist, we would have to invent it."[89] Blackbourn observes, "The demagogy of the old elite, in Wilhelmine as in Weimar Germany, was perilous precisely because it was not an act of manipulation, repeatable at will, but an attempt to harness forces that could not be fully controlled."[90]

However, the same government officials that sought to harness nationalist feeling complained when it went too far, contrasting a steady, deliberative, and rational foreign policy with self-defeating, Pan-German chauvinism that actually undermined German interests. Bülow stated: "Public opinion is the strong current that ought to drive the wheels of the mill of the state. However, when this current threatens to drive the wheels in the wrong direction or even to destroy them, then it is the obligation of any government worthy of that name to oppose that current, regardless of any unpopularity it may incur. There are greater garlands than those the Pan-German League has to bestow, namely the consciousness that one is being guided simply and exclusively by the genuine and lasting interests of the nation."[91] The chancellor was drawing a contrast between a cold-hearted realist, who remained "on the terra firma of reality" and a hot-blooded nationalist.[92] "I well know that the efforts of the Pan-German League have the benefit of keeping national feelings alive and of counteracting the inclination of the German philistine toward wooly-headed cosmopolitanism or narrow-minded confessional politics" but while there were "warm-hearted patriots in this organization … in questions of foreign policy, a clear head counts for more than a warm heart, and the heart of the patriot ought to manifest itself not just in indiscriminate wrangling with all foreigners … and even less in bold dreams about the future – dreams which only complicate things for us in the present and provoke mistrust of us everywhere."[93] Officials liked to equate the Pan-Germans with the loudmouths one would find at a tavern.[94]

---

[88] Blackbourn, *Populists and Patricians*, 232.   [89] Ibid, 233.   [90] Ibid, 219.
[91] Chickering, *We Men Who Feel Most German*, 67.
[92] Frankel, *Bismarck's Shadow*, 62.
[93] Chickering, *We Men Who Feel Most German*, 221.
[94] Eley, *Reshaping the German Right*, 191.

The Chancellor complained, "I cannot conduct foreign policy from the standpoint of pure moral philosophy ... nor can I from the perspective of the beer hall."[95]

The Pan-Germans were overly bellicose, even to the right. Bethmann-Hollweg said of the nationalists: "War, screaming for war, and with eternal armaments."[96] His predecessor evoked Bismarck's example, whose greatness "did not exist in the clinking of spurs ... and not in the rattling of the saber, but rather in a sober assessment of men and of things."[97] The Pan-Germans did not recognize the limits of the achievable as the Iron Chancellor had done.[98] They were "a cross for our foreign policy to bear," one which accomplished "nothing practical" but "managed to provoke all the other nations at the same time."[99] For their part, the nationalists considered Realpolitik equivalent to an excuse for inaction on the part of those with "weak heart and lack of vision," which brought German honor into question.[100]

William, the Timid: The Pan-German League and the Second Moroccan Crisis

We observe these dynamics, efforts by the government to instrumentalize the energy of the pan-Germans only to make matters worse at home, most clearly in the second Moroccan crisis. The PGL was jubilant at the deployment of the Panther gunboat to Agadir; it was just the sort of bold foreign policy move they had long advocated. They would later name an organizational periodical after the ship. The *Rheinische-Westfälische Zeitung*, a prominent nationalist paper, wrote of 20 years "full of humiliations ... as though we were not the most populous nation in Europe, as though we could not base our justified claims to power on an army of five million men ... as though we were not a nation whose efficiency and supreme effort had enabled it increasingly to outbid the century old world nations on the markets of all continents."[101]

[95] Frankel, *Bismarck's Shadow*, 62.
[96] Chickering, *We Men Who Feel Most German*, 276.
[97] Frankel, *Bismarck's Shadow*, 68.   [98] Ibid, 63.
[99] Chickering, *We Men Who Feel Most German*, 253.
[100] Class, *Wenn ich der Kaiser wäre*, 184.
[101] Fischer, Frtiz. 1975. *War of Illusions: German Policies from 1911 to 1914.* New York: Norton, 74.

When the British Chancellor Llloyd George made his Mansion House speech (described in the last chapter), the crisis took on a much more public character that drew in a larger variety of political actors, making agreement more difficult. Kiderlen-Wächter told the French that "Germany ... is too great and too powerful to yield to threats and public opinion would stand no Foreign Minister who had even the appearance of doing so."[102] He told the British, mentioning the Mansion House address, that the "outcry through all Germany that the Imperial Government had yielded owing to menaces from France and England" made it impossible to compromise. He would be accused "on all sides of sacrificing German interests and yielding to foreign pressure."[103]

Part of this was by design. Immediately after taking office, the foreign minister had called in Class to discuss a "division of labor between the foreign ministry and nationalist organizations" so that on the issue of Morocco he could say to German rivals "yes, I am conciliatory, but public opinion must be taken into account."[104] Even before the *Panthersprung*, the foreign minister was telling the nationalist organizations and press to put pressure on the government. "Just blame me, scold me. That is necessary and I have a thick skin." Kiderlen-Wächter promised Class, "You can be assured that you will be pleased with Moroccan policy – You will be satisfied." Class recorded: "We will stand firm in Morocco for certain; possible, that we must appear to take a step back; that should not disappoint you – in any case, we will see each other beforehand."[105] The foreign minister called this a strategy of "letting all the dogs bark."[106] Class began, in consultation with the foreign ministry, to put together a propaganda pamphlet on the importance of Morocco for Germany and agreed to put nationalist newspapers into service of this cause. On the day that the Panther was dispatched, Class was at the Foreign Ministry and one of the first to know. State Secretary Zimmerman told him of the German rhetorical pretext.

The nationalist groups, however, did not want compensation elsewhere in Africa. They wanted a piece of Morocco. When State Secretary Zimmerman told Class that Germany might settle for the

---

[102] BD VII, no. 429; also BD VII, no. 481. BD is *British Documents on the Origins of the War: The Agadir Crisis*, Vol. VII. London: His Majesty's Stationary Office, 1932.
[103] BD VII, no. 579.   [104] Bundesarchiv ADV 408, Bestand R/8048 (19.4.11).
[105] Ibid.   [106] Chickering, *We Men Who Feel Most German*, 263.

French Congo, the latter said: "Oh God, no. Morocco is our land of destiny."[107] Kiderlen-Wächter and the foreign ministry complained that they could not control the nationalist press.[108] He wrote in his diary on 12 August, "Public opinion is becoming more and more inflamed – through colonial league and pan-German propaganda. Despite my peaceful intentions, I cannot hold it back if attacks continue from the other side. Everyone thinks I am mistaken about the mood in England! No! If I wanted to make myself popular, I would push for war, which would be easy. But I don't have this honor."[109]

For their part, the Pan-Germans thought they were helping the national cause by contradicting guidance they were receiving from the government to tone down their rhetoric. A member of the organization's board wrote Class, "If the Foreign Ministry wants to have success, it must instead [of backing down] push the press so that Kiderlen-Wächter can make reference to public opinion."[110] The foreign ministry must stick to the "marching route."[111] Class published his pamphlet, "*Westmarokko deutsch*! (western Morocco for Germany!), which sold 50,000 copies. The foreign ministry could only convince him to remove the salacious demand to annex eastern France.[112]

More outrageous to the German nationalists, however, was German weakness. The nationalist organizations and press morally condemned their own leaders, particularly the emperor, for lacking resolve. A prominent nationalist newspaper attracted international attention by attacking the emperor, calling him "Guillaume le timide" (Wilhelm, the timid), and asking "what has happened to the Hohenzollerns, who count as their ancestors a Great Elector, a Frederick William I, a Frederick the Great and an Emperor William I?" The article spoke of "this moment of unspeakable shame, of deep national ignominy, far deeper than that of Olmutz!" (a reference to a previous diplomatic capitulation in 1850). The paper asked the foreign minister to resign in protest rather than "subscribe to this national humiliation."[113] The paper lamented, "Are we dead to all

---

[107] Bundesarchiv ADV 408, Bestand R/8048 (1.7.11).
[108] Chickering, *We Men Who Feel Most German*, 265.
[109] Kiderlen-Wächter, *der Staatsman und Mensch*, 138.
[110] Bundesarchiv ADV 408, Bestand R/8048 (8.7.11).   [111] Ibid (5.7.11).
[112] Chickering, *We Men Who Feel Most German*, 265.   [113] BD VII, no. 462.

feelings of national honour, have we lost all sense of political responsibility, or political foresight? Has Germany become a mere object of ridicule for foreign nations to laugh at?" Through his lack of leadership, the emperor was acting disloyally to his own nation. "Are we to regard our Emperor as the strongest support of France, a support worth more than 50 French divisions? Are we to look upon him as the hope of France? We dare not and will not believe that such is the case."[114] The official governmental newspaper took notice and chastised the authors for their lack of patriotism, by which they meant something else: an insufficient moral commitment to authority. It was "unprecedented for a Conservative and nationally minded paper to make a violent attack on the Emperor himself."[115]

The Kaiser seemed particularly sensitive to public critique, which we must understand as a moral condemnation of his leadership. Directly after the article appeared, the emperor rattled the saber, telling the English ambassador: "I do not want any territory in Morocco whatever, but if I give France a free hand there I must have proper compensation. I have laid my demands on this head [sic!] before the French Government, and if they do not accept them I will have the status quo after Algeciras, and see that every French soldier in the interior and coast towns and the Shawia district is turned out of Morocco, and if I can't get them out by peaceable means I will turn them out by force."[116] He told the French of the importance of supporting "one's politics with the sword" and boasted of having the best army in the world.[117] As an indication of the domestic pressure it was under, the German government even forbade the English from publicly revealing its private assurances that no German crewmen had left the Panther for land, fearing that it would make Germany look weak and irresolute at home, as "groveling" as Lloyd George put it.[118] It was not "consistent with their dignity, after the [Mansion House] speech of the Chancellor of the Exchequer, to give explanations as to what was taking place at Agadir" in light of the "tone of their communication."[119]

[114] Ibid.   [115] Fischer, *War of Illusions*, 82.   [116] BD VII, no. 476.
[117] BD VII, no. 490.
[118] GP XXIX, no. 10626, also no. 10625. GP *is Die große Politik der europäischen Kabinette 1871–1914. 1927*. Berlin: Deutsche Verlagsgesellschaft für Politik und Geschichte.
[119] BD VII, no. 419.

The allies recognized what was going on. The French premier diagnosed that Kiderlen-Wächter had raised expectations in the public for gains that he could not deliver. Having deliberately excited opinion in the country, he was finding it impossible to back down.[120] "These circumstances constitute dangers to the mainte-nance of peace," believed the French ambassador Cambon,[121] a con-cern shared by the British.[122] "I thought it possible that the German Government, having excited public opinion, and the appetite for territory, might perhaps be carried away and press their demands to the point of covert menaces of war," wrote the English ambassador to Paris.[123] The English noted the emperor's "irritation caused by the charges of timidity and hesitation which have been so freely brought against him by the Pan-German papers."[124] The press was accusing him, the French recognized, of "cowardice," causing him to dig in his heels.[125]

An agreement was eventually found, but not before doing irre-vocable damage to Anglo-German and Franco-German relations. France and Germany engaged in a territorial swap of colonial ter-ritories in Africa (Germany receiving interior parts of the French Congo), and Germany committed to relinquishing any claims to influence in Morocco provided the open door was maintained. Germany came out ahead in terms of square kilometers, although much of what it obtained was economically useless. The French could claim that they had not bought off the Germans at the point of a gun since there had been "exchange" of African properties, important "solely for the gallery" in their words.[126] It was a "make-believe exchange," as the Germans put it.[127] The French had their domestic audience too.

The National Opposition: The Origins of an Oxymoron

The Moroccan crises had two effects that would contribute to the out-break of the Great War. Internationally, it cemented the antagonism between Germany and England and thereby consolidated the Entente Cordiale. This had begun already with the first crisis, in which "the

---

[120] BD VII, no. 488.   [121] BD VII, no. 510.   [122] BD VII, no. 533.   [123] Ibid.
[124] BD VII, no. 486.   [125] BD VII, no. 510.   [126] GP XXIX, no. 10674.
[127] BD VII, no. 419.

diplomatic alignment began to form which prevailed during the First World War."[128] The British ambassador to Bavaria (still a kingdom that was part of imperial Germany) observed after the second: "The hard and disconcerting fact has been realized that the Franco-British entente, so far from having been undermined by the Morocco question, has been cemented by the trial. In other words the Morocco affair is believed to be about to end in a diplomatic defeat and that defeat is ascribed to the interested support given to France by Great Britain. Among those with whom I have the opportunity to converse I have noticed a difference of tone since the beginning of the year, and a reluctance on the part of those who formerly confessed to British sympathies to parade them now."[129]

During the Reichstag ratification debate, the Conservative leader, von Heydebrand, directed most of his outrage not at France, but at England, particularly the threat to German honor and dignity that was the Mansion House speech. "Like a lightning bolt in the night it showed the entire German people where its adversary resides. The German people now knows, if it wants to expand in this world, if it wants to take its place in the sun, which is its right and destiny – who will ... allow this or not.... We Germans are not used to that, and the German people will know how to give the answer."[130] Class demanded, "Not only must this disgraceful process never be repeated, but German policy must, at the first opportunity, freely choose the opportunity so that England shows its colors again. If it decides again in an unfriendly manner, then we have to pick up the gauntlet – then it is clear that the German-English question cannot be solved by committee pronouncements and friendly visits but rather only through blood and iron."[131]

Second, domestically, the second Moroccan crisis saw the final emancipation of what historians call the "nationalist opposition," up to that point a contradiction in terms, which would be one of the most powerful forces in the coming war and was even important for

---

[128] Rich, *Friedrich Von Holstein: Politics and Diplomacy in the Era of Bismarck and Wilhelm II*, 745.
[129] BD VII, no. 602.
[130] *Verhandlungen des deutschen Reichstags.* XII. Legislaturperiod. II Session. Band 268. Stenographische Berichte. 201 Sitzung. Berlin: Druck und Verlag der Norddeutschen Buchdruckerei und Verlags-Anstalt, 7721.
[131] Class, *Wenn ich der Kaiser wäre*, 146.

its outbreak in the first place.[132] Smith argues that the "attack on the sellout of 1911 clearly tied the hands of the government in diplomacy during the ensuing years. It could never again afford to brave a repetition of such an assault, which had a severely restrictive effect on the range of options open to it in diplomacy."[133]

During the Reichstag debate on ratifying the Franco-German Treaty settling the crisis, the traditional governmental parties of the right – Conservatives, Free Conservatives, and National Liberals – all forcibly criticized the government's foreign policy.[134] This showed "the extent and depth of the crisis among the very sections of the population which by tradition loyally supported the government's foreign policy."[135] Most shocking was von Heyderbrand's speech. Contradicting the chancellor's assertions that Germany could have not obtained anything more without war, one which would have dissipated the strength of a largely territorial (rather than world) power, he said menacingly, "that which assures peace is not concessions, nor agreements or understandings, but only our good German sword and simultaneously the feeling ... that we hope to see a government that is resolved not to allow this sword to rust."[136] Heydebrand made a thinly veiled threat to the government: "We Germans will be prepared ... to make sacrifices if necessary. We expect the German government also to be guided by these feelings ... unworthy is the nation that does not do everything for its honor."[137]

Von Heydebrand's speech demonstrates how Pan-German ideology was penetrating some of the oldest elements of the old guard. The Conservatives were the party of the east Elbian aristocracy, historically more Prussian in identity than German, among the most loyal to the establishment and the emperor, and less tempted by the material gains to be had from an active Weltpolitik and confrontation with

---

[132] Blackbourn, *Populists and Patricians*, 237; Chickering, *We Men Who Feel Most German*, 265; Smith, *The Ideological Origins of Nazi Imperialism*, 137.
[133] Smith, *The Ideological Origins of Nazi Imperialism*, 138.
[134] Eley, *Reshaping the German Right*, 323.
[135] Fischer, *War of Illusions*, 89.
[136] *Verhandlungen des deutschen Reichstags*. XII. Legislaturperiod. II Session. Band 268. Stenographische Berichte. 201 Sitzung. Berlin: Druck und Verlag der Norddeutschen Buchdruckerei und Verlags-Anstalt, 7721.
[137] Ibid, 7722.

England. Von Heydebrand's speech was applauded in the Reichstag gallery by none other than the heir to the throne, the crown prince, signaling an end of an ethical era in which the emperor was the undisputed director of German foreign policy. This was the culmination of a moral revolution in German society, one in which the link between ingroup loyalty and deference to authority was severed forever.

For the Pan-Germans like Class, Morocco marked a breaking point. The compromise, which they saw as a capitulation, demonstrated "psychological and political short-sightedness without comparison for people at the pinnacle of a state, simply an outrage."[138] Its effects on the "people's soul [were] particularly fateful."[139] The "giving away of the Congo to France is ... a political sin against the future of our people," a "political sacrilege," "a moral collapse."[140]

This led Class, albeit it anonymously, to draw much more radical conclusions concerning the monarchy. "The humiliations of last fall have reinforced doubts, and precisely the truest friends of the empire are asking how these concerns can be laid to rest. They ask themselves whether the emperor has insight into the great questions of the time ... whether all the dangers that the concerned patriot has long recognized are also seen by his emperor."[141] Class concluded, "The time of God's grace," by which he meant the principle of divine right, "are over. Criticism shines into every corner," even that of the emperor, and "asks only whether what prevails is reasonable and practical ... whether it serves to benefit the whole or whether something better could not be found."[142] Class hoped "that there will never be any doubt as to whether another form of government would be more beneficial to the people." However, he warned: "As firmly established as the loyalty of the Germans to their rulers is based on the merits of their ancestors, as unshakable as their attachment to the living heirs of such deeds appears, one does not dare to deny that the accumulated mistakes of the crown and the permanent inefficiency of its bearers could lead our people to wonder why they should continue to accept a form of government that wants to force them to endure a useless head."[143] There was a reason this book was published under a *nom de plum*.

---

[138] Class, *Wenn ich der Kaiser wäre*, 13.   [139] Ibid, 9.   [140] Ibid, 14.
[141] Ibid, 222.   [142] Class, *Wenn ich der Kaiser wäre*, 220.   [143] Ibid, 222.

The most forceful expression of national opposition, however, occurred in an article later that year in which the nationalist paper, the Rheinisch-Westfälische Zeitung, finally reached the logical conclusion of the country's nationalist turn: "If the Imperial throne and the Empire are not to collapse the nation must take its fate into its own hands and just as in 1813 it defeated the Napoleonic regime, it must today free itself from the personal regime."[144]

During the Moroccan crisis, Class had scribbled a note: "War as the only cure for our people. The influence of foreign policy on domestic policy."[145] Often taken as evidence for the social imperialist hypothesis, it is actually evidence against it. In its linking of the need for group solidarity in the face of external threat, it was a perfect statement of binding morality. The Pan-German leader was articulating what he thought his country needed, not his social class, and would continue to do so as the country plunged into war. Untethered by any remaining ethical deference to the Kaiser, the Great War unleashed the power of the German nationalists, whom the government was no longer able to control. As we will see, this new moral force, more than any other, was responsible for Germany's tragic fate. The emperor would fall, but so would the empire.

Hidden Virtues Survey: Resolve as Ethical Trait in the American Public

Can we really claim that accusations of weakness and timidity are moralistic epithets? Generally, we do not treat resolve as an ethically laden concept. However, in situations of conflict between groups, particularly for those who see the world as a dangerous place, will and determination take on moral meaning. To show this more clearly, I conducted a survey experiment of roughly 1,800 American residents on the M-Turk platform in May 2020. I asked respondents the extent to which a number of different traits were "extremely useful in determining whether someone is a [moral OR competent] person," randomizing whether the attribute was being assessed on the basis of ethics or capability. Each trait was evaluated on a ten-point scale in which 0 indicated "not at all useful" and 10 was "extremely

---

[144] Fischer, *War of Illusions*, 93.
[145] Eley, *Reshaping the German Right*, 323.

useful." I included the familiar traits that generally score highest as predictors of morality – fair and just, principled and honorable, compassionate and forgiving, generous and kind, and honest and trustworthy. We recognize these as some of the most universal of moral values. However, I also included three characteristics venerated by the ethics of community – obedient and respectful, loyal and faithful, and brave and courageous – as well as four indicators of resolve: disciplined and hardworking, strong-willed and determined, tough and strong, and persistent and resolute.[146] The resolve attributes are generally understood as indicators of "competence" in frameworks like Fiske's seen in our first empirical chapter.[147] However, I expect that the moral understanding of will and determination varies by individuals and by the situation. In some clearly identifiable instances and for some specific people, resolve will take on an ethical valence.

Since in binding morality, members of a group are supposed to fall in behind a strong leader, I also randomized whether the person in question was an ordinary citizen or a "leader of our country." The expectation is that authority figures in particular will be morally judged by their resolve. In addition, I randomized the context, with roughly half the respondents receiving an additional prime to make their assessment about what constitutes an ethical or competent individual "during a time of war, crisis and great threat to the United States." The expectation is that resolve will be more important in determining moral character in a situation of danger. The result is a 2 × 2 × 2 fully crossed design.

Table 7.1 presents the mean rating of all the traits across the competence and morality treatments, again on a ten-point scale. As we can see, the resolve traits score much higher as competence markers than morality markers, suggesting that respondents were indeed paying attention to what was being asked about these traits and not just ranking them based on a generic evaluative sense of good or bad. In contrast, our typical ethical characteristics – fair and just, honest and trustworthy, generous and kind, compassionate and forgiving – score higher as indications of moral qualities, as we would expect. This is in keeping with the previous findings.

---

[146] The traits were listed randomly, so as to avoid any order effects.
[147] Fiske et al., "Universal Dimensions of Social Cognition."

Table 7.1 *In general, resolve is used to judge competence and morality to judge ethics*

| | | Mean value of trait | | |
		As reflecting competence	As reflecting ethics	Difference
BINDING VALUES	Loyal and faithful	7.1	7.2	.1
	Obedient and respectful	6.1	6.0	.1
	Brave and courageous	6.6	6.1	−.5***
RESOLVE	Disciplined and hardworking	7.9	7.0	−.9***
	Strong-willed and determined	7.3	6.1	−1.2***
	Tough and strong	6.4	5.3	−1.1***
	Persistent and resilient	7.6	6.2	−1.4***
UNIVERSAL MORAL VALUES	Fair and just	7.9	8.3	.4***
	Honest and trustworthy	8.1	8.4	.3***
	Generous and kind	7.0	7.7	.7***
	Compassionate and forgiving	7.0	7.7	.7***
	Principled and honorable	7.8	8.0	.2*
	N	820	876	

Entries are based on a ten-point scale. Difference is value of first column subtracted from second column. Significance of two-tailed t-test. ***p >. 001, *p >.01, *p > .05.

However, this belies important differences induced by experimental treatments and dispositional variables. Table 7.2 estimates the predictors of whether each of our traits are useful for judging whether someone is moral or not (excluding those who received the competence treatment). In addition to dummy variables for our other two experimental treatments, I also include individuals' beliefs in a dangerous world (DWB). I used four items from the DWB scale (Cronbach's alpha = .80) and constructed an additive scale that was subsequently standardized for use in the regression model. The text of the questions was based on a five-category Likert scale ranging from "strongly agree" to "strongly disagree," in Online Appendix 4.1.

Table 7.2 *Resolve is virtuous for leaders and for those who hold dangerous world beliefs*

	BINDING VALUES				RESOLVE			UNIVERSALLY ACCEPTED MORAL VALUES				
	Loyal and faithful	Obedient and respectful	Brave and courageous	Disciplined and hardworking	Strong-willed and determined	Tough and strong	Persistent and resilient	Fair and just	Honest and trustworthy	Generous and kind	Compassionate and forgiving	Principled and honorable
DWB	.37***	.53***	.41***	.29***	.40***	.40***	.23*	-.06	-.06	-.11	-.13	.10
Citizen vs. Leader	.14	.18	.26	.37*	.88***	.76***	.75***	.15	-.04	-.35*	-.35	.15
Peace vs. War	-.22	-.08	.01	-.10	.26	.28	.44*	.05	-.18	-.20	-.16	.17

Table entries are OLS regression coefficients. DWB is a standardized variable so that coefficients indicate the effect of a change in one standard deviation on the dependent variables, which are based on a ten-point scale. N = 876. Analysis includes the demographic controls for college education (dummy), age, sex, white (dummy), and Southern residence (dummy), but results are not reported here.

Table 7.2 shows the effects of treatments and DWB on assessed importance for judging others' morality (but not competence). The coefficients for DWB's effect on disciplined and hardworking, strong-willed and determined, tough and strong, and persistent and resilient are substantively large, positive, and for the most part strongly statistically significant. As we would expect, those who score high on DWB also regard the attributes of loyal and faithful, obedient and respectful, and brave and courageous as particularly relevant for determining moral character, all traits that strengthen ingroup solidarity in situations of intergroup threat. This is all the more remarkable in that the model included ideology as a control, which we might have expected to absorb a significant amount of DWB's impact. All of these are robust to the inclusion of a seven-point ideology scale in the analysis as well as a dummy variable for Southern residence (a control for the "honor" culture thought to influence resolve[148]), although the table does not report the coefficients for these controls and others.

DWB has no statistically significant effect on the five more universal moral traits, buttressing my claim that these are the most basic and foundational of moral values. Even those who embrace the worldview that leads individuals to feel the need to bind together are not devoid of more basic human moral impulses.

There is also a strong positive treatment effect of our layperson versus leader manipulation. Leaders, more than ordinary citizens, are judged morally on their resolve. The coefficients for strong-willed and determined, tough and strong, and persistent and resilient are the strongest in the regression analysis. In addition, there is a negative effect of this treatment on generous and kind and compassionate and forgiving, likely because of the capacity for tough love that respondents might find virtuous in a leader.

Our peace versus war treatment has smaller effects, but again these are found exactly where we might expect – on the resolve traits. Persistent and resilient takes on a particularly strong ethical valence in a situation of crisis and threat. Strong-willed/determined and tough/strong have positive coefficients but are not statistically significant.

---

[148] Dafoe and Caughey, "Honor and War."

A factor analysis of all scores of traits as indicating morality, not reported here, reveals a two-dimensional structure in which the binding traits load on the same dimension as the resolve traits. The other dimension is composed of our more general indications of ethical behavior. Only "loyal and faithful" straddles the two dimensions, unsurprisingly since the recipient of this loyalty is unidentified. To the extent that respondents might be thinking, for instance, of fidelity in a relationship, it is not surprising that this trait does not load fully on the binding dimension. This suggests again that resolve is a moral attribute that arises out of the binding foundations.

8 Biting the Bullet
Binding Morality, Rationality, and the Domestic Politics of War Termination in Germany during World War I

One of the great puzzles of the Great War is why this "war that no one wanted" lasted as long as it did. Germany is at the center of that mystery since its leaders prosecuted the war beyond the point which their society could bear. The result was a total collapse – the overthrow of the monarchy and the creation of a parliamentary democracy for the first time in united Germany's brief history, one instantly tested by communist insurrections and violence between left- and right-wing paramilitary forces. Why did Germany decide to fight on in vain, prolonging the country's great suffering, as opposed to biting the bullet and ending the war?

The decision seems irrational. Rationality dictates that when we are in a hole, we stop digging.[1] This is the essence of the rational war termination literature, which accounts for the duration of conflict as a function of private information. Costly conflict might begin because opposing sides have incentives to dissemble about their relative power and resolve. The act of fighting reduces this informational asymmetry, exposing who is more powerful and separating the resolved from the irresolute. Rationality would dictate that while settlement, particularly in the face of losses, is emotionally painful, leaders will still behave in a consequentialist manner and settle on the lesser evil. Better not to throw good soldiers after bad.

Sometimes that does not happen though, and the rationalist war termination literature offers a number of corollaries to explain the

---

[1] I should stress that I am referring to rationality in its procedural and instrumental forms as distinct from Weberian "value rationality" in which the pursuit of a goal is rational in and of itself regardless of the chances of success. This is the standard of rationality and reasoning I apply in Rathbun, Brian C. 2019. *Reasoning of State, Realists, Romantics and Rationality in International Relations.* Cambridge University Press, 134–135. This is distinct from Weberian "value rationality," in which the pursuit of a goal is rational in and of itself regardless of the chances of success.

stubborn persistence of the losing side. First, warring parties might face a commitment problem in which the winner cannot credibly commit to abiding by a settlement, setting up the loser for future exploitation. Second, although battlefield outcomes become public information showing the distribution of power, resolve is still somewhat private, and the pursuit of a diplomatic solution might indicate a lack of determination. Fearing that an approach will undermine bargaining leverage, leaders might persist in a losing effort. Third, leaders might have a parochial incentive to resist settlement for fears that any compromise will lead the regime to collapse, threatening elite prerogatives. Instead, they "gamble for resurrection," even increasing their war aims as a last-ditch effort to compensate for the mass public's privations during protracted conflicts.

Rationalists have struggled, themselves in vain, to account for German behavior during the Great War, resisting the evidence to make self-destructive decisions, both for the country and even the policy-makers themselves, seem reasonable and reflective of deliberative thinking. Reiter argues that commitment logic necessitated that Germany obtain gains in the West so as to guard against any future attack from England and France. This explains why the country made one last push to break through the Western Front in March 1918 after the Russian revolution had forced the Soviet Union to accept harsh terms in the east. Any peace without some kind of control of Belgium was unenforceable. Goemans formalizes a line of argumentation that self-serving conservative forces in the country – heavy industry, large agricultural estate holders, and the monarchy, but particularly the military – continued the war well past the point at which Germany had any real chance of winning major annexations in a desperate bid to buy off the masses that elites feared would otherwise overthrow the regime.[2] This meant that as Germany's position declined on the battlefield, its war aims actually increased. Ordinary Germans had to be compensated for their sacrifices in some form other than reform.

What in fact explains the refusal of German decision-makers to bite the bullet is something virtually unseen in accounts of war

---

[2] Goemans, Hein E. 2000. *War and Punishment: The Causes of War Termination and the First World War*. Princeton: Princeton University Press; Reiter, Dan. 2009. *How Wars End*. Princeton: Princeton University Press.

termination: morality. More specifically, German intransigence was a reflection of the ethics of community. We generally think of morality as something that places breaks on conflict. This can be true of liberal and humanitarian morality, which is the benchmark for moral progress for both skeptics and optimists about morality's pacifying effects. However, binding morality has within it a number of features that can lead to extreme stubbornness, even irrational unwillingness, to come to terms in a conflict. This is yet another indication that what we know as power politics, of which Wilhelmine Germany was a key practitioner, is hardly amoral but it is soaked in ethics, just not the types on which we typically focus. Thought to be the ultimate example of "might makes right," Germany did not bend to might precisely because of right.[3]

As argued previously, binding morality is premised on a particular understanding of the world as a dangerous place in which bad people want to do good people harm. Meeting both external and internal threats necessitates that groups demonstrate solidarity, with individuals sacrificing for the whole and deferring to authority. Binding morality leads to a highly moralized conception of international relations in which threats are deserving of moral condemnation. Adversaries are not simply threats to a country's interest. They are dishonest, murderous, and unjust. Since these threats are inherently bad and evil, binding moralists are predisposed to a framing of conflicts akin to the "deterrence model" of international relations in which signs of weakness and lack of resolve will inevitably be exploited.[4] This gives conflicts the character of a commitment problem and precludes diplomatic approaches even in situations of clear relative loss during war. In other words, it leads naturally to the first two "rational" exceptions to the updating rule. Yet, these are actually highly subjective framings of the situation, not objective fact as is assumed in rationalist models. No moral condemnation, no commitment problem.

---

[3] I should stress that this phenomenon was not confined in World War I to Germany; nor are authoritarian moralists the only who fall prey to these dynamics. In wartime situations, all fall to some degree into this trap. Binding moralists, however, exhibit a greater propensity. If such a moral dynamic emerges dyadically, the results will be particularly catastrophic, as World War I was.

[4] Jervis, *Perception and Misperception in International Politics*.

Binding moralists will also be predisposed to oppose democratic reform within their own countries, especially during conflict situations, when the country must act cohesively. Demands for individual rights are, for authoritarian moralists, expressions of excessive self-concern that are particularly inappropriate when the group is under attack. They also indicate a lack of the resolve necessary to prevail over immoral adversaries bent on destruction. Therefore, what might appear to be a parochial interest in authoritarian survival can in fact be an expression of authoritarian ideology and its moral foundations.

As established previously, binding morality is primarily, but not exclusively, found on the political right. It is "conservative" or "authoritarian" morality. In the German case study that follows, it becomes evident that those who feared commitment problems and the opening of diplomatic negotiations were predominantly found on the right of the political spectrum, which dominated decision-making during the war. The left in Germany, from the beginning of the conflict, declared itself against the annexationist goals the right thought necessary to solve the commitment problem. While it also saw the struggle as one of self-defense, it sought no annexations but instead a "peace of understanding" and "renunciation" of German gains. In 1917, following the defection of the Center Party, the Reichstag disavowed a peace of conquest publicly, despite fears by the right about the deleterious effect on perceptions of German resolve. The domestic politics of wartime Germany therefore revolved around the issue of war aims. With its different moral foundations, based on liberal humanitarianism, the left sought to end the pointless bloodshed of the war. Its calls for reconciliation indicated a lack of moral condemnation of the other side. By glossing over these differences, Reiter mistakenly attributes rationality to the rightist German leaders that guided the country's war effort, treating their framing of the situation as universal and therefore objective.

The evidence shows that the military's concern about the demands of the left for greater political voice, thought to explain Germany's leaders' persistence, was itself an outgrowth of the same framing of the war as a struggle against immoral enemies. In such a war of attrition in which compromise was not an option, Germany had no choice but to continue to fight. The outcome of the war would hinge on the resolve of German society, its willingness to bear the hardships of the war. Demands for greater rights were, to the German military leadership, indications of a lack of loyalty to the country in its time of need, which would weaken the resolve necessary to prevail. Again we see the moralization of will and determination on the part of the German right seen in Chapter 7. There is little evidence that conservative forces in Germany (particularly the military, against whom these charges are genuinely leveled) opposed a reform of the Prussian franchise and the parliamentarization of the German executive branch simply to hold on to power. Overall binding morality parsimoniously accounts for all the varied actions of supposedly rational German decision-makers.

In taking this course, however, Germany's establishment was digging its own figurative grave, bringing about the very outcome that it ostensibly most feared. The working class and its representatives, from the beginning, made clear that it had no interest in the war booty that the right thought would pacify it. Germany's military, in particular, might have been acting rationally in light of its beliefs, but its beliefs were fundamentally irrational; they had no objective basis in the situation prevailing in the country.

Since they represented different portions of German society though, the irrationality of the German right is best seen not by contrasting left to right, but by comparing the latter's beliefs and behavior to the Realpolitik of the German Chancellor, Bethmann-Hollweg, a part of the conservative establishment by any standard. Authoritarian foreign policy is fundamentally different from Realpolitik. As explored in Chapter 3, the realist embraces an ethics of responsibility, in which difficult decisions, such as conceding in the face of a stronger power, is the essence of good decision-making. The realist, who makes decisions unemotionally and rationally, is a pragmatist and a consequentialist. Realists engage in little moral condemnation. Realism cautions leaders to avoid moral crusading as a dangerous emotional distraction from the pursuit of the national interest. The realist is more inclined to behave according to the most basic rationalist mechanism of war termination – seek peace when one's side is losing. However, not everyone is a realist. Indeed I believe they are quite rare. Nevertheless, realism provides an important baseline by which to assess the rationality of binding moralists.

Bethmann-Hollweg, too, wanted to forestall revolution and unlike the left was not guided by any internationalist inclinations or cosmopolitan humanitarianism, only the German national interest.

However, his rational thinking style led him to take fundamentally different positions. Without the moral condemnation more typical of his rightist counterparts, he adjusted his expectations for what Germany could rationally expect as its battlefield situation deteriorated. In other words, he demonstrated the consequentialism expected of a rational thinker. The same was true in domestic politics. Bethmann-Hollweg accurately predicted that the resistance to internal reform would undermine the German war effort and lead to the very outcome the German right most feared: revolution, democracy, and the overthrow of the monarchy. He advocated pragmatically for reforms that would solidify the loyalty of the German working class and thereby avoid the worst possible outcome, a collapse of the monarchy.

In the following sections, I lay out the expectations of a baseline rationalist model of war termination in which war aims are a function of the information revealed by the progress of the conflict. War aims should increase as countries win and should decrease as they lose. I then describe three features of a conflict that might lead to exceptions to this process – commitment problems, fears of domestic revolution, and the costs of diplomatic conversation. Domestic politics explanations have a corollary, the expectation that semi-authoritarian regimes will actually inflate their aims over time, a claim I take up in the next chapter. I offer a counterargument reducing these considerations, at least in the German case, to authoritarian ideology, particularly binding morality. Each of these three gambles for rationalist theoretical resurrection is considered in turn in light of the evidence from the German case.

Gambling for Theoretical Resurrection: Explaining Departures from Rational Thinking in the Face of Loss

Rationalist models of war termination all draw on Fearon's bargaining model of conflict.[5] He argues that war arises due to private information about resolve and power. Although war is ex post costly for all sides, they nevertheless have incentives ex ante to conceal their reservation price and their relative power from the other side. War reveals this private information. In a process of rational updating, the

---

[5] Fearon, James D. 1995. "Rationalist Explanations for War." *International Organization* 49(3): 379–414.

weaker and/or less resolved side should lower its goals and seek peace, the stronger and/or more resolved side should persist and even raise its war aims. This is the baseline bargaining model of war.

However, rationalists maintain that there are three reasons why states who are losing in a conflict – or better said, to whom battlefield outcomes have revealed they will not reach their war aims – continue to fight. These are all efforts to explain why what might seem like irrational behavior is in fact rational.

First, as originally formulated by Fearon and subsequently refined by Reiter, states might face commitment problems.[6] Even if a country is losing a war, it might nevertheless have an incentive to keep fighting if it cannot trust the opposing side to credibly commit to a settlement. If a states' leaders rationally believe that the country will face exploitation in the future, it can be rational to continue fighting. Reiter argues that Germany faced such a situation in the last years of World War I. Its future security depended on control of the Belgian coast, which explains its last-ditch effort in 1918 to break through its adversaries' western lines.

Second, the very pursuit of peace might reveal a lack of resolve to the opposing side, what Mastro calls the "costs of conversation."[7] She explains: "States are concerned that the enemy may perceive a move to an open diplomatic posture as a *concession* made because of weakening resolve, degraded military capabilities, or reduced war aims."[8] Turning to diplomacy reveals even more private information to the opposing side than the outcome of battles to that point. Leaders will only turn to diplomacy, she argues, when they are in a position of strength so as not to appear weak.

Third, what might be irrational for the state as a whole might be rational for individual leaders, particularly in what Goemans calls "semi-repressive" regimes.[9] Elites in such institutional settings might fear that even a moderate loss in a conflict will lead to an overthrow of the regime and the loss of all their prerogatives, even their own imprisonment or execution. In such cases, it might be rational to "gamble for resurrection," damn the consequences for the country. Goemans' central case for this argument is Germany during World War I. German

---

[6] Fearon, "Rationalist Explanations for War"; Reiter, *How Wars End*.
[7] Mastro, Oriana Skylar. 2019. *The Costs of Conversation: Obstacles to Peace Talks in Wartime.* Ithaca and London: Cornell University Press.
[8] Ibid, 12.   [9] Goemans, *War and Punishment*.

elites, particularly the military, were so desperate to avoid internal reform, such as a revision to the franchise and the accountability of the executive branch to the parliament, that they engaged in "high variance" strategies, risky gambles that had little chance of succeeding but could decisively alter the war's outcome if they did.

All of these models, given their rationalist foundations, presume that leaders' framing of the situation is an objective evaluation, not a highly subjective one unique to a particular part of the political spectrum.[10] What all of these models describe as rational behavior in light of deteriorating conditions I argue is better characterized as ideological thinking based on a particular understanding of the situation, one in which rapacious enemies will stop at nothing to reach their goals. This is the framing of the binding moralist, based on moral condemnation. Those who share this particular set of moral foundations will have a way of responding to loss in an international conflict that is distinctly irrational. Rationalist models are themselves efforts at gambling for resurrection, trying to make the irrational rational.

As maintained in previous chapters, binding morality goes hand in hand with a "deterrence model" mindset, the mental model whose "central argument [is] that great dangers arise if an aggressor believes that the status quo powers are weak in capability or resolve."[11] This mindset creates a preoccupation with generating a reputation for toughness. Even small acts of weakness might, it is feared, create the impression that one is irresolute.[12] Any rapprochement or effort to avoid spiraling conflicts will not only go unreciprocated; it will be exploited.

We generally consider the deterrence model as a highly rational and therefore phlegmatic approach to foreign and security policy. However, the deterrence model, as Jervis notes, rests on a dispositional understanding of an adversary's motives; they are a function of the actor's characteristics, not its environment, and certainly not based on any previous provocation that might shift the moral blame.

---

[10] I have explored this phenomenon in other work, such as how some frame the same situation as either a prisoner's dilemma or a coordination game. See Rathbun, Brian C. 2011. "The 'Magnificent Fraud': Trust, International Cooperation, and the Hidden Domestic Politics of American Multilateralism after World War II." *International Studies Quarterly* 55(1): 1–21.

[11] Jervis, *Perception and Misperception in International Politics*, 58.

[12] Schelling, *Arms and Influence*.

An image forms of the other as "hostile" with "aggressive intentions."[13] Aggressiveness, research shows, is one of the traits most associated with an immoral and unethical character.[14]

Moral condemnation makes more and more situations into perceived commitment problems in which no cooperation or compromise is possible given the nature of the adversary. While rationalists explain decision-making as a calculated response to objectively given circumstances, leaders subjectively frame the same situations differently based on assumptions about others' intentions. Where some see an assurance game, for instance, others see a prisoner's dilemma.[15] Binding moralists will be predisposed toward seeing commitment problems.

If binding moralists understand the adversary as insatiable and therefore incapable of compromise, the situation is by definition a commitment problem. Those who morally judge their adversaries will be inclined to believe that they could never be trusted to bury the hatchet. Since nothing will satisfy the enemy's desires in the long term, there is simply no choice but to continue fighting, even when the chances of success are low. Since the adversary can be given no quarter, this gives rise to a fixation on resolve, the application of Jervis' "deterrence model." War becomes a test of will between good and evil. This is the logic of Weisiger's model of unconditional surrender.[16] When others are evil, the only acceptable outcome is total victory. I am arguing here that some are more predisposed to such a dispositional understanding of the adversary than others.[17]

---

[13] Jervis, *Perception and Misperception in International Politics*, 68.

[14] Goodwin et al., "Moral Character Predominates."

[15] Rathbun, "The 'Magnificent Fraud'."

[16] Weisiger, Alex. 2013. *Logics of War: Explanations for Limited and Unlimited Conflicts*. Ithaca and London: Cornell University Press.

[17] Readers will note similarities to classic works by Van Evera and Snyder on the impacts of nationalism and the "myths of empire" on European decision-making, German in particular, during World War I, although they are primarily interested in explaining the causes rather than the duration of war. Both, however, treat these ideological factors as being instrumentally manipulated by cynical self-serving elites. In this way, they are of a feather with Goemans' account. In addition, coming to terms with binding morality helps explain the package of beliefs that guided German but also other European decision-makers during this period. For instance, why did moral condemnation go together with the belief in a big stick and nationalism? Evera, Stephen Van. 1985. "Why Cooperation Failed in 1914." *World Politics* 38: 80; Snyder, *Myths of Empire*.

This mindset applies in both the use of force and diplomacy. I argue elsewhere that binding moralists practice a particular type of diplomacy, coercive bargaining, predicated on a competitive heuristic in which others are seen as keen to exploit any perceived weaknesses. This precludes the information exchange that allows for the creation of win–win outcomes, making even coming to the table difficult. Coercive bargainers inflate their reservation point in negotiations, make heavy use of "positional commitments" in which they threaten never to compromise past a certain point, and "reactively devalue" others' offers, deriding them as insufficient and insulting. They also insist that others make concessions first so that they can pocket them and demand more, assuming the other will do the same.[18] Just as one must never show weakness and must always show resolve in conflict, the same will be true in negotiation. Coercive bargaining is simply the diplomatic manifestation of the deterrence model mindset, as argued earlier.

Even the resistance to internal reform can be understood as a function of binding morality. Binding moralists believe that in situations of threat, societies must act in a unified and hierarchical manner so as to maintain the cohesion necessary to defeat adversaries. The nation can only maintain and indicate its resolve if all sacrifice their own personal interests for the sake of the broader community. The pursuit of internal reform in such a mindset is a self-serving and disloyal enterprise, even more so during a period of war in which the nation must dedicate all its energies toward victory. Moreover, it signals a lack of determination to the adversary, indicating that if it pushes harder, the country will collapse. In situations of threat, resolve becomes a virtue for the binding moralist, an expression of sacrifice and commitment to the group, as we see in the previous chapter. Conversely, a lack of determination indicates selfishness and free-riding. Those who do not demonstrate such perseverance are liable to moral condemnation from inside the group. Of course, such claims might be self-serving, instrumental, and even disingenuous, but ultimately this is an empirical question.

My argument expects the baseline expectations of rationalist models, in which political decision-makers revise their goals upward or

[18] Rathbun, Brian C. 2014. *Diplomacy's Value: Creating Security in 1920s Europe and the Contemporary Middle East. Cornell Studies in Security Affairs.* Ithaca and London: Cornell University Press.

downward based on the battlefield situation, will apply, but mainly to rational thinkers. Since the "rational" exceptions to this baseline dynamic identified by rationalist theorists are, according to my argument, actually the manifestation of ideological thinking that might lead to suboptimal outcomes, rational thinkers will consciously avoid them. Realist practitioners, those with high levels of procedural rationality, share the national focus of authoritarians in a way that the more cosmopolitan left does not; comparing their behavior and cognitive processing to the authoritarian right allows us to control for variation in interests while testing the importance of cognitive style. As System II processors, realists will more easily engage in the emotionally costly act of updating information when it is unfavorable; they will be constantly assessing whether the time for conversation is ripe; and they will apply their thinking style to domestic politics as well. As pragmatists, they will question whether resisting democratic reform actually impedes the war-fighting effort by undermining national solidarity.

I focus my attention on the most important realist in World War I Germany: the chancellor, Theobald von Bethmann-Hollweg. I compare the substance and rational cognitive style of his Realpolitik with that of his political allies before the war. While it is challenging to assess thinking style independent of decisions, there is no way around it. Otherwise, we make the same tautological mistake as rationalist analyses that assume rationality and work backward from decisions to construct a set of beliefs that make choices seem appropriate. The chancellor's cognitive style becomes evident independent of the willingness to bite the bullet in three ways: (1) Numerous scholars of the chancellor have identified his rational thinking as a key characteristic evident long before the war began,[19] (2) as we will see, the chancellor

---

[19] See citations in Jarausch 1973, who reviews the literature of authors who describe Bethmann-Hollweg as "contemplative, judicious," a "stoic" with a "pensive nature" (5) who walked a tightrope between "reason and public pressure." This thinking style translated into "pragmatic opportunism, adaptable to changing constellations" (67). Ritter writes, "Cautious and conscientiousness, he was slow to make up his mind" (1972, 73). This System II approach made him a practitioner of the ethics of responsibility: "Invariably he sought to do what he thought reasonable and necessary, as the responsible head of the Reich government" (485). Jarausch, Konrad. 1973. *The Enigmatic Chancellor: Bethmann-Hollweg and the Hubris of Imperial Germany.* New Haven: Yale University Press.

modeled his approach after the greatest German realist, Otto von Bismarck, and (3) in a way not true of his authoritarian opponents at home, Bethmann-Hollweg explicitly describes his thought process separate from the decisions he makes in private sources reviewed in the following text. Table 8.1 compares my argument to that of the four rationalist mechanisms for war persistence during loss and fore-shadows the empirical findings.

Bethmann-Hollweg's home was on the right of the political spectrum and he saw his responsibility as safeguarding German interests and German interests only.[20] His family was part of the establishment, having parlayed its commercial success into nobility. The Kaiser hunted at his family home. When he entered politics, the young Theobold tried first as a Reichstag candidate for the Conservative and National Liberal parties, the pillars of the right, eventually taking up ministerial office in the conservative Prussian cabinet. As chancellor he pursued a *Sammlungspolitik* that allied these parties with the Catholic Zentrum party in a blue–black coalition.[21] In this way, he had the same interests in preserving the status quo as other right-wing figures.

The literature on World War I, particularly its outbreak, is immense and marked by controversy; I cannot do it justice; I focus my attention on the narrow(er) question of German war aims, drawing in many sources of primary documents generally neglected. Rather than presenting a narrative of chronological events, I organize the case study into three sections, each corresponding to one of the rationalist explanations for German persistence in Table 8.1. I consider the war aims inflation argument in the next chapter. The case study concerns itself primarily with events up until July 1917, when Bethmann-Hollweg was forced out through threat of resignation by the top military leadership for his putative lack of resolution. This is regarded by almost all historians as a decisive turning point in the war, one which sealed the fate of the regime.

---

[20] Craig, Gordon Alexander. 1978. *Germany, 1866–1945*. Oxford: Clarendon Press, 365; Jarausch, *The Enigmatic Chancellor*, 1, 28. He was known as well for his sense of duty over ambition. Jarausch. 1973, 67, 71, something the Kaiser recognized. After the war, he volunteered to be tried in the emperor's place, claiming he bore full responsibility for his government's actions.

[21] Jarausch, *The Enigmatic Chancellor*, 38, 46, 73.

Table 8.1 *Rationality, morality, and the termination of war*

		Rationalist War Termination Argument	Binding Morality Authoritarian Ideology Argument	Empirical findings of Germany in World War I WWI
Departures from Rational Baseline	Information Updating (rationalist baseline)	State leaders will become more willing to seek settlement and lower war aims as their battlefield situation deteriorates	Realists with a more rational thinking style and a commitment to consequentialist ethics will become more willing to seek settlement and lower war aims as their battlefield situation deteriorates whereas binding moralists will not	Only realist chancellor Bethmann-Hollweg and the German left are more willing to seek settlement and lower war aims as tide turns against Germany
	Commitment Problem	States leaders will not lower their war aims when there is a commitment problem	Binding moralists will be predisposed to frame conflicts as a commitment problem due to morally laden view of adversary in a way not true of realists and the left	Commitment problem framing is predominant in the German right, whereas left seeks reconciliation in later years of conflict

Costs of Conversation	State leaders will not seek diplomatic accommodation even if they are in a position of weakness for fear of revealing a lack of resolve	Binding moralists will be resistant to diplomatic negotiation even if they are in a position of weakness for fear of revealing a lack of resolve to a ruthless adversary	German right resists efforts by German left to declare that Germany has no annexationist aims and opposes any expression of willingness to negotiate as indications of lack of resolve to insatiable enemy
Fear of Domestic Punishment	Rational leaders in semi-repressive regimes will gamble for resurrection so as to avoid internal political reform or revolution to preserve their political prerogatives	Binding moralists will resist democratic reforms for fears of weakening internal unity and projecting an image of lack of resolve, whereas realists will make endorse pragmatic concessions to maintain unity and avoid the worst	German right opposes democratic reform as expression of disloyalty undermining German unity in a time of great threat and resists pragmatic efforts of chancellor aimed to reform institutions in order to prevent revolution and save monarchy
War Aims Inflation	Rational leaders in semi-repressive regimes will increase their war aims in an attempt to buy off domestic opponents through spoils of war	Binding moralists will increase war aims as costs increase so as to compensate for loyal sacrifices of soldiers, whereas others will adjust expectations downward	As war drags on and German casualties mount, German right calls for ever greater annexations to honor fallen heroes, whereas Bethmann-Hollweg revises expectations downward

Commitment Problem?: The War Aims Movement of the German Right

Reiter explains German persistence during World War I as the manifestation of a commitment problem, a rational decision in light of Germany's strategic dilemma during the war. "Germany doubted the willingness of France or Britain to accept a peace deal into the future. The Germans believed it critical that they shore up their Western borders to neutralize the long-term Anglo-French threat. Accomplishing this task required a peace settlement permitting German control of Belgium."[22] Therefore, even as the western front stagnated and the country struggled to feed its own people, it had no choice but to keep fighting. Some expansion in the west was necessary for future German security.

The German Right

However, this was not the way by which all German elites, much less the masses, understood the war. When Reiter refers to "Germans" or "Germany," he is eliding an enormous chasm that separated the left and the right in German domestic politics on war aims, differences that can be traced to alternative moral foundations. From the early days of the conflict, a war aims movement (*Kriegszielbewegung*) emerged to advocate for an annexationist peace through pressure on the government and public propaganda. The movement, which united virtually the entire German right, was held together by a common diagnosis: that Germany was surrounded by hostile and immoral adversaries, a situation that required an expansion of its borders and an improvement in its economic and strategic position to avoid another world war that threatened its very existence. They called this a "Hindenburg peace," after the German general tasked with leading the country's eastern forces and later brought in to lead the entire war effort. The movement incorporated intellectuals, rightist parties in the Reichstag, economic interests who stood to gain from annexationist goals, and military leadership. Its work was closely linked to the Pan-German League (*Alldeutscher Verband*). Ritter explains: "The psychological background to the so-called 'war aims movement' was formed precisely by the German people's unshakable conviction that they were

---

[22] Reiter, *How Wars End*, 147.

taking the field in 1914 as victims of a malicious surprise attack, a systematic encirclement by envious rivals, especially Britain – in other words, that this purely defensive war had been forced on them."[23] The clearest statement of this point of view is found in the petition of the Pan-German League to the government, authored by the group's leader, Heinrich Class, originally censored and only officially published in 1917.[24] Since Germany's adversaries were bent on the fatherland's destruction, only expansion could provide economic and military security. "It is clear that there are no more Germans on the soil of the empire who are not of the view, after the envy and hate, the terror and recklessness of our enemies that forced us into this existential struggle without precedent, that such a terribly difficult and dangerous situation must never again be allowed and that therefore our enemies must be opposed and weakened to such an extent that our existence never comes into question again."[25] The world was a dangerous place. "Our external security demands the weakening of enemies; the type, means and scale … follows from the size of the peril that we now have to endure, and from the justified aspiration to never again be exposed to such a danger of a similar scale."[26] Class set out a variety of annexationist goals, justifying all of them as necessary defensive measures in light of the moral transgressions of Germany's enemies.

The military also endorsed this highly ideological point of view, something that became particularly important after July 1917. In his memoirs, Erich Ludendorff, second in command as of August 1916 but the de facto head of the German armed forces, wrote that given the unrelenting demands of Germany's enemies, it had no choice but to outlast its adversaries. An understanding with Germany's opponents was "impossible in view of the enemy's determination to destroy us."[27] They had a "lust for our destruction."[28] He wrote of "England's defiance of the laws of nations in employing the blockade against our very

---

[23] Ritter, Gerhard. 1972. *The Sword and the Scepter: The Problem of Militarism in Germany*, Vol. III. Coral Gables: University of Miami Press, 24.

[24] Class, Heinrich. 1917. *Zum deutschen Kriegsziel, eine Flugschrift*. München: J. F. Lehmann. On this memo see Gatzke, Hans. 1978. *Germany's Drive to the West*. Westport: Greenwood Press, 39–47, 54; Smith, *The Ideological Origins of Nazi Imperialism*, 177; Craig, *Germany, 1866–1945*, 360–363.

[25] Ibid, 8.   [26] Ibid, 13.

[27] Ludendorff, Erich. 1919. *My War Memories, 1914–1918*, Vol. 1. Hutchinson & Co., 8.

[28] Ibid, 372.

flesh and blood." It was an "inhuman enemy."[29] All parties of the right in the Reichstag also endorsed annexations based on the need for security.[30] Bethmann-Hollweg identified the Pan-Germans and the military as his primary opponents domestically during the war.[31]

Annexationism and commitment problem framing grew directly out of moral condemnation. The "Petition of the Professors" of July 1915, signed by over 1,300 artists, writers, academics, professionals, teachers, and theologians, accused German enemies of "plans that amount to the annihilation of the German empire," such that "mere defense is no longer sufficient." They also identified a commitment problem. "We want to never repeat such an attack from all sides ... and we want to position ourselves so firmly and so broadly on a secured and enlarged homeland territory, that guarantees our independent existence." Germany was only protecting itself "against the barbarian flood from the east and the revenge and longing for domination from the west." Belgium was "nothing other" than a launching point for "English aggression, the shield behind which our enemies will again collect." For its part, France was obsessed with revenge, having responded to efforts at reconciliation with "the most extreme fanaticism." In contrast, Germany was a peaceful force in international politics, "having preserved peace up to the limits of its national honor and existence. Germany has never thought of overstepping the narrow borders of its continental, European possessions through conquest despite the growth of its population and power."[32]

---

[29] Ludendorff, *My War Memories, 1914–1918*, Vol. II, 453.
[30] Grumbach, S. (ed.). 1917. "Erklärung aller bürgerlichen Parteien im Reichstag." In (ed.). 1917.*Das annexionistische Deutschland: Eine Sammlung von Dokumenten, die seit dem 4. August 1914, in Deutschland öffentlich oder geheim verbreitet wurden.* Lausanne: Verlag Payot, 33.
[31] Ritter, *The Sword and the Scepter*, 476.
[32] "Petition der Professoren an den Reichskanzler. In Grumbach, *Das annexionistische Deutschland,* "Erklärung aller bürgerlichen Parteien im Reichstag," 132–142. This petition, called the "Seeberg address" was spearheaded by Class. The Conservative leader Cuno von Westarp describes its purpose, "to give more emphasis to the petitions of the economic organizations through support of large sections of the population, in order that the propagation of far-reaching war aims on the part of the economic organizations would not give the impression that these aims were based exclusively on selfish, materialistic, and non-patriotic feelings" (Gatzke, *Germany's Drive to the West,* 117). These intellectuals were the "brain trust" of the Kriegszielbewegung, and it seems hard to trace their position back to some crude personal economic interest in German expansion. The fact that such a petition was thought

All parties of the right endorsed annexations based on the need for security. A joint declaration of the "bourgeois parties" on December 9, 1915 stated that "we also want to end this war forced upon us" but also demanded that the peace ensure "the military, economic, financial and political interests of Germany ... including the necessary territorial acquisitions."[33] The board of the Conservative party called for Germany "not to be scared of any further sacrifices that are necessary to bring to war to a lasting, honorable peace that secures that basis for a peaceful German future. Naturally the board will advocate for the expansion of required territorial expansion necessary for this purpose."[34] This was again couched in the need for security. The Center Party, the second largest in the Reichstag behind the Social Democrats, issued a resolution in October 1915 stating the need for "increased security against the military and economic annihilation plans of its [Germany's] enemies. The terrible sacrifices imposed by the war on our people call for strengthened protection of our country in west

necessary indicates that even for the most crass egoists, in a wartime situation one can never avoid the need for a strong moral rationale. It is also important to note that Class himself was the originator of the petition of the six economic associations, indicating that this was the ideological tail wagging the material dog more than a cloaking of economic interest with a moral mantle (Gatzke, *Germany's Drive to the West*, 39–47, 54; Smith, *The Ideological Origins of Nazi Imperialism*, 177; Craig, *Germany, 1866–1945*, 360–363).

[33] "Erklärung aller bürgerlichen Parteien im Reichstag," In Grumbach, *Das annexionistische Deutschland*, 33.

[34] "Erklärung aller bürgerlichen Parteien im Reichstag." In Grumbach, *Das annexionistische Deutschland*, 40. Particularly noteworthy is the Conservative party's fixation with England as Germany's main enemy. A purely materialist interpretation of German party motives, common in the literature, identifies the party as the representative of large agricultural interests largely in the east, the Prussian Junker, and predominantly interested in the acquisition of land suitable for farming through annexations of Russian territory. The party mentioned such Lebensraum goals in its public statements but reserved most of its ire for England, so much so as to draw rebukes from the Agrarian League, the economic lobbying arm of the Junker (Gatzke, *Germany's Drive to the West*, 103). England was primarily a threat to Germany's western economic interests, given its geographical proximity. The Weltpolitik that industrialists favored given the need for global shipping lanes and colonial acquisitions also identified England as the main competitor. Russia was the primary threat from the east, and Germany's agricultural interests had little interest in exporting abroad given their lack of competitiveness. Yet the board of the party describes as "the most important [goal]: striving with all means to defeat England, which is responsible for the war and will never cease to threaten our position in the world and prevent our further development in the future." The materialist case is weak.

and east, that prevents our enemies from overrunning us again."[35]
The central board of the National Liberal Party proclaimed on August
15, 1915, "The result of the present war can only be a peace that by
expanding our borders in the east and the west and overseas protects
us militarily, politically and economically from new assaults and the
enormous sacrifices, that the German people have endured and are
determined to endure until the final victorious end."[36]

Because binding morality predisposes its adherents to think in terms
of commitment problems, even defensive conflicts become offensive
ones. If the adversary is insatiable and bent on annihilation, then war
aims do not change based on a country's successes or failures on the
battlefield. As one petition to the government endorsing extensive war
aims argued: "[A]n unfavorable or insecure war situation *would not
change anything....* Because the goal can only be realized by fighting
for a peace that secures our border in west and east, a broadening of
the foundation of our maritime possibilities and the possibility of an
unhindered and strong development of our economic power."[37]

Class explicitly rejected liberal morality with its emphasis on disinterested justice. "In evaluating and establishing the conditions for
peace the first rule for us must be: dismiss all cosmopolitan thinking,
a political tendency of the Germans, to place itself in others' shoes,
all dangerous 'objectivity' in favor of foreigners that has caused us to
wrong ourselves, that has made us short-sighted at the expense of the
advantage to our own people."[38] However, this was not the expression
of a more general amoralism; the actions of Germany's adversaries justified a violent response. In light of the behavior of Germany's adversaries, the country could no longer be concerned with "humanitarian
regard."[39] "Our opponents show us the example."[40] He invoked negative reciprocity, asking rhetorically, "Where was the humanity of the
French and the Belgians when they committed in the most ignominious
way the most gruesome type of assassination against our officers and
soldiers, when the Russians permitted abominations against unarmed

---

[35] "Erklärung aller bürgerlichen Parteien im Reichstag." In Grumbach, *Das
annexionistische Deutschland*, 35.
[36] Ibid, 36.
[37] "Petition der sechs Wirtschaftsverbände an den Reichskanzler." In Grumbach,
Das annexionistische Deutschland, 124.
[38] Class, *Zum deutschen Kriegsziel*, 13.
[39] Ibid, 14.   [40] Ibid, 6.

seniors, women and children?"[41] The lesson of the war, Class argued, was that "a Volk has to rely on itself; it bears the responsibility to guarantee its existence and its future alone – self-preservation is the highest obligation.... From this follows the right and the duty, following victory in battles forced upon us, to judge the price of victory only on the basis of the needs of one's own people, without regard for the wishes or the opinions of the defeated peoples."[42] The need to provide physical and material protection drives binding morality. Its purpose is to protect. In wartime situations, there is "justifiable self-seeking."[43]

The German Left

Much is made of the fact that the Social Democratic Party in Germany, like leftist parties in other European countries, endorsed the war effort at the onset of the conflict. This is evidence of the war fever that gripped the Continent and extended across the political spectrum.[44] In Germany, this was known as the *Burgfrieden*, literally the peace within the besieged castle. While the left did abstain from undermining the war effort, this fact obscures important differences between left and right that became increasingly acute as the wore dragged on. While the Social Democratic Party (SPD) also saw Germany as defending its "national existence and independence ... against a world of enemies," its caucus in the Reichstag declared itself on the first day of the war to "condemn any war of conquest" and to "recognize the right of every people to independence and self-defense."[45] As other parties and organizations put forth their designs for conquest, in December 1915, the Reichstag caucus came out against "all annexation plans ... that rape other peoples. These would weaken the national strength and unity of the German empire, damage its foreign relations and become the germ of new wars."[46] This program became known as the "Scheidemann peace," after the party's caucus leader. In August 1915, the SPD party conference demanded the restoration

---

[41] Ibid, 14. [42] Ibid, 13. [43] Ibid, 10.

[44] See, for instance, Maehl, W. W., 1952. "The Triumph of Nationalism in the German Socialist Party on the Eve of the First World War." *Journal of Modern History* 24(1): 15–41.

[45] "Die Erklärung vom. 4. August 1914." In Grumbach, *Das annexionistische Deutschland*, 432.

[46] "Die Fraktionserklärung vom 21. Dezember 1915." In Grumbach, *Das annexionistische Deutschland*, 434.

of Belgium as necessary "from the standpoint of German interests not to mention justice."[47] Rejecting continued war credits for the war, Ttwenty Socialist members of the party even splintered off and formed the Independent Social Democratic Party.[48]

What explains the different position of the SPD? The left in Germany believed in the possibility of a peace of "reconciliation" (*Versöhnung*) and "understanding" (*Verständigung*) that the right, which engaged in more moral condemnation, could not envision. In other words, second-order moral beliefs were the primary source of the differences that separated the two sides of the political spectrum. Engaging in less moral outrage allowed the SPD to foresee the potential for mutual forgiveness. In a petition to the chancellor, the SPD party board decried the petitions of economic interests and political leaders described previously, declaring it "our duty, to remind [Germans] that ... we want a peace that allows for friendship with neighboring peoples.... Peace must bring us more sympathy, not more enmity."[49] For this, they were predictably condemned by the right for being unpatriotic.[50]

Another reason that the left might have taken a different position, of course, is that it represented different constituencies in German society, most importantly those average Germans paying the ultimate price on the battlefield. As this is not central to my argument, I did not try to establish whether left-wing motivations as publicly stated were genuine, although even if they were not, it still begs the question as to why such internationalist and renunciationist justifications were politically necessary. More crucial for the argument about how binding morality contributed to the war's duration is a comparison between the German nationalists and the realist chancellor, himself part of the conservative establishment.

The Chancellor's Realpolitik
The task of negotiating these domestic differences, and much more, fell to German Chancellor Bethmann-Hollweg, whose sober, unemotional,

---

[47] "Resolution des Parteiausschusses an der Reichstagsfraktion." In Grumbach, *Das annexionistische Deutschland*, 431.

[48] See "Die Erklärung der Zwanzig." In Grumbach, *Das annexionistische Deutschland*, 434.

[49] "Petition des Parteivorstandes an den Reichskanzler." In Grumbach, *Das annexionistische Deutschland*, 429–430.

[50] Jarausch, *The Enigmatic Chancellor*, 213.

and morally consequentialist Realpolitik provided a great contrast to both the left and the right. Bethmann-Hollweg was on the right of the political spectrum and saw his responsibility as safeguarding German interests and German interests only.[51] In that sense, he shared the interests and morality of the right. However, in his mind, German annexationists, because of their moral exuberance and hot-headedness, made this task more rather than less difficult. The chancellor's approach shows us not only what a hard-headed pursuit of interests, stripped of moral condemnation, looked like but also how politically unpalatable it often is. No one loved this political realist, something realists often lament.[52]

The chancellor insisted that Germany's war aims should be dictated by German military success. The Germans should "take what we can according to the military situation"[53] but not get ahead of themselves. He told the Prussian ministry of state in the fall of 1914 that "we can only talk about peace conditions after victory. They depend on the degree of our military strength."[54] He told Conservatives in the Prussian Landtag: "It does not seem right to propose aims when we are trying to save our skins.... If we are strong enough when peace comes we shall reap great rewards. But our strength will not increase by proclaiming large goals."[55] It was "useless to discuss the distribution of the fruits of victory before we have won it,"[56] he wrote privately, fruits that "will solely depend on our military situation at the conclusion of peace."[57] He saw himself as following Bismarck's example: "I believe he would have turned his famous riding boots first against the political agitators who, greater in words than in thought, wanted to force him to unfurl banners which he might have had to pull down again at any time."[58]

---

[51] Craig, *Germany, 1866–1945,* 365.

[52] Gilpin, Robert G. 1996. "No One Loves a Political Realist." *Security Studies* 5(3): 3–26.

[53] Jarausch, *The Enigmatic Chancellor,* 227.

[54] "Sitzung des Staatsminnisteriums am 28. November 1914." In *Die Protokolle des Preußischen Staatsministeriums 1817–1934/38.* Hildesheim: Berlin-Brandenburgischen Akademie der Wissenschaften, Band 10, no. 123. Hereafter, "Protokolle." The protocols in question can be found in the Prussian State Ministry Libraries under the following signature: I. HA Rep 90 A, Nos. 3260–3622.

[55] Jarausch, *The Enigmatic Chancellor,* 217.   [56] Ibid, 203.

[57] Bethmann to Weizsaecker, Nachlass Loebell, N 1045 (10 November 1914). All Nachlässe (the letters from an estate) are located at the Bundesarchiv (German Federal Archive) location in Koblenz.

[58] Jarausch, *The Enigmatic Chancellor,* 215.

This was a manifestation of Bethmann-Hollweg's rational Realpolitik. "Since politics will always remain the art of the possible, nobody can foresee today if we shall reach all the goals we have set for ourselves."[59] This was his own personal morality: "Can one in politics call something objectively right which is impossible? I believe not."[60] It was "blasphemous to force the hand of providence."[61] He wrote, "The German empire as master of the continent and the world by dispossessing England, annexing Belgium, northern and eastern France, and the Baltic states and Poland would be a dream – and since unrealistic, perhaps not even a beautiful one."[62]

Even in 1914, the chancellor did "not believe that we could gain a peace which would allow us to dispose of the world," and cautioned that "even fighting to a standstill against such an enormous coalition would be a success that would provide for the protection of the peace in the future."[63] He was also cautious, as Bismarck had been during the Austro-Prussian War in 1866, of biting off more than Germany could chew. Just as Bismarck, following German victory, had passed on forcefully annexing populations, such as the Bavarian Catholics, that would be hard to immediately incorporate into the new German body politic, the chancellor noted the difficulties of annexing the Walloon portion of Belgium, which would "mean an enormous weakening of Germany."[64] He advised, "The goals should not only be measured according to what is obtainable but also what is really useful to us."[65]

As the war became one of attrition, the chancellor argued that it was his responsibility to end the war on a pragmatic basis, what he called a "moral duty."[66] He spoke of annexing "whatever the soldiers and sailors absolutely demand and what even a reasonable man cannot deny to unreasonable Germans. But as little as possible."[67] According to the ethics of responsibility, "If the opportunity for peace arises anywhere we are duty bound to seize it."[68] War aims could not be allowed to intrude: "We do not want to prolong the war one day more than necessary because of wild annexations." Under his

[59] Ibid, 220.   [60] Ibid, 229.

[61] Bethmann to Loebell, N 1045(2 January 1915), Nachlass Loebell.

[62] Jarausch, *The Enigmatic Chancellor*, 202.

[63] "Sitzung des Staatsminnisteriums am 28. November 1914," in *Protokolle*, no. 123, Band 10.

[64] On Bismarck, see Rathbun, *Reasoning of State, Realists, Romantics and Rationality in International Relations*, 134–135.

[65] Jarausch, *The Enigmatic Chancellor*, 199.

[66] Ibid, 251.   [67] Ibid, 199.   [68] Ibid, 250.

consequentialist logic, "If we offer the chance for peace to return, our conscience will be clear before God and our nation."[69] Biting the bullet would be the right thing to do.

While Bethmann-Hollweg still placed most of the blame for the outbreak of the war on German adversaries, somewhat alone among rightist politicians he also acknowledged Germany's role. Since the Kaiser ascended the throne, "we have often done the opposite of that which would have lightened our burden."[70] The problem was a lack of rational calculation, leading to self-encirclement. He complained just before hostilities began: "A Turkish policy against Russia, Morocco against France, fleet against England, all at the same time – challenge everybody, get in everyone's way, and actually, in the course of all this, weaken nobody." For this he blamed the "'national' parties" for making a "hullabaloo about foreign policy."[71] As the carnage began, he maintained that the "wild demands of our annexationists bear part of the responsibility for the protraction of the war."[72] This conviction even affected his public pronouncements. Ritter writes. "Reading his wartime speeches in the Reichstag today, one clearly senses that despite his often exaggerated charges against the policies of Germany's enemies and his polemics centered on speeches by enemy leaders, Bethmann Hollweg deliberatively avoided lapsing into fanatical preachments of hatred.... They were of tempered militancy, but never inflammatory in effect."[73]

This put the chancellor at odds with his previous political allies, the nationalists in Germany, who accused him of defeatism. He chastized this "hydra of Pan-German annexationist fury" for indulging in emotionally driven fantasizing rather than calm, sober, and rational consideration of what was truly possible.[74] The "policy of a great empire cannot be directed according to the recipe of a few hotheads." Pan-German visions were "utopias." They suffered from "illusory hubris." His task, as he saw it, was "keeping a group of madmen on the road to reason or, if that is impossible, taking the least idiotic way and acting as if it were the path of rationality."[75] He complained of the six

---

[69] Ibid, 251.
[70] Bethmann to Oettingen, N 1688 (30 August 1914), Nachlass Oettingen.
[71] Craig, *Germany, 1866–1945*, 337.
[72] Jarausch, *The Enigmatic Chancellor*, 229.
[73] Ritter, *The Sword and the Scepter*, 21–22.   [74] Ibid, 193.
[75] Ibid, 186, 199, 229, 231.

economic associations: "I cannot enlighten the petitioners about the military position. Either they accuse me of defeatism, or they become frightened. We need neither. Only military events themselves can gradually *sober* them."[76]

Bethmann's goals were also different *qualitatively*. Even at his most annexationist, he envisioned an economic bloc of Central European countries with Germany at its core, satisfying its economic needs and need for greater security without overt annexations.[77] These were the ideas that drove his September program, which is not the plan for conquest that Fritz Fischer originally maintained but rather a program for an informal empire driven primarily by economic considerations.[78] Again, Bethmann-Hollweg believed that Bismarck would have agreed.[79]

Bethmann-Hollweg's approach had the support of another group of intellectuals who, in response to the annexationist petition mentioned earlier, mobilized in favor of a largely defensive war and the creation of a customs union.[80] This pragmatic approach, however, did not attract nearly as many followers. The number of signatories of the "Delbrueck-Derburg" petition was a tenth of the Seeberg proposal, another indication of how moralization had overtaken positions on both sides of the war aims debate, leaving realists like Bethmann-Hollweg in a relatively unpopulated center.

[76] Jarausch, *The Enigmatic Chancellor*, 203.
[77] This was a longstanding concept in German foreign policy thought, the notion of *Mitteleuropa* (Central Europe) in which the country sought its destiny through economic (and therefore political) preeminence in the heart of the continent in which other states voluntarily acquiesced due to the economic advantages for them (Gatzke, *Germany's Drive to the West*, 106). Germany was to be the industrial hub, technological innovator and source of capital, and a customs union of protective tariffs that would include Austro-Hungary, Poland, Denmark, Holland, and Belgium. Peripheral states would provide raw materials and agricultural goods (Smith, *The Ideological Origins of Nazi Imperialism*, 170). See also Ritter, *The Sword and the Scepter*, 30.
[78] Craig, *Germany, 1866–1945*, 365. Mommsen writes, "To those who have studied the sources it is disturbing that Bethmann-Hollweg's bitter opposition to the Pan-Germans and the industrialists and ultra-conservatives behind them, which greatly increased is difficulties, is dealt with by Fischer as if it were of merely secondary importance. There was after all a world of difference between Bethmann's September Programme and Class' first big memorandum on war aims; it is misleading to suggest that the two are identical in attitude." Mommsen, "The Debate on German War Aims."
[79] Jarausch, *The Enigmatic Chancellor*, 215.
[80] "Die Delbrück-Dernburg Petition." In Grumbach, *Das annexionistische Deutschland*, 410.

Costs of Conversation?: The Debate over the Peace Resolution

Mastro argues that state leaders will be reluctant to negotiate from a position of weakness, fearing that declaring willingness to engage in diplomatic talks will be taken as an indication of a lack of resolve.[81] This phenomenon also occurred in Germany, but again it was largely confined to the right wing of German politics. Such a perspective on diplomacy, known as coercive bargaining, is founded on the same dangerous world beliefs as the deterrence model in which others will inevitably exploit one's weaknesses. It is an expression of binding morality and moral condemnation.[82] This is best seen in the context of debates on war aims within the Reichstag.

On April 11, 1917, the SPD issued a manifesto demanding peace "without annexations or indemnities." Soon after, a dramatic about-face by the Center Party, led by Matthias Erzberger, created a new majority in the Reichstag for a renunciationist peace. A new alliance of the Center Party, the Progressive Party, and the Social Democratic Party announced plans to introduce a "peace resolution" before the Reichstag, calling for a "peace of understanding and a lasting reconciliation of peoples. Any violations of territory, and political, economic and financial persecutions are incompatible with such a peace."[83] A successful vote would indicate that parties representing a majority of the German public supported peace without annexations, a Scheidemann peace.

In the subsequent debate in early July 1917, the parties of the right described the peace resolution "not only as useless, but dangerous and erroneous to the highest degree," in the words of the Free Conservative parliamentarian, Warnuth.[84] It was an indication of a lack of resolve to evil enemies bent on German destruction. Von Westarp, of the Conservatives, warned that "the will of our enemies to annihilate us is not broken; every indication of our readiness to make peace, every appearance of renouncing the fruits of victory will still be seen as a sign of our breakdown." He argued that "Germany's goals could not

---

[81] Mastro, *The Costs of Conversation.*   [82] Rathbun, *Diplomacy's Value.*
[83] *Verhandlungen des deutschen Reichstags.* XIII. Legislaturperiod. II Session. Band 310. Stenographische Berichte. 116 Sitzung. Berlin: Druck und Verlag der Norddeutschen Buchdruckerei und Verlags-Anstalt, 3596.
[84] Ibid, 3585.

be reached through reconciliation, which rested solely on the good will of her enemies."[85]

Given what the National Liberal representative described as a "world of enemies,"[86] the country had no choice but to persist until Germany's inevitable victory. This included expansion to provide for security against "England, which is leading the whole world against us, month after month." Westarp also demanded that "our [eastern] borders be protected for all time; East Prussia must never again be subjected to the atrocities of a Russian invasion."[87]

Yet this was now the minority position. The sponsors of the resolution had an entirely different moral understanding of the war premised on cosmopolitan, humanitarian ethics. For Scheidemann of the SPD, the war "is a tyrant, that oppresses all peoples. But if all countries fight against it, and if we help to prepare the end ... then we are not weak but rather we are strong. It is out of weakness that this disastrous war drags on."[88] Von Payer, speaking for the Progressive People's Party, explained, "This resolution grows out of the discovery that at the end of three years of war not only Germany and its allies, but the whole of humanity desires peace.... We are concerned how many million people, if no peace arises, will have lost their lives, what enormous, irreplaceable things of value will have been destroyed, not only by our enemies, but unfortunately by us and our allies."[89]

Scheidemann explicitly advocated ending the moral condemnation that drove the conflict, asking foreign peoples to "close their ears to the warmongers, who – just like ours – continually point to new indications that on the other side 'over there' they will fight to the end, and that it will only require one last push to strike the opponent to the ground. No more will we defeat you in a few months than will you defeat us."[90] Both Scheidemann and von Payer acknowledged that their own government no longer had credibility with foreign countries, so the point of the peace resolution was to demonstrate to foreign audiences the will of the German people: not to conquer but rather only to protect what was theirs. The resolution passed 212 to 116.

Bethmann-Hollweg found himself again trying to walk a tightrope between the left and the right with his realpolitik approach. On the one hand, grandiose plans strengthened the fighting spirit in enemy

[85] Ibid, 3584.   [86] Ibid.   [87] Ibid.   [88] Ibid, 3575–3579.
[89] Ibid, 3579–3584.   [90] Ibid, 3575–3579.

nations, so he avoided them. "If you read the speeches which I made in the Reichstag ... then you will find that this thought of working upon the emotions of the peacefully-inclined minorities in the enemy countries occurs again and again," he later testified.[91] However, he was opposed to an explicit renunciation of war aims since appearing to be too eager to achieve peace would also be dangerous. "We cannot proclaim no annexations, status quo. Then they will say: we are through.... We need a sign of strength and unity in a form which reinforces the enemy's desire for peace."[92] The chancellor thought it was best to say little at all. "Neither annexationism nor a pacifism provoked by it facilitated the tasks dictated by the war situation to increase the enemy's inclination towards peace. German desires for conquest as well as German renunciation of claims were the most valuable allies of our enemies," he later explained.[93] In a May 15, 1917 speech to the Reichstag, he declared that the establishment of any concrete aims to be "inimical to the national interest" since both the left and the right's approach was bad for the national interest.[94] This was his reasoning for banning public discussions of war aims earlier in the war. However, the right, particularly the Pan-German League, came in for more private criticism than the left.[95]

The military unsurprisingly disagreed, lobbying against the peace resolution and demanding a positive statement of annexationist war aims. The head of the armed forces, Hindenburg, protested that the peace resolution "would intensify the existing unrest in the army and would be regarded as a sign of internal weakness at the present moment."[96] Like the other right-wing forces in Germany, the military leadership thought a unilateral declaration of a renunciationist peace was dangerous in light of the immoral character of German enemies. Ludendorff wrote at the time, "A strengthening of our internal spirit

---

[91] *Official German Documents Relating to the World War*, Vol. 1, Fourth Session. New York: Oxford University Press, 1923, 332.
[92] Jarausch, *The Enigmatic Chancellor*, 212.
[93] Bethmann-Hollweg, Theobald von. 1921. *Betrachtungen zum Weltkriege*, Band 2. Berlin: Verlag von Reimar Hobbing, 29.
[94] Bethmann -Hollweg, *Betrachtungen zum Weltkriege*, 225.
[95] Jarausch, *The Enigmatic Chancellor*, 201; Gatzke, *Germany's Drive to the West*, 53.
[96] Asprey, Robert. 1991. *The German High Command at War: Hindenburg and Ludendorff Conduct World War I*. New York: William Morrow and Company, 328.

would be the most rapid way to convince our enemies that prolonging the war will endanger their way of life to the point of destruction. On the other hand, every complaint of disappointed expectations, every sign of exhaustion and longing for peace on the part of us and our allies, any talk of the alleged impossibility of surviving a further winter campaign, can only have the effect of prolonging of the war."[97]

In response to the Social Democratic renunciation announcement, the army responded directly by summoning a conference at Kreuznach at which, as Goemans notes, the most extreme aims of the warwere declared even though Germany's position had never been worse: the outright annexation of Lithuania, Estonia, eastern Poland, the ore and coal basin of Longwy-Briey, Luxembourg, and the southern tip of Belgium among other baubles.[98] As the Reichstag was scaling goals downward, the army was upping its aims. Bethmann-Hollweg only agreed to this program because he made his support conditional on Germany's ability to "dictate the peace," which he knew was impossible.[99] These demands were "fantasies,"[100] and he vowed, "If the slightest chance of peace opens up anywhere, I shall pursue it."[101] "A decision as to whether and on what basis we were willing to negotiate or might be forced to negotiate could only be made at the moment when the possibility of entering into negotiations presented itself – and this would depend upon the general situation existing at a given time,"[102] he explained later. Again we see the contrast between System II and System I thinking, mentioned in Chapter 3.[103]

[97] Asprey, *The German High Command at War*, 326. See also Ludendorff, *My War Memories, 1914–1918*, Vol. 2, p. 458 and Vol. 1, p. 5.

[98] Craig, Gordon. 1955, *The Politics of the Prussian Army, 1640–1945*, 325; Jarausch, *The Enigmatic Chancellor*, 224; Gatzke, *Germany's Drive to the West*, 178; Kitchen, Martin. 1976. *The Silent Dictatorship: The Politics of the German High Command under Hindenburg and Ludendorff, 1916–1918*. New York: Holmes and Meier, 102; Ritter 1972, 419.

[99] Craig, *Germany, 1866–1945*, 383.

[100] Kitchen, *The Silent Dictatorship*, 106.

[101] Ritter, *The Sword and the Scepter*, 419.

[102] *Official German Documents Relating to the World War*, 1923, 339.

[103] Skeptics of my account might point to the rationality of persisting given the likely resistance of Germany's adversaries to any peace initiative. After all, France and England dismissed Germany's offer of negotiations in December 1916. This peace feeler, however, was marked by the same dynamics highlighted here. In approaching the Entente, the German government made no substantive concessions, particularly on Belgium, that would have induced its adversaries to come to the table. The initiative came from

Fear of Revolution?: Domestic Reform as Indication of Disunity and Lack of Resolve

According to the rationalist regime survival account of Germany's persistence during the war, authoritarian elites feared that any loss would lead to a collapse of the Reich and the end of their traditional prerogatives. The argument centers on the actions of the military, the institution with perhaps the most to lose. The Supreme Command (die oberste Heeresleitung or OHL), jointly led by Hindenburg and Ludendorff, "gambled for resurrection," preferring a "high variance" strategy to a negotiated peace that they felt would certainly end with the loss of their prerogatives and perhaps their lives.[104] Since they were going down in any case, they might as well give it one last shot.

Bethmann-Hollweg based on rational considerations, the judgment that "our condition and that of our allies did not inspire confidence that the continuation of the war into the next year would create more favorable circumstances than now" (Jarausch, *The Enigmatic Chancellor*, 251). Ludendorff complained about it: "Our whole position compelled us to adopt a tone of confidence. I advocated this from the military point of view also. Our troops had done marvels. What would they do if we adopted any other tone? It was essential that the peace offer should not impair the fighting capacity of the army" (*My War Memories*, Vol. I, 310). Bethmann-Hollweg describes a compromise "due to our anxiety on the point of giving an appearance of weakness and which represented a compromise between the military and political points of view" (*Official German Documents Relating to the World War*, 335). Perhaps crucially, particularly for a public document, the approach continued to lay the blame on Germany's enemies, as the Central Powers declared they must "solemnly disclaim responsibility for [the outbreak of the war] before humanity and history." Outraged, the British government dismissed the approach as a ploy for public sympathy at home and abroad (Lanoszka and Hunzeker, "Rage of Honor"). Ludendorff morally condemned the Entente's answer, claiming it left "no doubt of their intention to annihilate us" (Ludendorff, *My War Memories*, Vol. I, 310). The chancellor's position at home was entirely undercut. He later recalled, "On the 9th of January [when Germany received the Entente's reply], it was absolutely impossible for me to say: 'No, we will not launch the U-boat war, I will guarantee that we shall enter upon peace negotiations in the immediate future.' Every word of the joint note of the Entente of the 30th of December would have closed my lips" (*Official German Documents Relating to the World War*, 342–343). Shortly afterward, Germany removed all restrictions on submarine warfare. The minutes of the Prussian state ministers on 15 January 1917 report that the chancellor could not persuade the Kaiser not to embark on this "unpredictable" course. No. 190, Band 10 of *Protokolle*.

[104] Goemans, *War and Punishment*, ch. 4.

What was irrational for the country was rational for the military.[105] The OHL was far more powerful than the Kaiser during the war, who pathetically remarked: "If Germany believes that I lead the army, it is mistaken. I drink tea and cut wood, go for walks, and then find out from time to time what has been decided."[106]

At issue was the government's unaccountability to the Reichstag and the lack of universal equal suffrage in the Prussian state, which contrasted with the universal male suffrage used in federal elections. The parliament under the Reich constitution played no role in the creation or dismissal of the cabinet, which was a prerogative of the emperor. The Prussian state government had a disproportionate influence in Germany given its population and preeminent position in the Bundesrat, the upper house of the legislature created by Bismarck at the time of unification to retain Prussian hegemony. Legislation had to pass both houses, and the chancellor of Germany was simultaneously the head of the Prussian government. The capital of Prussia, Berlin, was a major home to the industrial working class whose influence was restricted by the greater weighting of the votes of those who had higher incomes and paid higher taxes.

Yet again, the behavior of Germany's generals is best understood as a reflection of binding morality. For Hindenburg, Ludendorff, and other military leaders, the desire for internal reform was an indication of the disintegration of German unity, the key element of the resolution that would be decisive in a struggle against evil enemies bent on German destruction. This is most clearly seen in a famous memorandum written in March 1917 by Ludendorff's right-hand man, Max Bauer, to his superiors but which receives no attention in regime survival accounts.[107] Bauer was described by none other than the Crown Prince of Bavaria as a "dangerous fanatic."[108] Yet, his views captured the prevailing "wisdom" among military leaders.

Cohesion and resolve were one and the same. Ludendorff later recounted: "Our Army and Navy are rooted in the Nation, as is the

---

[105] This is in some ways a wartime corollary of the social imperialist argument, that elites used nationalism as a way to distract from the gross inequalities and lack of democracy in the empire.

[106] Jarausch, *The Enigmatic Chancellor*, 265.

[107] It was included by Bauer in his memoirs. Bauer, Max. 1921. *Der grosse Krieg in Feld und Heimat: Erinnerungen und Betrachtungen aus der Zeit des Weltkriegs*. Tübingen: Osiander, 134ff.

[108] Ritter, *The Sword and the Scepter*, 457.

oak in German soil. They live upon the homeland, and from it they draw their strength. They can keep, but cannot produce, what they need, and can only fight with the moral, material and physical means which the country provides. These means make possible victory, faithful devotion and unselfish self-sacrifice in the daily battle and the miseries of war. They alone could secure Germany's final success."[109] Hindenburg wrote to the chancellor that Germany's enemy "is counting on the collapse of Germany and her allies before its own. It perhaps hopes for a military victory on land, but above all, it expects it from economic and internal political causes, that is, shortages of food and raw materials, dissension, discontent, and the victory of German Radical Socialist Democrats. They base this expectation on the decline of our morale, the growth of international sentiments, our food situation and the desire for peace that is unfortunately loudly proclaimed from many sides."[110] In order to prevail, "The whole German nation must live only in the service of the fatherland," insisted Hindenburg.[111] Ludendorff presaged Churchill: "Every individual had to give his very utmost, if we were to win. We had literally to fight and work to the last drop of blood and sweat and yet maintain our fighting spirit and, above all, our confidence in victory."[112]

As the war wore on, the "duo" at the OHL constantly fretted that this resolve, predicated on a willingness to subordinate individual desires and interests to the collective whole – that is, binding morality – was waning: "Blockade and propaganda began gradually to undermine our moral resolution and shake the belief in ultimate victory. The very natural longing for peace began to assume forms that bordered on weakness, led to divisions among the people and lowered the *moral* [e] of the army. Poisonous weeds grew on this soil."[113]

This was moral condemnation from the perspective of the ethics of community. Excessive and exclusively selfish behavior is unethical in all moral foundations. "All German sentiment, all patriotism, died in many breasts. Self came first.... The idea of revolution, preached by enemy propaganda and Bolshevism, found the Germans in a receptive frame of mind, and gained ground in the army and navy.... Pernicious

[109] Ludendorff, *My War Memories, 1914–1918*, Vol. 1, 3.   [110] Ibid, 325.
[111] Asprey, *The German High Command at War*, 286.
[112] Ludendorff, *My War Memories, 1914–1918*, Vol. 1 (1919), 2.
[113] Ibid, 359.

doctrines spread among the masses. The German people, at home and the front, had received its death-blow."[114] He lamented this moral failing: "Profiteering, pleasure seeking, the thought of self, crowded out all noble aspirations, and privations made men callous.... It is with deep emotion that one looks back and sees how the German sense of truth and honesty, spotless personal purity and devotion to the Fatherland gave place to something else, something quite foreign to Germans– love of self, which became the highest law."[115] What others called Prussian militarism, he thought to be "the spirit of unselfish loyalty, of the surrender of the individual to the conception of the state."[116] Bauer wrote: "The war demanded the utilization of all domestic forces. It is the basic duty to help the fatherland and stifle all selfish impulses," which a portion of the country was not doing.[117]

Students of the OHL conclude that the military leadership relied on "a caricature of the German worker at home living a life of luxury and idle opulence, in contrast to the brave men at the front sacrificing their lives for their country for little recompense."[118] "There are thousands of childless soldiers' wives who are only a burden on the finances of the state," Hindenburg complained to the chancellor. "In addition there are thousands of women and girls at large who are doing nothing or are engaged in quite useless calling. The principle that 'he who does not work shall not eat' is truer than ever in our present situation, even as applied to women."[119] Ludendorff lamented: "In some places wages are so high that there is no longer any inducement to work. On the contrary, disinclination to work, love of pleasure and high living are on the increase. Workmen often lounge about all day."[120] Bauer indicted unions for exploiting the situation for better wages with no concern for the real heroes, those risking their lives in the field.[121]

For the German right and the military leadership, demands for internal reform were therefore selfish acts of disloyalty and disobedience being indulged by the government at a time when, somewhat literally, all hands needed to be on deck. Bauer's memo reads: "The careful observer cannot escape the fact that ... German loyalty, morality and sense of duty is declining monstrously. In every profession and

---

[114] Ibid, 359, also 369.   [115] Ibid, 369.   [116] Ibid, 360.
[117] Bauer, *Der grosse Krieg in Feld und Heimat*, 136.
[118] Kitchen, *The Silent Dictatorship*, 249.
[119] Asprey, *The German High Command at War*, 285.   [120] Ibid, 403.
[121] Bauer, *Der grosse Krieg in Feld und Heimat*, 135–136.

group there is a search after gain, profiteering, pleasure-hunting and waste. *Hand in hand with this goes remarkable presumption, demand for rights, extension of the powers of parliament at the expense of the Throne, and a complete indifference to the burdens of those fighting the war.*"[122] He accused self-interested social democratic and liberal forces for leading the masses astray with promises of democracy based on narrow partisan considerations. They were "enemies of the state" who had always wanted Germany to lose the war.[123] "The greater the prominence given to questions of internal politics, the lower the warlike ardour," Ludendorff believed. Instead, "home politics should have been dominated and directed by consideration of the effect on the enemy."[124] He equated "questions of internal politics and thoughts of self," which meant the "ruin of our country."[125] Bethmann-Hollweg noted this genuinely held belief: "[E]ven if it seemed erroneous to me, the other side was of the inner conviction that domestic reforms were signs of disintegration and therefore also of defeat."[126] High-ranking officers like Wilhelm Groener who worked with industry and labor to supply the war effort tried to convince the military of the necessity of internal reform to bolster unity but were demoted and dismissed.[127] Bauer accused him of not standing up to workers in the armaments factories.[128]

Democracy, argued Bauer, was incapable of meeting Germany's challenges because it could not act in a unified manner. "A parliament is anything but the selection of the most noble and most capable, but for the most part a collection of ambitious, egoistic, average people with narrow horizons ... obstinate in their party politics."[129] Only strong leadership by the emperor could lead the Germans through. He advocated greater rights, but only for those who had served their country. Bauer distinguished between "social democratic policy" and "social policy," endorsing the latter, especially state support for those injured or widowed during the war.[130]

---

[122] Feldman, Gerald. 1966. *Army, Industry, and Labor in Germany, 1914–1918.* Princeton: Princeton University Press, 371 (emphasis added).

[123] Bauer, *Der grosse Krieg in Feld und Heimat*, 134ff.

[124] Ludendorff, *My War Memories, 1914–1918*, Vol. 1, 447.   [125] Ibid, 5.

[126] Bethmann-Hollweg, *Betrachtungen zum Weltkriege*, 36.

[127] Feldman, *Army, Industry, and Labor in Germany, 1914–1918*, 368, 455.

[128] Bauer, *Der grosse Krieg in Feld und Heimat*, 134.   [129] Ibid, 137.

[130] Ibid, 137–138.

Historians consider this irrational behavior. Asprey concludes, "The Duo did not get the message. Justified protest to them was only the stuff of mutiny, the work of deserters, shirkers, war profiteers and socialist-communists who believed the lies of evil conditions at the front spread by disgruntled soldiers invalided home."[131] Ritter writes, "With characteristic militarist blindness, Ludendorff and his propagandists believed they could counteract this disaffection by appeals to patriotism and discipline."[132]

With the ethics of community in mind, the quotes consistently marshaled as evidence for the regime survival argument reveal a different reality. One consistent favorite is from Wolfgang Kapp, a Prussian civil servant who later gained notoriety in an aborted attempt to overthrow the Weimar republic. He warned of "the democratic swamp into which we should be drawn undoubtedly after a lukewarm peace."[133] Kapp's quote is taken from a propaganda pamphlet criticizing Bethmann-Hollweg's leadership, rather than some secret document revealing an elite plot to maintain its prewar privileges. Moreover, the document is an expression of the ideology of binding morality. Kapp cautioned that the government "must not let the reins be taken from its hands by political parties; otherwise it is to be feared that unity of action will be destroyed." The democratic swamp into which Germany will sink in the event of an incomplete victory is contrasted to the "Empire of highest splendor [that] will arise which will empower Germany to the greatest, political, economic and cultural productivity," not an elite playground.[134] If anything, the specter of revolution was raised instrumentally to stiffen the resolve of the civilian government.[135]

The Realpolitik of Innenpolitik: Bethmann-Hollweg's Pragmatic Domestic Reform Strategy

The rational, pragmatic course for regime survival was actually taken by Bethmann-Hollweg, who realized that by perpetuating the conflict beyond which the masses could bear, the army and other conservatives

---

[131] Asprey, *The German High Command at War*, 402.
[132] Ritter, *The Sword and the Scepter*, 446,
[133] Gatzke, *Germany's Drive to the West*, 129.   [134] Ibid.
[135] Craig, *The Politics of the Prussian Army*, 364.

would ensure the very revolution they were supposedly trying to fore-stall. He told leaders of the six major economic associations that Pan-German agitation was contributing to the same unrest that these "truly monarchist circles are warning against."[136] Outside observers came to the same conclusion. The Austro-Hungarian foreign minister, Count Czernin, observed, "I do not think that the internal situation in Germany is widely different from what it is here. I am only afraid that the military circles in Berlin are deceiving themselves in certain matters. I am firmly convinced that Germany too, like ourselves, has reached the limit of her strength, and the responsible political leaders in Berlin do not seek to deny it.... If the monarchs of the Central Powers are not able to conclude peace within the next few months, it will be done for them by their peoples, and then will the tide of revolution sweep away all that for which our sons and brothers fought and died."[137]

Bethmann-Hollweg recognized that some internal reform was an inevitable consequence of the war, the fair payment its citizens would expect for their sacrifices. In 1917, he wrote that "the decisive consideration for me was and is that any suffrage which does not offer political rights to the masses to the same degree as the duties demanded by this war will clash with the justified desire for a government embodying the will of the people." He referred to parliamentarization: "The desire that the personal composition of the government express the will of the people manifest in parliament is such a naturally necessary result ... of the war that it cannot be refused in the long run."[138] This was a pragmatic, consequentialist compromise of the type expected from a realist. "Not for a moment do I deny the gravity of such a step, but I ask myself whether it is wise to oppose the natural consequence of this struggle of nations."[139]

As this was an inevitability, he wanted to get ahead of the problem. He stressed that the step should come now when it "could be presented as a free act," rather than wait until when it was forced "to concede under the greatest external pressure."[140] By initiating reforms he hoped the government could gain credit, contain excesses,

---

[136] Gatzke, *Germany's Drive to the West*, 206. [137] Ibid, 176–177.
[138] Jarausch, *The Enigmatic Chancellor*, 347. [139] Ibid, 344.
[140] "Sitzung des Staatsministeriums am 8. Juli 1917," No. 204, Band 10 in *Protokolle*.

and forestall major social unrest. "My most important duty was the preservation of the crown's leadership in order to guard it against the fate so dangerous to all monarchies. Inevitable reforms, if too long delayed and finally forced through, irredeemably weaken the royal principle instead of strengthening it."[141] He warned the Prussian Landtag, which was hostile to voting reform, "Woe unto the states-man ... who fails to read the signs of the times, who thinks he can simply pick up where he left off, after a cataclysm such as the world has never seen before."[142]

Bethmann-Hollweg's goal was to reform the German state so as to preserve the monarchy. He explained to his Prussian state minis-ters: "The decisive reason for the reform lies in foreign policy, with its strong threat to the state of the monarchy and the dynasty. The monarchy must present itself as a popular one."[143] The chancellor again explicitly invoked Bismarck, who during the Austro-Prussian war, a step toward German unification, promised universal, equal suf-frage so as to attract liberal, nationalist allies who had to that point been the domestic adversaries of the monarchy (even though as a con-servative he had been consistently to that point anti-democratic).[144] "In 1866 Bismarck put the proclamation of universal suffrage onto the scales of fate to create the German Reich. Today this action is perhaps necessary to preserve Prussia and the Empire."[145] Bethmann-Hollweg successfully lobbied the Kaiser to issue what became known as the "Easter message" on 7 April 1917 to maintain the working class' "support of the monarchy."[146] Wilhelm II promised to abolish the three-class suffrage system in Prussia.[147]

By making such pragmatic concessions, Bethmann-Hollweg hoped to hold the country together long enough to secure an adequate peace. He later wrote that the "broad masses could only hold out with the cer-tainty that their brothers and sons are fighting only for the defense of

---

[141] Nachlass Thimme, No. 61, N 1058.
[142] Ritter, *The Sword and the Scepter*, 448.
[143] "Sitzung des Staatsministeriums am 5. April 1917," No. 198, Band 10 in *Protokolle*.
[144] On Bismarck, see Rathbun, *Reasoning of State, Realists, Romantics and Rationality in International Relations*, 112–115.
[145] Jarausch, *The Enigmatic Chancellor*, 333.
[146] Feldman, *Army, Industry, and Labor in Germany, 1914–1918*, 122, 334.
[147] Gatzke, *Germany's Drive to the West*, 173; Craig, *Germany, 1866–1945*, 323.

the country and that the victors will be ensured of a future of political and social liberation."[148] He called this Realpolitik of domestic politics a "policy of the diagonal," "the only available policy in order to maintain the unity of the people," yet one that satisfied neither moral extreme. The chancellor wrote in his memoirs, "Especially in times of passion and excitement, in which extremes battle each other and even escalate, such a policy is thankless. It will be attacked by both sides but must consistently seek allies from situation to situation and lacks both the glamor and the momentary impact that a policy of reckless determination has. As long as the German people possess now inner spiritual and national unity ... the German empire, whether republic or monarchy in times of emergency have to resort to the policy of the diagonal as the only possible one."[149] The chancellor understood the necessity for the victory of maintaining working-class support and the backing of the home front, just as the military did. However, he did not think it could be simply willed.

By "reckless determination," the chancellor had in mind the military's position, what they would have valorized as resolve. Ludendorff said of electoral reform in Prussia: "I always hope that the Prussian franchise falls through. If I didn't have that hope, I would advise the conclusion of any peace. With this franchise we cannot live."[150] This is often mistakenly taken as an admission of the military's parochial aims.[151] Yet Ludendorff's quote continues, "Let the disturbances come. I would rather endure a terrible end than endless terror. Are there no more fighters left? Can the best among us be frightened by the bogie of 'internal unrest?' To look the danger straight in the eye and then at it! Only thus can we win; and if we should lose it would be better than acting against one's conviction." Ludendorff was making clear that he viewed the fight against electoral reform as a fight for national unity, on which one could not compromise, just as strength was the only way to win on the battlefield. The general proclaimed in his memoirs: "I am neither a 'Reactionary' nor a 'Democrat.' All I stand for is the prosperity, the cultural progress and national strength of the German people, authority and order."[152] He equated "breaking up the unity of the German Empire and separating Germany

---

[148] Bethmann-Hollweg, *Betrachtungen zum Weltkriege*, 36.   [149] Ibid, 35.
[150] Craig, *Germany, 1866–1945*, 393.   [151] Goemans, *War and Punishment*.
[152] Ludendorff, *My War Memories, 1914–1918*, Vol. I, 8.

from her ruling house, and her dynasties and governments from their people" with "revolution pure and simple."[153] Ludendorff complained that the Easter message was "kowtowing before the Russian Revolution," which exposed Germany's weakness to its enemies and encouraged them.[154]

In the next chapter, we will see the consequences of this stubborn commitment to authoritarian morality, the most irrational behavioral tendency of the German military and other conservatives: escalating aims as the domestic and international situation deteriorated. Once Bethmann-Hollweg was removed – at the military's insistence, precisely because of his pragmatic positions – there were no more guardrails to prevent the collapse of the very form of government the authoritarians were so desperate to keep.

---

[153] Ibid, 360–361.   [154] Ritter, *The Sword and the Scepter*, 454.

9 Dying in Vain
Authoritarian Morality Causes the German Empire to Collapse

Binding morality can sometimes be pathological, as the previous chapter shows. Yet, we have not yet seen its most irrational expression: not just the tendency to resist giving in but to set aims higher in the face of loss, to literally throw good soldiers after bad. This tendency, which we know as the sunk cost fallacy, defies rational thinking by all standards, yet of course is quite common in everyday life. In war, I argue, it is most pronounced for binding moralists.

The rational war termination literature has an answer for this, a gamble for theoretical resurrection. Goemans locates the source of this behavior in a desperate effort by self-serving elites to compensate those who would otherwise punish them for their wartime privations.[1] Losing a war can lead threatened leaders to actually inflate rather than reduce the extent of their ambitions, that is, their reservation price. In semi-authoritarian regimes, he maintains, leaders will face severe punishment regardless of how badly their country loses, so it is rational to fight to the last man. German aims reached their high point in 1917 after the situation had decisively turned against them. The evidence for this claim, however, is strikingly weak. The previous chapter has shown that the working class and its representatives in the parliament were precisely those forces pushing for an early settlement of the conflict without annexations. It is possible that the military thought they could buy them off after the fact to save their hides, but there was no rational reason for thinking so.

I show, instead, that binding morality leads elite decision-makers to inflate their war aims precisely at the moment when rationality dictates that they lower their expectations. Since binding morality venerates sacrifice to the group, an admission that such sacrifices have been in vain is particularly emotionally costly. Instead, authoritarians are inclined to raise their aims to compensate for national losses in light of the price

[1] Goemans, *War and Punishment*.

paid by the fallen. This is where we see the irrationality of binding morality most clearly.[2] Those who sacrifice their lives for a country have demonstrated ingroup loyalty, the greatest moral virtue. In order for their contribution not to have been in vain, something must come of the conflict. As the costs of a war rise, binding moralists should be inclined not to pragmatically adjust their expectations based on the logic of consequences but actually to increase their demands so as to compensate for the human toll. This is an emotional mechanism, not a rational one, a manifestation of loss aversion and the sunk cost fallacy, which the "behavioral economics literature has explicitly demonstrated ... violates the expectations of rational choice theory."[3] Rational thinkers should separate their valuation of gains from past losses. I argue that binding moralists are particularly prone to this bias in war.

In Germany, rather than gambling for resurrection, authoritarian German leaders gambled to morally compensate for the price paid by its fallen soldiers, with disastrous consequences. Bethmann-Hollweg, as a more rational and pragmatic thinker, tried to avoid such a pitfall. His war aims rose and fell with Germany's battlefield situation. However, given the intense ideological divisions in the country, which only increased during the war, the chancellor found himself in a moral no-man's land, a figurative no-go zone that paralleled the literal strip of land between the fighting forces. For his efforts, he earned the ire of both the right and the left. As the generals moved to oust him in July 1917, he had no allies to help him. Germany was left, on the one hand, with an exhausted population and parliament that had moved to endorse a peace of understanding without annexations and, on the other hand, a military leadership intent on fighting to the last man with no more institutional checks on its blind crusade. The result was predictable: the total collapse of the imperial regime that authoritarian leaders so feared. I tell this story in the first half of this chapter.

---

[2] There are other likely non-rational motives for the continuation of war, most notably honor concerns, although I do not address them here. See Dolan, "Demanding the Impossible"; Lanoszka and Hunzeker, "Rage of Honor."

[3] Johnson, Dominic and Dominic Tierney. 2018. "Bad World: The Negativity Bias in International Politics." *International Security* 43(3): 111. This is related to the familiar risk acceptance in the domains of losses, first systematically applied to international relations by McDermott, Rose. 1998. *Risk-Taking in International Politics: Prospect Theory in American Foreign Policy.* Ann Arbor: University of Michigan Press.

To demonstrate that such a process is not unique to Germany or political elites, I combine this qualitative reading with a panel survey experiment of the Russian public designed to replicate the strategic circumstances of Germany in World War I – a protracted war with extensive casualties in which Russia falls behind in a fight with the United States. I am able to elicit the same dynamics seen in that historical case in this semi-authoritarian country. Respondents split between those who quickly seek peace and those who fight on to the end, and commitment to binding morality is highly predictive of the latter. In the sample as a whole, a framing highlighting the need that soldiers do not die in vain has much less effect than a framing stressing the need to avoid sunk costs, indicating how natural the former is and likely why Bethmann-Hollweg found himself so isolated. Those who choose to persist at each stage of the conflict, even as the war turns against Russia, raise rather than lower their reservation price, that is the outcome for which they are willing to settle. This tendency, long established as irrational, is exacerbated by an ethical framing of the decision that highlights soldiers' sacrifice. Other moral foundations do not have an effect. In both the modern Russian public and German history, it is binding and not humanitarian morality that is most crucial for war termination, indicating how important it is that we widen our conception of the ethics that play a role in war.

In short, the pairing of a Russian experiment with a close reading of the German World War I case reveals a general process of conflict persistence that likely applies much more broadly. Of course, the survey is artificial and superficial, but that is precisely the point. It is possible to evoke the same dynamics even in such a stylized instance.

The Prize for Victory?: Rewarding Sacrifice and War Aims Inflation

Not only did the military leadership resist internal reform and peace abroad as seen in the previous chapter; they raised their demands over time. The regime survival account argues this was an effort to buy off the working class with the spoils of war instead of reforms. Quite crudely, this price increased as the bodies added up. As Craig describes, conservative forces in the state were "determined to prevent [reform] and hoped to do so by debauching the working classes with a grandiose programme of territorial acquisition."[4]

The most obvious problem with the regime survival account, as should be clear from the discussion in the previous chapter, is that the working class was entirely uninterested in war aims; in fact, the more that conservative forces talked about annexation, the more internal discord they created. In June 1915, the chancellor's office wrote to the head of the emperor's secret cabinet: "The longing for peace among the workers is very great, and is only kept from breaking out openly through the efforts of their leaders. The violent agitation of the Right feeds the suspicion, that the government might continue the war – out of desire for conquests – longer than the protection of the Fatherland requires."[5] In July 1917, the Office for Social Policy found in its survey of public opinion: "The temper of the masses is at present so bad in many places, that every mention of a war aim beyond the *status quo* ... would result in numerous voters going over to the [renunciationist] minority."[6] If the army was peddling payoffs in the form of lower taxes or small farmsteads in annexed territory in the east, as Goemans argues, no one was buying.[7] In March 1915, a Social Democratic Party member argued that the working classes would have to be bought off with internal reforms in order to support annexations![8] The chancellor warned that "if we claimed as much [as the annexationists] we would find ourselves opposed to the broad masses fighting for the fatherland, and not for such a policy of expansion."[9] Ritter finds that it would have been "difficult and even dangerous" for the social democratic politicians "to preach patriotism to the masses" by 1917.[10]

Precisely because of this domestic constraint, Bethmann-Hollweg talked ambiguously about German war aims. "Open debate would split the nation internally and endanger eventual success by the

---

[4] Craig, *Germany, 1866–1945*, 341.
[5] Gatzke, *Germany's Drive to the West*, 110. Bethmann-Hollweg noticed this as well. Bethmann-Hollweg, *Betrachtungen zum Weltkriege*, 29.
[6] Gatzke, *Germany's Drive to the West*, 109.
[7] Goemans, *War and Punishment*, 109.
[8] Jarausch, *The Enigmatic Chancellor*, 208.
[9] Ibid, 217. Also Gatzke, *Germany's Drive to the West*, 166, Bethmann-Hollweg, *Betrachtungen zum Weltkriege*, Vol. 2: 30; Ritter, *The Sword and the Scepter*, 22.
[10] Ritter, *The Sword and the Scepter*, 445.

fixation of aims, which can prove mistaken and impossible at any time in such an unprecedented war," the chancellor believed.[11] He later admitted, "I tried to suppress the public dispute over war aims as much as I could."[12] For these reasons, the government legally forbid the public discussion of annexation and war aims so that petitions like those reviewed previously had to be distributed privately. The government even pursued legal action against open annexationists like Heinrich Class. They also, however, restricted peace propaganda.

Bethmann-Hollweg consistently stressed the self-defense that commanded domestic agreement, never reaching further than the need for vague "securities" against future attack, particularly in regard to the status of Belgium, that were vague enough not to amount to an explicit endorsement of either the left or right's aims.[13] After the war, he explained this as more Realpolitik than Innenpolitik: "With us in Germany, the rift between those parties who believed that the future security of our country depended upon the attainment of war aims of more or less scope looking towards annexation, and those circles which were opposed to such measures, had become constantly deeper and wider … which, in my opinion, constituted a serious menace to the resisting power of far-reaching circles of society…. [T]he constant reiteration of the fact that the war was not being carried on for fantastic purposes was shown to be not only practical, but necessary, from the standpoint of domestic politics."[14]

Consistent with his realist and rational approach, Bethmann-Hollweg's sense of what Germany might demand rose and fell with Germany's battlefield successes and failures in a way that was not true of the German right, including the military. The chancellor behaved in the way that the baseline rationalist model of bargaining predicts. His ambitious September Program of 1914, first revealed in Fischer's book *Griff nach der Weltmacht*, reveals the chancellor's aims at the height of Germany's position on the battlefield.[15] At the pinnacle of

---

[11] Jarausch, *The Enigmatic Chancellor*, 215.
[12] Bethmann-Hollweg, *Betrachtungen zum Weltkriege*, 29.
[13] Official War Documents 1923, 311. He also thought of his Mitteleurope constellation as consistent with this policy of the diagonal in that it expanded German influence and security without annexation. Jarausch, *The Enigmatic Chancellor*, 215.
[14] Bethmann-Hollweg, *Betrachtungen zum Weltkriege*, 311.
[15] Published in English as Fischer, Fritz. 1967. *Germany's Aims in the First World War*. New York: WW Norton.

German armed success in the early days of the war, he did give up
the idea of pure defense and looked for security guarantees through
adjustments to the status quo ante.[16] As Germany's military stalled, he
adjusted his expectations. By 1915, he was maintaining: "You will not
accuse me of defeatism. But serious, victory-conscious soldiers today
think that defense against this overpowering coalition would already
be enough. If God gives us more, we shall accept it gladly, but we
cannot count on it."[17] By 1916, he wrote: "We should not think of
something very wonderful in connection with this famous discussion
of war aims. Our situation at the end of the war will not be such that
we can choose freely among a series of entirely different possibilities.
We shall rather try to make of the situation whatever we can. As far as
there will be a choice, it will be limited by the fact that Belgium, colonies, and a large indemnity cannot all be had. The value of colonies
and an indemnity will have to be balanced against the value of Belgian
guarantees."[18] He told the Reichstag foreign affairs committee that
"the glowing hopes we entertained in the years 1914–1915 are now
probably beyond fulfillment. Unfortunately the war has not gone the
way we had expected."[19] There was only an "illusion of a fat peace,"
he chided Hindenburg.[20] The chancellor's updating, compared to the
nationalist right, meant that in private he increasingly criticized the
right more than the left, whom he thought to be more reasonable.[21]
By the end of 1916, his hypothetical peace terms "came close to a
straightforward restoration of the status quo ... almost tantamount to
total renunciation."[22] He explained to the military that politics is the
"art of the attainable."[23]

In making the case for a peace feeler in October 1916 to the
Prussian state ministry, the minutes of the chancellor's remarks read:
"According to Bethmann-Hollweg, it is not to be expected that the
continuation of the war into the next year will bring any improvement

---

[16] Ritter, *The Sword and the Scepter*, 33.
[17] Bethmann to Loebell, N 1045(2 January 1915), Nachlass Loebell.
[18] Gatzke, *Germany's Drive to the West*, 73.
[19] Ritter, *The Sword and the Scepter*, 279.
[20] Bethmann to Hindenburg, DZA Po. Rkz., no. 2446 (25 June 1917).
[21] Ritter concludes about the Fischer thesis, "it is simply untrue that this
    memorandum formed the basis for Bethmann Hollweg's entire war aims
    policy, to which he clung in all essential points right down to the day of his
    fall" (1972, 39).
[22] Ritter, *The Sword and the Scepter*, 277.   [23] Ibid, 292.

in the situation. Now the psychological moment has come for a positive step towards peace. The military situation and the lack of our allies capacity for resistance." He then went on to note, "The mood of the people, which is asking for peace and accusing part of the government for being at a loss and passive." The chancellor knew that the public could not be appeased with annexations. A Hindenburg peace would require, he thought at the time, compulsory labor for men 15 to 60, which was entirely unfeasible. It would amount to a "declaration of bankruptcy."[24]

Therefore, the right's thinking that the masses would be more willing to fight if more exaggerated war aims were identified seems, if genuinely held, to have been (especially after 1917) irrational, "contrary to simple common sense" as Bethmann-Hollweg later described. A desire for an annexationist peace was "removed from reality" and "born of hollow fantasy.... Like at home, in the army, willingness to fight and goals of conquest were independent from one another."[25] Historians of the oberste Heeresleitung (OHL) agree on this.[26] The military leadership engaged in classic, non-rational motivated reasoning in which it sought out information to bolster its beliefs rather than test them. The chancellor complained that "these gentlemen at the front do not and cannot rightly evaluate political life as it has developed here during the war. Our officers ... politicize now more than ever. They prefer to read the conservative newspapers.... If one wants to go on in the old way without any consideration for what's going on in the world, then one will come to disaster."[27] Asprey writes, "Had either Hindenburg or Ludendorff or their staff officers deigned to talk to the front-line soldiers, they would soon have discovered that most of them did not give a damn for postwar gains. Their one interest was to leave the subhuman trench life of mud and shit, of lice and rats and foul food, of death hovering about like the unwanted visit of a hated relative.... Other than trying to stay alive, their major interest was when the war would end and postwar gains be damned."[28]

[24] "Sitzung des Staatsministeriums am 27. Oktober 1916," No. 180, Band 10 in *Protokolle*.
[25] Bethmann-Hollweg, *Betrachtungen zum Weltkriege*, 29–30.
[26] Asprey, *The German High Command at War*, 341; Craig, *Germany, 1866–1945*, 358.
[27] Feldman, *Army, Industry, and Labor in Germany, 1914–1918*, 336.
[28] Asprey, *The German High Command at War*, 341.

Yet, if not a rational effort to gamble for resurrection, how do we explain this demand for ever greater gains precisely when Germany's position was deteriorating, which was true not only of the German military but the right more generally? As argued previously, binding morality contributes to the irrational inflation of war aims. In this ethical mindset, the country owes it to its loyal soldiers and even citizens that their sacrifices should not have been in vain. This has the effect of escalating war aims as the costs of war in terms of blood and treasure increase, which is precisely the moment at which pragmatism should dictate setting one's sights lower. This explains why the government was trying to "reward" German society and soldiers with presents they were not asking for.

To fail in its task was a betrayal of the blood shed by loyal soldiers defending the country, the Pan-Germans argued. It would be a "sin against Germany's future."[29] The people were owed a *Siegpreis* (victory reward) that corresponded to the sacrifices they had made in the war, Class wrote.[30] "The opponents, who put us in such tremendous danger should not be surprised, when at the end of the war, they are asked to give satisfaction that corresponds to the scale of the threat and the mass of victims that we had to sacrifice so as to victoriously defend attacks from all sides."[31] Class summoned his readers to harden themselves to the necessity of demanding a price proportional to the "blood sacrifices."[32] The Petition of Professors used the same "reasoning": "The military results of this war, with so many victims, should be exploited to the outer limits of the possible."[33] Rather than trying to buy off the masses, the German right thought they were obligated to win gains for them, even if it ultimately came at their expense.

Johnson and Tierney also take issue with the rationality of the German generals, yet attribute their behavior to a loss aversion that was especially pronounced given their responsibility for the outcome.[34] However, such an account fails to explain why the right as a whole, even those parliamentarians whose accountability was substantially lower, would endorse the same inflation of war aims for the same

---

[29] Class, *Zum deutschen Kriegsziel*, 5.   [30] Ibid, 12.

[31] Ibid, 13.   [32] Ibid, 15.

[33] "Petition der Professoren an den Reichskanzler." In Grumbach, *Das annexionistische Deutschland*, 132–140. See also in the same volume: "Petition der sechs Wirtschaftsverbände an den Reichskanzler," p.124.

[34] Johnson and Tierney, "Bad World: The Negativity Bias in International Politics," 137.

reasons. In response to the social democratic renunciation of conquest, bourgeois parties issued a common counter-proclamation calling for "a peace commensurate with the sacrifices." The National Liberals, Center Party, and Free Conservatives each emphasized the same in separate party resolutions.[35] The Free Conservatives "were of the firm and unanimous conviction that the heavy sacrifices of property and blood that the German people willingly and enthusiastically accepted and will continue to accept should not be in vain. They require as the goal of peace a Germany whose power position is strengthened and expanded beyond its present borders through the greatest possible retention of presently occupied areas.... Our borders must be secured against any attack from east and west...."[36]

These statements, all made in 1915 as party leaders were buoyant about German successes on the battlefield, might be seen as rational reflections of the distribution of power at the time. However, as the position of German forces stalemated and even deteriorated, these rightist politicians did not adjust their war aims, instead often inflating them. Only the centrist parties updated, and this took considerable time. Still in 1916, a Centrist deputy to the Reichstag, asserted: "The continuance of the war has required such tremendous sacrifices that we must increase our demands."[37] The chancellor complained, "In rash underestimation of our foes, everyone thought the end of the war near, the enemy beaten, and believed he could revise the map of Europe according to his whim" but that "the less hopes for a quick and decisive victory were fulfilled, the more our chauvinists believed they had to prove their bravery and loyalty by proposing the most power-hungry war aims and smearing everybody who refused to follow their lead as subversive weaklings."[38]

The Castle Falls: The Chancellor's Resignation, the Collapse of the Burgfrieden and Military Dictatorship

The issues of war aims and domestic reform came to a simultaneous head in the spring and summer of 1917. The debate over the peace resolution came on the heels of the Kaiser's Easter message, creating

---

[35] "Erklärung aller bürgerlichen Parteien im Reichstag." In Grumbach, *Das annexionistische Deutschland*, 35–36, 39.
[36] Ibid,39.   [37] Gatzke, *Germany's Drive to the West*, 111.
[38] Jarausch, *The Enigmatic Chancellor*, 213.

a sense of panic in right-wing circles. Threatening to resign if the emperor did not dismiss the chancellor, Hindenburg and Ludendorff forced his ouster. His failing, in their eyes, was a lack of resolve. Hindenburg wrote the Kaiser on 26 June: "Our greatest anxiety at this moment ... is the decline in the national spirit.... The question arises whether the Chancellor is capable of solving these problems – and they must be solved, or we are lost!"[39] In their particular conception of ethics, indecisiveness was a moral fault. Ludendorff recalled: "The Government had lost the determination to win and its faith in German strength, which had so brilliantly manifested itself in the past three years and had only commenced to totter for want of leading. So the army did not receive what it needed for victory. I no longer believed that a change would take place under that Chancellor.... So I wrote out my resignation."[40] As Craig writes of the army: "Unprepared by their previous experience to deal with subjects which possessed any degree of political delicacy, they were apt to operate on the assumption that *all problems could be solved by firmness*. When this was not the case, they had a natural tendency to attribute lack of determination to civilian officials, to the ministers, and ultimately to the Chancellor," who they accused of a failure of "leadership."[41] The critique was genuinely held, if preposterous, and tensions had been brewing for a long time. In his internal OHL memorandum, Bauer criticized the government for not maintaining the *Burgfrieden*, allowing "anti-monarchical and anti-state social democrats" and those with "internationalist tendencies" to gain the upper hand.[42] "Instead of creating order by firm action and instruction, the government permits itself to be led and directed by those groups who even in peacetime had been recognized as a danger to the state and the monarchy," he complained.[43]

As Ritter notes, the chancellor's "irresolution" was the right's interpretation of his deliberative and objective thinking style. The chancellor

[39] Parkinson, Roger. 1978. *Tormented Warrior: Ludendorff and the Supreme Command*. London: Hodder and Stoughton, 131.
[40] Ludendorff, Vol. 2, 454.
[41] Craig, Gordon. 1955. *Politics of the Prussian Army, 1640–1945*. Oxford: Oxford University Press, 318.
[42] Kitchen, The Silent Dictatorship, 84.
[43] Bauer, *Der grosse Krieg in Feld und Heimat*, 134ff; Feldman, *Army, Industry, and Labor in Germany, 1914–1918*, 371.

demonstrated "unswervingly lucid and objective insight into Germany's true situation.... What Bethmann-Hollweg's grasp of political realities showed him, in sharper focus than was seen by most of his fellow countrymen, was that Germany's position in the world was desperate and ultimately hopeless.... He was not the kind of man ... who leaps over all doubts, problems, and dangers by taking swift and risky decisions.... Thus he did make an irresolute impression on some who were not close to him."[44] Because there was no easy path, he was always considering the appropriate option for the situation.

By virtue of the morally polarized nature of the conflict, brought about by the irrational behavior of the German right, the pragmatic Bethmann-Hollweg had no strong allies on either side of the political spectrum even though a majority in the Reichstag now agreed with his program. The right called him a "traitor," a "defeatist," and a "*Flaumacher*" (wet blanket or killjoy),[45] while the left doubted his true commitment to a peace of reconciliation.[46] This left him in an ideological no man's land of moral consequentialism. In domestic politics, "The left was not content with vague promises, the right felt that the chancellor now believed in parliamentary democracy."[47] In foreign policy, as his contemporary observed, "the Chancellor could satisfy neither the Right nor the Left."[48] The right wanted a formal declaration of war aims, the left an explicit renunciation of war aims.

The dismissal of Bethmann-Hollweg is by all accounts a decisive turning point in the war, ushering in a period of what was effectively military dictatorship.[49] Subsequent chancellors were stooges who lacked the courage to stand up to the generals, allowing the OHL to plunge Germany into the abyss and bring about all the revolutionary changes they were supposedly so afraid of. The chancellor was the "one political figure who, if no match for the strong personalities of Hindenburg, at least was powerful enough to delay the complete ascendance of the military authorities over the political affairs of the

---

[44] Ritter, *The Sword and the Scepter*, 486.
[45] Gatzke, *Germany's Drive to the West*, 220.
[46] Jarausch, *The Enigmatic Chancellor*, 370; Gatzke, *Germany's Drive to the West*, 175.
[47] Kitchen, *The Silent Dictatorship*, 128.
[48] Gatzke, *Germany's Drive to the West*, 182.
[49] Craig, *Politics of the Prussian Army*, 328; Gatzke, *Germany's Drive to the West*, 193.

nation."[50] His dismissal "represented a significant turning point in the constitutional history of imperial Germany," striking a "blow at the very foundations of monarchical system. It is ironical that that blow should have been delivered by the army, which had so steadfastly opposed political and social reform precisely because it might weaken the power of the Crown."[51] With the chancellor's departure, institutional reform in Germany was stillborn, and the peace resolution was ignored by the intentionally weak chancellors chosen to follow Bethmann-Hollweg. The chancellor later noted his "peculiar fate," "that my fall was brought about by a combination on the part of the parliament with the military authorities at the very moment when *for the first time* it was made possible for me to defend my policy, supported by a majority of the parliament."[52]

Reiter argues that these leaders rationally assessed the military situation following the Treaty of Brest-Litovsk with Russia. He argues that German decision-makers, freed of constraints on the eastern front, decided that a final military push on the western front in March 1918 was necessary to neutralize Belgium, without which Germany could not be secure.

No doubt that the Duo thought that the two countries were bent on Germany's destruction. Yet this was an ideological belief, based on moral condemnation. There is unanimity on the irrationality of this course in the historical literature. "The OHL and its supporters still lived in the dream world of the annexationist peace, but the essential precondition for the realization of such plans did not exist. Germany could not defeat the Entente."[53] Asprey asks, "How could Hindenburg have permitted Ludendorff to go on with his insane offensives in the spring of 1918?.... His was increasingly a dream world remote from reality."[54] Isabel Hull's book, the most thorough consideration of military thinking in the literature to date, concludes: "[M]ost historians agree with Bethmann that the war was definitively lost [in April 1917].... But it was lost more quickly and spectacularly because of the March offensive of 1918.... By 1918 Germany lacked both the manpower and mobility to convert a breakthrough into a strategic victory;

[50] Gatzke, *Germany's Drive to the West*, 193.
[51] Craig, *Politics of the Prussian Army*, 328.
[52] *Official German Documents Relating to the World War*, 335.
[53] Kitchen, *The Silent Dictatorship*, 250.
[54] Asprey, *The German High Command at War*, 406–408.

the March offensive demanded the impossible. The alternative most suitable to Germany's eroded position in 1917–18 would have been the strategic defensive and the simultaneous pursuit of nesgotiations. But OHL never seriously considered this alternative, and no institutions or civilian or military leaders were strong enough to stop the decision for self-destruction."[55]

The military leadership demonstrated a striking lack of rational thought: "The risks were apparently too great to allow realistic assessment of danger, making the risk takers unwilling to admit when the gamble had failed.... [I]nstead, the unrealistic conviction of professional superiority, wishful thinking, belief in miracles or in *Kriegsglück* (the fortunes of war), and compulsory optimism created a working atmosphere in which admitting defeat became almost impossible."[56] When questioned before the spring offensive by Prince Max von Baden, who would soon take over as chancellor, about the slim chances for success, Ludendorff replied, "You have to believe in victory."[57] Even in his memoirs, Hindenburg does not have a good explanation. "It is a reasonable question: What justified our hope for one or more sweeping victories? The answer is easy to give, but hard to explain.... It was the trust a leader feels when he sends his troops into enemy fire, convinced that they will bear the utmost burden and make the seemingly impossible possible." One could not "trust in numbers or external strengths."[58]

Indeed even Reiter admits as much; while claiming that "Germany's recognition of Belgium as important to international security and power was *probably reasonable*," he ultimately concludes pages later that the "German leadership refused to accept the half a loaf of western Russia, *its enduring paranoia of Britain and France* pushing it to grab Belgium to provide long-term security."[59]

Bringing the point home, in the very last days of the war, after the allies finally broke through German lines on the "Black Day of the German Army," Ludendorff and Hindenburg demanded that Germany fight on when President Wilson demanded what they regarded as excessive concessions for an armistice. Ludendorff insisted that Germany "make up

[55] Hull, Isabel V. 2005. *Absolute Destruction*. Ithaca and London: Cornell University Press, 299.
[56] Ibid, 291.   [57] Ibid, 303.   [58] Ibid.
[59] Reiter, *How Wars End*, 171, 185.

its mind to fight out the struggle for our honor to the very last man."[60]
Vice Chancellor Friedrich von Payer described the arguments made
by the military to the cabinet: "[T]here were lots of hopes and fears,
surmises and reckonings, that were half-reasonably, half-emotionally
expressed, but then taken back or otherwise contradicted; they gave
no satisfactory base for objective judgment."[61] The military had no
rationale for its preferences. Hull concludes, "Honor was therefore a
shorthand formula standing for the entire way of thinking that had just
failed, so it was not, as Payer sharply observed, an actual argument; it
substituted for one."[62] When Chancellor von Baden complained that
by fighting on, Germany would have to "face even worse," Ludendorff
replied, "There can be no worse."[63] Only then was he forced out by
the Kaiser, but too late for the monarchy.He wrote privately at the
time, "A people that accepts humiliation and conditions that destroy its
existence without having done its utmost is ruined. If it is forced to do
the same after making a last, extreme exertion, then it will live."[64] This
is the same valorization of resolve that is so common in authoritarian
ideology, now not as a means but as an end in itself.

Panel Experiment of the Russian Public

The case study of German decision-making raises serious questions
about the validity of rational war termination arguments. Exceptions
to the rational adjustment of goals in light of deteriorating battlefield
situations seem to apply mostly to authoritarians guided not by parochial considerations of domestic politics but instead by ideological predispositions that lead them to frame situations in terms of the familiar
deterrence model of international politics. However, the case study I
present has significant limitations. First, are the dynamics I uncover
more generalizable or unique to Wilhelmine Germany? Second, there
is the question of measurement precision. Binding morality is hard to
capture precisely qualitatively. Third, while the abovementioned evidence suggests that the authoritarian German right was acting based
on a particular, subjective framing of the situation, how can we say

---

[60] Asprey, *The German High Command at War*, 479.
[61] Hull, *Absolute Destruction*, 317.   [62] Ibid.
[63] Asprey, *The German High Command at War*, 471.
[64] Hull, *Absolute Destruction*, 318.

for sure that its understanding was any less objective and deliberate, and therefore less rational, than that of others? Perhaps this is simply a function of the subjective framing of a highly ambiguous situation susceptible to multiple, equally justifiable interpretations.

In the following section, I present results from a survey of the Russian mass public meant to address some of these weaknesses. The study is a "panel experiment" that places respondents into conditions and measures their responses over time as they receive new information within the same survey. The study was designed to mimic the dynamics of Germany in World War I in which a war of attrition gives way to a losing effort with disproportional casualties. By measuring binding morality directly through a dispositional survey, we can precisely estimate its effect. Experiments allow us to control information so as hold background knowledge constant and establish the objective situation. In addition, I prime binding moral concern through an experimental manipulation so as to judge its effect on the sample as a whole.

The study is also constructed in such a way as to distinguish rational from non-rational behavior by allowing us to observe the presence of a sunk cost fallacy. Goemans argues that self-serving elites in a semi-repressive regime have an incentive to raise their war aims as their situation deteriorates in a desperate effort to compensate those who would otherwise punish them for their wartime privations. But perhaps binding morality alone can explain this escalation of demands, without any recourse to institutional incentives. As the costs of a conflict rise, binding moralists (or those so primed) should be inclined not to pragmatically adjust their expectations based on the logic of consequences but actually to increase their demands so as to justify the human costs. As has been seen, it has been argued that German elites differed from one another by virtue of their personal, egoistic stakes in the outcome of the war. This is something we do not have to worry about in a survey of the mass public, and we can directly measure the moral commitments of all respondents in exactly the same way. We can also directly capture reservation price, which is normally private information only approximated, even in careful historical research. A direct measure of reservation price allows us to establish whether decision-making is rational.

Some might express concern that findings about the mass public have no bearing on the behavior of elites who are much different from ordinary citizens. If this is really the case, however, then evidence showing convergent behavior among these very different populations is all the more compelling. Moreover, the claim that elites and publics are radically different is under increasing stress now that it is being submitted to actual empirical testing.[65] Given that research shows that morality structures the very ideological cleavages that exist in societies, it seems a strong candidate for the type of force that drives both mass and elite behavior and in similar ways.[66] It has become increasingly common to combine tests of theoretical microfoundations based on data from ordinary populations with case studies and even large-N analyses of conflict behavior.[67]

As seen in earlier chapters, in early March 2020, I conducted a survey on a sample of approximately 1,200 members of the Russian public selected to reflect the population's distribution in terms of region, age, and gender. Russians are members of a semi-authoritarian society that more resembles Wilhelmine Germany than contemporary Western democracies, the latter being a more typical source of subjects for public opinion surveys. Before beginning, subjects completed the "moral foundations questionnaire," translated into Russian by Russian scholars, which measures binding morality, a combination of deference to authority and ingroup loyalty, as well as the moral foundations of "harm/care" and "fairness/reciprocity," which capture a general liberal ethical orientation and humanitarian commitment.[68] Other typical demographic information was also collected, although nothing politically sensitive. All respondents were presented with a "hypothetical situation our leaders may face in the future." They were further instructed: "We will describe one approach Russian leaders might take and ask whether you approve or disapprove of that approach." The prompt was based on a vignette employed by Gottfried and Trager.[69] The exact text and translation are in Online Appendix 5.4.

The United States and Russia have a longstanding dispute over a resource-rich area in the Arctic.

[65] Kertzer, "Re-Assessing Elite-Public Gaps."
[66] Kertzer et al., "Moral Support."
[67] Kertzer, *Resolve in International Politics*; Renshon, *Fighting for Status*; Rathbun, *Reasoning of State.*
[68] Сычев, Олег А., Ирина Н. Протасова, and Константин И. Белоусов. 2018. "Диагностика моральных оснований: апробация русскоязычной версии опросника MFQ." *Российский психологический журнал* 15(3). The English version is in Online appendix #2.
[69] Gottfried and Trager, "A Preference for War."

Over 25% of the world's undiscovered oil and gas are beneath the Arctic Ocean and portions of the ice contain materials that will become the world's next alternative energy source. Both Russia and the United States claim that the area lies inside their continental territory according to international law. The United Nations has decided that the scientific evidence is unclear.

The Russian President wants to make sure that Russia has rights to at least 50% of the area.

Respondents were then asked to identify the minimum share of the area that they would be willing to accept as a negotiated settlement, a direct measure of reservation price, on a scale of 0 to 100.

All respondents were then told:

Following several months of negotiations, the Russian president announces that negotiations have broken down and the American navy moves into the area. Russia responds by also sending its navy.

All respondents were asked to identify their level of support for this action by the Russian President on a seven-point scale ranging from strongly oppose to strongly support and for a second time to identify their reservation price.

From this point, respondents were randomized into three different conditions. One continually stressed the moral importance of cutting losses and emphasized the human costs of the conflict. Another highlighted the moral importance of persistence, focusing on loyalty and the importance of having something to show for Russian sacrifice. A control condition presented information without any ethical framing at all.

Respondents were then given new information: *After a standoff, both forces fire at each other. Over 1,000 Russian troops, and a similar number of American troops, die in the exchange.*

Participants were given a dichotomous choice of whether to continue fighting or to withdraw. This choice was framed differently depending on the treatment condition.

<u>Control condition</u>: *Do you support withdrawing the Russian navy or continuing the fight?*

<u>Cutting losses</u>: *The Russian President must decide whether to continue the military operation or withdraw to avoid the deaths of more Russian soldiers in a fight that Russia might not win. Do you support withdrawing the Russian navy or continuing the fight?*

<u>Moral escalation</u>: *The Russian President must decide whether to withdraw from an operation that Russia might not win or continue to fight so*

that its soldiers will not have sacrificed their lives for nothing. Do you support withdrawing the Russian navy or continuing the fight?

No further questions were asked of respondents who chose to withdraw. Those who chose to continue were asked their reservation price again, and then updated identically on developments: *In another fierce battle, another 5,000 Russian troops and 5,000 American troops die.* However, there were three different framings depending on the treatment condition.

Control: *The Russian President must decide whether to continue the military operation.*

Cutting losses: *The Russian President must decide whether to continue the military operation or withdraw in order to avoid the deaths of more brave Russian soldiers in a stalemate that might continue to lead to unnecessary loss of life.*

Moral escalation: *The Russian President must decide whether to withdraw from an operation that has so far resulted in a stalemate or continue the fight to honor the service of these 6,000 fallen soldiers.*

Again, no further questions were asked of respondents who chose to withdraw. Those who chose to continue the fight were asked their reservation price and given a subsequent update in which the battlefield situation took a decisive turn for the worse. This was meant to mimic the strategic situation of Germany in the later years of World War I: *The Americans are now gaining a decisive advantage in the conflict with the sinking of a Russian battleship and the death of another 5,000 Russian soldiers.*

The three different framings depended on the treatment condition.

Control: *The Russian President must decide whether to continue the military operation despite the setback.*

Cutting losses: *The Russian President must decide whether to continue what some are describing as a senseless bloodbath or withdraw.*

Moral escalation: *The Russian President must decide whether to continue the fight or withdraw, betraying the memories of the more than 11,000 soldiers who died for Mother Russia.*

This was the last stage in the experiment, meaning that respondents were given a chance to continue to fight up to three times after Russian casualties of 1,000, 6,000, and 11,000. Those who chose to persist were asked a final, fifth time, for their reservation price.

My authoritarian morality argument has a number of distinct expectations. First, binding morality – both as a dispositional trait and a treatment condition – should be associated with a tendency to persist. Second, in keeping with the rarity of pragmatism and rationality, I expect that the cutting loss treatment will have a greater effect than the moral escalation treatment since the latter is more normal and natural. Individuals as a whole will have to be reminded not to put good soldiers after bad, whereas sunk cost tendencies are a universal human bias. Third, I expect that those who endure to the end will also simultaneously raise their reservation price over time rather than lower it, a departure from rationality by all accounts.

Figure 9.1 provides a "heat map" showing the distribution of respondents and the association between their total endurance score (ranging from 0 to 3 based on how many times they chose to continue fighting) and their initial level of support for intervention before any casualties were reported. Darker areas are those more populated by the individuals in the sample.

The data show a largely bifurcated population. The largest categories are those who weakly supported the President's deployment of the navy and who chose never to continue to fight when given the chance

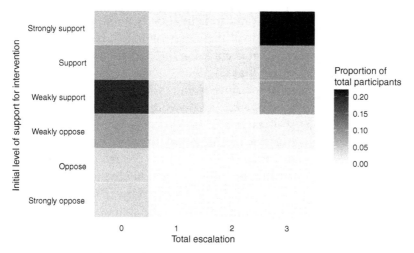

Figure 9.1 *Distribution of respondents by support for initial intervention and choices to stay in conflict.*

Table 9.1 *Binding morality causes Russians to stay in conflict, reminding them to avoid the sunk cost fallacy to withdraw*

	B	Hazard Ratio
Cut Losses	.15*	+16%
	(.07)	[2.2%, 32.2%]
Moral Escalation	–.01	0%
	(.07)	[–13.3%, 14%]
Binding Morality	–.79***	–54.4%
	(.21)	[–31.8%, –69.3%]
Humanitarian Morality	.01	+1.2%
	(.22)	[–64.6%, +58.6%]
N		1257

Table entries are coefficients and hazard ratios from Model 2 in Online appendix 5.2 Results for age, education, and gender are not reported. Robust standard errors for coefficients and 95 percent confidence intervals for hazard ratios, expressed in percentages, are in parentheses. Continuous variables scaled from 0 to 1. $***p < .001$; $**p < .01$; $*p < .05$. The neutral information treatment is the excluded category. The two individual-level moral variables are based on factor scores from a factor analysis with a two-dimensional solution reported in Online Appendix 5.1

on the one hand and a group of respondents who strongly supported the initial deployment and chose at every point not to withdraw on the other hand. Just under half (47.7%) choose to withdraw at the first chance, whereas 41% continue to fight at every point. Only 11.2% of the population falls outside of these extremes. This is very similar to the strong polarization that occurred in the German population in the real-world case of World War I.

Table 9.1 presents the results from a Cox hazard model, which measures the likelihood of a hazard (leaving the fight) based on treatment variables as well as individual-level covariates. Based on the two-dimensional structure of the moral foundations, indicated by the factor analysis in Online Appendix 5.1, I created two continuous moral variables – humanitarian morality and binding morality – standardized to vary between 0 and 1. Positive hazard ratios indicate that a variable has a positive effect on leaving the conflict, whereas negative hazard ratios indicate that the variable has a negative effect on leaving the conflict – that is, standing firm. B is the coefficient, whose sign indicates the direction of its effect.

The individual-level binding morality variable has an extremely large effect on the willingness to stay in. Moving from the minimum to the maximum of this variable is associated with a 54.4% lower risk (hazard ratio) of exiting the conflict at any stage. In other words, our highest binders are over twice as likely to stay the course than our lowest binders. Humanitarian morality, in contrast, has no statistically significant effect at all.

There are a number of pathways through which binding morality should affect the persistence behavior of participants in the panel experiment. As I have shown already, binding moralists likely place significant weight on the need to demonstrate resolve in international relations. Authoritarian ideology and binding morality are premised on high threat sensitivity, which should, in turn, generate concern about maintaining credibility. I utilize agreement or disagreement with a question that forms part of the construct of "militant internationalism," an index introduced in Chapter 4: "Russia must demonstrate its resolve so that other countries do not take advantage of it" (Россия должна продемонстрировать свою решительность, чтобы другие страны не использовали ее в своих интересах).

Binding morality also induces a felt need to bind tightly in a group, which should create a strong sense of national identity in the context of foreign policy. I used a frequent measure of nationalism: "When someone speaks badly of Russians, how strongly do you feel that this applies to you personally?" (Когда кто-то плохо отзывается о россиянах, насколько сильно вы чувствуете, что это относится лично к вам?)

Finally, it is important to establish whether or not binding morality has an effect beyond merely setting one's sights high in a military conflict. Binding morality is likely associated with a higher reservation price, but causal mediation analysis allows us to judge whether its effect is solely through that pathway. Therefore, I undertake a mediation analysis using the first reservation price, the share of the territory respondents believe necessary to have before backing down (Table 9.2).

A non-parametric mediation analysis with all the variables in model 2 of Online Appendix 5.2 reveals that binding morality partially works through a belief in resolve (10.8%) and national identification (32.7%). Although it also operates through higher reservation prices (26.2%), it

Table 9.2 *Non-parametric analyses of binding morality's indirect effects*

	Direct effect of binding morality	ACME	Total effect	% of Total effect mediated
Belief in Resolve	.42	.05	.47	10.8
	[.22, .59]	[.02, 09]	[.28, .63]	[8.1, 18.2]
National Identification	.32	.16	.47	32.7
	[.11, .50]	[.09, .23]	[.29, .63]	[24.8, 51.2]
Original Reservation Price	.33	.12	.45	26.2
	[.12, .51]	[.07, .17]	[.26, .61]	[19.4, 45.1]

Effects based on logit model in which escalation variable was dichotomized, with those who escalated zero or one time coded as 0 and those who escalated two or three times coded as 1. 95% confidence intervals in parentheses. Each row represents a separate mediation analysis as the method can only include one mediator at a time.

cannot be reduced to simply having higher aims. The variable's direct effect is high in substantive and statistical significance.[70]

Turning to the effects of the experimental treatments, we see that a loss-cutting framing has a positive effect on the hazard ratio; those reminded of the human costs have a 16% greater inclination to exit the conflict at any point. When we subset the analysis to those who support the initial dispatch of Russian soldiers, the effect of the cutting loss treatment rises substantially. The hazard ratio rises to 29% and the treatment has a significance level of $p = .002$. Being reminded of sunk costs is of course not likely to affect those who are uninterested in entering in the first place; this is preaching to the choir. Moral escalation, however, has no effect. This seems to indicate that respondents have to be specifically prompted to avoid the sunk cost fallacy. They naturally move in the direction of persistence. This can explain the uphill battle Bethmann-Hollweg faced in urging pragmatism during World War I, even in a losing situation.

Those who choose to persist in the conflict (a process predicted by binding morality) also tend to raise their reservation price over time,

---

[70] Online Appendix 5.3 reports the results of how sensitive the results are to the sequential ignorability assumption.

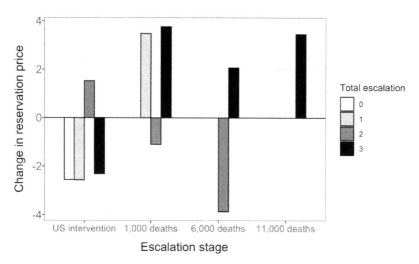

Figure 9.2 *Those who escalate further increase their reservation price as casualties mount and Russia begins to lose the war.*

even as absolute and relative costs rise. Figure 9.2 plots the change in reservation price compared to the previous round at four stages of the conflict, separating respondents by their ultimate escalation level at the end of the survey. For our purposes, it is at the final stage, when casualties begin to turn decidedly against the Russians, where we can observe the inflationary dynamics we saw in Germany. Those who chose to keep fighting every time (the black bars), on average increased their acceptable compromise settlement by three points from the next-to-last to the last round after hearing about the 11,000 casualties. A paired *t*-test shows this is a highly significant difference (p < .001).

Casualties seem to be driving the results. Earlier, after being told about the deployment of the Russian navy but before being told about the first round of conflict and attendant battle deaths, this super-resolute group actually lowers its reservation price, a difference significant again at p < .001. However, it raises its demands after every round in which Russians are killed. Those who persist only until Russian casualties rise well above American casualties demonstrate a much more rational updating style. Prior to withdrawing after being informed that 11,000 Russian soldiers in total had been died, those with an escalation score of 2 have begun lowering their reservation price by almost 4 percentage points of the territory.

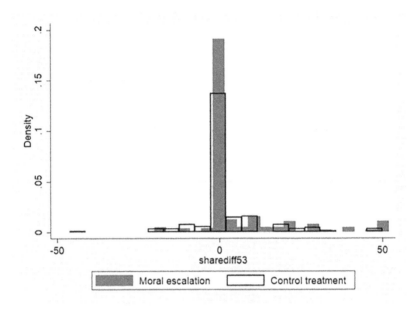

Figure 9.3 *Moral escalation framing causes super-escalators to increase their reservation price even further.* N = 516.

This is indicative of the same process observed among German escalators during World War I. While those who endure to the end make higher initial demands than those who do not (results not reported), they also increase those demands at precisely the moment where rationally they should lower them given the prospects for victory. Nor is this a small portion of the sample. As mentioned, 40% of the sample fights to the end. By the end, the average reservation price for the fifth query is 72 out of 100, an increase from an average of 59.6 the first time respondents are asked, although readers should bear in mind that the sample has changed, with many having opted out of the fight.

Also consistent with my argument is the effect of the moral escalation treatment on this same group of super-persisters. While there is no substantively or statistically significant effect of this treatment on the sample as a whole, there is an effect on those who end up fighting on at every point in the conflict. For instance, for those who choose to stay in at every casualty and battlefield update, the moral escalation treatment, compared to the control, induces an increase of reservation price of 2.8% between the 1,000 and 11,000 casualty stage, significant at p = .03. Reminding respondents of binding moral stakes exacerbates existing loss aversion. Figure 9.3 shows a histogram comparing the difference between super-persisters who received the control and those primed with moral escalation. We see that most primed to think of honoring soldiers' sacrifice do not change their reservation price very much; virtually none lower their reservation price; and quite a few raise it. The group presented with casualty data neutrally has more subjects that lower their demands and fewer who raise it substantially.

10 | Daily Bread
Hitler, Moral Devolution, and Nazi Foreign Policy

Hitler marked a decisive break in German foreign policy, a shift from a moralistic and self-righteous foreign policy predicated on an understanding of the world as a dangerous place to an amoral foreign policy entirely devoid of humanitarian considerations in which all are engaged in a competitive and brutal struggle for survival. The rise of Nazism was a moral revolution in German foreign based on a fundamentally new conceptualization of the forces that bind groups together, one in which group loyalty was owed to race rather than culture or nation and which demanded absolute deference to the *Führer*. However, it was also a moral devolution, a revolution of immorality. Whereas binding morality typically justifies its ingroup favoritism by reference to the need to protect wrongdoers from both within and without, Hitler (at least privately) entirely eschewed moral condemnation as irrelevant in a dog-eat-dog world in which only the strong survived. This was a perversion of what generally constitutes binding morality and drove a fundamentally different foreign policy agenda: Germany must pursue *Lebensraum* in the east through a war of conquest, providing for the material needs of the German people without even the slightest humanitarian constraints. Whereas those with dangerous world beliefs must justify (even if speciously) the harm they do to others as necessary to protect the ingroup, those with competitive world beliefs (CWB) are under no such obligation. In power, they are able to practice a ruthless egoism in foreign policy often assumed but rarely seen. If we were to pursue the notion of a "world apart" or an "autonomous moral sphere" to its logical conclusion, Hitler would be the norm rather than the exception. And even Hitler, as we will see, operated under the shadow of morality.

Yet curiously, the conventional wisdom, at least in recent political science accounts of Nazi foreign policy, stresses the continuity between

Hitler and his predecessors.[1] Structural accounts locate that consistency in the geopolitical environment Germany faced, which had not decisively changed. The genocidal aspects of the Nazi regime are treated as peripheral to German war aims, a question of how Germany fought the war but not why. What distinguished Hitler, Copeland argues, was the way in which the war was conducted, particularly Hitler's simultaneous pursuit of Lebensraum and racial extermination. In his argument, the complexion of World War II was different because of Hitler but not the decision to initiate – that is the "how" and not the "whether."[2] "German geopolitical vulnerability and the desire to eliminate the Russian threat would have existed with or without Nazi ideology." Racism "appears to be neither a sufficient nor even a necessary condition," he concludes, "best thought of as an accentuating condition, one that turned the Second World War into the most devastating and chilling war the world has ever seen."[3] In other words, the only unique thing about Hitler was the Holocaust.

Constructivist accounts maintain that Hitler was driven by the same set of ideas, nationalism and militarism in particular, that motivated the Wilhelmine regime. Legro argues that after World War I, the country "returned to roughly the same ideas that had fueled the conflict. German thinking about international involvement featured a set of beliefs favoring armed expansion that prioritized the utility of armed force and territorial acquisition in the heart of Europe."[4] There was "considerable continuity in German foreign policy ideas from Wilhelm to Hitler."[5] The latter was again unique only in his racial policies. He "built on that legacy in an abhorrent form, especially in the genocide of the Jews and other minorities and the mass killing and enslavement of 'subhuman' Slavs (and here there is a

---

[1] Many historians, particularly the "Fischer school," point to continuity as well, arguing that German war aims in the first and second world wars were highly similar, owing to the pathologies created by Germany's stunted democratic development and the persistence of feudal elites desperate to resist any infringement on their prerogatives. Fischer, *Germany's Aims in the First World War*.

[2] Copeland, Dale C. 2001. *The Origins of Major War*. Ithaca and London: Cornell University Press, 119.

[3] Ibid, 120.

[4] Legro, Jeffrey W. 2005. *Rethinking the World: Great Power Strategies and International Order*. Ithaca and London: Cornell University Press, 84.

[5] Ibid, 86.

notable difference between Wilhelmine and Nazi Germany), but the foundation of his expansionist ideas was aligned with the prior pattern."[6] Hitler's was a "traditional orientation that favored territorial expansion."[7] The Führer might have been quantitatively different, but he was not qualitatively different from previous German leaders. He was a "hypernationalist," but this was simply a question of degree. It was only with Germany's collapse and subsequent democratization under Western occupation that (West) Germany fundamentally revised the ideas guiding its foreign policy.

These accounts do not come to terms with the unique nature of Hitler's worldview and its moral (and immoral) foundations. Germany's foreign policy under Hitler and the Kaiser was indeed nationalistic, militaristic, and expansionist. But these overly elastic concepts obscure enormous differences in the kind of nationalism that drove Hitler and those who came before him and therefore the uses to which military force would be applied. Noting that both Hitler and Wilhelmine elites or other Weimar-era politicians wanted to expand territorially is like noting that Baptists and bootleggers both want to abolish the legal sale of alcohol.

The Nazi Party proposed a qualitatively different type of nationalism, a racialized and materialist version rather than a cultural and linguistic one, based on a vision of the world as a competitive environment of existential struggle in which groups fought to secure their *tägliches Brot* (daily bread). The group was bound together not by culture, language, or history but by blood. The ultimate aim of foreign

---

[6] Ibid, 88.

[7] Ibid, 97. Snyder makes a more nuanced argument, claiming that Hitler was a true believer of national myths propagated instrumentally during the Wilhelmine period to justify militaristic policies economically favored by narrow interest groups. However, the implication is that the ideas driving Hitler were mere retreads of the previous epoch. The Nazis were "true believing victims of the stew of strategic myths that the Wilhelmine and wartime radical right concocted and over time spiced up" (107), what he calls "ideological blowback from the strategic mythmaking of the Wilhelmine area" (93). Hitler was "politically socialized" during this period (107). Snyder notes that Nazi strategic concepts made use of notions of self-sufficiency, social Darwinism, and Lebensraum but argues these were already present before World War I, thereby denying any special role for them in Nazi Germany. In the end, Hitler embraced the same notions as previous elites: that countries respond to force. The use of a big stick cowers paper tigers and leads other states to bandwagon with the stronger (93). Snyder, *Myths of Empire*.

policy grew out of this biologized understanding of the human experience, the securing of *Lebensraum* (living space) that would ensure the necessary material resources – most importantly, agricultural land – for the Aryan race to survive and prosper. All collective enterprises of any size require morality to bind the group together, and Hitler made use of all the binding values to ensure cohesion; he demanded obedience, celebrated authority, and venerated sacrifice, this time to the race rather than the nation.

The continuity argument does not distinguish between dangerous world beliefs (DWB) and competitive world beliefs (CWB) (described in Chapter 5) and the distinct foreign policy aims they identify for their holders. The central challenge for those who believe in a dangerous world is to neutralize threats from immoral others. The fundamental social problem in a competitive world is scarcity, which is the basis of material value and generates zero-sum conceptions of social life.[8] In a competitive world, there is no distinction to be made between relative and absolute gains. Individuals will seek dominance and hierarchy, since power and security are one and the same. CWB describes an individual-level worldview in which individuals go through life taking everything they can. Hitler saw racial groups as doing so as well, situating the racial nation in a dog-eat-dog international environment.

Hitler's racial beliefs and the pursuit of Lebensraum grew out of the same underlying biological worldview. The former was not merely a graft onto the existing nationalism of the Wilhelmine period. "The struggle to destroy the power of international Jewry, the struggle to annihilate Marxism, and the struggle to obtain 'living space' for Germany at the expense of Russia amounted in effect to three forms of expression of the same integral thought," writes Kershaw, one of the foremost historians of Hitler. "And this was embedded in, and took its justification from, an understanding of history which ... dogmatically held to a view of historical development as the unfolding of a constant struggle between races – ethnic, biological peoples."[9]

As Duckitt maintains, CWB of this type are associated with, and enabled by, a lack of basic humanitarian values that Haidt calls the

---

[8] Hamilton, E. J., and B. C. Rathbun. 2013. "Scarce Differences: Toward a Material and Systemic Foundation for Offensive and Defensive Realism." *Security Studies* 22(3): 436–465.

[9] Kershaw, Ian. 1991. *Hitler*. London: Routledge, 28.

harm/care foundation. Those with CWB are therefore less limited by moral compunctions of any sort, removing any moral restraint on the use of instrumental violence for simple material gain. In the pursuit of the people's daily bread, the Nazis disavowed any Christian ethical commands found in the Lord's Prayer. For Hitler, these humanitarian sentiments were social constructions with no basis in the material world. The Nazi leader justified this anti-humanitarianism in crude and now debunked evolutionary terms. Organisms do not work for the benefit of their species as a whole, as he falsely believed, but rather the survival of their own, individual-level genetic material. More importantly, of course, is the set of findings on which this book is based – the altruism at which Hitler scoffed is a necessary condition for the progress and astonishing success of the human species.

Hitler was highly dismissive of the foreign policy goals of Wilhelmine German foreign policy as well as the plans offered by his right-wing Weimar counterparts before his seizure of power. The earlier generation of German nationalists, who had challenged the status-quo-oriented Wilhelmine elites, sought to protect the German people by binding together and resisting the designs of Germany's immoral adversaries. While this might require expansion, it was for defensive purposes in their mind. These views were the outgrowth of a moralistic understanding of the environment as a dangerous rather than a competitive world; it was fixated on the wrong done to Germany by other countries. This tendency continued after the war with the now traditional nationalists demanding that Germany be given back what was rightfully hers. At the most they wanted to expand Germany to include territories such as Austria so that all Germans would be contained in one Reich, a goal based on a predominantly cultural understanding of what constituted the Volk.

Hitler, in contrast, did not morally condemn Germany's adversaries at all, except for propaganda purposes. Consistent with his competitive worldview, he did not think the world owed countries anything except what they had the strength to take. No people, even the Germans, had any right to any particular territory. He set his sights on greater goals: Lebensraum that would provide for the sustenance of a racially defined German people. For the Nazis, the mere return of lands lost in the war and the unification of all German speakers in one empire were not enough to provide for their biological needs. This living space could only be found in the east. Its attainment required a showdown with the Soviet Union and a decisive break with the pre-1914 Weltpolitik that had needlessly antagonized England. Hitler's foreign policy aims were not defensive at all, except in the sense that if life was a bitter struggle for survival some other race would take the territory it needed if Germany did not get there first. By not distinguishing between DWB and CWB, Copeland falsely equates the pursuit of living space with security against Russia, while Legro places both Wilhelmine and Nazi aims under the general category of "expansionism" that marked German foreign policy in both World War I and World War II.

Just as accounts in political science and even history miss the revolutionary character of national thinking in the Wilhelmine period, thereby overstating the extent of continuity and the ways by which the new nationalists posed a threat to the conservative establishment, the same is true of the interwar year period. By shifting the basis of the Volk from culture and language to race, the Nazis marked a significant departure with foreign policy implications. They challenged the new establishment right, those nationalists who had displaced the monarchical old guard of their time. This again shows that an evolutionary account does not enable us to predict the myriad ways by which binding morality or CWB might manifest.[10] Ideological movements and cultural change are essential. Hitler's agency came in the form of integrating racial ideas percolating at the time with nationalism. However, whereas the rise of the nationalist right in the Wilhelmine period was a moral revolution, the rise of the racist right in the interwar period was both moral revolution (in its shift from nation to race) and moral devolution (in its dismissal of humanitarianism), a perversion of binding morality.

Even Hitler acted under the shadow of morality, however. While he thought that the traditional nationalist right was overly fixated on restoring the status quo and the injustice of Versailles, which for him were overly moralistic goals, he largely hid his lack of moral condemnation of Germany's historical antagonists from public view. In fact, the surge of Nazi popularity in 1930 likely owes to the parroting

---

[10] A non-racialized understanding of the world as a cut-throat struggle for survival is also possible.

of this very critique. Hitler also largely downplayed his dismissal of basic humanitarian values and his crude evolutionary views. As he became a factor in German politics, he almost never mentioned these central concepts, confining his discussion of race largely to his virulent anti-Semitism.

In the sections that follow, I present an intensive analysis of Hitler's worldview, focusing first on his understanding of the world as an amoral struggle for survival in which humanitarian morality plays no role.[11] I then examine the shift from traditional German nationalism, based on culture (*Kultur*), to groups defined in terms of race (*Rasse*), and the cleavages this created in the German right. I show how Hitler embraced many elements of binding morality – a focus on national cohesion and a hostility to democracy and socialism – but that his racialized conception of the nation and CWB led to fundamentally different foreign policy concepts, most importantly the need for Lebensraum. I then demonstrate how Hitler's foreign policy agenda differed from the nationalists of the Wilhelmine and the Weimar period, noting the implications of his complete dismissal of moral condemnation and national entitlement.

Hitler's shielding of his true beliefs likely contributed to British uncertainty about Hitler's motives, which I show in the final section. A look at the deliberations of the British Cabinet indicates that they were unsure as to whether the Nazis represented a new breed of German racist intent on continental domination or a traditional nationalist one aiming only at repossessing Bohemia and the Polish corridor. The question, as they noted, was crucial. Yet by postponing any firm conclusion, they lost crucial time in confronting the Nazis. Historians and political scientists are not the only ones to have missed this crucial distinction.

---

[11] I focus on Hitler's views, rather than those of the Nazi Party, because of what we tragically know about history. The Führer's ideology, articulated clearly in his two books and speeches from the 1920s, decisively affected German foreign policy. They offered a blueprint he followed in power. Hitler stayed to these publicly articulated beliefs throughout the war. Although I focus on his statements before his seizure of power, I periodically point out in footnotes where he expressed identical thoughts during a set of private dinner-time discussions at his wartime headquarters. Hitler, Adolf. 1981. *Hitler's Secret Conversations, 1941–1944.* New York: Octagon Books, 21. These reveal *Mein Kampf* to be his genuine worldview.

Constant "Kampf": Biology, Struggle, and the Illusion of Humanitarian Morality in Nazi Ideology

Hitler grounded his worldview in basic evolutionary principles,[12] that humans have two primary drives that are the "rulers of life": hunger and love.[13] "While the satisfaction of eternal hunger guarantees self-preservation, the satisfaction of love assures the continuance of the race."[14] These "two passions ... the drive for life, to sate hunger, and to preserve the species, the impulse for self-preservation and the impulse for procreation ... are the primary urges that guide every life."[15] Hitler acknowledged the mystery of why life existed at all, "but one thing is clear. As soon as a lifeform sees the light of this earth, it clings with all its power to this life."[16]

While it is hard to deny the human urge to procreate and survive, the most important element of Hitler's evolutionary worldview (and where, in terms of human beings, he went fundamentally wrong) is his belief that these impulses inevitably lead to struggle – in German, "Kampf." "We must realize that the satisfaction [of these drives] is only possible through struggle, that it is an eternal fight, that the satisfaction of these two drives is solely an eternal battlefield and will remain so."[17] For Hitler, this was because of scarcity. There is simply not enough to go around for everyone. "These beings must come into conflict with one another at the same moment at which the basis on which the development of these drives takes place is limited."[18] This means that "the one being only lives from the other; that the life of

---

[12] Hitler, Adolf. 1961. *Hitlers zweites Buch: ein Dokument aus dem Jahr 1928*. Stuttgart: Deutsche Verlags-Anstalt, 47; Weikart, Richard. 2009. *Hitler's Ethic: The Nazi Pursuit of Evolutionary Progress*. New York: Palgrave-Macmillan.
[13] Weinberg, Gerhard L. 1980. *The Foreign Policy of Hitler's Germany: Starting World War II, 1937–1939*. Chicago: University of Chicago Press, 47.
[14] Hitler, *Hitlers zweites Buch*, 46.
[15] "Tageskampf oder Schicksalskampf" (3 March 1928) in Hitler, Adolf. 1994. *Reden, Schriften, Anordnungen: Februar 1925 bis Januar 1933. Von der Reichstagswahl bis zur Reichspräsidentenwahl Oktober 1930–März 1932*. Munich: Saur, 723. Also "Was ist Nationalsozialismus?" (6 August 1927) in Hitler 1994, 439.
[16] "Tageskampf oder Schicksalskampf," 722; also "Was ist Nationalsozialismus," 439.
[17] "Was ist Nationalsozialismus," 441.
[18] "Tageskampf oder Schicksalskampf," 723.

one being causes the death of the other; that the question is: Which of you two wants to live, either you or me ... because one only lives from the other."[19] Struggle was of course such an important concept for Hitler that it formed the title of his ideological manifesto and auto-biography before he achieved any significant political power: "Mein Kampf" or "my struggle."[20] Hitler concluded: "[I]t is a cruel, heart-less world, a terrible world, if one considers that this earth gives birth to beings who can only be preserved forever through the death of the other being by eating it."[21]

In this way, Hitler thought that humans were no different from any other species, as much as they wanted to believe otherwise. "Nothing that is made of flesh and blood can escape the laws which determined its coming into being."[22] A human being must "never fall into the lunacy of believing that he has really risen to be lord and master of Nature" but must "understand the fundamental necessity of Nature's rule, and realize how much this existence is subjected to these laws of eternal fight and upward struggle. Then he will feel that in a universe where planets revolve around suns, and moons turn about planets, where force alone forever masters weakness, compelling it to be an obedient slave or else crushing it, there can be no special laws for man there. For him, too, the eternal principles of this ultimate wisdom hold sway. He can try to comprehend them; but escape them, never."[23] "Just as the smallest worm receives its weapons for the struggle for life from nature," he wrote, "so man must preserve his life through the application and use of the means that nature has given him."[24]

This equating of humans to other animals led Hitler to the conclu-sion that most distinguished Nazism from previous right-wing ide-ologies and which would be directly responsible for the tremendous destruction that Germany would cause under his leadership: there was no such thing as humanitarian ethics. Animals know no morality in their struggle for life, and Hitler believed the same to be true of humans since all organisms operate under the same universal laws. "We all

[19] Ibid, 724.
[20] Hitler, Adolf. 1971. *Mein Kampf* (R. Manheim, trans.). Boston & New York: Houghton Mifflin (Original work published in 1927).
[21] Ibid, 724.   [22] Hitler, *Hitlers zweites Buch*, 46.
[23] Hitler, *Mein Kampf*, 245.
[24] "Tageskampf oder Schicksalkampf," 722.

know," he said, "that when a tiger tears up a human being, this tiger per se, from a higher point of view, cannot be found guilty; he acts unconsciously, not badly, blindly, no differently than any spider that eats the little insect that goes into its yarn, acts no differently than the human being who eats the other animals to survive."[25] He noted in Mein Kampf, "you will never find a fox who in his inner attitude might ... show humanitarian tendencies toward geese, as similarly there is no cat with a friendly inclination toward mice.... [T]he struggle among them arises less from inner aversion than from hunger and love. In both cases, Nature looks on calmly, with satisfaction, in fact. In the struggle for daily bread all those who are weak and sickly or less determined succumb, while the struggle of the males for the female grants the right or opportunity to propagate only to the healthiest."[26]

This is the connection between CWB and amorality drawn by Duckitt. Humanitarianism and liberal morality were for Hitler merely social constructions, illusions that men lived under to distract from the brutal realities of life. "When the nations on this planet struggle for existence ... then all considerations of humanitarianism or aesthetics crumble into nothingness; for all these concepts do not float about in the ether, they arise from men's imagination and are bound up with man. When he departs from this world, these concepts are again dissolved into nothingness, for Nature does not know them.... Humanitarianism ... would vanish even from a world inhabited by man if this world were to lose the races that have created and upheld these concepts."[27] He wrote of the "principal discovery that there is no humanism, only eternal struggle, which is the precondition for the development of all of humanity. The line between man and animal is drawn by man himself."[28]

Hitler was contemptuous of these most universal of moral values, decrying "loathsome humanitarian morality."[29] "In the end," reads Mein Kampf, "only the urge for self-preservation can conquer. Beneath

---

[25] "Was ist Nationalsozialismus?," 462. He expresses the same privately during the war (Hitler, *Hitler's Secret Conversations, 1941–1944*, 33).
[26] Hitler, *Mein Kampf*, 285.   [27] Ibid, 177–178.
[28] "Der Nationalsozialismus als Weltanschauung, der Marxismus ein Wahnsinn!" (2 April 1927) in Hitler 1994, 229. He says the same in his wartime, "secret" conversations (Hitler, *Hitler's Secret Conversations, 1941–1944*, 57).
[29] Hitler, *Mein Kampf*, 42.

it so-called humanity, the expression of a mixture of stupidity, cowardice, and know-it-all conceit, will melt like snow in the March sun. Mankind has grown great in eternal struggle, and only in eternal peace does it perish."[30] He longed for the time in which "our people were not yet sickened by pacifism and humanism" but instead "filled with the healthy spirit of striving for world domination."[31]

For Hitler, there was only the right of the stronger (*Recht des Stärkeren*). Humans, like any other species, had no right to life.[32] They had to fight for it. Hitler wrote of "the rigid law of necessity and the right to victory of the best and stronger in this world. Those who want to live, let them fight, and those who do not want to fight in this world of eternal struggle do not deserve to live."[33] "So long as there is an earth," he wrote, "and so long as life beings exist on it … so long as we have recognized history, right has never won, but rather strength alone."[34] Might makes right. "On this earth there is the right of the stronger, the right of struggle and the law of victory; if you claim that right rules, then you are deceiving yourself. When two fight with another and one of them is right and the other is in the wrong, but the former is defeated, where is the right?.... [D]o not look at the universe from the standpoint of your little laws. The universe does not recognize them. When someone loses despite his right, this is because he was weaker."[35] Rights other than those of strength were to him "paper rights" of no use.[36] "The world does not concern itself with paper rights but only with power that stands behind rights."[37]

This was an explicit rejection of liberal ethics. "Mankind did not reach its current position as ruler of the world through arbitration courts, treaties, peaceful conflict resolution, or regulating relations based on equal compensation but through struggle," he argued.[38] He

---

[30] Ibid, 135.

[31] "Die soziale Sendung des Nationalsozialismus" (19 December 1925) in Hitler 1994, 240.

[32] See his expressions of this viewpoint privately during the war as well (Hitler, *Hitler's Secret Conversations, 1941–1944*, 33).

[33] Hitler, *Mein Kampf*, 288.

[34] "Tageskampf oder Schicksalkampf," 727.

[35] kampf oder kampfIbid, 726.

[36] "Zukunft oder Untergang" (6 March 1927) in Hitler 1994, 168.

[37] "Tageskampf oder Schicksalkampf," 727.

[38] "Was ist Nationalsozialismus," 442.

rejected the notion of a progressive expansion of humanitarian concern and a growing recognition of the equality of man. "The pacifist-humane idea is perfectly all right … when the highest type of man has previously conquered and subjected the world to an extent that makes him the sole ruler of this earth…. Therefore, first struggle and then we will see what can be done."[39]

For Hitler, the goal of the National Socialist movement was to remind the German people of what they had forgotten or pretended to no longer know, "to bring our people back to a clear, healthy way of thinking, … to give back the natural instinct that has been artificially buried, this natural self-preservation instinct to those people who have to struggle hard for their daily bread and thereby for their existence."[40] The truth was right in front of them, he thought. Sophisticated ladies, he observed, might sit at lunch, observing a spider eating a fly and comment on its cruelness, while simultaneously eating a blood sausage.[41]

---

[39] Hitler, *Mein Kampf*, 288. "Was Hitler simply a realist?. The endogeneity of morality to power, captured in the aphorism that "might makes right" is after all a common realist theme. As I have discussed in previous chapters, however, realist morality is consequentialist in nature. The nature of international relations poses difficult ethical tradeoffs that the leader cannot avoid, and he or she chooses the lesser evil. Hitler, in contrast, did not lament the right of the stronger as a disagreeable fact with which one must come to terms. He embraced it, even pointing consistently to its role in promoting progress as he saw it. "Anyone who would banish this struggle from the Earth forever would perhaps abolish the struggle between men, but he would also eliminate the highest driving power for their development," Hitler wrote, "exactly as if in civil life he would want to eternaliseeternalize the wealth of certain men, the greatness of certain business enterprises, and for this purpose eliminate the play of free forces, competition. The results would be catastrophic for a nation." (Hitler, *Hitlers zweites Buch*, 55). Without the struggle for existence, man would become a "lazy, degenerate brute." "Tageskampf oder Schicksalkampf," 726. To restrain the struggle for existence was to "sin against the will of the eternal creator…. The stronger must dominate and not blend with the weaker, thus sacrificing his own greatness. Only the born weakling can view this as cruel, but he after all is only a weak and limited man; for if this law did not prevail, any conceivable higher development of organic living beings would be unthinkable." Hitler, *Mein Kampf*, 285.

[40] "Tageskampf oder Schicksalkampf," 719.

[41] Ibid, 726.

Folk Theory: From Kultur to Rasse as the Basis of German Nationalism

Hitler did not eschew all morality, however. Rather he refashioned elements of binding ethics in a way consistent with his racialized worldview. He defined the bonds that held the nation together differently than traditional nationalists. Just as German nationalists in the Wilhelmine period had reordered elements of our evolutionary-based toolkit to create an entirely new cultural construction, so did the Nazis.

In his emphasis on the binding moral foundations, Hitler appealed to the ethics of community in the same way that previous German nationalists did. In this amoral struggle of racially defined peoples, absolute unity was necessary, he believed. Logically, this makes sense as a deduction from his core beliefs. A scarce world is one of bitter competition in which others are always out to take what you have, in which the best defense is a good offense. This requires collective resistance.

Individuals had an obligation to serve the greater whole. "As much as the individual is initially tormented by his fate, we find that there is actually no particular individual fate. The fate of the individual derives from the fate of the whole. The primary concern is the fate of the whole."[42] Nationalism was itself a moral value. "We recognize that there are noble values in nationalism.... Nationalism is an eternal sacrifice to the people. The highest nationalism is synonymous with a deep dedication for this totality of 62 million people."[43] Yet this obligation stopped at the Volk's edge: "The highest National Socialist is the person who gives the most for the well-being of all his fellow citizens, and who in this struggle is closer to the last fellow citizen than to the highest man who is outside of his group of fellow citizens."[44] He spoke of a "community of fate, in which one frees oneself from feeling as an individual person, and understands oneself as part of a community of millions of which you are only a small fraction."[45] Like Ludendorff and Hindenburg had done during the war, he decried "unidealistic egoism, the most primitive selfishness, most pronounced

---

[42] "Die soziale Sendung des Nationalsozialismus," 720.
[43] "Tageskampf oder Schicksalkampf," 737.
[44] "Was ist Nationalsozialismus," 458.   [45] "Zukunft oder Untergang," 165.

in the ordinary criminal whose standpoint is that his life is more important than those of others, even if he has to stab the other.... The hero says: what difference does my life make if I can save the collective, the criminal: who cares about the collectivity if I can save my own life?"[46]

Hitler held out for special praise binding values such as "blind obedience and submission" as well as courage, industriousness, and resolve.[47] And as it was for all German nationalists, betrayal was the worst offense. "We also want the nation to give you what you are due. Therefore we have the right to say: your whole people stands up for you; if you do not stand for your people, you can expect no mercy from us.... [W]e will oppose you as the implacable avengers of our fatherland, our nation!"[48] He embraced the common *Dolchstoss* or "stab in the back" myth, which maintained that Germany had not lost militarily but rather was betrayed by forces inside of Germany, its "internal defilers," a "collection of Marxist, democratic pacifistic, destructive traitors" responsible for the "November crime."[49]

As the German nationalists of the Wilhelmine period and the interwar years did, Hitler lamented the domestic conflicts, particularly over class, that divided the left and right, preventing both from acting together on behalf of the community in its struggle with other nations. "German power is worn down by internal struggles" so that it is "missing as a means of power abroad."[50] "Power can only be created again through a people striving for power with unity and determination, through a people that carries within itself the noble thoughts of the national community, of the indissoluble connection in all questions concerning blood, race and national tradition. Power is created through a body of the people that does not allow itself to be distracted by less important disputes, but which represents a community of fate from the right to the left and the left to the right in all matters concerning the existence and non-existence of the Volk."[51]

---

[46] "Tageskampf oder Schicksalkampf," 350.
[47] "Appel an die deutsche Kraft," 352–333; "Die soziale Sendung des Nationalsozialismus," 259.
[48] "Die soziale Sendung des Nationalsozialismus," 259.
[49] Hitler, *Hitlers zweites Buch*, 52.
[50] "20 millionen Deutsche zu viel" (7 May 1927), 292 in Hitler 1994.
[51] "Die soziale Sendung des Nationalsozialismus," 259. He called it a "fantasy if we believe that our people will rise again in this world if it does not celebrate its inner resurrection, if it does not recognize its mutual necessity

Hitler, however, conceived of the Volk as primarily a racial grouping rather than a cultural and linguistic one. For Hitler, groups were based on common biological characteristics. Where struggle was his "first law," the competition between races was his second. "As a National Socialist, I stress that no man is identical to another.... Each has its own ... specific worth.... The same is true for peoples. It is natural that a people will decline in comparison to another if any processes eliminate or remove its most valuable single specimens. If a people loses its best blood carriers over the course of centuries, the collective specific worth of the people will decline."[52] A Volk is a "body of flesh and blood," he maintained.[53] "A nation is only a multitude of more or less similar individual beings."[54]

As is well known, Hitler believed in a racial hierarchy. He argued that "who we today understand as the victor over the animal world is not man himself but rather a particular kind that consistently catches our eye, the Aryan." Aryans were a "community of similar blood,"[55] who, because of their greater racial value, were responsible in his mind for all the great cultural achievements of the world.[56] "Take away the Nordic Teutons," he proclaimed, "and all that is left is monkey dances."[57] "Wherever this man has arrived, he has become the lord of other forms of life, while the rest of mankind lags behind in desperate struggles with other life forms."[58]

---

and togetherness" ("Zukunft oder Untergang," 174). He asked rhetorically whether the German people "were in a position to unite and come together" and "finally exercise the power abroad that is required to attain its freedom and gain victory for itself rather than delivering it to others outside?" ("Zukunft oder Untergang," 178). Germany needed the masses. "These 15 million people, they are 30 million fists, who stand in the factory, and work on this earth for us, and who are also employed on the land. If these 15 million socialists were not here, we could not exist" ("Zukunft oder Untergang," 172). When Germany had acted in a unified manner, such as in the time of Bismarck, it had achieved great things. When it allowed its internal divides to undermine national solidarity, as was the case during the religious wars, for instance, it had failed in foreign policy.

[52] "Appel an die deutsche Kraft" (4 August 1929) in Hitler 1994, 346.
[53] "Tageskampf oder Schicksalkampf," 346; also Hitler, *Hitlers zweites Buch*, 47.
[54] Hitler, *Hitlers zweites Buch*, 46.
[55] "Tageskampf oder Schicksalkampf," 728.
[56] "Die soziale Sendung des Nationalsozialismus" (19 December 1925), 258.
[57] "Der Nationalsozialismus als Weltanschauung," 229.
[58] "Was ist Nationalsozialismus," 440.

Politics was the struggle for existence among these Völker, which led to the creation of the state. "Just as the individual being is dominated by the urge to live, we find the same in the collectivity with the Volk. Here lies the most fundamental law that compels individual beings to unite to form the state. For the state represents nothing other than the organization of individuals for the common struggle of the collectivity for its life, whose expression is politics."[59] Hitler saw the National Socialist mission as educating the German in "correct, clear, selfish thinking: selfish not in the sense of the individual, but in the sense of the whole, the national community, which has the same blood, the same language, the same mental disposition of those who have to fight together on this earth for daily bread."[60]

This was a revolutionary departure from previous conceptions of nationalism. Eley writes, "When German politicians referred to the Volk at the turn of the century, they meant the people."[61] The "preponderance of opinion held that the determination of ethnic identity were language, culture and religion."[62] Indeed following its founding, the Pan-German League clarified its understanding: "Das Volkstum ties a bond – spiritual, moral and linguistic – around all Germans, wherever they may be."[63] The term "Rasse" (race) was used, but as a synonym for ethnicity and cultural affinity. Hitler inverted this understanding; culture became an "index of racial purity." Racial superiority was equated with *Bildung* (cultivation).[64]

Biological racism of course was very much present in the Wilhelmine period. There was a state-funded eugenics research foundation called the German Institute for Racial Hygiene.[65] Anti-Semitism was becoming particularly pronounced in the German right before World War I. The Nazis drew on social Darwinistic ideas that had been emerging since the late 1800s, not just in Germany but across Europe. However, the biological-based conception of racism was at first used primarily as a "scientific" justification for existing patterns

---

[59] "Tageskampf oder Schicksalkampf," 723.
[60] Ibid, 719.
[61] Eley, Geoff. 1991. *Reshaping the German Right: Radical Nationalism and Political Change after Bismarck*. Ann Arbor: University of Michigan Press, 185.
[62] Chickering, *We Men Who Feel Most German*, 234.   [63] Ibid.
[64] Ibid, 234, 243; Hitler, *Hitler's Secret Conversations, 1941–1944*, 385.
[65] Schafft, Gretchen E. 2004. *From Racism to Genocide: Anthropology in the Third Reich*. Urbana and Chicago: University of Illinois Press.

of hierarchy and inequality. The earliest biological racists, in other words, were already paternalistic and culturally oriented racists, as German historians note.[66] With the Nazis, this became true belief, the real "ideological blowback" of the interwar years.[67]

There is "no question" that racist ideas were present in nationalist ideology before the rise of National Socialism, but Eley argues it is "doubtful whether they carried the weight of explanatory importance some historians have tried to attribute to them. These efforts misdirect our attention to idealist continuities." He warns, "if we talk too uncritically of some distinctive völkisch ideology ... later Nazi meanings may be misleadingly read back into an earlier and different discourse."[68] There were "radical discontinuities of ideology and practice which endowed some of the possibilities for a German fascism," and "an over-simplified view of linear continuity between the Second and Third Reich ... skates over all the interesting problems of the transition from one kind of right-wing politics to another." Hitler was quite conscious of how different his ideas were: "In coming before the people as National Socialists with this conception of the real strength of a Volk, we know that today the whole of public opinion is against us. But this is in the deepest sense the meaning of our new teaching, which as a worldview separates us from others."[69] He maintained that "nationality, or rather the race, is not rooted in the language but in the blood."[70]

The Nazis' real antithesis though was the left. International solidarity and bonds came at the expense of racial solidarity in the völkisch community.[71] Marxists, for instance, "imagine a world ... that goes

[66] Smith, *The Ideological Origins of Nazi Imperialism*, 146, 153; Chickering, *We Men Who Feel Most German*, 238.

[67] Snyder, *Myths of Empire*.

[68] Eley, *Reshaping the German Right*, 186–187. As Smith writes, "It is important to note that, although we normally think of notions of racial and cultural superiority as part of the same ideological package because of the prominence of both ideas in post-1918 radical conservatism, the two concepts were, in fact, not initially entirely compatible" (1989, 151). There were "significant and readily apparent contradictions between the materialist, biological foundations of racism and the cultural idealism inherent in much völkisch ideology" (1986, 91).

[69] Hitler, *Hitlers zweites Buch*, 65.

[70] Staudinger, Hans. 1981. *The Inner Nazi: A Critical Analysis of Mein Kampf*. Baton Rouge: Louisiana State University Press, 47.

[71] "Die soziale Sendung des Nationalsozialismus," 252.

so far as to say: the man of a foreign people who shares my worldview is closer to me than a compatriot of my own blood who does not share my worldview. That indicates that the common bond, the blood bond of the people, has been cut.... And what is the result?.... [T]he entire strength of the German people is not sufficient at the moment in which major foreign policy issues are to be dealt with, in which it concerns securing the sustenance of the German people."[72] Hitler complained of those on the left who "say, we want nothing to do with this Volk, we are citizens of the world, international citizens. Everyone is our brother."[73] He complained, "Instead of referring to the primordial right of our sense of struggle, we refer to the world spirit, world humanity, to world citizenship."[74]

More Patriotic than Thou, Redux: Racist versus Cultural Nationalism on the German Right

Hitler's particular racial brand of nationalism came with dangers for the now more traditional nationalists. He directed almost as much criticism at the "bourgeois" parties, ostensibly the parties of national solidarity and loyalty, for what he regarded as their fake, superficial, and self-serving nationalism. The German National People's Party (DNVP) was the heir to the National Liberal and Conservative parties of the Wilhelmine period and the home of this nationalist right.

In order to create unity in German society, the masses had to be won over to the national cause, and this required that the right demonstrate concern for the fate of average Germans. The nationalist right until then, however, was only concerned with maintaining its class privileges, indifferent to others' plight, he claimed.[75] Hitler accused the bourgeoisie of hypocrisy, an act of moral condemnation. "It is not sufficient to hold national speeches while thinking of the Kaiser, in order to be able to say that you are a nationalist."[76] Through their hypocrisy, Hitler claimed, German elites had made "national, pan-German, and

---

[72] "Was ist Nationalsozialismus," 450.   [73] "Zukunft oder Untergang," 172.
[74] "Tageskampf oder Schicksalkampf," 737.
[75] "Zukunft oder Untergang," 173.
[76] "Tageskampf oder Schicksalkampf," 737.

German" dirty words in the circles of the working class, since they were associated forever with bourgeois class interests.[77]

There is a direct parallel to the Second Reich. Just as Wilhelmine nationalists had accused the emperor of insufficient national commitment, the Nazis leveled the charge of deficient patriotism at the German nationalists. "Hand offs of our people," he told the bourgeois right. "We have the right to lead this fight, because we are more nationalist than you."[78] Hitler was morally condemning German elites for their inadequate fidelity to binding principles. He expressed identical views during the war in his "secret conversations."[79] What was good politics was also his genuine feeling.

Mass buy-in to the national, racial project was necessary for successful outcomes in an interracial struggle. "If the masses do not feel part of the national body, the nation has lost the most formidable source of power because they represent the brutal will for survival, in which lies dormant the power of the struggle for existence in this world. Sad if these masses ... instead go their own way, which is no longer in the direction of the national interest. They were not taken care of.... How did one think German power could be maintained if the millions of workers were alienated by power instead of becoming converts?"[80] He mocked the traditional right: "And one day you want to step in front of this people and be able to say: Workers, leave your workshop now, shoulder your rifle and go to death, the fatherland demands it! German mother, give your child away, it now belongs to the fatherland! Wife, renounce your husband, he now belongs to the fatherland! And then you talk about sacrifice?! As long as you count your money as a sacrifice, you cannot expect others to give their blood."[81]

This mobilization task had two separate parts that account for the name of the movement itself: making socialists into nationalists and nationalists into socialists. "Germany could only free itself from the yoke of bondage if its 16 million men of the left become fanatical nationalists and its 14 million right-wing supporters become supporters of social justice."[82] In fact, Hitler went so far as to claim that one could not be a nationalist without being a socialist or vice versa.[83] "To

---

[77] "Die soziale Sendung des Nationalsozialismus," 247.
[78] Ibid, 259.
[79] Hitler, *Hitler's Secret Conversations, 1941–1944*, 15, 17, 31, 110, 208, 209, 267.
[80] Ibid, 243.   [81] "Die soziale Sendung des Nationalsozialismus," 260.
[82] Ibid, 260.
[83] "Was ist Nationalsozialismus," 458; "Zukunft oder Untergang," 185.

be national is identical with being social. There is no separation here, the one requires the other. There is no socialism that does not find its most vivid expression in the most ardent admiration and love for the people ... which alone is the bearer of the fatherland and provides for the social welfare of its children."[84]

Hitler promised a classless society but not an egalitarian one. Germany would select its most racially valuable from all strata, since "the qualities of a people do not lie in their classes or professions, but rather are simply either in the blood of individual persons or not. It is necessary to bring these qualities to light ... and build the core of a new community, in the conviction that a people leads itself when its best forces lead it."[85] Just as races were of radically different values, the same was true of individuals. Hitler called the higher worth of a particular class of superior individuals "personality," and this struggle for dominance among them, even within the same race, was his "third law."[86]

This was a different kind of hierarchical society, one based on racial qualities rather than the bourgeois criteria of *Bildung* and *Besitz* (education and property) discussed in Chapter 7. This aspect of Hitler's ideology was more threatening to the traditional right than the left. National socialists were socialists, he explained, "not out of sentiment or out of fear that this class will otherwise rise up and become revolutionary, but because it is necessary, because we know that it contains the most valuable forces of our people that would otherwise perish."[87] In the "smallest factory worker might be found in the bud the highest value for the nation, because of his race he might be able to produce a son who may at some point become one of the geniuses of his people."[88] Beck explains: "In Nazi eyes, the DNVP was the embodiment of the bürgerliche (bourgeois) world ... a despised cosmos of rules and conventions that excluded those who had not imbibed them with their mother's milk; a universe of entitlement ... that required formal education, standardized tests and schooling ... as preconditions for social

---

[84] "Die soziale Sendung des Nationalsozialismus," 259; also "Tageskampf oder Schicksalkampf," 738; "Was ist Nationalsozialismus," 458.
[85] "Appel an die deutsche Kraft" in Hitler 1994, 351.
[86] "Der Nationalsozialismus als Weltanschauung," 229; "Was ist Nationalsozialismus," 440.
[87] "Wesen und Ziele des Nationalsozialismus" (3 July 1927) in Hitler 1994, 406.
[88] "Wesen und Ziele," 407.

advancement. It runs counter to the often implied community of interests between Nazis and their conservative allies that Nazis – storm troopers and intellectuals alike – hated the conservative bourgeoisie with consuming passion."[89] The Nazis were populist, and the German National People's Party (DNVP) paternalist.[90]

Scarcity, Competitive World Beliefs, and the Pursuit of "Living Space": Nazi versus Wilhelmine Nationalist Foreign Policy

As we have seen, Duckitt makes a crucial distinction between dangerous world beliefs and CWB. For those who hold the former, the "social world is a dangerous and threatening place in which good, decent people's values and way of life are threatened by bad people." For the latter, the social world is a "competitive jungle characterized by a ruthless and amoral ... struggle for survival." The central problem in a dangerous world is to provide security against those bad individuals or groups who would do us harm. This is the highly moralized worldview associated empirically, as we have seen, with binding morality. However, the more that international politics, indeed life, assumes a zero-sum quality in which there is not enough to secure basic needs, the more that scarcity becomes the key foreign policy problem. An acutely scarce world inevitably invites aggression as cooperation cannot resolve the dilemma of a pie that is too small. The natural strategy in such an environment is the maximization of power to take the maximum amount of resources.

Hitler depicted international relations, indeed life in general, as a competitive struggle for scarce material resources in which moral obligation could not intrude. This was different from the dangerous world beliefs of more traditional German nationalists, who as we have seen framed Germany's challenge as negotiating a world of hostile and immoral adversaries. Those who argue for continuity across these distinct periods of German history fail to distinguish between a dangerous and competitive worldview, and the way by which different moral values (or their complete absence) contribute to different foreign policy goals and means.

[89] Beck, Hermann. 2008. *The Fateful Alliance: German Conservatives and Nazis in 1933*. New York: Berghahn, 149.
[90] Ibid, 21.

Combining a competitive world view and a racialized conception of the national community, Hitler defined the "ultimate goal" of foreign policy as the "winning of the basis of a Volk's sustenance,"[91] the "creation of the most necessary prerequisites for life."[92] For Hitler, foreign policy, like life, was fundamentally material. "What is the goal of the National Socialist movement or party? To summarize briefly, we can say it in one sentence: preservation and advancement, nourishment and security of our people and the most valuable race elements on which these people are based. That is the exclusive and only goal! We are there for the struggle of this people, not for the realization of beautiful ideals that hover above the peoples."[93] Whereas "some say to us: the world of the spiritual is your greatness ... by nature you are the people of thinkers and poets,"[94] Hitler insisted that the "struggle for daily bread stands at the forefront of all vital necessities. To be sure, brilliant leaders can hold great goals before a Volk's eyes, so that it can be further diverted from material things in order to serve higher spiritual ideas." However, "if these ideals are not to result in the ruin of a Volk, they should never exist unilaterally at the expense of material nourishment so that the health of the nation is threatened by them."[95]

What were these (literally) vital necessities for Hitler, the basic material conditions for survival and propagation of the Volk defined in racial terms? Hitler answered this consistently: the need for territorial expansion to create living space (*Lebensraum*) that would provide the soil for cultivation necessary to sustain and nourish a growing people. Land provided for Germans' daily bread. Many international relations scholars have noted this key concept in Nazi thought but without understanding how it originates out of Hitler's crudely biological worldview or its implications for German foreign policy, particularly the departure from previous tendencies in German foreign policy that were also nationalistic and militaristic.

Hitler's emphasis on territorial expansion was a deduction from his belief in the perennial problem of material scarcity that affects all species, not just humans: "Countless are the species of all the Earth's organisms, unlimited ... in their instinct for self-preservation ... yet

---

[91] Hitler, *Hitlers zweites Buch*, 70.   [92] Ibid, 78.
[93] "Die soziale Sendung des Nationalsozialismus," 258.
[94] "Appel an die deutsche Kraft," 349.   [95] Hitler, *Hitlers zweites Buch*, 53.

the space in which the whole life process takes place is limited. The struggle for existence and continuance in life waged by billions upon billions of organisms takes place on the surface of an exactly measured sphere. In the limitation of living space lies the compulsion to engage in the struggle for existence but also the basis for evolution."[96] This is one of the most consistent themes in Hitler's speeches in the 1920s, particularly his two books.[97] "We can justly say that the whole life struggle of a Volk, in truth, consists in safeguarding the territory it requires as a general prerequisite for the sustenance of the increasing population. Since the population grows incessantly, and the soil as such remains stationary, tensions perforce must gradually arise which at first find expression in distress, and which for a certain time can be balanced through greater industry, more ingenious production methods, or special austerity. But there comes a day when these tensions can no longer be eliminated by such means. Then the task of the leaders of a nation's struggle for existence consists in eliminating the unbearable conditions in a fundamental way, that is, in restoring a tolerable relation between population and territory."[98]

Hitler thought this problem was particularly acute for Germany[99] and so "politics was nothing else than the pursuit of creating a lasting equivalence between population and territory (*Bodenfläche*, literally 'floor space')."[100] He argued that when the German peoples had expanded in the past, particularly to the east, they had prospered. When they had not, as was the case since Bismarck, they had suffered from overpopulation. In this way, Hitler recast German history not as one of triumphs and glory but rather the simple pursuit of territory driven by material need.[101] "When our people came from the east and hit the gates of Rome, it was not to reap triumphs, but it was need, need, and again need that drove them because they needed space to settle somewhere. Necessity pushed the migration of nations forward. It was later under the banner of need that the empire's Ostmark was colonized. Everywhere the same picture of need compels a people

---

[96] Ibid, 46.
[97] "Tageskampf oder Schicksalkampf," 723; "Zukunft oder Untergang," 166; "20 millionen Deutsche zu viel," 291.
[98] Hitler, *Hitlers zweites Buch*, 54.   [99] "20 millionen Deutsche zu viel."
[100] "Tageskampf oder Schicksalkampf," 729.
[101] Ibid, 240; "Tageskampf oder Schicksalkampf," 732; "Zukunft oder Untergang," 167.

to push their limits further, to fight for their daily bread."[102] Hitler's materialism precluded any romantic understanding of history. "Entire tribes have bled to death, not because they possessed the romantic drive to do so," but because "they were compelled to begin new migrations.... It was always their own need"[103] Hitler literally equated "destiny" with "nature."[104]

Foreign policy therefore equated to the acquisition of territory. "[W]e National Socialists must hold unflinchingly to our aim in foreign policy, namely, to secure for the German people land and soil," the only action that "would make any sacrifice of blood seem justified ... since we have been put on this earth with the mission of eternal struggle for our daily bread, beings who receive nothing as a gift, and who owe their position as lords of the earth only to the genius and the courage with which they can conquer and defend it."[105] And because Lebensraum was finite, the Volk had no choice but to use violence. Struggle was unavoidable, just as for other forms of nature. The pursuit of space required a "determination to fight and the risk of bloodshed."[106] "It is up for the fist to take."[107] History for Hitler was the story of different groups taking territory, cultivating it, only to later lose it.[108]

Lebensraum could only be found in suitable amounts to the east, particularly in Russia, a theme of both Hitler's books that of course guided his policy during the war.[109] "[O]nly through a territorial policy in Europe can the human resources shifted there be preserved for our Volk.... An additional 500,000 square kilometers in Europe can provide new homesteads for millions of German peasants, which will make available millions of soldiers for the power of the German Volk at the moment of decision. The only area in Europe that could be considered for such a territorial policy [during WWI] was Russia."[110] In *Mein Kampf*, he wrote, "If land was desired in Europe, it could be obtained by and large only at the expense of Russia, and this meant that the new Reich must again set itself on the march along the road

---

[102] "Tageskampf oder Schicksalkampf," 732.
[103] "Was ist Nationalsozialismus," 444.
[104] "Die soziale Sendung des Nationalsozialismus," 240.
[105] Hitler, *Mein Kampf*, 652. [106] Hitler, *Hitlers zweites Buch*, 54.
[107] Hitler, *Mein Kampf*, 138. [108] "Was ist Nationalsozialismus," 444.
[109] The same strategy is revealed privately during the war. Hitler, *Hitler's Secret Conversations, 1941–1944*, 28, 43. Nothing had changed.
[110] Hitler, *Hitlers zweites Buch*, 202.

of the Teutonic Knights of old, to obtain by the German sword sod for the German cow and daily bread for the nation."[111] He called on Germany to pursue a "clear, far-sighted territorial policy," in which "she abandons all attempts at world industry and world trade, and instead concentrates all her strength" in order to secure "sufficient living space for the next hundred years.... Since this territory can be only in the east, the need to be a naval power also recedes into the background. Germany tries anew to champion her interests through the formation of a decisive power on land."[112]

While Hitler was the primary (pseudo-) theoretician of German racism, all of these elements were present in the earliest statement of Nazi party goals, its 1920 program of 25 points. Its third point reads, "We demand land and territory (colonies) to feed our people and to settle our surplus population," its fourth that "only members of the nation may be citizens of the State. Only those of German blood, whatever their creed, may be members of the nation. Accordingly, no Jew may be a member of the nation."[113]

Land as Security or Securing Land? Lebensraum and War Aims

By missing the difference between a dangerous world in which one must defend against those who might attack and a scarce world marked by a competitive struggle in which conflict is assured, Copeland mistakenly concludes that the foreign policies of Germany leading up to and during World War I and World War II were fundamentally similar. The error results from equating the Lebensraum strategy, which he recognizes as central, with the pursuit of international security, particularly from Russia, when in fact Hitler's aim was to ensure the necessities of life at the expense of Russia because that was where the living space was. "Fear of the rise of Russia was a primary and probably dominant force pushing Hitler and his generals to war. The causes of war in 1939 thus parallel those in 1914," he writes.[114] But Hitler's motives were offensive not defensive, and offensive because of his understanding of the world as an amoral struggle among racially defined peoples. Copeland recognizes that the "sheer horror of what Nazi Germany

---

[111] Hitler, *Mein Kampf*, 140.   [112] Hitler, *Hitlers zweites Buch*, 163.
[113] See, for a translation: https://encyclopedia.ushmm.org/content/en/article/nazi-party-platform.
[114] Copeland, *The Origins of Major War*, 119. Copeland is by no means the only person to have missed this crucial difference, only the most explicit.

wrought in Europe is so overwhelming that to emphasize the security side of German policy seems to temper our conviction that this was one of the most evil regimes in history."[115] Normatively, this is surely true, but empirically his conclusions are wrong, precisely because it is this very evil, Hitler's utter lack of humanitarian morality, that explains his goals.

At no point in Hitler's exposition of his views do we see any concern for security. Hitler was not driven by fear of Russia but by lust for its territory. He might not have described his aims as greedy since in his twisted mind Germany was only pursuing the means of survival. The continent was not big enough for both of them. At most the Soviet Union was an ideological threat to Germany through its export of Bolshevik ideology.[116] Hitler actually thought it would be easy to defeat racially inferior Slavs, particularly now given his preposterous but genuinely held belief that Soviet Russia was governed by inferior Jews.[117] "The gigantic empire in the East is ready to collapse," he predicted.[118] Hitler noted that the Germans had dispatched the Russians before with relative ease.[119] The country was ripe for conquest, he believed.[120] Weinberg argues, against Copeland's conclusions, that even the army "was at no time seriously concerned about the Soviet menace that was supposedly keeping the German general staff awake at night."[121] The Soviets would of course be the major foe in a new war given Hitler's aims, but Russia needed to be destroyed not because of what it would do to Germany but because of what Germany needed to do to it.

Hitler explicitly contrasted his expansionist aims with those of his Wilhelmine predecessors. In Mein Kampf, he declared that "we National Socialists consciously draw a line beneath the foreign policy tendency of our pre-war period.... We take up where we broke off six hundred years ago. We stop the endless German movement to the south and west, and turn our gaze toward the land in the east. At long

---

[115] Ibid, 118.   [116] Hitler, *Hitlers zweites Buch*, 153.
[117] On his view of the Slavs as racially inferior, "brutes in the state of nature," see Hitler, *Hitler's Secret Conversations, 1941–1944*, 23, 34.
[118] Jäckel, Eberhard. 1981. *Hitler's World View: A Blueprint for Power*. Cambridge: Harvard University Press, 38.
[119] Weinberg, *The Foreign Policy of Hitler's Germany*, 13.
[120] Kershaw, "Hitler," 28.
[121] Weinberg, *The Foreign Policy of Hitler's Germany*, 43.

last we break off the colonial and commercial policy of the pre-war period and shift to the soil policy of the future. If we speak of soil in Europe today, we can primarily have in mind only Russia and her vassal border states."[122] Hitler blamed traditional German nationalists for the needless deaths of millions of German soldiers during the war in pursuit of aims not worth the sacrifice. Of "the necessity of winning the ore basin of Longwy and Briey ..., possessing the Belgian fortresses on the Meuse River, and so on.... Truly for such baubles a Volk should not have been kept for even an hour longer in a war whose battlefields had slowly become an inferno. The sole war for which that monstrous bloodshed would have been worthy could consist of only the assurance to German soldiers of so and so many hundred thousand square kilometers, to be allotted to front line fighters as property, or to be placed at the disposal of a general colonization by Germans."[123]

Amorality and the Social Construction of National Borders: Nazi versus Weimar Nationalist Foreign Policy

Hitler's aims were also fundamentally different from those of his right-wing counterparts (and competitors) in the Weimar era. Those who stress the continuity in German foreign policy maintain counterfactually than any German leader was likely to pursue a revisionist foreign policy.[124] However, a comparison of Nazi conceptions with those of other right-wing forces shows just how different Hitler's foreign policy was. Most importantly for our purposes, those differences reflected different moral foundations.

---

[122] Hitler, *Mein Kampf*, 654.

[123] Hitler, *Hitlers zweites Buch*, 104–105. He also faulted the prewar policy of Weltpolitik, predicated as it was on economic exchange that put Germany at the mercy of other nations for obtaining fundamentally scarce resources (Hitler, *Hitlers zweites Buch*, 53); "Was ist Nationalsozialismus," 447; Hitler, *Mein Kampf*, 138; "Tageskampf oder Schicksalkampf," 734; Hitler, *Mein Kampf*, 48). Moreover, the policy created unnecessary conflicts with the greatest maritime power in the world, England, the country that had perfected Weltpolitik, which he expected would acquiesce to German expansion provided it were eastward and land based (Hitler, *Hitlers zweites Buch*, 107, 162–163, 171; Hitler, *Mein Kampf*, 140).

[124] See the discussions of Weimar Germany in Copeland, *The Origins of Major War* and Legro, *Rethinking the World*.

Revisionist and militarist in its demands that the unjust seizure of German territories by France, Belgium, and Poland be returned to Germany, the DNVP's most ambitious aim was the incorporation of the German vestiges of the Habsburg empire. The DNVP was vitriolic in its hatred of France and Britain since these were the parties behind the Versailles Treaty and the occupation of the Rhineland. The party was the most prominent opponent of Foreign Minister Gustav Stresemann's policy of "fulfillment" and "understanding" during the 1920s, which aimed to restore Germany's position by creating trust and mutually beneficial economic exchange with the allies.[125] The DNVP based its resistance largely on moral condemnation and outrage; Germany had been treated unjustly, exploited by Britain and France. National honor necessitated resistance. These nationalists demanded an immediate evacuation of the Rhineland without any German concessions that would threaten German dignity, and voted against the Locarno Treaty in which the country renounced any claims on the Alsace-Lorraine. Without the biological and racial understanding of foreign policy that Hitler had, however, their desire for revision was fundamentally different. Their aim was national unification of a culturally and linguistically defined people living in historically German lands.[126]

In its first electoral program of 1919, the DNVP started with the same principles as the Nazis did: the demand for the unification of all Germans in the same state. The DNVP made special note of lost territories with German inhabitants. However, the platform made no mention of race as the basis of the German *Volksgemeinschaft*, demanding instead the restoration of the German monarchy and a "strong and steady foreign policy defined exclusively from a German point-of-view." The DNVP called for cultural unity to be promulgated through religion and education. Religion would solidify binding morality: "Through the deepening of Christian consciousness we expect the moral rebirth of our Volk, something which is a fundamental requirement for its political resurgence. Religion is a national issue.

---

[125] Grathwol, Robert P. 1980. *Stresemann and the DNVP: Reconciliation or Revenge in German Foreign Policy, 1924–1928*. Lawrence: University Press of Kansas; Jacobson, Jon. 2015. *Locarno Diplomacy: Germany and the West, 1925–1929*. Princeton: Princeton University Press. Rathbun, Brian C. 2014. *Diplomacy's Value*. Ithaca and London: Cornell University Press.

[126] Chickering, *We Men Who Feel Most German*, 38.

The purity of the family, the development of the youth, the reconciliation of social antagonisms, the health of the state, all depend upon the
dynamic absorption of Christian-religious forces." Education would
promote a feeling of Germanness:. "Education should lead to the spiritual unity of the nation. To a much greater extent than in the past, we
must shape will and character so that they reflect a conscious German
identity [*Deutschtum*] and a spirited state ethos."[127]

Hitler was contemptuous of DNVP foreign policy thinking. He complained their "concept of a national attitude was in the end only a
purely patriotic dynastic one. It had almost nothing to do with völkish
insights."[128] "The National Socialist Movement is distinguished from
previous bourgeois parties," Hitler explained, in that "the foreign policy of the national bourgeois world has in truth always been only a
border policy whereas in contrast the policy of the National Socialist
Movement will always be a territorial one. In its boldest plans, the
German bourgeoisie aspires to the unification of the German nation,
but in reality it will finish with a botched up regulation of the borders."[129] The pursuit of Germany's old boundaries would not solve
its fundamental problem, "For even the utmost success of this policy
of the restoration of the borders of 1914 would bring only a renewal
of the economic situation of the year 1914.... [T]he question of
sustenance which then, as now, was completely unsolved, will imperi-
ously force us onto the tracks of world economy and world export."[130]
Germany's pre-1914 borders "were anything but logical. For in reality they were neither complete in the sense of embracing the people
of German nationality, nor sensible with regard to geo-military
expediency."[131]

Consistent with his radically different right-wing ideology, Hitler
did not invest particular territory with any meaning, something that
differentiated his views from more traditional nationalists.[132] German
romanticism, out of which German nationalism grew, maintained an
organic connection between particular landscapes and the peoples who
had long inhabited them.[133] Hitler saw land more instrumentally, as

---

[127] https://arplan.org/2021/03/24/program-german-national-peoples-party-dnvp/.
[128] Hitler, *Hitlers zweites Buch*, 87.   [129] Ibid, 78.
[130] Ibid, 121–122.   [131] Hitler, *Mein Kampf*, 648.
[132] During the war, he said the same. See Hitler, *Hitler's Secret Conversations,*
      1941–1944, 214.
[133] Mosse, *The Crisis of German Ideology*, 15–19.

the simple basis for sustenance. Therefore, there was no inherent value in getting back what Germany had lost, what for those like the DNVP was a matter of national honor. "[T]he slogan of the restoration of the German borders as an aim for the future is both stupid and dangerous, because, in reality, it in no way encompasses any useful aim worth striving for. The German borders of the year 1914 were borders which presented something incomplete in exactly the same way that the borders of all nations are at all times incomplete." Lebensraum came and went. "The territorial distribution of the world at any time is the momentary result of a struggle and a process which by no means is concluded, but one which clearly continues further. It is stupid to take the border of any sample year in a nation's history, and, without further ado, to represent it as a political aim."[134] He complained that the bourgeois right "lives only in the past ... their backward gaze does not extend beyond their own times. The law of inertia binds them to a given situation and causes them to resist any change in it."[135]

Liulevicius notes a shift in conceptual categories between the prewar and interwar years in which the terms "Land" (country, land, and countryside) and "Leute" (people) were replaced by "Volk" (folk) and "Raum" (space). Territories were "no longer understood as ... areas with history and internal coherence, organization and meaning all their own." Raum is "neutral," "stark," "emptied of historical content," and "triumphantly ahistorical, biological, and "scientific." The implication was that "the lands and peoples were stripped of any legitimate claim to independent existence and stood bare as objects and numbers, resources to be exploited and exhausted."[136]

Mad but not Mad: Hitler's Lack of Moral Outrage

This view was a natural corollary of Hitler's amoral conception of the struggle between races. No one had any right to any particular territory.[137] "[E]very healthy, vigorous Volk sees nothing sinful in territorial

---

[134] Hitler, *Hitlers zweites Buch*, 114.   [135] Hitler, *Mein Kampf*, 650.

[136] Liulevicius, Vejas Gabriel. 2000. *War Land on the Eastern Front: Culture, National Identity, and German Occupation in World War I.* Cambridge: Cambridge University Press, 252.

[137] He expresses this later during the war as well Hitler, *Hitler's Secret Conversations, 1941–1944*, 23.

acquisition, but something quite in keeping with nature."[138] He denied that "one can regard the current distribution of territory on earth as rightfully given... Peoples had appropriated land in proportion to their superiority over others."[139] No nation or people had any eternal, moral claim to any territory. Just like humanitarian principles, borders were social constructions. "I must sharply attack those foolish pen-pushers who claim to regard such an acquisition of soil as a 'breach of sacred human rights'... no people on this earth possesses so much as a square yard of territory on the strength of a higher will or superior right.... State boundaries are made by man and changed by man. The fact that a nation has succeeded in acquiring an undue amount of soil constitutes no higher obligation that it should be recognized eternally. At most it proves the strength of the conquerors and the weakness of the nations. And in this case, right lies in this strength alone."[140]

Hitler was also contemptuous of sentiments of national honor expressed by those like the DNVP, moral concepts that held no value to him. "National honor requires that we restore the borders of the year 1914. This is the tenor of the discussions at the beer hall evenings, which the representatives of national honor hold.... [N]ational honor has nothing to do with the obligation to conduct a stupid and impossible foreign policy. For the result of a bad foreign policy can be the loss of a Volk's freedom, whose consequence is slavery, and which certainly cannot be viewed as a condition of national honor."[141] Foreign policy was a simple matter of space and population, not moral righteousness. "I most solemnly protest against the claim that a duty of national honor exists which compels us to have two million men bleed to death on the battlefield in order that, under the most favorable result, we may be able to enter a total of a quarter million men, women and children on our books," by which Hitler meant the incorporation of the southern Tyrol, a favorite goal of more traditional German nationalists that added no significant Lebensraum.[142]

Perhaps most remarkably, Hitler also held no grudges against Germany's recent enemies. The implication of Hitler's amoral

---

[138] Hitler, *Hitlers zweites Buch*, 55.   [139] "20 millionen Deutsche zu viel," 292.
[140] Hitler, *Mein Kampf*, 652–653; also Hitler, *Mein Kampf*, 134; "Tageskampf oder Schicksalkampf," 730; Hitler, *Hitlers zweites Buch*, 54.
[141] Hitler, *Hitlers zweites Buch*, 115.   [142] Ibid, 118.

worldview, devoid of humanitarianism or liberal ethics, was a lack of moral condemnation when it comes to the actions of other countries. Since nature compels all peoples to seek territory for their nourishment, others cannot be blamed for their use of force and coercion. Stripped of ethics, Hitler did not have the same sense of righteous indignation vis-à-vis England and France. This had dramatic consequences for his foreign policy strategy, leading to a de-emphasis of previously salient adversarial images.

Not only did Hitler not demonize Germany's recent enemies, he expressed an understanding of their actions. Were we not to recognize the uniquely amoral nature of his ideology, we might otherwise find this strange for a rabid nationalist. Hitler located the source of English enmity in Germany's own Weltpolitik. He wrote, "The course of the anti German attitude of the English parallels our development on the seas, rises with our colonial activity to an overt antipathy, and finally ends up with our naval policy in a frank hatred. One cannot take it amiss that in England a really solicitous State leadership scented a threatening danger for the future in this development of a Volk as efficient as the Germans." In fact,the Germans should learn from the English: "We must never apply our German sins of omission as a measure for judging the actions of others. The frivolousness with which post Bismarckian Germany allowed her position in terms of power politics to be threatened in Europe by France and Russia, without undertaking any serious countermeasures, far from allows us ... to denounce them in moral indignation, if indeed they attend to the vital needs of their own peoples better."[143] In discussing England's actions, both past and present, Hitler spoke in terms of necessity, not monstrosity. "One completely forgets, that in 1914 we were forced to fight because others could no longer break the competition through peaceful means, but had to use the sword.... [T]oday it is not greed or petty envy, rather England is struggling for the same reasons as we are. England has too many people, and these people must also be fed; and whoever takes the sales for his product away from an English worker is the enemy in England."[144] The Great War was driven by the zero-sum nature of world politics, in which no moral judgments could be made.[145] "England did not do this because we were bellicose, but because we

---

[143] Ibid, 169.   [144] "Was ist Nationalsozialismus," 447.
[145] "Wesen und Ziele des Nationalsozialismus," 169.

wanted to survive, and England also wanted to survive. Because now the competitive struggle came, decided not by right, but ultimately only power.... [W]e were beaten."[146]

Nor did Hitler, by the same reasoning, condemn the French. "I do not believe for a moment that France's intentions with respect to us can ever change because they have their deepest motive nowhere but in the French nation's sense of self-preservation," he wrote. "Were I a Frenchmen myself, and were France's greatness as dear to me as is Germany's sacred, then I could and would not act otherwise than [French President] Clemenceau himself did in the end."[147]

What is striking is what we do *not* see in Mein Kampf and Hitler's Zweites Buch. In over a thousand pages of writing, Hitler only mentions the Versailles Treaty and the infamous war-guilt clause in passing. He does not present the German people as more righteous, moral, or trustworthy than those of the country's former enemies or current adversaries. As Welch trenchantly notes, "For Hitler, neither Versailles nor the borders it established were unjust – they were merely unacceptable."[148]

Indeed Hitler morally condemned Germans more harshly than the allies for the country's defeat: "No enemy had so reviled the German Army as it was defiled by the representatives of the November crime.... I frankly confess that I could reconcile myself to any of the former enemy, but that my hatred against the betrayers of our own Volk in our ranks is and remains irreconcilable. [T]he wrong committed by the men of the November crime is the most dishonourable, the basest crime of all times."[149] Strikingly, he commented in 1925, "unfortunately the military defeat of the German people is not an undeserved catastrophe, but the deserved chastisement of eternal retribution. We more than deserved this defeat."[150]

Hitler thought such moral outrage against foreign adversaries as inhibiting the creation of expedient but necessary alliances in the future – most notably, with England. "Only a bourgeois national German politician can manage to refuse a useful alliance."[151] And France was of no particular importance to him, unlike for traditional

---

[146] "Tageskampf oder SchicksalKampf," 733.
[147] Welch, *Justice and the Genesis of War*, 132.   [148] Ibid, 134.
[149] Hitler, *Hitlers zweites Buch*, 115–116.
[150] Jablonsky, David. 2014. *Churchill and Hitler: Essays on the Political-Military Direction of Total War*. New York: Routledge, 284.
[151] Hitler, *Hitlers zweites Buch*, 174.

nationalists, for whom France was Germany's bitter enemy. The völkisch movement "has no right to sulk about the past."[152] Germany would simply need to knock France out of any future war first. A "reckoning with France" would "remain ineffectual in the long run if it represented the whole of our aim in foreign policy. It can and will achieve meaning only if it offers the rear cover for an enlargement of our people's living space in Europe. For it is not in colonial acquisitions that we must see the solution of this problem, but exclusively in the acquisition of territory for settlement."[153] Whereas the rest of the right was fixated on the injustice of Versailles and the powers behind it, Hitler wrote, "The struggle against Versailles is the means, not the end of my policy. I am not in the least interested in the former frontiers of the Reich."[154]

With the rise of Hitler, traditional German nationalists were presented with a dilemma, much as dynastically oriented elites had been in the Wilhelmine period. Should they attempt to ally with this new force in politics and harness its larger mass appeal? After all, they shared a hostility to socialism and democracy and an affinity for foreign policy revisionism, even if of a different sort. Like the Kaiser and establishment elites had done before World War I, traditional German nationalists attempted to co-opt this new movement for their own purposes, only to find themselves swallowed whole. Hitler was appointed Chancellor legally with the support of traditional German conservatives like President Hindenburg in 1933, but within the year the DNVP, like every other German party other than the National Socialist Party, was banned. This *Gleichschaltung*, essentially a purge of non-Nazi elements, was aided by intimidation and violence not just against the left but also the right.[155]

Speaking No Truth to Power: Hitler under the Shadow of Morality

Even arguably the most evil madman in human history, at least measured in terms of the tremendous death and destruction Hitler wrought, felt the need to conceal his true beliefs about morality.

[152] Ibid.   [153] Hitler, *Mein Kampf*, 653.
[154] Jablonsky, *Churchill and Hitler*, 281.   [155] Beck, *The Fateful Alliance*.

The Nazi Party leader made little public mention of his matter-of-fact views about the Versailles Treaty. Weinberg speculates that his criticism in his second book of other nationalists, on whom Hitler would have to rely to come to power, explains why it was never published. And in the 1930s, Hitler almost never spoke about the biological groundings of his worldview and their ethical implications. Hitler's utter lack of humanitarian morality and his lack of interest in castigating Germany's enemies for their unjust treatment were politically untenable. In order to be successful under the ubiquitous shadow of morality, Hitler would have to hide his moral nihilism. No one, even the Führer, could avoid its cast.

As much as Hitler did not blame the Versailles powers for acting in the manner they did, he understood the indispensability of such a tool for building a mass movement. "What could have been done with this peace treaty of Versailles?.... [I]n the hands of a willing government, it could have become an instrument for whipping up the national passions to fever heat. With a brilliant propagandist exploitation of these sadistic cruelties, the indifference of a people might have been raised to indignation, and indignation to blazing fury!"[156] What the government was unwilling to do (at least in Hitler's eyes), he took upon himself. In recounting the early days of the Nazi movement in Mein Kampf, he notes how he focused in particular on the peace treaties. "Beginning with the 'War Guilt,' which at that time nobody bothered about, and the 'Peace Treaties,' nearly everything was taken that seemed agitationally expedient or ideologically necessary. Especially to the peace treaties themselves the greatest attention was given," which were presented as "a shame and a disgrace ... an unprecedented pillaging or our people.... [H]ow immeasurably great was the blame on another side!"[157] Hitler would compare the terms of the Treaty of Brest-Litovsk imposed by Germany on Russia after the Bolshevik revolution removed the latter from the war, and Versailles in moral terms, "the actual boundless humanity of the one treaty compared to the inhuman cruelty of the second."[158]

Hitler made clear that he did not necessarily believe this rhetoric: "The function of propaganda is ... not to weigh and ponder the rights of different people, but exclusively to emphasize the one right which

---

[156] Hitler, *Mein Kampf*, 655.   [157] Ibid, 454.   [158] Ibid, 468.

it has set out to argue for. Its task is not to make an objective study of the truth, in so far as it favors the enemy, and then set it before the masses with academic fairness; its task is to serve our own right, always and unflinchingly."[159] This applied for instance to the issue of war guilt, a fixation of more conventional nationalists. It was "absolutely wrong to discuss war guilt from the standpoint that Germany alone could not be held responsible for the outbreak of the catastrophe; it would have been correct to load every bit of the blame on the shoulders of the enemy, even if this had not really corresponded to the true facts."[160] He credited England with its effective propaganda during the war, "as ruthless as it was brilliant."[161]

Hitler understood the connection between morality and emotion, even as the former was largely alien to him. "As soon as our own propaganda admits so much as a glimmer of right on the other side, the foundation for doubt in our own right has been laid. The masses are then in no position to distinguish where foreign injustice ends and our own begins. The people in their overwhelming majority are so feminine by nature and attitude that sober reasoning determines their thoughts and actions far less than emotion and feeling. And this sentiment is not complicated but very simple and all of a piece. It does not have multiple shadings; it has a positive and a negative; love or hate, right or wrong, truth or lie, never half this way and half that way, never partially, or that kind of thing."[162] He bragged that in his speeches denouncing the postwar settlement, "three hours later I had before me a surging mass full of the holiest indignation and boundless wrath."[163]

It is Hitler's use of moral indignation against the allies that seems to explain his political surge, not his amoral view of dog-eat-dog struggle or even his anti-Semitism. The Nazis' major breakthrough in national politics only came in 1930 after Hitler had his big break. He formed a coalition with the more traditional DNVP to campaign against the Young Plan, a renegotiation of German reparations obligations that presented another opportunity to make hay of Germany's poor treatment at the hands of its enemies after the war.[164] Hitler imitated the rhetoric of the DNVP, railing against the injustices of the peace treaty.

Following this breakthrough, in which the Nazi party increased its vote share in September 1930 from 2.6% to 18.3% and became the

---

[159] Ibid, 205.   [160] Ibid, 182.   [161] Ibid, 183.   [162] Ibid.   [163] Ibid, 468.
[164] Ward, *Status and the Challenge of Rising Powers.*

second largest party of the Reichstag (now far more powerful than the DNVP which received only 41 seats to the Nazi's 107), Hitler's materialist rhetoric about the right of the stronger disappeared entirely, as did references to his biologically based conceptions of politics. In an analysis of searchable databases comprising the two main compendia of Hitler's writings, speeches, and proclamations – *Reden, Schriften, Anordnungen: Februar 1925 bis Januar 1933*; and *Reden und Proklamationen 1932–1945*[165] – I searched for keywords indicative of his evolutionary views – Selbsterhaltung, biologisch, Auslese, Menschenwert, Lebenskraft, Volkswertes, Lebensbedürfnisse, Ernährung, Hochwert, Menschenmaterials, Blutsvermischung, Rassensenkung, Blutswertes, Lebenswiderständen, minderwertig – as well as those indicating his amorality – Macht des Stärkeren, Gesetz des Stärkeren, Recht des Stärkeren, Kampf des Stärkeren. All major speeches based on his crude evolutionary thought, in which he dismissed the very existence of humanitarian ethics, were made before the 1930 elections. After this point, Hitler never made a public speech outlining his Darwinian views, even after he took power. Only behind closed doors in his secret speech before leading industrialists on January 26, 1932, did he return to these themes. Even after Hitler consolidated power in perhaps the most totalitarian dictatorship the world had ever seen, he avoided these topics suggesting that he strategically understood how such rhetoric could undermine his rule. He confined his racial rhetoric to the virulent anti-Semitism that had a long history in Germany. We see no mention of natural selection in any public comments until 1943, as the war was turning against the Nazis.

Goddard systematically evaluates the nature of Nazi "legitimation" strategies used abroad – the ways by which Hitler justified calls to revise the Versailles Treaty following his ascent to power. Hitler made virtually no reference to Lebensraum but instead appealed to the values of equality and self-determination. She estimates that throughout the Rhineland and Munich crises, 43% of legitimating phrases referenced a need for equality and 20% the right of Germans to collectively

---

[165] Both are available in a centralized database at www.degruyter.com/view/db/ hitq.

determine their destiny as a nation.[166] After the Munich conference, when Hitler began his military bid for Lebensraum, those justifications were used in less than 3% of speeches. Instead Hitler shifted to a self-defense rhetorical strategy condemning the aggressive designs of England in particular, which, while a bit rich, actually proves my point again. Even Hitler, perhaps the most immoral leader of all time, leading one of the most totalitarian states of all time, felt compelled to justify his foreign policy morally before domestic and foreign audiences.

"The Racial Theory": British Appeasement and the Ambiguity of German Nationalism

The failure to distinguish between these two different nationalisms had profound consequences. Nazi goals overlapped considerably with those of the nationalist right in the sense that Hitler saw the incorporation of those of German ethnic (and therefore, for him) racial origin as a first step, just not a sufficient one. In the early Weimar period, he wrote, "the Reich encompassed only a part of the German Nation, even though the largest. It would have been self-evident that even if the new State had not possessed any great foreign policy aim of a völkish character, at least as a so called bourgeois national State it should have kept in view further unification and consolidation of the German Nation, as its minimum foreign policy aim."[167] This made the Nazi plan difficult to distinguish from that of the more traditionally nationalist DNVP, especially when Hitler began to decisively shift his rhetoric in the 1930s as he moved from a peripheral political player to a major force.

Hitler confused his international adversaries long enough to gather German strength. The British, perhaps the most important potential check on Nazi ambitions, were unclear whether Hitler was a garden variety German nationalist like those in the DNVP, merely aiming to bring all Germans into a single Reich, or a megalomaniac bent on the pursuit of Lebensraum. Indeed their confusion is evident in the way they described the two possibilities. They called the *former* possibility, not the latter, the "racial theory," indicating they had not connected Hitler's biological racism with his program for territorial expansion.

---

[166] Goddard, *When Right Makes Might.*   [167] Hitler, *Hitlers zweites Buch*, 82.

Hitler's initial revisionist probes aimed at precisely those territories that would not reveal his type in comparison with those like the DNVP: first, the annexation of Austria and second, the incorporation of the Sudetenland, the Czech area with a sizeable German population. The latter provoked the famous Munich conference at which the British acquiesced to the Nazi annexation. Prime Minister Neville Chamberlain observed in a cabinet meeting: "The crucial question was whether Herr Hitler was speaking the truth when he said that he regarded the Sudeten question as a racial question which must be settled, and that the object of his policy was racial unity and not the domination of Europe. Much depends on the answer to this question."[168] While at Munich, Chamberlain tried to ascertain from Hitler whether his Czechoslovakian aims were limited to the Sudetenland.[169] The Foreign Secretary, Viscount Halifax, recognized Germany's "racial efforts" to unify all ethnic Germans "could not be doubted," but for him it was not clear whether Hitler had "lust for conquest on a Napoleonic scale."[170] It was reckless to act, Halifax thought, before more evidence was accumulated.

It was not until the British government concluded for sure that Hitler wanted more than the rectification of post–World War I borders and the incorporation of Germans in one Reich – that is, that he was more than a traditional German nationalist – that appeasement came to an end. Nazi occupation of the rest of Czechoslovakia, where there was no German minority, revealed Hitler's biologically driven, materialistic ambitions. Whereas in February 1938, the foreign secretary did not think that "Hitler's racial ambitions are necessarily likely to expand into international power lust,"[171] he changed his mind in March 1939 when German troops entered Prague. For Halifax, this was a genuine signal of German intentions. The "rape of Czechoslovakia" indicated that Hitler's goals were much grander in scope. On March

---

[168] Parker, Robert A. C. 1993. *Chamberlain and Appeasement: British Policy and the Coming of the Second World War.* Basingstoke, UK: Macillan, 169.
[169] Gilbert, Martin and Winston S. Churchill. 1977. *The Prophet of Truth, 1922–1939.* Boston: Houghton-Mifflin, 875.
[170] Gilbert and Churchill, *The Prophet of Truth, 1922–1939*, 922; Charmley, John. 1993. *Churchill: The End of Glory, a Political Biography.* London: Sceptre, 335.
[171] Roberts, Andrew. 1991. *The Holy Fox: A Biography of Lord Halifax.* London: Wiedenfeld and Nicolson, 301.

16, 1939, Halifax said in a Cabinet meeting that he considered the military occupation of Czechoslovakia "significant" since "this was the first occasion on which Germany had applied her shock tactics to the domination of non-Germans."[172] He wondered whether "if in fact events show that [Hitler] had reached already the decision to attempt at this moment the execution of a policy much wider than that of finding a remedy for the grievances of the Sudetendeutsch."[173] Halifax later wrote in his memoirs that "evidence seemed to accumulate that Hitler was not interested merely in the re-assembly of racial elements accidentally separated from the parent stock. Something much larger than this was being born and taking shape in that evil mind. After March and the final rape of Prague, it was no longer possible to hope that Hitler's purposes and ambitions were limited by any boundaries of race, and the lust of continental or world mastery seemed to stand out in stark relief."[174] Henderson, the former Foreign Secretary, concurred: "The absorption of Czecho-Slovakia has clearly revealed Germany's intentions. It marks the first departure from the Nazi racial theory."

In fact, Hitler was acting consistently with his racial theory, which was about much more than bringing together ethnic Germans. He had shown himself, however, not to be a nationalist like those in the DNVP who might be content with smaller concessions. It was at this point that the British took the fateful step of guaranteeing the integrity of Poland, the attack of which began World War II.

[172] Ibid, 142. [173] Ibid, 116.
[174] Halifax, Edward. 1957. *Fullness of Days*. New York: Dodd, 207–208.

11 | From Demonizing to Dehumanizing War under Hitler and the Implications for Humankind

More often than not, violence between states in the academic field of international relations (IR) is understood in amoral and instrumental terms. Not only are states thought to be acting purposively in the pursuit of some tangible object; they are also treating those in their way as objects, albeit calculating ones. In violence of this sort, "perpetrators have no destructive motive like hate or anger. They simply take the shortest path to something they want, and a living thing happens to be in the way. At best it is a category by exclusion: the absence of any inhibiting factor like sympathy or moral concern." Others are simply "part of its environment like a rock or a river or a lump of food."[1] Instrumental violence is "characterized by perpetrators who do not necessarily desire to harm victims, but who knowingly harm them in order to achieve some other objective."[2]

As the expression of unbridled egoism, instrumental killing is susceptible to social sanction precisely because of the phenomenon of morally judging audiences. As a result, it is typically accompanied, deliberatively or unconsciously, by efforts to make the targets less human. While we generally associate dehumanization with the sadistic pleasure taken in harming others, it might actually more often involve indifference. Instrumental violence is amoral, but it is only with dehumanization that we can really create an autonomous political sphere. As we have seen, psychologists and now many international relations scholars are increasingly rejecting this instrumental conception of state behavior as the norm, distinguishing instrumental from virtuous violence, in which coercion and killing are morally justified.

As I will argue below, Duckitt's dual-process model (see Chapter 5) tells us that such dehumanization is most likely perpetrated by those

---

[1] Pinker, *The Better Angels of Our Nature*, 509.

[2] Rai, Tage S., Piercarlo Valdesolo, and Jesse Graham. 2017. "Dehumanization Increases Instrumental Violence, But Not Moral Violence." *Proceedings of the National Academy of Sciences* 114(32): 8512.

who hold competitive world beliefs (CWB), those who assert dominance over the weakest and most vulnerable without humanitarian compunction. Those who think the world is a dangerous place instead practice virtuous violence, punishing evildoers. Yet only human beings have moral agency, so virtuous violence resists dehumanization. We cannot judge others for acting immorally if they are not capable of being moral.

Not surprisingly then, if one really wants to know what a complete and amoral disregard of humanitarian morality (and even indifference to moral condemnation) looks like when combined with a potent military machine, we can see it in Hitler. The Nazis are the ultimate example of instrumental, amoral killing. Yet the fact that Hitler is the exemplar of this kind of violence indicates again the rarity of this type of behavior thought to be so common in international relations scholarship. Hitler is the exception that proves the rule. When realists are cavalier about throwing about notions like the "autonomy of the political sphere," they do not tend to realize how exceptional this is, and how devastating the exception can be. Hitler's exceptionality not only demonstrates Pinker's point in the epigraph that starts this book about the relative paucity of amoral violence but also reminds us how a world truly devoid of morality might look. Rationalist and structural realist accounts that depict international relations as a moral void assume that inhumane action is ubiquitous because their accounts are inhuman. They are not based on a real understanding of human nature. As should be clear by now, however, just because most foreign policy action is morally motivated does not mean that international relations is any more peaceful or humane than any other form of social interaction. Human beings are plenty capable of doing barbarous things when they believe they are in the right.

A comparison in this chapter between the occupation regimes in Eastern Europe of the German army during World War I and World War II brings home the singularity of Nazi amoralism. Just as many maintain continuity between the foreign policy goals of Wilhelmine and Nazi Germany, many point to the similarities in their treatment of foreign populations under occupation. Some maintain that World War I offered a laboratory for the brutal exploitation of occupied lands in World War II. In discussing German atrocities in Belgium in 1914, in which 6,000 Belgian civilians were killed in just a few weeks, Lipkes writes, "To anyone familiar with activities in Nazi-occupied

Eastern Europe, there will be a striking sense of déjà-vu."[3] He claims the "Nazi was also a restoration.... [A] predisposition to force and fraud and a contempt for the rights of civilians and for due process characterized the German polity decades before the Nazi era."[4] Less obliquely, he concludes that "the invasion of Belgium precipitated a long chain of events that resulted in the murders of untold millions of civilians."[5]

The actions of the German army in Belgium and Eastern Europe from 1914 to 1918 were indeed ruthless and extractive. Yet they pale in comparison to Nazi behavior and plans in terms of their quantitative damage because they were premised on qualitatively different moral bases. Both the old and the new type of German nationalists thought of the occupied, largely Slavic peoples, as racially different. Ludendorff wrote decades before in terms identical to Hitler of building a defensive "wall" of Germans against racially different peoples.[6] However, this similarity conceals the fundamentally different types of racism underlying the two different right-wing ideologies. Different racisms are associated with different types of (and therefore indirectly, levels of) violence.

Tasked with administering conquered Baltic territories in the wake of Russian retreat in 1915, the German military launched an extensive program of what they saw as civilizing culturally inferior native inhabitants, whether they liked it or not. The authoritarianism of the traditional German nationalist in the Wilhelmine period, so dominant in the German military and one of the most vehement expressions historically of its kind, enabled extreme violence against perceived enemies; yet even it did not indulge in that brutality as a matter of general policy. German behavior in World War I was incredibly inhumane, but not dehumanizing. In the same areas twenty years later, with a biological rather than a cultural understanding of racial differences, the Nazis treated what they regarded as inherently inferior local populations as mere physical impediments to their goals of extracting

[3] Lipkes, J., 2007. *Rehearsals: The German Army in Belgium, August 1914*. Leuven: Leuven University Press.
[4] Lipkes, *Rehearsals*, 13.   [5] Ibid, 19.
[6] Liulevicius, Vejas Gabriel. 2000. *War Land on the Eastern Front: Culture, National Identity, and German Occupation in World War I*. Cambridge: Cambridge University Press, 95. Hitler, Adolf. 1981. *Hitler's Secret Conversations, 1941–1944*. Octagon Books, 21.

resources from the region and cleansing it racially for Nordic resettlement. While we should not refrain from morally judging the policies of World War I Germany, it is important to recognize that its actions were much less evil in terms of their sheer humanitarian cost. Given the consequences were so dire, it is dangerous not to conceptually distinguish between these various sins going forward.

The empirical finding that Hitler and the Nazis marked a decisive break of the kind with no previous parallels in history (at least in terms of size and scale), combined with others in the book, has great normative implications. As much as moral philosophy seeks to maintain a separation between the way the world is and the way that it should be, all normative arguments rest on (even if only implicitly) empirical claims about what is possible. In Kant's words, "ought implies can," "what one has a moral obligation to do is limited by what is possible – and this must include what is politically possible – in the circumstances," as Rodin explains.[7] "Normative theorizing cannot escape some degree of empirical description," Price agrees.[8] If morality requires us to give every one of our belongings to the most needy, even at the expense of our family, then we would conclude that such ethical standards are impossible to meet and therefore cannot be appropriate ethical standards at all. If all governments behaved like the Nazis, we would similarly have to conclude that morality in foreign affairs is simply non-existent and normative theorizing therefore pointless. The normative and the empirical are linked in the minds of everyone, not just moral philosophers. Indeed, the essence of the dual-process model is that fundamental beliefs about what is right and wrong come with concomitant understandings about the moral nature of others in the world they confront. Hitler believed that the material nature of the world meant that morality was a mere social construction. We know by the empirical rarity of those who think like him that he was mistaken, and therefore, that normative theorizing still has a place.

The case of Hitler raises another crucial question. Anyone who takes the position that morality has no biological basis runs up against the "problem of foundations." One of the central questions in moral philosophy has and continues to be the objective justification of moral

---

[7] Rodin, *War and Self-Defense.*
[8] Price, "Moral Limit and Possibility in World Politics."

values. How do we *know* what is right and wrong? How do we *prove* ethical benchmarks? Since all logic must proceed from some assumptions that themselves cannot be subject to normative debate, many have settled on a social constructivist solution. Morality is whatever a community decides it is at any particular time. Rather than looking for an irrefutable logical basis in objective fact, constructivists recognize ethics as an intersubjective phenomenon. However, this cultural relativism should make us uneasy since it implies that morality is nothing but a figment of our imaginations and that there is no external standpoint for assessing right and wrong. If we believe this, the dangers are clear. That is the lesson of Nazism.

However, evolutionary theory tells us that this is not the case at all. There is a basis for morality, one that we know from empirical research, that helps solve the problem of foundations without having to conclude that any definition of right and wrong is just as good as any other. Once we understood where Hitler's crude struggle-based biological determinism went wrong, by failing to recognize what is uniquely about humans among other animals, biology buttresses rather than undermines liberal ethics. Wright agrees: "Altruism, compassion, empathy, love, conscience, the sense of justice – all of these things, the things that hold society together, the things that allow our species to think so highly of itself, can now confidently be said to have a firm genetic basis."[9]

The normative cost of this recognition is that our humanitarian impulses are not our only ingrained ethical tendencies. We also exhibit a propensity toward ingroup favoritism and moral condemnation, which, when combined, can ravage international relations. This raises a difficult question: Are we forced to conclude that Hitler's actions were perfectly morally defensible from the standpoint of binding morality? If ingroup favoritism is a biological by-product cemented with the emotional force of loyalty, are we not denied the basis by which to condemn the Nazis since we cannot help but favor those like us?

We are not. Empirical research is again our solace. Binding morality rarely entails complete indifference to the fate of others outside of our community. Outgroup hate is far too present in international relations as in any other sphere, but nothing we have discovered so far empirically tells us it is automatic, ingrained, or universal. Biology

[9] Wright, *Moral Animal*, 12.

tells us what we already intuitively knew. Hitler and the Nazis were perversions of humankind, stunted human beings without a full moral sense. Most binding morality expresses itself differently, as the protection of the group from those who would do it harm. Nazi-style dehumanization and predation of the kind reviewed in this chapter is not as uncommon as we would like, but it is certainly not common. This suggests the problem of ingroup conflict is most often one of fear driven by second-order beliefs about the morality of others rather than an utter absence of morality. We can do terrible things to one another and feel virtuous about it. As I have argued previously, Wilhelmine Germany needlessly prolonged the greatest conflict the world had ever known based on irrational moral beliefs about its adversaries. However, this does not compare to what we do when we feel no sense of ethics at all.

In the text that follows, I connect scientific findings on instrumental violence, dehumanization, the dual-process model, and varieties of racism. After demonstrating how this literature exposes the pronounced differences between the occupation policies of Germany during the two wars, I address the implications of the findings for longstanding normative questions. I make the case that evolutionary ethics should leave liberal, humanitarian-minded readers to breathe more easily, rather than less. Biology provides the foundation for moral foundations.

Humanizing International Relations Theory: Instrumental Violence and Racism

Instrumental violence for pure egoistic ends goes hand in hand with dehumanization. Treating others as less than human allows for "moral disengagement."[10] Dehumanization mitigates moral objections that emerge from basic humanitarian values and our moral conscience, "sympathy toward fellow human beings, whom we feel are entitled to rights and protections that prohibit violence against them."[11]

---

[10] Bandura, Albert, Claudio Barbaranelli, Gian Vittorio Caprara, and Concetta Pastorelli. (1996) "Mechanisms of Moral Disengagement in the Exercise of Moral Agency." *Journal of Personality and Social Psychology* 71(2): 364.

[11] Rai et al., "Dehumanization Increases Instrumental Violence," 8511. See also Valentino, Benjamin A. 2004. *Final Solutions: Mass Killing and Genocide in the Twentieth Century.* Ithaca and London: Cornell University Press.

This is the sort of violence that we take for granted in international relations, even if we do not explicitly recognize what it entails in terms of its treatment of other human beings.

Virtuous violence, in contrast, resists dehumanization since "victims must be capable of thinking and having intentions, feeling pain and other sensations, and experiencing moral emotions" for the punishment to provide satisfaction.[12] We want bad guys to suffer for the wrong they did. Morality is a quality that humans assign only to other humans, not to objects or even other animals. Rai et al. find that using dehumanizing language rather than humanizing language increases the willingness to harm strangers for money but not to harm them for their immoral behavior. And individuals spontaneously dehumanize strangers when they imagine harming them for money but not for their immoral behavior.

Those who hold competitive world beliefs (CWB) are much more likely to engage in dehumanization than those who hold dangerous world beliefs (DWB). Duckitt argues that prejudice deriving from a motivation to neutralize threat and danger is directed at those social groups and categories of persons viewed by societies or groups as threatening their stability, cohesion, security, order, traditions, and values. These groups are viewed as unethical, unjust, and immoral. This implies they have moral agency in the first place, which is a human trait. In contrast, prejudice deriving from CWB is directed against those social groups and categories who are low in power status and driven by a desire to dominate the inferior.[13] Nothing about them is considered at all. Whereas DWBers demonize, CWBers dehumanize.

Duckitt and Sibley find that social dominance orientation (SDO) (but not right-wing authoritarianism (RWA)) – predicts dislike of the mentally handicapped, the obese, and immigrants. SDO is strongly associated with CWB. RWA (but not SDO), in contrast, predicts dislike of those who "make society dangerous" or "disrupt safety and security" as well as "terrorists" and "violent criminals."[14] RWA is strongly associated with DWB. It does not predict, as SDO does,

---

[12] Rai et al., "Dehumanization Increases Instrumental Violence," 8511. See also Fiske and Rai, Virtuous Violence.

[13] Duckitt, "A Dual-Process Cognitive-Motivational Theory," 98.

[14] Duckitt, John and Chris G. Sibley. 2007. "Right Wing Authoritarianism, Social Dominance Orientation and the Dimensions of Generalized Prejudice." *European Journal of Personality* 21(2): 120.

dislike of housewives but is associated with dislike of drug dealers (whereas this is not true of SDO).[15] For binding moralists, as right-wing authoritarians are, the former are productive members of a cohesive society, the latter a scourge corrupting innocent children.

Threat-driven prejudice is characterized by fear and anger, whereas dominance-based prejudice is associated with the emotion of disgust. Haslam writes, "Disgust and revulsion feature prominently in images of animalistically dehumanized others: Represented as apes with bestial appetites or filthy vermin who contaminate and corrupt, they are often viscerally despised."[16]

Not all outgroup derogation is racially based, but biological racism is the most obvious manifestation of dominance-based prejudice. Those high in SDO (and CWB) are specifically marked by their dislike of and disgust for groups based on their physical qualities and other attributes over which these targets of prejudice exhibit little agency. SDO is associated with contempt, in the Duckitt and Sibley study, for the unattractive, mentally handicapped, obese, and psychiatric patients. Tellingly, "Africans," so frequently the target of racist dehumanization, load high on this same dimension as well.[17]

These contrasts are essential for grasping the discontinuity of German foreign policy. Nazi racism was dehumanizing, premised on a delusional racial hierarchy in which other human beings were closer to animals than they were to Aryans. Such dehumanization was a natural corollary of the Nazis' amoral indifference to humanitarian morality and their depiction of the world as a brutal struggle for scarce resources among races. The Holocaust is the most obvious and well-known consequence, of course; yet Hitler's treatment of the Jews was just the most dramatic act of a regime with contempt for humanitarian values.

Wilhelmine-era racism, in contrast, largely understood racial superiority in cultural terms and was more paternalistic and patronizing than dehumanizing, particularly vis-à-vis those populations it encountered as occupiers rather than adversaries (the latter being largely demonized). Paternalism was an expression of what Kinder

---

[15] Ibid.

[16] Haslam, Nick. 2006. "Dehumanization: An Integrative Review." *Personality and Social Psychology Review* 10(3): 258.

[17] Duckitt and Sibley. "Right wing Authoritarianism, Social Dominance Orientation and the Dimensions of Generalized Prejudice," 120.

and Sears[18] coined *symbolic* racism, prejudice based on the perception that "minorities' different moral values threaten their own culture."[19] Symbolic racists look down at other groups that are not as "civilized" and as they are. Such superiority is associated with child-like rather than animalistic metaphors.[20] Whereas, for instance, the biological racist in the United States believes that white Americans are inherently biological superior to black Americans, the symbolic racist feels morally superior. The latter's intolerance is based on stereotypes of the ethical failings of minority groups, such as lacking a work ethic or discipline, thereby justifying in his or her mind the privileged position of whites in America. The prejudice is – at least, ostensibly – directed at the (stereotypical) actions and behaviors, not the DNA or skin color, of minority groups. In the former, minority racial groups do not fit into the dominant culture and threaten its cohesion. This is the natural racism of those with DWB, although just because it does not dehumanize does not mean that it does not brutalize.

Such civilizing missions can no doubt be and have been vicious, coercive, and hierarchical, but to the extent that others are regarded as human, a significant break is placed on the use of state violence. Others must be cultivated, cleaned up, and educated, not stepped on and exterminated. Indeed authoritarians do not believe themselves to be lacking in humanitarian sensibilities.[21] Racial hierarchy is expressed in the form of a paternalistic obligation to others over whom they exercise legitimate authority. Nothing of course precludes both demonization and dehumanization; indeed both were present in the treatment of indigenous Americans by European settlers, as well as other native populations especially in settler colonies.

By comparing Nazi occupation policies in Eastern Europe to those of its predecessors, we again see Hitler's exceptionality. The case allows

---

[18] Kinder, Donald R. and David O. Sears. 1981. "Prejudice and Politics: Symbolic Racism versus Racial Threats to the Good Life." *Journal of Personality and Social Psychology* 40(3): 414–443.

[19] Hiel, Alain Van and Ivan Mervielde. 2005. "Authoritarianism and Social Dominance Orientation: Relationships with Various Forms of Racism." *Journal of Applied Social Psychology* 35(11): 2327.

[20] Haslam, Nick, Paul Bain, Lauren Douge, Max Lee, and Brock Bastian. 2005. "More Human than You: Attributing Humanness to Self and Others." *Journal of Personality and Social Psychology* 89(6): 937; Haslam, "Dehumanization," 252–264.

[21] Altemeyer, "The Other 'Authoritarian Personality,'" 47–92.

for a focused comparison: How did the two regimes treat the same conquered populations, judged in both cases to be racially different? It is, however, difficult to read. The dismissiveness, disdainfulness and superiority of the Wilhelmine regime still leaves me breathless, and as much as we theoretically understand the brutality of the Nazi regime, we are still unprepared to see their dehumanization on the page.

"Civilizing" and "Cultivating": The Occupation Regime of the German Army during World War I

In the great advance of 1915, German forces took northern Poland and much of the territory along the Baltic Sea, including the Courland (southern Latvia) and much of Lithuania. With the Russian army retreating rapidly, and in its wake a further million inhabitants of the region, the Germans found themselves in control of an area the size of France, about 15% of Russia's imperial territory. The three million civilians remaining were a patchwork of nationalities: Lithuanians, Poles, Latvians, Russians, Tatars, eastern Jews, Belarusians, and Baltic Germans. Poland was divided up between the Austro-Hungarian and German empire. In the east and north to the Baltics, the Germans created what was essentially a military colony called Ober Ost and placed under the leadership of Hindenburg, commander of Germany's eastern forces, and his right-hand man, Erich Ludendorff, who became the real decision-maker. The German army was one of the strongest bastions of nationalist thinking in the empire, and Hindenburg and Ludendorff were arch reactionaries. "Upper East" was "a laboratory for the utopian war aims of the German occupation which enjoyed far-reaching powers to experiment and act autonomously."[22]

In Ober Ost, in the words of Ludendorff, the German military took "up ... the Kultur work which Germans had done in those lands over many centuries."[23] This conception of its mission permeated the German army, from newspaper theater critics down to grunt soldiers. One of the former wrote in a military paper, "It is not a question of entertainment alone, which is to be solved here, rather it is a great mission of culture [Kulturmission], which German art has to

---

[22] Kramer, Alan. 2007. *Dynamic of Destruction*. Oxford: Oxford University Press, 47.
[23] Ludendorff, *My War Memories, 1914–1918*, 178.

fulfill.... Here we finally have for once the opportunity to show by deed that we are capable of bringing salvation to other peoples, to be leaders for them out of the darkness of un-culture [Unkultur] and un-education [Unbildung] to the light of an ideal existence truly worthy of humans."[24] More crudely, troop transport trains were chalked with slogans such as "Tsar, it's an almighty shame, that we first have to disinfect you and your gang. And then thoroughly cultivate you."[25] To this end, in addition to the millions of soldiers who served in the area, between 10,000 and 18,000 worked in the administration of Ober Ost, including archivists, professors of theology and philosophy, art historians, writers, and artists.[26]

The civilizing conception of occupation rested on a highly paternalistic conception of Germany's role. Ludendorff thought that "the population, made up as it is of such a mixture of races, has never produced a culture of its own."[27] Liulevicius writes, "Overall, native populations of the East were often seen as dirty, undisciplined, lazy and undeveloped.... This whole area was condemned as ... barbaric."[28] Eastern peoples were not so much dehumanized as they were infantilized. A German commander said that Lithuanians were as able to rule themselves independently "as well as for example my daughter Ilse."[29] Eastern Europe had not matured. "The scenes of the East also seemed lost in time, out of tune with the modernity of the rest of Europe, and a journey back in time."[30] Local inhabitants were treated roughly, even brutally, much like children who should be seen but not heard.[31] The German military instituted compulsory bathing and disinfecting stations, literally cleansing the locals, which sometimes included vaccinations without any effort to explain their purpose. Ludendorff later bragged that "German love of order and knowledge of hygiene carried the day."[32] Kramer writes, "The German occupation in eastern Europe saw itself as a colonial regime with a civilizing mission, to transform

---

[24] Liulevicius, *War Land on the Eastern Front*, 140.
[25] Ibid, 141. [26] Ibid, 57.
[27] Ludendorff, *My War Memories*, 1914–1918, 179.
[28] Liulevicius, Vejas Gabriel. 2010. *The German Myth of the East: 1800 to the Present*. Oxford: Oxford University Press, 141.
[29] Ibid. [30] Ibid, 138.
[31] Liulevicius, *War Land on the Eastern Front*, 105; Kramer, *Dynamic of Destruction*, 47.
[32] Ludendorff, *My War Memories*, 1914–1918, 206.

savages into decent Europeans.... Yet this was not racism in the sense of race hatred; it was rather the common western European or north American sense of a natural differentiation between races."[33]

The German military did not try to stamp out local cultures or languages, as had been done by the Russians before the war, but rather develop them within a larger, culturally superior German framework. Typical of the conception of nationalism that prevailed at the time, German decision-makers thought of each nationality as having a certain character or essence that the Germans could identify and foster. Von Gayl, in charge of Ober Ost's interior ministry, described this as the "gentle guiding by the reins," in which, for instance, the Lithuanians "could certainly be led to a higher level of culture and a satisfactory life of their own ... in the framework of the German cultural sphere, without giving up their own national properties."[34]

The "Chief Principle" of the "Order of Rule," the Ober Ost's constitution, instructed that "the divergent people-tribes of the area under command are to be treated by all German officials on equal terms."[35] After the war, Ludendorff boasted, "No restrictions were imposed on anyone in the practice of his religion," that educational plans were "conceived in a lofty spirit and respected the rights of each denomination and race," and that juridically the "German judge administered foreign laws to the poor, vermin-infested villages of Lithuania in the same spirit of justice and impartiality that he would have shown in Berlin."[36] Local Jewish populations fared much better than they had under Russian control, and indeed the German troops reported more favorable impressions of Jews than other ethnic groups since they could understand Yiddish much more easily than the other languages they encountered.[37] Hindenburg ordered that education be based on the "national school" principle, in which instruction would take place in children's "mother tongue," which overturned previous Russian policy (although was never fully implemented before the war concluded since almost all teachers had fled).

This *Kulturpolitik* (cultural policy) often conflicted with the simultaneous policy of pacifying, modernizing, and ordering the occupied

---

[33] Kramer, *Dynamic of Destruction*, 48.
[34] Liulevicius, *War Land on the Eastern Front*, 127.   [35] Ibid, 122.
[36] Ludendorff, *My War Memories*, 1914–1918, 203–204.
[37] Liulevicius, *War Land on the Eastern Front*, 119.

area for military activities, what was called *Verkehrspolitik*. The German military intensively exploited the area's resources and man-power, which involved the use of forced labor. Travel was highly limited and censorship was strict. Inhabitants "experienced the occu-pation as a system of violent, arbitrary rule."[38] Labor camp workers lived on starvation diets. However, Alan Kramer, the foremost expert on German wartime atrocities, concludes that "it would be mistaken to see the occupation as a pilot programme for the Third Reich."[39] For one thing, as he writes, the "policy of deporting Polish civilians to work in Germany ... was identical to the deportation of French and Belgian citizens" and was dedicated to the prosecution of total war.[40] No distinctions were made based on race. Indeed Ludendorff used the lessons drawn from Ober Ost to develop the policies implemented in Germany itself under the Auxiliary Labor Law, meant to fully exploit German manpower and resources after the Duo took over command of the entire war effort in the OHL.

Ludendorff bridled in his memoirs at accusations that the German military was brutal in its occupation, complaining of "enemy propa-ganda [that] denounced us as Huns to the world at large."[41] He insists, "What we accomplished together before my departure at the end of July 1916 was admirable in every respect, and worthy of the German character. It benefited the army and Germany as well as the country and its inhabitants."[42] It was "a work for civilization" that improved the lot of subject peoples compared to their time under Russian domi-nation."[43] It wasn't and it didn't. Yet it reveals what we will see was not true at all of Hitler, Ludendorff's sensitivity to claims of acting against humanitarian norms. This is an indication that the Wilhelmine right's racism was fundamentally different from the Nazis.

Expropriating and Exterminating: The Occupation Regime of the National Socialists during World War II

During World War II, after the Nazi-Soviet pact essentially divided Poland into German and Russian spheres, the Nazis carved out two new Gaus (districts) – Danzig-West Prussia and the Wartheland. More

---

[38] Kramer, *Dynamic of Destruction*, 47.   [39] Ibid, 49.   [40] Ibid.
[41] Ludendorff, *My War Memories*, 1914–1918, 203.   [42] Ibid, 189.
[43] Ibid, 206.

than a million Poles were forcibly expelled from these Gaus into the remaining area, designated again the Government-General of Poland. Over a million ethnic Baltic Germans from the areas newly occupied by the Soviets were to be relocated, by agreement, into these new districts. After Hitler attacked the Soviet Union and moved further east, the Nazis established new Reich Commissariats for Ukraine and a territory called Ostland that largely overlapped with Ober Ost. Hitler appointed Heinrich Himmler, the Reichsführer of the Schutzstaffel (SS), as Commissar for the Strengthening of the German Race, giving him the power to remake the occupied territories according to the Nazi vision. Whereas in World War I, the German military had been given free reign over the occupied Ober Ost, in World War II this role was given to the SS, essentially the Nazi branch of the army composed of the most vehement believers in Nazi racial ideology. Hitler also created an Ostministerium led by Alfred Rosenberg, a key racial theorist, but its incompetence precluded it from having much influence.

The Nazi occupation regime was fundamentally different. In private conversations during the war, Hitler explicitly objected to any civilizing mission for the east of the kind pursued during World War I. "We do not want any of this enlightenment nonsense, propagated by an advanced guard of persons! What is the use of talking about progress to people like that ... what on earth does it matter if one or two more locals get run over by the trains."[44] He objected to paternalism: "Russian and Ukrainian towns are not in any circumstances to be improved or made more habitable. It is not our mission to lead the local inhabitants to a higher standard of life."[45] Citing many of the measures pursued by the Ludendorff regime, he admonished: "We're not going to play at children's nurses; we're absolutely without obligations as far as these people are concerned. To struggle against the hovels, chase away the fleas, provide German teachers, bring out newspapers – very little of that for us! We'll confine ourselves, perhaps, to setting up a radio transmitter, under our control.... These are views that will have to be completely readjusted."[46] Hitler maintained that in the past, "The German made himself detested everywhere in the world, because wherever he showed himself he began to play the teacher. It's not a good method of conquest."[47] He modeled his plans after the British, whom he claimed

[44] Hitler, *Hitler's Secret Conversations*, 1941–1944, 478.   [45] Ibid.
[46] Ibid, 57.   [47] Ibid, 20.

had dominated the world for so long because they had no plans for civilizing: "The reason why they've kept it so long is that they were not interested in washing the dirty linens of their subject peoples."[48] High-ranking officials got the message. In his diary, Hans Frank, under whose control occupied Poland had been placed, wrote, "The imperialism we are developing here is beyond all comparison with the miserable efforts undertaken by former weak German governments in Africa.... [W]e are free of any obligation to Germanize. The Führer further stated explicitly that we had no obligation to create German conditions of life here, that there was no room for Germanizing efforts."[49]

Instead, the Nazis had a different understanding of Germanization, one predicated on race rather than culture and nationality. Hitler announced in Mein Kampf: "The National Socialist Movement ... knows no Germanising or Teutonising, as in the case of the national bourgeoisie, but only the spread of its own Volk. It will never see in the subjugated, so called Germanised, Czechs or Poles a national, let alone Volkish, strengthening, but only the racial weakening of our Volk. For its national conception is not determined by earlier patriotic ideas of government, but rather by ... racial insights. Thus the point of departure of its thinking is wholly different from that of the bourgeois world."[50] Rather than assimilating foreign peoples, he aimed to remove them. "The Volkish State, conversely, must under no conditions annex Poles with the intention of wanting to make Germans out of them someday. On the contrary, it must muster the determination either to seal off these alien racial elements, so that the blood of its own Volk will not be corrupted again, or it must without further ado remove them and hand over the vacated territory to its own National Comrades."[51] Himmler explained, "Our duty in the East is not Germanization in the former sense of the term, that is, imposing German language and laws upon the population, but to ensure that only people of pure German blood inhabit the East." In fact, "it is a crime against our blood to worry about them and give them ideals.... We are not bringing these people civilization."[52]

Wartime documents have revealed the outlines of the Nazis' Generalplan Ost, an apocalyptic vision of a racially purified Eastern

---

[48] Ibid, 39.   [49] Liulevicius, *The German Myth of the East*, 188.
[50] Hitler, *Hitlers zweites Buch*, 78.   [51] Ibid, 81.
[52] Liulevicius, *War Land on the Eastern Front*, 268 (emphasis added).

Europe in which tens of millions of conquered peoples would be expelled from the region, mostly to Siberia and other parts of east, to make room for a hundred million Nordic settlers of ostensibly racially superior quality. The Nazis would ethnically cleanse through extermination and deportation. A draft of the plan from 1942 foresaw the expulsion of 31 million non-Germans within twenty-five years.[53] Liulevicius writes, "German identity, no longer national, would be superceded by racial engineering, in programs of breeding, domination and extermination."[54] Himmler liked the plan, and wanted to show it to Hitler, only stressing that it did not go far enough; it had to entail Estonia and Latvia.[55]

Before these massive deportations, however, the Nazis planned to screen out the most racially valuable, those with ostensibly observable Germanic and Aryan traits. Only these individuals might be Germanized.[56] Hitler described the process: "The only problem is to make sure whether the offspring of any race will mingle well with the German population and will improve it, or whether, on the contrary (as is the case when Jew blood is mixed with German blood), negative results will arise."[57] Himmler wrote of "racial screening, which must be the foundation of our considerations, to fish out the racially valuable from this mush and bring them to Germany to assimilate."[58] Already during the war, the Nazis divided up the Polish population into four categories of "racial value," and took the most exceptionally "promising" children away from their parents, giving them to the Nazi Lebensborn organization.[59]

Those estimated 14 million deemed more racially valuable but not Aryan in origin would remain in the occupied territories, essentially serving as a slave labor population.[60] Rather than providing Kultur to those less civilized, as had been the stated goal of the German army during World War I, the Nazis saw occupied populations as

---

[53] See "Bericht über die Sitzung am 4.2.1942 bei Dr. Kleist über die Fragen der Eindeutschung," 293–296 and "Stellungnahme und Gedanken zum Generalplan Ost des Reichsführers SS," 294–324, both in *Vierteljahrshefte für Zeitgeschichte* 6(3), published in 1958.

[54] Liulevicius, *The German Myth of the East*, 269.

[55] Dokument Nr. 3 (NO-2255) in *Vierteljahrshefte für Zeitgeschichte* 6(3) 325.

[56] Hitler, Hitler's Secret Conversations, 1941–1944, 57.   [57] Ibid, 384.

[58] "Denkschrift Himmlers über die Behandlung der Fremdvölkischen im Osten (Mai 1940)," *Vierteljahrshefte für Zeitgeschichte*, 5(2), 194–198.

[59] Liulevicius, *War Land on the Eastern Front*, 191.   [60] Ibid, 268.

instruments to be put to use. Hitler described the Slavs as a "mass of born slaves, who feel the need of a master."[61] Himmler planned, "This population will be available as a leaderless workforce providing Germans with migrant workers and special projects (streets, quarries, buildings) every year."[62] Frank was more blunt: "What we have here is a gigantic labor camp."[63] Himmler admitted, "Whether nations live in prosperity or starve to death interests me only insofar as we need them as slaves for our Kultur; otherwise it is of no interest to me."[64] These "culture-less" inhabitants "will work together on these eternal cultural deeds and buildings under the strict, consistent and fair leadership of the German people."[65] Hitler said the same: "Our guiding principle must be that these people have but one justification for existence – to be of use to us economically. We must concentrate on extracting from these territories everything that is possible to extract."[66] He contrasted that conception with that of the previous occupation regime: "[W]e must not try too ardently to impose our own German ideas of personal cleanliness on the local inhabitants and attack them daily with curry-comb and polish. It really does not matter to us whether they wash and sweep their houses daily; we are not their overseers, all we are there for is to promote our own interests."

Uncivilizing the Conquered (and the Conqueror): Hitler's Reduction of Human Beings to Animals

Hitler consistently warned against any sentimentality, empathy, or even paternalistic humanitarianism vis-à-vis these conquered peoples.[67] "[A]bove all, no remorse on this subject!" he proclaimed.[68] He warned that "anyone who talks about cherishing the local inhabitant and civilizing him goes straight off into a concentration camp."[69] He wanted to "avoid all danger of our own people becoming too

---

[61] Hitler, *Hitler's Secret Conversations*, 1941–1944, 28.
[62] "Denkschrift Himmlers über die Behandlung der Fremdvölkischen im Osten,"195–198.
[63] Liulevicius, *The German Myth of the East*, 188.   [64] Ibid, 269.
[65] "Denkschrift Himmlers über die Behandlung der Fremdvölkischen im Osten,"195–198.
[66] Hitler, *Hitler's Secret Conversations*, 1941–1944, 343, also 29.
[67] Ibid, 384.   [68] Ibid, 57.   [69] Ibid, 501.

soft-hearted and too humane towards them."[70] Instrumental violence is made possible through amoralization.

Hitler explicitly forbade any provision of basic health care to the occupied populations, such as the (forced) vaccinations that occurred during World War I.[71] German settlers would simply remain safe by simply walling themselves off from others, which would also prevent fraternization and racial mixing.[72] "In the field of public health there is no need whatsoever to extend to the subject races the benefits of our own knowledge. This would result only in an enormous increase in local populations, and I absolutely forbid the organization of any sort of hygiene or cleanliness crusades in these territories. Compulsory vaccination will be confined to Germans alone and the doctors in the German colonies will be there solely for the purpose of looking after the German colonists."[73] The only exception was contraception, which Hitler wanted to encourage so as to tame the birth rates of non-Germans, threatening to cut the head off of anyone who defied him on this score.[74]

Such callous humanitarian disregard cannot be understood without reference to the racial categories used by the Nazis. Those occupied were "Untermenschen" or "subhumans."[75] The Nazis consistently equated the Slavs with animals, "brutes in the state of nature."[76] Hitler said privately, "As for the ridiculous hundred million Slavs, we will mold the best of them to the shape that suits us, and will isolate the rest of them in their own pig-sties."[77] Tellingly, while scornful, Hitler claimed not to hate those he thought racially inferior, consistent with his dehumanization. He could not detest them any more than one hates an animal. "[W]e don't hate them. That sentiment is unknown to us.... In this business I shall go straight ahead, cold-bloodedly."[78] This was not virtuous violence.

For the Nazis, civilizing was wasted on the racially inferior, just as it would be on an animal. Instead of unleashing the "German school-master on the Eastern territories," he maintained that "the ideal solution would be to teach this people an elementary kind of mimicry.

---

[70] Ibid, 478.   [71] Ibid, 345, 477.   [72] Ibid, 20, 46.
[73] Ibid, 345.   [74] Ibid, 477.
[75] "Denkschrift Himmlers über die Behandlung der Fremdvölkischen im Osten,"195–198.
[76] Hitler, *Hitler's Secret Conversations, 1941–1944*, 34.
[77] Ibid, 501.   [78] Ibid, 57.

One asks less of them than one does of the deaf and dumb."[79] He said dismissively, "I am not a partisan, either, of a university at Kiev. It's better not to teach them to read. They won't love us for tormenting them with schools."[80] Education should not be "forced ... down the throats of subject races."[81] Hitler endorsed elementary education in reading and writing in German to facilitate administration, such as the reading of road signs, but not training in mathematics.[82] Education was also dangerous. Hitler declared, "It would be a mistake to claim to educate the native. All that we could give him would be a half-knowledge – just what's needed to conduct a revolution."[83] Himmler identified an exception. Parents might apply to the SS to allow their children to go beyond the fourth grade. Permission might be granted to "racially spotless" applicants, who would then be forced to relocate to Germany so as to avoid improving the local blood stock and seeding future resistance. Himmler also imagined a yearly evaluation of all six- to ten-year-olds in Poland for "valuable and non-valuable blood" to determine who might be granted the chance at any education.[84]

Not only did the Nazis dehumanize the Eastern populations whose land they occupied, but they also sought to strip any remaining humanity from them by erasing their national identities. Whereas the Ober Ost regime envisaged the development of local culture within the framework of German tutelage, the Nazis set out to eradicate national feeling. Hitler explained, "It is furthermore essential to avoid doing anything which might give rise to a feeling of superiority or of racial pride among the natives. This is of the utmost importance, for it is only by the creation of the very reverse state of mind that we shall be able to prepare the ground for the accomplishment of our plans."[85] Himmler wrote, "In just a few years – I imagine, in four to five – the concept, for example, of Kashubians must be unknown so that there is no longer a Kashubian people."[86]

Therefore, when in the wake of the Russian retreat, Baltic peoples began to establish provisional governments with the hope of obtaining independence as they had during World War I, "it quickly became

---

[79] Ibid, 288.   [80] Ibid, 29   [81] Ibid, 344.   [82] Ibid, 478.   [83] Ibid, 28.
[84] "Denkschrift Himmlers über die Behandlung der Fremdvölkischen im Osten,"195–198.
[85] Hitler, *Hitler's Secret Conversations, 1941–1944,* 478.
[86] "Denkschrift Himmlers über die Behandlung der Fremdvölkischen im Osten," 195–198.

clear that they had not understood the intervening changes in the occupier's ideology."[87] In Hitler's words, "It was we, who in 1918 created the Baltic countries and the Ukraine. But nowadays we have no interest in maintaining Baltic States, any more than in creating an independent Ukraine."[88]

It is unclear, with so many historical records destroyed by the Nazis before the regime's collapse, just how far plans like Generalplan Ost had proceeded. Nor can we know how far Hitler would have gone. However, internal deliberations among the relevant ministries expose the degree to which racial conceptions had penetrated the thinking of German decision-makers. Memos reveal that the goal of a racially Germanized Eastern Europe was taken for granted. The only points of debate concerned the hurdles and practical difficulties of implementing a plan of this enormous scale. Some of the best windows into Nazi planning were written by Dr. Erhard Wetzel, a functionary in the Ostministerium (eastern Ministry), who objected to the overzealousness of the SS. Wetzel complained that the Generalplan Ost underestimated the number of people who would have to be moved to Siberia and overestimated the number of Germans who would be willing to settle the new territories. He raised issues with the arbitrariness of the criteria for racial purity and advocated that local inhabitants be offered incentives to allow for voluntary relocation so as to avoid the political complications and resistance that would accompany any efforts to racially screen and divide the population.[89] However, at no point did he or anyone else raise questions about the objectives of the plan itself. Wetzel wrote, "It goes without saying that only those foreign peoples who are racially valuable to us should be considered for Germanization. Racially valuable for our people are essentially only those foreigners who themselves or whose tribe show the characteristics of the Nordic race in their external appearance as well as in their demeanor and performance."[90] His main objection was that such a judgment was impossible without considerable study.

---

[87] Liulevicius, *War Land on the Eastern Front*, 266.

[88] Hitler, *Hitler's Secret Conversations, 1941–1944*, 29.

[89] "Bericht über die Sitzung am 4.2.1942 bei Dr. Kleist über die Fragen der Eindeutschung," 293–296 and "Stellungnahme und Gedanken zum Generalplan Ost des Reichsführers SS," 294–324.

[90] "Stellungnahme und Gedanken zum Generalplan Ost des Reichsführers SS," 301.

In the end, this complaint was minimal. Wetzel got his hackles up that the SS estimated the percentage of racially valuable in Poland was not 5%, as he believed, but 3%.[91] The absurdity is tempered by our knowledge of the horrific consequences of Nazi dehumanization and amorality.

What Are the Foundations of Moral Foundations? Biology as Solution to the Problem of Moral Relativism

The Nazis have given biological thinking a bad name. Evolutionary theory has significant political baggage given the perverse uses by which it has been put in the past, most notably the crude material determinism of the Nazis but also the use of social Darwinism to justify cruel practices even in advanced, liberal societies like the United States, such as forced sterilization. Moreover, biological theory has a deterministic reputation. To the extent that moral progress requires active change and agency, the application of evolutionary logic sometimes seems to imply and even excuse the ethical status quo. If ought implies can, and we (falsely!) conclude that human beings are not capable of much when it comes to moral behavior, then we are already living in the best of all possible worlds. Moreover, morality implies agency. We can only morally judge others and ourselves to the extent that we have a choice in our actions. This is why we can watch nature programs without outrage. The scorpion cannot help stinging the frog; after all, it is in his nature.

Properly understood, however, the study of evolutionary ethics does not give us much to fear. As maintained in previous chapters, the crude social Darwinism of Hitler misses the central role played by morality in human evolution, among other misapplications. Basic human experience, not to mention the historical record, tell us that there is nothing fixed about morality; the social constructions of time and place play huge roles in the development of moral rules and norms, even if cultures are working with a fixed set of ingredients highlighted in biological and psychological research. These particular flavors can be combined in any number of ways and explain the paradox of human ethics: while human beings differ markedly across time and place, by and large the actions

---

[91] "Bericht über die Sitzung am 4.2.1942 bei Dr. Kleist über die Fragen der Eindeutschung," 294.

of others are intelligible, if not justifiable to us. To use the example of Hamarabi's code, it seems cruel and unacceptable to impose a penalty of death for stealing, but we still understand how theft is a moral violation, something that links us to the civilizations of the past.

Not only are evolutionary ethics, properly understood, not nearly as dangerous as is commonly believed, but an understanding of the biological foundations of humanity's moral sensibilities actually leaves liberal normative theory on stronger footing. One of the central problems of moral philosophy has and continues to be the justification of moral values. Why is it right to be humane? Because it is wrong to harm others, the liberal might respond. It causes them pain. But that doesn't answer the question, a moral skeptic replies. Why does others' pain concern me? Because we are part of a human community, the liberal retorts. Who says? asks the skeptic. All efforts to reason our way to values, not just those of liberals, suffer from this "problem of foundations," as Donnelly calls it.[92] The problem, as Hume long ago surmised, is that we are trying to infer an "ought" from an "is," a normative statement from one of fact. Physical harm causes pain is a factual statement; causing pain is wrong is a normative statement, and we cannot get from one to the other. We either feel their pain or we do not.

Roughly speaking, normative theorists have responded to this challenge in two ways: through reason and through relativism. There is a longstanding tendency in liberal theory to identify moral standards through a process of logical deduction. Such an approach offers what it considers an "objective" benchmark, by which is meant a universal standard that holds across time and place. Through reason we can determine what is moral. We derive moral universals by taking an external position, free from any particular cultural or historical context.[93] The tradition goes back to Kant who "sought to place morality beyond the realm of the human experience, custom and desire. For him, the only available answer to this was reason ... reason alone reveals the laws. They are not given by providence, or natural law.... Pure reason provides the only grounds for securing the moral realm against the vagaries of human experience, custom, habit and desire."[94]

[92] Donnelly, Jack. 2013. *Universal Human Rights in Theory and Practice*. Ithaca and London: Cornell University Press.
[93] Jefferey, *Reason and Emotion in International Ethics*; Erskine, *Embedded Cosmopolitanism*.
[94] Shapcott, *International Ethics*.

While Kant based his conclusions on deontological precepts about individuals' duties toward others, later utilitarians grounded theirs in a weighing of harms and benefits. Regardless, all stress the necessity of drawing moral conclusions from what Rawls calls an "original position," an objective viewpoint free of prejudice and bias. Later liberal theorists such as Habermas argued that such a process could not occur in isolation. Moral conclusions must be reached through a process of reasoned dialogue in which interlocutors exchanged arguments.[95] However, participants in such a hypothetical exercise must enter with an open mind, determined to discover the objective truth. As Jeffrey indicates, in this liberal tradition, this pursuit must be unemotional since emotion is assumed to be antithetical to reason. The "passions" are a source of bias and allow selfishness to contaminate ethical decision-making.[96]

However, we cannot reason our way to moral foundations; we can only take certain moral foundations as given and deduct from them prescriptive and proscriptive implications for good and bad behavior. For liberals, this starting point is the inherent worth and dignity of the individual, which cannot be proven. It is a feeling that one simply knows to be true. Debates among liberals, pitting deontologists against utilitarians, are fierce, considering that they start from the same locus of moral concern.

Morality from Within: Biology and the Communitarian Critique

"Communitarians" have long held that it is impossible to abstract away from particular subjective and intersubjective contexts so as to discover universal moral laws.[97] All individuals are embedded in thick cultures that constitute their members' moral understandings. From this perspective, individuals only come to have moral knowledge by inhabiting and participating in these local cultures. Erskine explains, "An account of moral reasoning as embedded presents the moral agent as constituted by particular ties and relationships. In other words, these associations define ... one's 'moral starting point'. Such

---

[95] Risse, "Let's Argue!"
[96] Jefferey, *Reason and Emotion in International Ethics*, 14.
[97] Shapcott, *International Ethics*, 52–58.

an understanding is meant to depart from a conception of the person as able to adopt an 'impartialist' perspective by which one temporarily removes oneself from consideration of particular affiliations in order to engage in moral deliberation."[98] Rather than adopting an external point of view, what is right and wrong can only be determined from within a particular culture, what Walzer calls the "view from the cave."[99] Without our social contexts, we lack the embodiment of who we are that is necessary to arrive at moral decisions.[100]

The implication is that there is no objective benchmark by which to compare and adjudicate between alternative understandings of what is right and wrong. All morality is relative, specific to concrete historical circumstances and incommensurable with other ethical understandings. Given the diverse moral understandings that define communities, communitarians argue that any effort to generate such universal rules will founder. They note that no liberal effort has been successful so far in generating universal acceptance, and not for lack of trying. Moreover, it would be morally objectionable to force individuals out of the particular cultural circumstances that are so dear to them. Human beings are not atomistic, nor do they want to be.

Communitarians accuse liberal, cosmopolitan normative theorists of confusing their own subjective understanding of what is right and wrong for an objectively derived one. "Cosmopolitanism does not sufficiently recognize that its abstract, idealized, supposedly impartial, principal standpoint is, in fact, the product of a particular history, context and culture, and not an impartial one.... The cosmopolitan commitment to impartiality with regard to different conception of the good life is itself an articulation of a particular conception of the good life."[101] Indeed in deducing moral rules logically through reason, all liberals adopt the starting point that all individuals are deserving of equal concern and respect, which is itself a moral principle, as seen previously. They do not reason to this fact but rather reason from it. From a modern, Western point of view, this is self-evident but not from others. In that way, liberalism does not solve the problem of "foundations" any more than religions do. Liberals do not always recognize that they are arguing from reified premises.

---

[98] Erskine, *Embedded Cosmopolitianism*, 25. [99] Ibid, 26. [100] Ibid, 25.
[101] Shapcott, *International Ethics*, 56–58.

I accept the communitarian critique. However, carried through to its logical conclusion, this constructivist account of ethics that humans make morality entirely as they choose is normatively alarming. If morality has no foundation except our intersubjective understandings, then humans can conceivably convince themselves that anything is ethical. There are no natural limits on ethical content. By such a standard, we have no choice but to regard Hitler's "ethic"[102] – his notion that what was ethically valuable was compliance with what nature intended, to brutally advance the species through a process of material competition – to be as morally justified as that of Mother Theresa.

It seems that resistance to this conclusion generates a tension in the norms literature in international relations, which embraces a particular liberal understanding of ethics by which to benchmark moral progress (as demonstrated earlier) while simultaneously utilizing a social ontology that implies there is no objective external standard to judge ethical behavior. Constructivists in the norms literature share the communitarian belief that morality is socially constructed and therefore historically specific and culturally relative, yet do not follow through. As Erskine points out, "[T]he way that liberal cosmopolitan positions tend to appeal to impartialist starting points does seem radically at odds with constructivism's own assumption that the identities of actors are defined by the institutionalized norms and values of their social contexts, making political agency (and arguably moral agency) radically situated and socially determined." Some constructivists admit as much.[103] "At the crossroads between the desire to embrace an ethical perspective with a global purview and the conviction that context and particularity are not only relevant but fundamental to moral reasoning, lies an apparent impasse, writes Erskine."[104] We can trace this "tension between constructivist scholars' historically contextual empirical theories of the rise of norms and the universalistic deontological commitments that some principled constructivists hold"[105] to an unwillingness to embrace the normative implications of their ontological position – that there is nothing inherently true about liberal morality.

---

[102] Weikart, *Hitler's Ethic.*   [103] Price, "Moral Limit and Possibility," 11.
[104] Erskine, *Embedded Cosmopolitianism*, 13.
[105] Snyder, Jack and Leslie Vinjamuri. 2012. "Principled Pragmatism and the Logic of Consequences." *International Theory* 4(3): 435.

I would argue that an understanding of ethics as having an emotional (and therefore a biological) basis helps constructivist theorists with liberal values out of this uncomfortable cul-de-sac in which their personal ethics and empirical understandings are at cross-purposes. Liberals are correct to note that all ethics require some degree of impartiality in the sense that moral rules are those meant to apply to all persons in particular categories, rather than just oneself. To say that something is right or wrong is to say that a general rule has been broken that is meant to regulate social behavior. However, we do not, indeed cannot, reach moral conclusions through reason alone. Evolutionary findings avoid the trap between a moral imperialism in which there is a single moral code and a moral relativism in which anything goes.

When we have no other response to the claims of the moral skeptics than "it is just wrong!" or "because that's the way it is," we have reached the point at which we realize that morality is a feeling, something that we "know" intuitively but cannot justify logically. Morality is embodied in our emotions. It comes literally from within. Without the feeling that harm to others is wrong, we cannot conclude that it is right to be humane. Hume called this "moral sentimentalism."[106] What is good or bad in moral terms cannot be described in the same way that we describe an elephant. It is a concept that cannot be broken down any further. It just is. Jeffery explains that this "sentimentalist cosmopolitan ethic thus contended that emotions can direct judgments of right and wrong and help to motivate responses to the experience of right and wrong that are not inherently selfish or self-serving."[107] Our emotions are not entirely untrustworthy when it comes to morality.

Because of this, inhumanity deserves moral condemnation not because we have logically proved that it is wrong, which we cannot do, but because of the terrible way it makes us feel. And since that outrage is such a universal human phenomenon (although perhaps not as universal as we would like it to be), we know when something is wrong, which provides the foundation missing in liberal thought. Every time that we feel sympathy for others we do not know, we are showing that we can, and therefore that we ought, to care for others. These feelings, like most of our physical and physiological features, have evolutionary origins. "[T]he selfish-gene revolution, far

---

[106] For a review, see Jefferey, *Reason and Emotion in International Ethics*.
[107] Jefferey, *Reason and Emotion in International Ethics*, 15.

from being a bleak and Hobbesian injunction to go out and ignore the good of others, is in fact the very opposite. It makes room for altruism after all."[108]

Fear of Fear Itself: The Moral Implications of Ingroup Favoritism

The normative cost of this recognition is that our humanitarian impulses are not our only ethical tendencies. Our propensity toward ingroup favoritism and moral condemnation, when combined, can ravage international relations. I suspect this is a potent source of resistance to biological arguments about ethics, one that is more normative than empirical. Indeed many of those who have applied the insights of biology have fixated on binding tendencies to the neglect of broader humanitarian impulses.[109] To point out the normative danger, might we be able to conclude that Hitler's actions were perfectly morally defensible from the standpoint of binding morality? If ingroup favoritism is a biological by-product cemented with the emotion of loyalty, are we not denied the objective viewpoint by which to condemn the Nazis?

Empirical results are again the way out of our moral conundrum. The findings on ingroup favoritism, as I argued in Chapter 3, have been wildly misinterpreted. Apropos is Robert Sapolsky, when he writes, "To understand the dynamics of human group identity, including the resurgence of nationalism – that potentially most destructive form of in-group bias – requires grasping the biological and cognitive underpinnings that shape them. Such an analysis offers little grounds for optimism. Our brains distinguish between in-group members and outsiders in a fraction of a second, and they encourage us to be kind to the former but hostile to the latter."[110] Yet the research indicates nothing of the sort, and Sapolsky (of all people) should know better. Sapolsky cites biological studies, claiming that oxytocin, the chemical in our bodies that promotes prosocial behaviors within groups, such as trust and identification, makes us "aggressive and xenophobic" toward outgroups. It "deepens the fault line in our brains between 'us'

---

[108] Ridley, *The Origins of Virtue*, 20.
[109] Lopez et al., "States in Mind, Coalitional Psychology, and International Politics"; Thayer, "Bringing in Darwin."
[110] Sapolsky, Robert. 2019. "This Is Your Brain on Nationalism: The Biology of Us and Them." *Foreign Affairs* 98(2): 42–47

and 'them'." However, oxytocin only generates a tendency toward "defensive out-group aggression," warding off outgroup threat.[111] It does not make respondents more likely to exploit cooperation by outgroups at all. By experimentally manipulating the suckering and the suckered payoffs, researchers have been able to show that oxytocin generates less cooperation with outgroups only when the latter is higher. In other words, fear rather than greed is at the heart of our ingroup bias. The overall takeaway of these studies is that oxytocin increases within-group cooperation, discouraging free-riding, but has no effect on inclinations to deprive resources from outgroups. These biological studies are particularly important since any understanding of what constitutes human nature when it comes to outgroups might be a reflection of modern, socially constructed values.

By failing to distinguish between hate, indifference, or derogation on one hand and fear, threat, and moral condemnation on the other, we have created a perception of a greater incompatibility between the ethics of community and the ethics of humanity than I believe the data warrants. This empirical is brought home in this chapter as we compare how different the German rights behaved in World War I and World War II. As De Dreu et al. write, "Out-group aggression may be driven by the desire to increase the in-group's relative status and power in the intergroup competition (henceforth 'out-group hate'). Alternatively, it may be driven by the vigilant desire to defend and protect the ingroup against real or perceived out-group threat."[112] To hate, we could also include outgroup indifference, in which we feel morally justified in simply taking from others since, well, they aren't us. Only ingroup defense seems so common as to be biologically innate, and even this varies, as we have seen, across individuals and cultures.

A world in which outgroup dislike and antagonism is a function of threat is much more amenable to change than one in which moral indifference and even hatred toward the other is hard wired and natural. While it does entail an admission that ingroup favoritism is a hard-wired tendency in human beings, that edge becomes softer when we highlight another consistent finding: the tremendous flexibility in which human beings draw group boundaries. The typical

[111] De Dreu et al., "The Neuropeptide Oxytocin Regulates Parochial Altruism."
[112] Ibid.

interpretation of the minimal group findings that form the basis of social identity theory is that the ease by which human beings are led to favor ingroups constructed on entirely arbitrary criteria with no evaluative force demonstrates just how dangerous group identity is. Yet the opposite seems more true. If we can form group identity on any basis, then the world is fundamentally less deterministic than we might believe it to be. The main thing we have to fear is fear itself. Our primary moral challenge, I believe, is to encourage groups to drop their guard. This means combating the impulse towards virtuous violence and the often irrational moral condemnation behind it.

These findings also indicate that no fully formed moral being can be indifferent to humanitarian morality. That is an empirical not a normative statement, although it has normative implications. We cannot simply say that there are those who love their ingroup and care nothing or are hostile to their outgroup and this is just as morally natural as any other combination. The empirical evidence, both of this book and in cognate literatures, indicates that binding morality is not defined in opposition to a more basic humanitarian morality but rather prioritizes the ingroup based on the perception of threat from an ethically challenged outgroup. It is an exception to broader humanitarian rules. Even World War I nationalists in Germany felt the need to justify, to themselves and others, the harm they did to others. Those distinctions might be constructed and exacerbated by self-serving elites to promote selfish motives. They might have no basis in reality. Yet they stop short of moral indifference to or hatred of anyone outside our group that Sapolsky falsely claims is innate.

Morality is Natural, Even in International Relations

Human beings are capable of doing terrible things to one another. Not everyone is a fully formed ethical person. If there were no immorality and if human beings did not have significant agency over their choices, we would have no language for ethics at all. Yet the fact that mass violence of the instrumental sort, dedicated only to the group's gain, is generally accompanied by efforts at dehumanization indicates just how unnatural (but certainly not impossible) this is for our species. Even Hitler could not be indifferent to our most basic human impulses. Even as he was arguing that liberal values had no basis in reality, but themselves were social constructions, he was dehumanizing others precisely because this was necessary to mobilize allies to achieve his goals. Binding foundations and ingroup favoritism were not enough precisely because there is more to human morality. Hitler was not free to reconstruct ethical rules entirely as he wished. We dehumanize others with far more ease than we would like to admit,[113] but the fact that we need to do so is the (very thin) silver lining of our worst actions.

One sees how contending ethical perspectives on international relations are themselves manifestations of universal human values. Communitarians are, as many note, making the case for the binding foundations. Himmelfarb argues if we try to strip individuals of the "givens of life: parents, ancestry, family, race, religion, heritage, history, culture, tradition, community and nationality," there is nothing left from which to make moral judgments. These particularities are "essential attributes. We do not come into the world as free-floating, autonomous individuals."[114] Note that all of these givens are virtues under the ethics of community, binding them together in a cohesive group. Beiser notes that the romantic conservative tradition that emerged in Germany had precisely such a historicist character, arguing against the assertion of any single ideal community standards deducible from reason. Instead, cultural values and morality were products of historical circumstances, in which values, beliefs, institutions, traditions, and language were linked in an organic and self-reinforcing whole. There were no "natural" laws. As we reviewed in Chapter 7, this tradition depicted societies as interdependent individuals, each with their own roles, deriving value from and contributing to the community.[115] In other words, communitarians are articulating basic human moral sensibilities, universal in character, captured by the ethics of community.

This is no less true of liberal theorists. De Waal writes that the great liberal theorist, John Rawls, is articulating basic human intuitions when it comes to morality: "I cannot escape the feeling that rather than describing a human innovation, [he] elaborates on ancient themes, many of which are recognizable in our nearest relatives. Of course, everything is more explicit in human society because of our

---

[113] Leyens, Jacques-Philippe, Stéphanie Demoulin, Jeroen Vaes, Ruth Gaunt, and Maria Paola Paladino. 2007. "Infra-humanization: The Wall of Group Differences." *Social Issues and Policy Review* 1(1): 139–172.
[114] Quoted in Erskine, *Embedded Cosmopolitanism*, 45.
[115] Beiser, *The Genesis of Modern German Political Thought*, 6.

ability to formulate rules of conduct, discuss them among ourselves, and write about them in exquisite detail. Still, it is safe to assume that the actions of our ancestors were guided by gratitude, obligation, retribution and indignation long before they developed enough language capacity for moral discourse."[116] Even academics, in other words, cannot escape our evolved moral instincts. We disagree because we have multiple moral impulses, and some are more prominent in us than others.

This should make us mindful of our own bias, both in empirical and in normative research on morality in international relations. My biological approach suggests that to establish whether ethical considerations do or do not drive behavior, we need a phenomenological empirical strategy, a willingness to see morality through the eyes of those doing the action rather than imposing a particular moral metric and assessing whether political actors measure up. It is objective, not in the false sense of establishing definitively universal ethical standards but rather in that it allows research subjects to define morality for themselves free from the preconceptions of the scholar. It is subjective not in the sense of concluding that morality is literally anything we might say it is but rather in allowing that empirically not everyone will agree on what constitutes right and wrong. Studying ethics objectively requires a deep understanding of subjectivity – that is, a realization that our morality might not be that of those we study.

When we do so, I believe that we actually reach some normatively pleasing conclusions. When we excuse or resign ourselves to certain tendencies with the shrug, "that's just human nature," we are concluding that we are innately wired to do bad things. Human nature and pessimism are synonymous, a legacy of realist thought but probably far older. Yet, human beings are by nature so much more than that. Wrangham writes of the "goodness paradox" that we are the nicest of species but also the nastiest.[117] There is a biological basis for both. Evolutionary ethics might not "leave our moral sentiments feeling as celestial as they used to. Sympathy, empathy, compassion, conscience, guilt, remorse, even the very sense of justice, the sense that doers of good deserve reward and doers of bad deserve punishment – all these can now be viewed as vestiges of organic history

---

[116] De Waal, *Good Natured*, 161.
[117] Wrangham, *The Goodness Paradox*.

on a particular planet."[118] Yet I agree with DeWaal, who asks,
"[W]hy should we let the ruthlessness of natural selection distract
from the wonders it has produced? Humans ... have been endowed
with a capacity for genuine love, sympathy and care – a fact that can
and will one day be fully reconciled with the idea that genetic self-
promotion drives the evolutionary process."[119] Morality is the most
natural thing in the world.

[118] Wright, *The Moral Animal*, 328.
[119] De Waal, *Good Natured*, 16–17.

Index

Cambridge Studies in
International Relations: 163

Printed in the USA
CPSIA information can be obtained
at www.ICGtesting.com
LVHW012315270823
756434LV00001B/52